The Global Financial Crisis

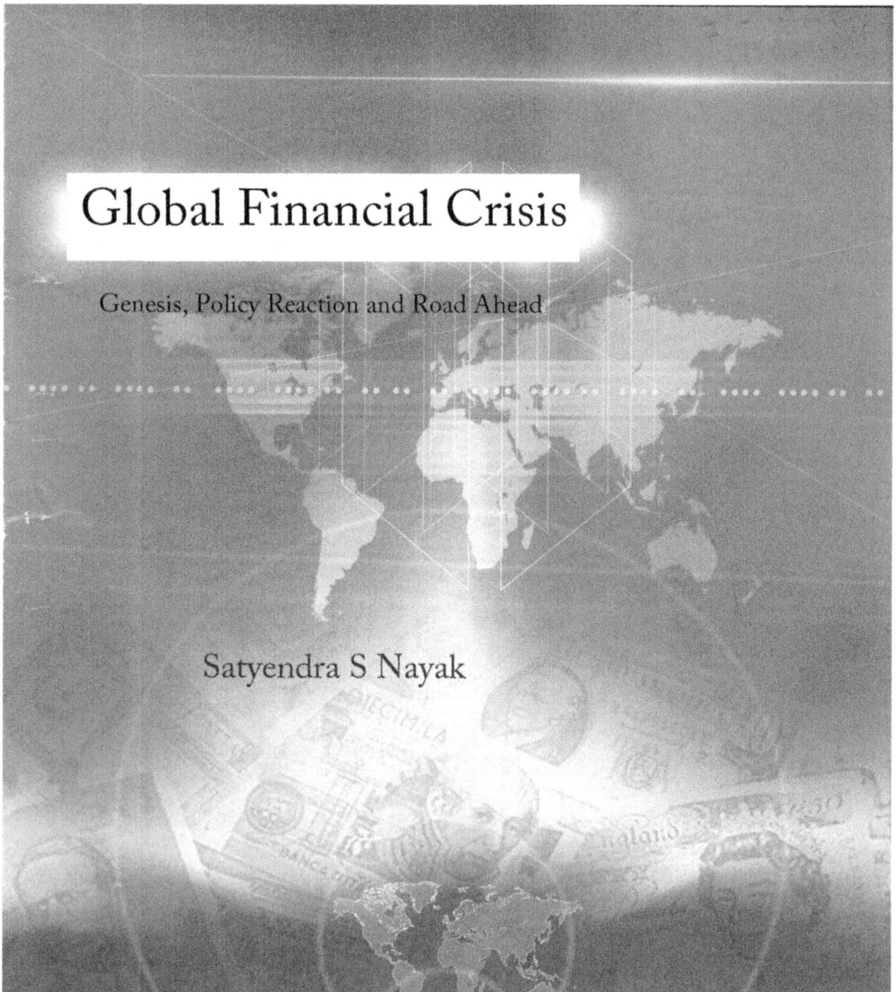
Global Financial Crisis
Genesis, Policy Reaction and Road Ahead
Satyendra S Nayak

Satyendra Nayak

The Global Financial Crisis

Genesis, Policy Response and Road Ahead

Springer

Satyendra Nayak
Center for Advanced Banking
and Finance Studies
ICFAI Business School
Mumbai, Maharashtra, India

ISBN 978-81-322-0797-9 ISBN 978-81-322-0798-6 (eBook)
DOI 10.1007/978-81-322-0798-6
Springer New Delhi Heidelberg New York Dordrecht London

Library of Congress Control Number: 2012956054

Printed on acid-free paper

Springer is part of Springer Science+Business Media (www.springer.com)

Preface

My earlier book on globalization was published in December 2007. It focused on the genesis and impact of major global economic policy change in the postwar period which has brought a dramatic shift in global trade, investments, and financing, thereby causing the most pronounced reduction in the global economic divide. It was time to move on to my next assignment which I was ruminating on and was my natural interest and obsession for years. The US Dollar at Crossroads was the theme I have been working on since the demise of the Bretton Woods. Although the floating exchange rates and globalization gave fresh lease for the US dollar, the institution of American capitalism was under stress. The New Deal formed the cornerstone of American capitalism since the Great Depression days of the 1930s. Despite some minor hiccups, the system continued to serve as the engine of economic prosperity. Communism collapsed as it took the shape of hierarchical, bureaucratic, and totalitarian machine devoid of market signals and individualism that engender innovation and enterprise. American capitalism succeeded as the invincible political economic doctrine but still remained under pressure to achieve its goal of sustained growth, full employment, and price stability. Yet nobody expected the major crisis as it did in 2008.

In September 2008, I had meetings in the IMF and with Paul Volcker giving presentation of my book. Coincidentally, in the same month later, the economy witnessed an unexpected bolt from the blue—the USA experienced its worst financial and economic crisis since the Great Depression of the 1930s. My op-ed on the subject titled "Keynes: Savior of Capitalism" was published in Washington Times on October 1, 2008. My attention for research and analysis naturally shifted from the future of dollar to much larger and more fundamental issues of the structure and dynamics of the US economy, American capitalism, backlash of globalization, and the need for the further reform of the global economy and monetary system. The global financial crisis, the function and dysfunction of dollar, and its future role became the focal point of the book.

The crisis demonstrated the weaknesses in the functioning of the economy, institutions that govern, and policies that direct and regulate the economy. It also underscored the need for introspection into the current state of knowledge and theoretical basis of economics that have molded the contemporary policies.

The draft of the book took shape in New York, Boston, and Mumbai, the nerve centers of the global and Asian financial markets. I benefitted immensely from the excellent collection of books of the New York Public Library (NYPL) and Boston Public Library (BPL).

The book is divided into three parts. The first part deals with the genesis of the crisis and policy measures that prevented the culmination of the crisis into another great global depression. It examines the microeconomic origins of the subprime debt crisis but also goes on to look into its macroeconomic roots. In dealing with both the approaches, it highlights the systemic lacunae and policy changes that triggered the crisis. Part two gives the backdrop of evolutionary view of the global economic and monetary system from the Bretton Woods of 1944 until the phase globalization that began in the 1980s. The phenomena of the Great Crash of 1929 and Great Depression of the 1930s are revisited in the light of the current crisis. The third part covers the structural aspects of the American capitalism and the global economy. It examines why and how the American capitalism survived the onslaught of several crises in the past and why it is at the crossroads now. The demise of communism in USSR and East Europe, and its reform in China are analyzed. In addition to the study of fundamental changes in the dynamics of the US economy, it highlights the implications of changing structure of global trade and investments. The issues of the global savings gap and liquidity reflux are compared. The fourth part deals with road map of reform for the future. Since the financial markets have been the focus of the crisis, it draws and articulates the peculiar features of the financial markets which make them more volatile and which need regulation. It shows why and how financial markets crash by introducing the concept of Niagara effect. It also deals with the limitations of the use of sophisticated models for pricing financial products for trading. There is an exercise on relearning from Keynes' writings in dealing with economic management. Finally, the last chapter, Agenda for Global Economic Reform, the New Bretton Woods, outlines the measures which the USA, China, IMF, and Eurozone need to take to evolve a sustainable crisis-free global economy. Coincidentally this draft was finished in the beautiful surroundings of the Bretton Woods, New Hampshire.

January 1, 2013 Satyendra S. Nayak

Contents

Part III Structural Gaps

Part I
The Crisis: Micro-Macro Perspective

Chapter 1
Pathology of the Crisis

> And there is the potential of a U.S. Crash, less likely because monetary and fiscal policy can respond, but never say never. Even with all the U.S. prosperity, the world today has had an overdose of finance, and hence it is far more likely that a serious accident can happen. And if it does, we can be sure the fallout is worldwide, and we must fear that the first instinct is to play the defensive and destructive strategies of the Great Depression.
>
> Rudi Dornbusch, *Keys to Prosperity – Free Markets, Sound Money and a Bit of Luck, 2000.*

The Crisis: Then and Now

Economies are large and complex organizational structures comprising three basic institutions, viz., households, businesses and corporates, and governments, which are the building blocks of all economic activities. They are all involved in economic activities such as production, consumption, saving, and investment. These four basic economic parameters that determine the behavior of any economy and its dynamics generate income and expenditure. Imports and exports are basically constituents of these parameters. All economies are targeted toward production and its growth. Economic growth measured in annual increase in gross domestic product (GDP) is the goal all economies aspire to attain. All economies are targeted and oriented toward achieving higher GDP growth. The emerging economies like China and India are aspiring to achieve 10% annual growth, while mature economies like the USA, Europe, and Japan are struggling to keep out of negative growth territory and targeting to achieve growth in the range of 2–4%. Although economic policies of every nation are aimed toward higher production, the end of all economic activity is consumption. It is this economic parameter, the consumption that drives production. The other crucial parameter that drives economic growth is investment. In an open economy where foreign trade is relatively important segment of the economy, exports also trigger and sustain growth. The classic example of this growth was in Japan and Germany, which are both export-driven economies, in the postwar period until the 1980s. In China and other smaller Asian Tigers, both exports and foreign investments fuelled economic miracle since the late 1980s.

S. Nayak, *The Global Financial Crisis: Genesis, Policy Response and Road Ahead*,
DOI 10.1007/978-81-322-0798-6_1, © Springer India 2013

The classical economics that dominated the economic policy for centuries before the 1930s ruled that production will determine consumption. The famous "Say's Law" proclaimed, "the supply creates its own demand." Whatever is produced will always be consumed, and an economy will never remain in excess capacity, high unemployment state for a long time. Underemployment, excess capacity equilibrium is not a normal possibility of a capitalist economy. The economy will move toward its fullest production capacity and full employment on the dynamics of the market economy of capitalist system. Whatever is produced at the full employment level will be consumed. There will not be any overall output surplus or production glut. It is the dynamics of the system that would move the economy toward the full employment equilibrium. The classical economics was also dominated by two other ideologies that dictated their economic policies in the pre-1930s period, viz., gold standard and balanced budget. The gold standard established fixed exchange rates between currencies and monetary policy oriented to balance the balance of payments (BoP). In many instances, the economic cycles were generated by this monetary discipline of the gold standard. Economic boom generated trade deficit which under the gold standard rule of fixed exchange rate needed to be corrected by monetary contraction. This gave rise to recession and unemployment. Natural endogenous economic cycles were both intensified or moderated depending on the character of the BoP behavior during the endogenous economic cycle. The third tenet of the classical economics, the doctrine of balanced budget, did not give any room for fiscal policy to be used for macroeconomic management. Deficit was a taboo.

In the late 1930s, Keynesian economics demolished the classical economics and all the three tenets of classical economic policy and ushered economic policies into the new age of noncyclical sustained economic growth that ruled the postwar economics. Yet, despite all the heroism of Keynesian economic policy, the economies did not remain free from sudden downturns and crises.

Over the span of last 100 years, there have been five critical times the US economy has manifested itself in deep crisis and due to its sheer size engulfing also the global economy.

1. The first one was the Great Crash of 1929 which later culminated into the Great Depression of the 1930s. The depression was cured over a prolonged period of a decade through the Keynesian prescription of abandoning laissez-faire economics, adopting deficit financing, and jettisoning the gold standard. The old-fashioned capitalism was institutionally transformed into new shade of capitalism led by the welfare state.
2. The second crisis was the dollar crisis of 1971 which represented mismatch between economic aspiration to grow faster and limitation imposed by the value country's gold reserves that determined the strength of dollar. The dollar was functioning under the false sense of security it gave behind the cloak of inadequate gold reserves. Higher growth required the US treasury to have more gold to preserve dollar's gold convertibility and also ensure financial security embedded in gold. The crisis was resolved by ending the convertibility of dollar into gold and demonetizing gold from the global monetary system. The USA and the

world moved to a fiat currency standard devoid of financial security gold provided for centuries. It was a crisis that required systemic adjustment and correction and was achieved by a smooth transition from fixed to floating exchange rates.

3. When the dollar lost its international convertibility anchored to gold at the price of $35 per ounce guaranteed by the Federal Reserve, another critical resource, the crude oil, staged sharp spikes in its price in 1974 and 1979. The cost-push inflationary spiral pushed the economy into stagflation, the third economic crisis with structural problems. Rate of inflation reached the record high level of 14% in 1980. The monetarist prescription by the Federal Reserve of raising the interest rates to the record level in 1980 tamed the inflationary fires and restored the confidence in dollar. The monetarism coinciding with Reaganomics comprising supply-side economics, economic deregulation, and philosophy of globalization drove the economy back into higher growth momentum through the 1980s and the roaring 1990s. The technology revolution of the 1990s and its jet-sped commercialization culminated into the technology, internet, and dot-com revolution also fuelling the bubble on the stock market.
4. The Black Monday of October 19, 1987 stock market crash with record 508-point drop in the Dow Jones Industrial Average from 2,246 to 1,738, 22.6% fall, wiping market capitalization by $1 trillion triggered by the program trading, was shock similar to 1929 crash. It was the worst crisis since the Great Crash of 1929 causing the largest single day fall in stock market history. The Dow's single day fall was nearly double the fall of 12.8% decline in 1929. The crash marked the end of a 5-year bull market which saw the Dow rising from 776 to 2,722. From the intraday high of 2,746 in August 25, 1987, to the low point on October 20 of 1,708, it was a steep fall of 37% with the decline of more than 1,000 points. December 1987 S&P 500 futures contract showed much steeper fall of 47%. The Brady Commission report identified macro factors such as rising rate of inflation, rising interest rates, declining dollar, increasing trade deficit, and divergent earnings estimates by analysts and the micro factors like unusual activity in the index futures and program trading by institutions practicing portfolio insurance, as the causes of the crisis.[1] The crisis did not cause much damage to the economy. The Fed handled the crisis with prompt action lowering the interest rate leading stock market and economic recovery by 1989.
5. The fifth crisis of the century erupted in 2000 with the culmination of the roaring 1990s into dot-com bubble burst causing widespread stock market collapse and sending recessionary aftereffects into the economy. Despite its impact on the stock market and the economy, the crisis did not have any adverse effects on the banking system and its viability. The ownership of technology stocks also covered only some segments of investors not affecting the average stock market

[1] Report of Presidential Task Force on Market Mechanism, Brady Commission Report, January, 1988.

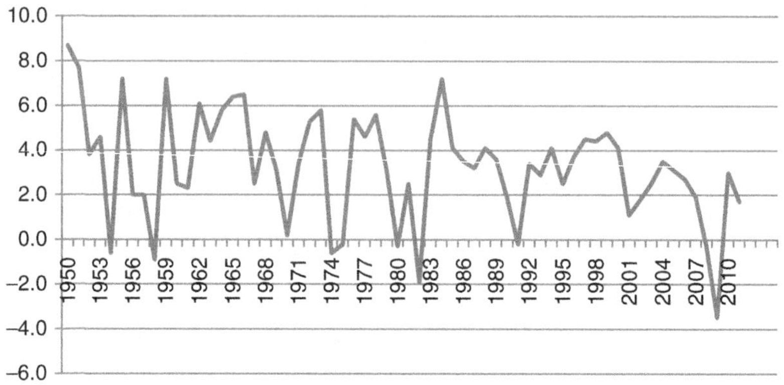

Fig. 1.1 US GDP growth (in percent in 2005 dollars) (Source: Bureau of Economic Analysis, US Dept. of Commerce)

investor. The dot-com crisis was not pervasive, and therefore, the economy recovered by 2003. It regained its growth momentum and speed, driving fast on the back of the housing and real estate boom (Fig. 1.1). The trend of GDP growth of the US economy for sixty years till 2010 can be seen from (Fig. 1.1).

6. The Fed's soft money policy facilitated the real estate boom of 2001–2006, which was largely fuelled by large-scale securitization of subprime debt, and its spread over the banking system in the USA and also globally. The concern about inflation forced the Fed to reverse its soft money policy and raise the interest rates. The slowdown in economic growth, slide in real estate prices, and defaults in housing loans caused by higher interest rates eroded the viability of holders of subprime debt securities. The year 2008 marked the onset of the century's sixth but major and the worst economic crisis which erupted from the subprime lending spree having much deeper and wider implications on the degree and coverage of its impact in the USA and the global economy.

US Economy Revives and Skips Depression: Thanks to Keynesian Wisdom

The mighty, the invincible, the heartland of capitalism had finally fallen prey once again, albeit after a long span of over 70 years, to the most devastating economic phenomenon last experienced in the 1930s. The signs of economic depression loomed large over the overpowering US economy. The financial economic crisis was reminiscent of the Great Crash of 1929 and the Great Depression that followed. When the economic boom of 1920s gave way to the biggest stock market crash in

October 1929, it led to severe banking crisis that culminated finally in depression taking heavy toll on economic life. The *laissez-faire* economic policy, gold standard discipline, and weak Federal Reserve Bank could neither rescue the banking system nor reflate the declining economy. It was not until 1933 with the New Deal, which abandoned obsolete economics of *laissez-faire* and gold standard and strengthened the Federal Reserve Bank, that the economy took a U-turn and resumed its course of recovery.

After the roaring 1990s of continuing high economic growth that was abruptly halted by the hiccup of Y2K dot-com bust, the US economy seemed fatigued and showed the signs of slowdown. Unprecedented and historically long phase of growth had no parallel in the US economic history. In the wake of slowdown caused by the weak consumer spending and lackluster investment demand, the low interest rate policy of the Fed since 2000 stimulated growth on the steam of the housing and real estate boom.

Onset of the subprime housing loan crisis in 2008 came like a bolt from the blue. Although it initially appeared to be a smaller localized problem, very soon it revealed its larger dimension and magnitude. The crisis was the center of gravity of a larger economic malaise. It was unprecedented in its size and magnitude of impact. No wonder was it a stark reminder of the gloomy economic days of 1930s. Further, the crisis did not restrict its coverage only to the USA but had penetrated other economies also making the crisis global in impact. This time, the government armed with the Keynesian economic weaponry of pump priming the government spending and stronger, more adept and proactive Federal Reserve, which by injecting record liquidity into the economy along with reducing the cost of credit to the near zero level for banks, averted the domino effect of the banking crisis and brought the economy on the recovery and growth path in the course of just two quarters of 2009.

The crisis evoked unconventional, unorthodox, and out of the rule book measures from the Fed to stem the rot before it spread and triggered its snowballing effects on the economy which was already recession prone. The Great Depression of 1930s has been the subject matter of research and analysis for over last many years for its causation. Among the several events that caused, precipitated, and aggravated the malady of depression, the banking crisis, which followed the stock market boom and crash of 1929, did the maximum damage. The current subprime home loan crisis was, therefore, taken in all seriousness with a prompt action from the Federal Reserve and Treasury in averting a larger banking crisis.

The worst seems to be behind. After suffering the worst fall in US GDP of 3.5% in 2009 following the marginal decline in growth of 0.4% in 2008, the effects of global action by way of fiscal stimulus by the governments and interest rate cuts to record low levels and also unprecedented liquidity infusion by the central banks showed visible signs on the growth figures. The year 2010 showed GDP growth of 2.4% followed by 1.8% in 2011. The year 2012 is expected to attain 2.5% growth.

In order to understand the chronology of the current crisis and its causation, it is essential to examine the longer term structural dynamics of the US economy and the anatomy of the housing and real estate boom that preceded the crisis.

American Economic Boom of 1990s: An Overview

One of the most outstanding features of the US economy in recent times has been the economic boom of 1990s. The economy enjoyed the longest, most vigorous, and unprecedented boom during this period. Although not subject to traditional, long, deep, and sharp economic cycle typical of the predepression capitalistic system, the US economy in the postwar Keynesian and later liberalization era that culminated in globalization did witness downswings in the economy periodically. What distinguished the modern American capitalism from its predepression edifice is the series of governmental instrumentalities and policies legislated through the Congress in reducing the systemic vulnerability of capitalism to its predisposed tendency toward any economic downswing following vigorous growth cycle. Bidding goodbye to *laissez-fairism*, balanced budget, and gold standard, the new economic policy beginning in the 1930s gave the capitalism a springboard to realize higher growth rates and a lever to skip the dirty phase of economic downswing.

The boom of the 1990s was longer and also much stronger than the one experienced in the 1960s. It lasted exactly 10 years, from March 1991 till March 2001, compared to the earlier long boom which lasted nearly 9 years, from February 1961 till December 1969.[2] The 1990s boom was punctuated by a short stint of recession of 8 months from March 2001 till November 2001. The recovery thereafter lasted up to December 2007. The earlier boom of 1980s which began in November 1982 to last till July 1990 was also followed by 8 months of recession, from July 1990 till March 1991. The sustained growth momentum of the US economy since mid-1980s, with only two recessions of 8 months each, demonstrates the benefits of globalization to the USA and global economies. The recessions of 1980 and 1982 were caused by tough monetary policy of high interest rates designed to combat intractable inflation emanating from oil price hikes and resultant cost-push inflation, while that in 1990–1991 was the fallout effect of savings and loan associations crisis.

Taking a longer look at the performance of the US economy since 1960s reveals that the economy experienced mild recessions in only 5 years. The declines in GDP in 1974 and 1975 of 0.6 and 0.2%, respectively, were caused by the oil crisis. Legendary Fed Chairman Paul Volcker's high interest rate policy broke the back of high and record inflation of 13.6% at the cost of GDP fall of 0.3% in 1980 and decline of 1.9% in 1982. By 1986, inflation rate had fallen to 1.9%. In 1991, GDP declined marginally by 0.2% under the adverse impact of savings and loan associations crisis.

Despite the sustained growth for a prolonged period of the 1990s, inflation was kept at bay. The supply of low-priced imported goods primarily from China and productivity growth were primary factors that kept the tight lid on price rise in 1990s.[3] During this period, the rise in oil prices was relatively moderate compared to earlier two oil shocks. The commodity prices showed a sharper rise but did not

---

[2] National Bureau of Economic Research, *Business Cycle Expansions and Contractions*, www.nber.org/cycles

[3] Bank for International Settlement, *75th Annual Report:* April 1, 2004–March 31, Basel, June, 2005, p. 15.

pose cost-push impact on general level of prices due to relatively stable energy cost. The impact of commodity prices on consumer price inflation was lower in the 1990s and later, compared to 1970s and 1980s.

There was considerable alteration in the structure of relative prices in the period. The share of energy and raw materials in the imports of industrial nations fell due the shift in production of manufactures to the emerging market economies. The supply elasticities of manufactured goods among the emerging economies were high due to large capacity buildup and intense competition among them to capture the markets of the developed nations. Despite rising raw material costs, the prices of manufactured goods continued to fall due to cost rationalization, increasing productivity, and lower markups and profit margins. Higher energy prices did not lead to rise in costs on account of steps to gain higher energy efficiency at each level. The wage costs remained stable due to migration of labor and relatively higher labor availability caused by displacement labor from closure of manufacturing in many industries in the USA and EU (European Union). Unprecedented productivity growth caused by new technologies in computers, internet, and telecommunications also contributed to lower pressure on prices. Finally, lower inflationary expectations and lower pass-through of exchange rate movements into import and consumer prices kept inflation at bay.

The decades of 1980s and 1990s recorded 3.8% GDP growth. However, the decade of 1980s was characterized by high inflation followed by high interest rate regime and 2 years of mild recession. Inflation had reached the record high rate of 13.6% in 1980 requiring one of the toughest monetary policies pursued by the Fed in the US history. The Fed funds rate reached the highest level of 20% in 1980–1981. The GDP declined by 1.9% in 1982, but high interest rates and negative growth reduced the excess demand in the economy and helped in checking inflation which declined to 3.2% by 1983. Since then, the USA enjoyed one of the longest period of low inflation through the 1990s and 2000s. The 1990s experienced sustained growth with only 1 year of recession and low average annual inflation of 3% compared to 5.5% in 1980s. The rate of inflation declined from 5.4% in 1990 to 1.6% in 1998. In the new millennium until 2009, the annual GDP growth rate slumped to 2.1% and inflation rate fell to 2.6%.[4] The highest rate of inflation of 5.5% was recorded during the new millennium in July 2008, when it rose consistently from 2.1% in January 2007.

The magnitude of the crisis can be gauged by the GDP fall it caused in 2009. The GDP fell by 3.5%, the record decline in GDP in the postwar US history. The unemployment also reached the level of 9.3%. Even a small negative growth in the US economy shows a sharp rise in unemployment. The earlier high decline of 1.9% in GDP in 1982 also brought record unemployment of 9.7% continuing in 1983 at 9.6, 7.5% in 1984, 7.2% in 1985, and 7% in 1986, even when GDP growth picked up to 4.5% in 1983 and 7.2% in 1984, 4.1% in 1985, and 3.5% in 1986. Despite high growth, the employment pickup was slow leading to unemployment still remaining above 7%. During the years of roaring growth of the 1990s, unemployment declined

---

[4] Bureau of Economic Analysis, US Dept. of Commerce and Bureau of Labor Statistics, US Dept. of Labor.

from 7.5% in 1992 to the lowest level of 4% in 2000. The technology boom succeeded in translating GDP growth figures into more employment and lower unemployment, a trend which did not occur in 1980s growth era. The technology growth of the 1990s offered large employment potential to absorb labor unlike in the 1980s. This experience of unemployment figures and its trend in the downturn shows that the US unemployment is very sensitive to growth. Even a small drop in growth or a marginal negative growth can cause high unemployment crossing 9% level.

Lower Inflation and Higher Unemployment Thresholds: 2-3-4% Economy

The perspective of more than half a century of the performance of the US economy reveals that while the inflation threshold of the economy has fallen, the unemployment threshold has gone up. The high and low unemployment rates which were 7.5 and 2.5% in 1950s were 7.1 and 3.4% in 1960s, went up to 9 and 3.9%, respectively, in 1970s, and to 10.8 and 5% in 1980s. The rates declined to 7.8 and 4% during 1990s boom. During the year 2000s, the unemployment crossed 10% again after the dot-com crisis but lowest rate remained at 3.9% (Fig. 1.2).[5]

Fig. 1.2 Inflation and unemployment, 1950–2010 (Source: Bureau of Labor Statistics, US Department of Labor)

[5] Bureau of Labor Statistics, US Department of labor.

The Bretton Woods period until 1971 showed the earlier decades enjoying high growth with relative price stability and also low unemployment rate. The era represented the fixed exchange rates and stable financial architecture. The 1950s recorded average annual real GDP growth of 4.5% with 2% rate of inflation, while the 1960s experienced 4.5% real GDP growth with 2.4% rate of inflation. The decade of 1970s represented the most uncertain era under which the global economy detached from the fixed rates financial environment was moving toward the floating rates system but had not yet got its firm anchor. The years were the years of transition and of struggle of price and rates adjustments. The price of crude oil, the critical ingredient of industrial economy with production monopolized by a few nations which cartelized the system, was beginning to assert in the market economy and test and discover its true value. The interest rates and exchange rates held together by central banks were finding market levels and adjusting rapidly. Threatened by the cost-push inflation, the economy failed to show growth and stagnated. The new economic phenomenon of stagflation, not experienced any time earlier, posed a fresh problem to the central bankers and economic policy makers. The conventional weapons did not yield results. The delinking of dollar from gold and resultant depreciation of dollar did set the process of economic adjustment of the USA with the rest of the world in motion. Yet inflation was raging and unemployment peaking. It was the Fed Chairman Paul Volker's policy of high interest rates in the early 1980s that finally succeeded in controlling inflation and restored the stability of the dollar in the international markets. The real GDP growth during 1970s slumped to a low of 3.2% with inflation peaking to 7.1%.

The new wave of globalization began in 1980s with the real GDP growth inching upward to 3.8% and inflation declining to 5.5%. The 1990s captured 3.8% GDP growth at lower inflation threshold of 3% with a flood of low-cost products from China and Asia, low-energy prices, outsourcing of skilled manpower from the emerging market economies, and record productivity growth emanating from the great technological revolution in internet, computer, and telecom industries. Hit by the dot-com bust in 2000 bringing the stock market crash and weak investor sentiment, the growth slowed down to 2.1% in 2000–2007, while the prices rise declined to 2.6%.

The above review shows that the US economy under the current phase of globalization until the onset of the subprime debt crisis has shown the inherent tendency to achieve 3% GDP growth, with inflation rate of 2% and unemployment rate of 4%. The US economy moved into 2-3-4% economic phase, 2% inflation, 3% growth, and 4% unemployment. Under the current institutional structure, natural endowments, and technological frontier, the USA shows the potential to continue to function into 2-3-4% economic trajectory.

Genesis of Real Estate Boom

With the end of the Bretton Woods era of fixed exchange rates and stable financial environment in 1971, the global economy entered a phase uncertain economic climate under the impact of falling dollar and record spurt in oil prices. The cost-push inflation and unprecedented imbalance in global payments structure caused by oil price hike beset the global economy with lower growth and recession in 1970s. In the 1980s, driven by the freer interplay of the market forces in the financial as well as the real sectors of the economies, the international economic and financial system ushered into a new phase of closer integration of economies and globalization. Removal of artificial economic policy restrictions and promotion of free trade and investment also characterized the phase of globalization. The change in the economic policy responses led by the USA and UK were followed by Europe as well as the emerging market economies. The resurgence of unprecedented growth in trade and cross-border investments galvanized the global economy with the highest ever economic growth for more than two and half decades driven primarily by the buoyant US economy.

In this new phase of global economic development beginning in mid-1980s and continuing in 1990s, America was financing globalization through cheap money policy, freer foreign trade and investments, transfer of technology, ongoing stream of technological innovations, booming stock market, and strong growth in consumer demand. The decade of 1990s was the decade of revolution in computer, internet, software, media, and wireless telecom technology that transformed the world and produced unprecedented gains in productivity. This spread its GDP growth by making other nations and global economy partners in its prosperity, albeit with some hiccups reflected in the crises in a few emerging market economies in the 1990s. The era of superfast growth of the US economy and speedier globalization came to an abrupt halt after the dot-com boom burst in 2000. The year also marked a near saturation of the big thrust and a change on the technological front. Although continuing stream of minor innovations in the sectors driven by intense competition among the main players became a routine matter, as in any other business, no major innovation was in the offing to drive big investment spend.

The new opportunities for large investments from the stream of technical innovations that had galvanized the investment climate during 1990s waned. The US economy seemed fatigued and showed the signs of slowdown. The stock market bust of 2000 had a negative wealth effect on consumer spending which grew fast during the 1990s under spell of rising stock prices. The adverse climate on both investment and consumer spending fronts were a drag on economic growth. Both the front and rear wheels of the economy that sped the growth in the earlier decades were slowing at a fast rate.

The GDP growth rate slumped from the peak of 4.8% in 1999 and 4.1% in 2000 to 1.1% in 2001 and 1.8% in 2002. Buoyant investment spending driving higher economic growth needed a new stream of technological discoveries and innovations. The technology had reached its limits of continuing to bring new discoveries for large-scale commercial exploitation. In the absence of any fresh technological breakthrough creating another investment boom, the economy was in search for a new driver for its growth.

In this somber investment and economic milieu, the housing and real estate market could kick-start the growth of the US economy again if finance was made available to the millions of prospective home owners at reasonable rates. The dream of every American to own a house had not been fulfilled by many, and millions did not and could not own one. The resource constraint did not permit the traditional mortgage banks, which were in this business, to finance larger number of houses year after year. Not many commercial banks had the technical expertise in housing and real estate financing but had adequate resources for lending. At the same time, comfortable domestic liquidity with the US banks and dollar liquidity with the foreign banks abroad due to rising current account deficit of the USA demanded lucrative outlet in lending. After the dot-com bust, there was a sudden decline in demand for credit. Despite low Fed funds interest rates of 1.75% during 2002, the bank credit failed to show growth. In this era of liquidity glut, the excess liquid funds of banks and financial institutions could be channeled into housing finance provided there was an efficient vehicle to do this.

On the supply side, there was a large pool of funds that could be channeled into housing at much better rates of interest. On the demand side, there was a large latent demand for houses not from traditional low-risk, high net-worth borrowers but from high risk, low and zero net-worth borrowers. The latter could be given loans which are usually not within the norms of traditional house mortgage financing. The subprime home loan mortgage asset-backed securitization was born out of this situation as an excellent tool for promoting home ownership among the population in lower strata of society and giving boost to the housing and real estate sector. The latter could kick-start and sustain the growth in the US economy.

The Fed's low interest rates policy, investment bankers' initiatives in developing securitization of subprime housing debt, and aggressive securitized lending by banks, along with and the mechanism for trading in these securities and their derivative products, created a rapidly expanding market for this new financial product. The lower income households could own houses promoting the government aim to distribute house ownership much wider. Unprecedented increase in home ownership triggered the housing and real estate boom, and cheap money raised demand for home loans further. The issue of these securities by the leading investment and commercial banks and rising real estate prices strengthened the ratings of these securities and promoted their secondary market trading. Everyone in the chain was a gainer, and the economy sustained higher growth rate. Global economy raced ahead without any interruption.

Housing and Real Estate: Driver of Economic Growth

Historically the real estate sector has been one of the largest sectors in the US economy. In 2010, it accounted for 12.5% of GDP compared to manufacturing at 12%. The housing and real estate sector grew very fast in the last two decades when the share of manufacturing declined from 16% of GDP in 1993. For capital formation in the US economy, also the housing and real estate have been overshadowing the manufacturing sector. In the year 1970, out of the total gross fixed capital formation of $182 billion at current prices accounting for 18% of GDP, the real estate investment was $52 billion, being the largest sector with 29% of total gross fixed investment. The manufacturing sector ranked second with $25 billion, 14% of investment in 1970. In 1980, the picture was similar, with real estate having 28% of total investment of $560 billion and the manufacturing remained at 14% of total investment. The rate of gross fixed investment rose to 20% of GDP. By 1990, under the effect of the first round of globalization that began in the early 1980s, the investment in manufacturing closed at $125 billion, with its share in total dropping to 13% of total investment of $999 billion. The rate of gross fixed investment in the economy fell to 17% of GDP. However, the real estate sector investment of $313 billion formed 31% of total investment and emerged as the rising and critical segment in the growth of the US economy. The trend of declining share of manufacturing and rising share of real estate was more pronounced in 1990s which carried much wider impact in the second round of globalization spreading faster than in the 1980s. By the year 2000, the investment in real estate rose sharply to $673 billion investment, accounting for 34% of total investment of $1,946 billion. The rate of investment rose back to 20% of GDP, but the share of manufacturing in total investment dropped to 11%.

The real estate boom that commenced in 2001 persisted till 2006 and was in fact generated by rising investments in the sector facilitated by the Fed's cheap money policy and promoted by the big wave of subprime lending. The process of securitization and spread of the portfolio of subprimes among larger and more diversified group of commercial banks within the USA and outside regenerated the resources of the original mortgage banks which could finance more homes at a faster rate. The securitization alone enabled the financing of mammoth $1.3 trillion for 7.5 million homes during this period.

One of the reasons for healthy growth in the economy during 2001–2007 was that the rate of fixed investment in the economy was maintained between at 18–19% with the investment in the real estate being primary source of growth. The real estate investment rose to $711 billion out of total investment of $1,870 billion (38%) in the economy in 2002 at the investment rate of 18% of GDP. Lower interest rates and rising real estate prices gave further boost to real estate investment. The ingenious method of subprime lending and its securitization ensured adequate funding for house purchases and rising demand for houses. In 2003, the real estate investment rose to $783 billion out of the total investment of $1,952 billion, 40%. The tempo of growth in investment continued in 2004 with real estate investment of $897 billion out of $2,147 billion total investment. The year 2005 witnessed the real estate investment crossing $1 trillion which was maintained in 2006. The investment in real estate declined in 2007 to $896 billion out of total investment of $2,521 billion. Under the influence of globalization, investment in manufacturing witnessed a declining trend and fell sharply to $185 billion, 7.5% of total investment in 2007.

In addition to the growth in consumer demand, real estate investment was the key driver of the tempo of economic growth. The globalization had brought a phenomenal reduction in the share of manufacturing and industry in the GDP in the USA. The service sector was rising and so was housing and real estate. The sharp drop in manufacturing was also reflected in the declining share of the sector in aggregate investment. In 2007, the investment in manufacturing was 7.5% of total investment, nearly half of 14% in 1980. The government needed to keep this huge gap in investment, arising out of declining investment in manufacturing, filled in order to keep the growth momentum of the economy. The housing and real estate sector was the only sector at the time most suited to fill this gap to maintain the momentum of the economy which was slipping in 2002 following a long boom of 1990s that culminated into Y2K bust in 2000. The housing sector, which was always the favorite of government for liberal assistance since the New Deal days, also fitted very well in the new growth strategy. A number of government initiatives paved the way for securitization of house mortgages for record lending in this sector which led to excessive demand and upward pressure on housing and real estate prices.

In a market economy, investment is allocated into sectors which have potential for growth and profitability. The real estate sector attracted investment due to rising demand for houses and commercial estate both of which witnessed rising prices. The trend of appreciation in housing prices and low interest rates raised the demand for houses and housing finance. In this buoyant environment in a low-interest era, home ownership was made accessible to those who did not fulfill the normal credit rating norms by relaxing the norms through the subprime mortgages.

Government Initiatives in Housing

Reckoning the critical importance of housing in the economy and the house ownership as a much cherished ideal or dream in the American society, the US government has played proactive and pivotal role in realization of American Dream of owning a house. To spread house ownership among all the families has been one of ideals of the government since the New Deal of 1933. The housing and real estate industry being a critical component of the economy also required the government to take a number of measures for the promotion and development of the industry by spreading home ownership across the country and across all sections of society. The government, therefore, played a significant role in the development and growth of housing markets. The initiatives of government in housing and real estate industry are not only large and developmental but also date back to the Great Depression days.

In order to promote housing through mortgage loans, the Federal Housing Administration (FHA) was created by the government in 1934 under the National Housing Act to insure the lenders against the loss on residential mortgages. The Fannie Mae (Federal National Mortgage Association) was created in 1938 to support the housing mortgage market by assisting the local banks and mortgages with low-cost federal funding. The financial support and guarantee from the government enabled Fannie Mae to establish and develop secondary mortgage market. Until 1968, Fannie Mae held the monopoly in the secondary mortgage market when it was privatized. However, it continued to carry the government guarantee.

The Ginnie Mae (Government National Mortgage Association), wholly owned government organization, was established in 1968 to promote the mortgage-backed securities (MBS) in a standardized format by pooling mortgages and their trading in the secondary market. In 1970, the Freddie Mac (Federal Home Loan Mortgage

Corporation) was created by the Congress to foster liquidity in secondary market for conventional mortgages. It eliminated the monopoly of Fannie Mae in the secondary housing mortgage market and made the market more vibrant and broader in geographic- and income-level coverage. The government also gave tax breaks to promote housing by allowing mortgage interest to be tax deductible. The US Treasury gives up annually revenue of nearly $150 million due to tax breaks enjoyed by 40 million home owners and taxpayers. The Community Reinvestment Act of 1977 also encouraged home ownership in low-income groups with credit subsidy.

Under the Tax Reform Act 1986, the government permitted creation of vehicles structured as corporations, partnerships, trusts, or pools of assets called real estate mortgage investment conduit (REMIC) for issuing MBS and gave them tax exemption at the issuer level on following the provisions of the act. This was a big boost to the growth of MBS. Unlike the ordinary bonds which are a plain vanilla debt obligation, MBS are complex instruments representing a pool of cash flows of underlying mortgage obligations. The complexity of the securities also arises from varying deal structure and set of rules that govern the cash flows. Hence, in many instruments, the inherent risk is masked or not apparent.

Based on the success of MBS, two large government-sponsored institutions, Freddie Mac and Fannie Mae, created their own MBS which were guaranteed by them. Both the Freddie Mac and Fannie Mae also went public in 1989 although they carried implicit government guarantee. Both the institutions were pivotal in the development secondary mortgage market which enabled primary financing agencies like savings and loan banks and mortgage banks to finance individual mortgages to promote home ownership at a greater pace. The rapid development of MBS in conventional fixed rate prime mortgages by Freddie Mac and Fannie Mae provided further support and funding for the housing and real estate market.

Housing and Real Estate Boom: 2002–2007

The year 2000 witnessed the dot-com bust leading to NASDAQ crashing from its peak of 5,048 in March to the low of 2,470 in December. Investors lost close to about $2 trillion in market value of new economy stocks. The collapse of the Twin Towers of the World Trade Center on 9/11 in 2002 from the terrorist attack marked the worst disaster that struck the US economy in the heart of the USA and global capital market and the citadel of American capitalism and the ideals it upholds. The economic scenario and investment climate was so badly damaged by these two events that Fed and the government had to resort to extraordinary measures to restore investment confidence and momentum of the economy to the levels experienced in the earlier two decades. GDP growth had slumped from 4.1% in 2000 to 1.1 in 2001. In order to revive the market sentiment and reinstate growth, the Fed pursued policy of reducing interest rates to record low levels. The Fed funds rate was from 6 to 1.75% in 2001 and to 1% by 2003. This low interest policy of the Fed popularly known as the "Greenspan Put" helped the stock market recovery and investment climate.

Historically, the housing industry and home ownership was adversely affected in the 1980s due to high interest rates. The annual interest rate on 30-year fixed mortgage exceeded 18% in the early 1980s during the Fed's high interest rate policy phase aimed to curb intractable inflation that had sprung up in the mid-1970s. On the Fed exiting the high interest rate policy in 1982, mortgage interest rate began declining and fell to a low of 8% by 2000. The Fed's policy of reducing Fed funds rate brought the 30-year fixed mortgage rate to the lowest level of 5.25% and remained within 6% through 2008. The ARM (adjustable-rate mortgage) further reduced the monthly payments of borrowers and enabled them to get larger loans and several new entrants to borrow and own house.

The low mortgage rates, innovations in mortgage lending, and securitizing them for refinancing enabled larger deployment of funds for home loans. Traditionally, the home loans disbursals were limited by the resources of the mortgage banks and other home loan financing institutions. Through the securitization of home loans, and selling them to banks, insurance companies and other financial and investment institutions helped the mortgage finance companies to increase their lending at much faster rate.

Being an important sector in the economy in the USA both at the micro as well as macro levels, the housing and real estate received special attention from the investment banking community for its development. It offered great potential provided the constraint of finance was overcome with innovative vehicle of financing. The subprime securitization filled this gap. The real estate boom followed.

The real estate boom of 2002–2007 was the result of the confluence of a number of favorable factors.

1. At the microlevel, increasing housing ownership especially among those who could not afford and were not traditionally eligible for housing mortgage loans enhanced the individual living standard, satisfaction, and a sense of well-being. At the macro level, it had a very significant impact on growth and employment due to skill-intensive nature of the industry and its share in the annual investment and income in the economy.
2. The second positive factor is the role of institutional framework of the government as well as the private industry in promoting the financing of mortgages which has been the cornerstone of its growth and dynamism.
3. Thirdly, the housing investment has been traditionally providing positive investment return over long periods. Despite exceptional fall in house prices for a few years, the trend in housing prices in the last 50 years has been upward.
4. Fourthly, the mortgage rates available during 2000–2007 have been the lowest ever. No other period in the past provided rates as low as prevalent in this period. The fixed mortgage rates which were consistently rising from 5.9% in 1963 to 8.9% in 1975 rose thereafter to 10.5% in 1979 and reached the peak of over 14% in 1981–1982. The rates came down to 9% in 1991, lowered further to 7.8% in 2000, and fell to 5% by 2005, lower than the ones prevalent in 1960s.
5. Fifthly, the provision of subprime loans increased the demand for houses from a large number of households who could not avail mortgages earlier. The innovations in securitization of subprime mortgages and aggressive marketing by

investment bankers spread the holding of these securities wider among banking, insurance, and investment institutions within the USA and also abroad. The speedier securitization enabled the primary mortgage lenders like local mortgage banks to finance mortgages at a faster rate.

6. Sixthly, the global liquidity glut and low interest rates promoted the investment in securitized debt by several international banks and investment institutions.
7. The rating of securitized mortgages by reputed US rating agencies provided level of comfort to the investors.
8. The OTC market for securities provided liquidity to the securities held by banks and institutions.
9. The lowest benchmark rate, i.e., 1% Fed funds rate, promoted risk taking and trading in risks. The trend of falling interest rates from 2000 till 2005 caused appreciation in the prices of debt securities enabling the holders to profit from trading.
10. The availability of credit default swaps (CDS) and its active market enabled the investors to insure against defaults and take higher risks.
11. In addition to the demand from first home owners, the rising home prices gave rise to investment for second home. The flippers and speculators also entered the market, buying homes for quick profit.

All these favorable factors combined in creating continuing demand for housing during 2000–2007 generating an unprecedented real estate boom. The record 8.2 million houses were sold in this period of boom. Due to the large magnitude of lending, securitization, and investment in the sector, the industry also emerged as the key driver of growth in the economy. The rising real estate prices also led to the wealth effect causing higher consumption either from second mortgages or from realized gains or simply higher spending from current income due higher home valuations. The consumption growth also remained high and helped the economy move at a faster rate.

The housing boom cycle which began in 2001 started reversing in 2007. The economy was overheating and worries about inflation rendered the Fed taking a review on interest rate and raising it to stall inflation. The Fed funds rate went up from 2.5% in 2005 to 5.25% in 2006. In February 2006, Ben Bernanke took over as the Fed Chairman from Alan Greenspan after his 18-year stint and continued the policy of raising the interest rates. The rising interest rates stalled the rising house prices which started showing declining trend. This trend lowered home sales. Higher interest rates increased the monthly payments under ARM and precipitated defaults. The defaults rose from 755,000 in 2005 to 1 million by 2006 and to 1.5 million in 2007 and 2.2 million in 2008, when 3% of households went on default.

Role of Debt Securitization in Housing Sales

The ingenious Wall Street investment bankers created and sold housing mortgage-backed securities of record proportion: $1.1 trillion in 2005, $1 trillion in 2006, and another $1 trillion in 2007. The process of securitization involves pooling of mortgages and slicing them into tranches according to risk. The investors in the senior tranches get paid first and hence get lower interest rate. The securities in the senior tranches also get higher rating. The lower tranches known as the middle-rated or mezzanine tranches carry higher risk, lower rating, and get higher interest rates. The senior tranche usually carries 80% face value of the issue and the mezzanine tranche 18% and remaining 2% is equity tranche with very high risk and higher return. The equity tranche is normally held by hedge funds.

In 1995, a median-priced home could be purchased in the USA with a monthly mortgage payment of $675. This was no greater than in 1980s due to the fall in mortgage rates. Despite some increase in the property prices, the declining mortgage rates by the late 1990s and early 2000s offered excellent opportunity for house purchases. By 2003, near the peak of housing boom, fixed mortgage rates had fallen to 5% and adjustable rates below 4%.[6] The mortgage financing, its refinancing by securitization, was at its peak. Between 2004 and 2006, more than $9 trillion mortgage loans were originated. At the peak of the housing boom in 2005, top 30 US banks, mortgage lender, and institutions accounted for half the loan originations of $2.8 trillion. The leading banks were Countrywide, Wells Fargo, Washington Mutual, Bank of America, Chase Manhattan, Citigroup, HSBC, and Wachovia. The investment banking firms securitized the housing mortgage debt and spread the debt over wider spectrum of banking, investment, and hedge fund industries in the USA and abroad. The leading investment bankers and broker dealers which were in forefront also as the market makers and dealers in the securitized debt were Goldman Sachs, Merrill Lynch, J P Morgan, Morgan Stanley, Lehman Brothers, Bear Sterns, HSBC, Citigroup, UBS, and Bank of America.

Housing boom had reached its peak in 2005. Among the areas which were more susceptible to speculative rise in prices were California, Florida, and the Northeast corridor, although the rising house prices was a nationwide phenomenon. In the real estate market "price to rent" (PR) ratio is what price to earnings (PE) ratio is in the stock market. During the housing boom, the prices were running faster than the rents, and the "price to rent" for the real estate had gone up to 25 by the end of 2005 compared to 18.5 in 2003 and the average of 16.6 for past quarter century and a low of 12.5 in 1980s.[7]

The residential mortgage debt outstanding which was $2.9 trillion in 1990 had increased to $5.5 trillion in 2000. The total mortgage debt outstanding rose to $7.8 trillion in 2003 and $11.9 trillion in 2007. During this period, the mortgages held by Fannie Mae and Freddie Mac rose from $2.3 trillion to $4.9 trillion. The mortgage-backed securities (MBS) held by them grew from $1.3 trillion to $3.5 trillion. In 2007, the two institutions held 41.3% of residential mortgage debt out of which 29% was securitized debt. In the first quarter of 2009, the total residential mortgage debt had reached $11.9 trillion with two institutions holding $5.4 trillion, 44.9%, out of which MBS of $3.7 trillion.

---

[6] Zandi Mark, pp. 160–1.

[7] Ibid, p. 164.

The yearly house sales in the USA which were below 600,000 in 1960s had risen to over 800,000 by 1977. It fell to low of over 400,000 in 1982 and went up to 750,000 in 1986. Until 1996, it hovered between 500, 000 and 750,000. The sales rose from 800,000 in 1997 to 880,000 in 1999. From 877,000 in 2000, the house sales went up consistently to 1,086,000 in 2003, 1,203,000 in 2004, 1,283,000 in 2005, 1,051,000 in 2006, slumped to 776,000 in 2007, and further to 485,000 in 2008.

The average sale price of mortgage financed house rose from $159,500 to $212,500, a rise of 33%. The price rose from $224,500 in 2000 to the high of $313,600 in 2007, a rise of 40%.

The home ownership in the USA which was 55% of all households in 1950 and had gone up to 64% in 1990 reached the peak of 69% in 2008. Out of 110 million households in the USA in 2008, 75.5 million were house owners. About 68% or 51.6 million have mortgages. It is estimated that due to decline in home prices since 15 million home owners, nearly 30% of home owners with mortgages were facing negative equity.

Favorable Trend in Fed Funds Rate

The only comparable period in which the Fed Funds rate was as low as in 2009 is the early 1950s. In 1954, the Fed funds rate hovered between 0.75 and 1.25%. It rose to 2.5% by end of 1955. The phase of rising interest rate had begun. The rate firmed up to 3% by the early 1957 and reached the peak of 3.5%. It had a short-lived decline to 0.63% by mid-1958 and started rising again and reaching 2.5% by the end of 1958. Thereafter, it rose persistently to 4% by 1959 end. Since then, the rates firmed up to reach the peak at 9% in 1969.

The decade of 1970s was fraught with volatility and uncertainty on global monetary front due to the weakness of dollar in the international market. The Fed funds rate had reached the high of 9% by 1969 end but declined thereafter to 3.5% in early 1972. It rose sharply to a high of 13% by mid-1974 when the oil crisis hit the world. The rate declined thereafter to a low of 4.50% by 1976 end. The 1980s were the decade of highest rates in the US monetary history. The concern about raging inflation which was becoming intractable needed extraordinary measures. Against this background, the Fed under the Chairmanship of Paul Volcker pursued very restrictive and high interest rate policy that has no precedent in US monetary history. Under the dear money policy, the Fed funds rate went on increasing from 14% in January 1980 to the highest level of 17.6% in April 1980. The rate declined to 9% by mid-1980 but rose again to reach the highest level of 19% in mid-1981. It began to decline to 8.5% in mid-1983. The rate rose again to 11% by mid-1985 but began to fall and reached the low of 6.75% by 1987 end and rose again to 9.50 by mid-1989. Since then, the rate began to consistently decline for a long period. The 1990s was a decade of lowest rate in recent US monetary history. From the level of 8.5% in 1989 end, the Fed funds rate fell consistently to a low of 3% in mid-1993 (Fig. 1.3).

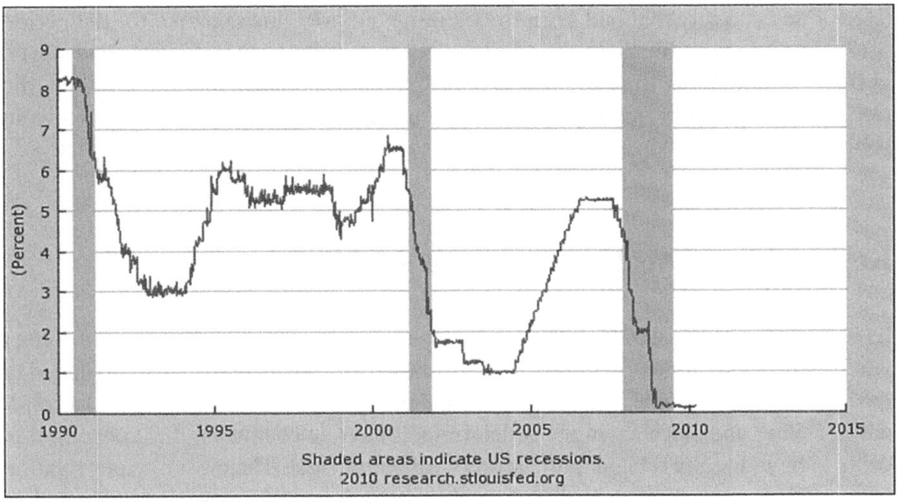

Fig. 1.3 Effective federal funds rate (FF). *Shaded areas* indicate US recessions. 2010 research.stlouisfed.org (Source: Board of Governors of the Federal Reserve System)

The decade of 1990s witnessed unprecedented stock market and economic boom and asset price inflation. From the level 2,300 in 1990, the Dow Jones crossed 6,000 mark in October 1996 and reached the high of 11,497 from the low of 2,365 in 1990. This became the cause of worry for the Fed. In December 1996, the Fed Chairman Alan Greenspan, one of the architects of 1990s boom, expressed his concern about rising stock prices terming the phase of the market as one of "irrational exuberance." The Fed began raising interest rates at a great frequency to curb the runaway growth in stock prices. The stock market boom was also fuelled by the dot-com phenomenon and irrationally high prices for the stocks of many startup companies without the underlying fundamentals of earnings but only expectation of high earnings growth. The monetary tightening resulted in the Fed funds rate going up and rising to 6% by mid-1995 from a low 3% in 1993. It declined to 5.5% in the beginning of 1996 and remained in the range of 5–5.5% until the end of 1998 and reached a high of 6.5% in mid-2000.

The dot-com bust in April 2000 created the panic in the stock market, but the Fed reacted only when the signs of a slowdown of the economy became visible on the macroeconomic front. In its attempt to preempt the sharp fall in growth rate of the economy, the Fed went ahead with its relentless cuts in Fed funds rate from 6.5% in mid-2000 to the lowest level of 1% in the beginning of 2004. It was the sharpest one-way declining movement in the Fed history. Throughout the 2002–2004 period, the Fed funds rate remained within the range of 1–1.75%. It is this phase of lowest interest rates that gave boost to the housing and real estate sector and fuelled the property boom.

The phase of rising rates began again in 2005 when Fed funds rate rose from 2% consistently to 5.25% by mid-2007. The first sign of subprime loan crisis was visible in mid-2007. The rate hike of 3.25% over a period of two and half years was a sharp rise for an economy that had been in declining and low interest zone for the period of 4 years. It is possible that the crisis may not have blown out if the rates had stayed in the range of 2–3% for a longer period. Realizing the gravity of the problem, the rate was reduced very quickly and dropped to 2% by mid-2008. When the blowout happened in September 2008, the rate was reduced to 1% and later below that.

Keynes Effect (Wealth Effect) and Real Balance Effect

In his path-breaking General Theory in 1936, Keynes discussed the wealth effect when he brought out the functional relationship, the propensity to consume related to the level of one's income. While the classical thought treated consumption as a residual of saving and since saving was determined the rate of interest, the consumption came to be indirectly related to the level of rate of interest. The most obvious relation of individual consumption with the level of his/her income was not established as firmly as Keynes did in economics and which was the most fundamental error of the classical economics whose reasoning and logic was resultantly short-circuited. It could, therefore, neither analyze the root cause of depression nor provide an effective remedy. Keynes first demonstrated the effect of stock prices on individual consumption expenditure in elaborating his concept of propensity to consume.

It is essential here to distinguish between the Keynes's wealth effect and Pigou's real balance effect. The real balance effect stipulates that the decline in prices of commodities and services during depression also causes an increase in the real money balances for consumers. It was argued that this real balance effect would cause rise in consumption that would reverse depression and initiate economic recovery. This did not happen during the Great Depression since the decline in GDP and loss in value of assets due to banking failure, steep fall in stock, and property prices were so large and the positive real balance effect was so insignificant that it was overshadowed by the negative wealth effect. Further, since cash balances are only a small part of the wealth or investment portfolio of an individual, the real balance effect is negligible in influence. This is evidenced also by the recent protracted recession in Japan which did not establish any recovery despite falling general prices that should have under real balance effect stimulated consumption. The negative wealth effect has been so dominant that the real balance effect has no influence in promoting consumption expenditure.

Keynes is the originator of the wealth effect, and it has been eloquently described by him in the *General Theory*. "Unfortunately a serious fall in the marginal efficiency of capital also tends to affect adversely the propensity to consume. For it involves a severe decline in the market value of Stock exchange equities. Now, on the class who take an active interest in their Stock exchange investments, especially if they are employing borrowed funds, this naturally exerts a very depressing influence. These people are even more influenced in *their readiness to spend by rises and falls in the value of their investments than by the state of their income*. With the stock minded public, as in the United States today, a rising stock market may be an almost essential condition of a satisfactory propensity to consume; in this circumstance, generally overlooked until lately, obviously serves to aggravate still further the depressing effect of a decline in the marginal efficiency of capital" [1, p. 139, Italics are mine].

Wealth Effect, Consumption, and Investment, 1990–2008

An increase in the valuation of assets of households has strong influence on their propensity to consume and their consumption levels. Hence, stock market or property boom also witnesses strong consumer sentiment and growing consumption. The impact of this wealth effect may vary from time to time. The decade of 1980s had shown much stronger wealth effect on consumption from the stock market boom of the decade. During the 1980s, the Dow Jones went up by 214% by contributing to the consumption spending going up from 80% of GDP in 1980 to 83% in 1990. During 1990–2000, the Dow Jones Industrial Average went up from 2,810 to 11,317, 304% rise, while the real GDP grew by 38% and GDP in nominal terms rose from $5.8 trillion to $9.8 trillion, 70%. The consumption expenditure grew from $4.8 trillion to $8.1 trillion, nearly same as the nominal GDP growth. The consumption expenditure which had gone up from 80% of GDP in 1980 to 83% in 1990 remained stable at 83% in 2000. But the growth during the decade of 1990s was fuelled more by rising investment primarily in internet, computers, software, telecom, and media and entertainment. The technology, media, and telecom (TMT) sectors were witnessing great breakthroughs and attracted record investments. The gross investment rate in the USA went up from 18% of GDP in 1990 to 21% of GDP in 2000.

The story in the new millennium is different. After the internet and dot-com bust in 2000, the avenues for fresh investments dried up. The gross investment rate fell from 21% in 2000 to normal 18% in 2007, the rate which the US economy incurred over a long period of last four decades. It was consumption growth during 2001–2007 that enables the US economy to achieve the average annual growth of 2.7% after coming out of the depressing effect of the stock market crash of April 2000. The bull market of 1990s did produce a pronounced wealth effect on the US consumers and had not been visible in the aggregate figures of consumption. One of the reasons is that during this period, the US budget which was showing record deficit turned into record surplus, and capital gains, whether realized or unrealized, were used to pay higher taxes. In contrast, the period of 2000–2007 showed GDP growing by 40% and consumption rising by 47% and from 83% of GDP to record 87%.

The negative performance of the stock market during 2000–2003 did affect consumption propensity adversely. The consumption expenditure, however, rose sharply to 87% of GDP in 2007 primarily due to low interest rates, low level of inflation, and booming housing prices. The strongest factor in favor of rising consumption was the rising housing and real estate prices. The primary reason why the investment rate in the economy did not fall sharply after the dot-com burst was that the real estate investment went up steadily since 2001 until 2007. The low interest rate policy, rising real estate prices, and increasing financing of real estate through subprime debt securitization all contributed to sharp rise in investment expenditure in housing, and real estate kept the gross investment rate from dropping below 18% of GDP.

The rise in consumption resulted from the wealth effect, interest rate effect, and real balance effect. The stock market during this period did not show any rise at all and in fact was in a mild bearish phase in the initial years. The real estate boom began in 2001 and lasted until 2007. The housing and real estate price as measured by the S&P/Case–Schiller House Price index of 10 cities rose from 100 in 2000 to the high of 227 in April 2007, a rise of 117%. The index for 20 cities during the same period rose from 100 to 206, showing 106% rise. Such an unprecedented rise did bring about a strong positive wealth effect which was seen in the buoyant consumption expenditure during those years. As the real estate prices started declining in April 2007, the consumption growth slowed down and the investment in real estate also plummeted. With the consumption and investment, both the wheels of growth, moving at a slower pace the economy, went into recession much before the eruption of the subprime in September 2008. The indices later dropped to the lows of 140 and 152, respectively, in May 2009 under the impact of housing market slump and the subprime crisis, showing 38 and 26% declines from the highs in these indices, respectively.

Lessons from Theories of Growth and Business Cycles

Post-Keynesian neoclassical growth theory elaborated on the determinants of long-term steady-state growth dynamics of a mature capitalist economy but could not throw more light on the deviations in growth in terms slumps and recessions [2].[8] "Many industrial capitalist economies go for long stretches of time without deviating by more than few percent from the trend of potential output. Over 30–50 year intervals the actual growth path is clearly dominated by supply-side factors like the increase of the labor force, the accumulation of physical and human capital, and advance of technology.... The observed growth paths are not smooth. They are punctuated by recessions, large and small, and by periods of excess demand" [2, p. 184]. The labor and capital, and the technology embedded in them determine the growth potential of an economy. But if growth falters below its longer term potential, it is caused by deficient effective demand. Yet growth economists were unable to unequivocally identify the causes of periodic blips in growth rates. Their frustration in this area was obvious. "What we used to call business cycles- or at least booms and recessions- are now to be interpreted as optimal blips in optimal path in response to random fluctuations in productivity and the desire for leisure.... I find none of this convincing.... I cannot imagine shocks to tastes and technology large enough on a quarterly or annual time scale to be responsible for the ups and downs of the business cycle" [2, p. xvi].

---

[8] The book in addition to outlining Solow's Steady State Growth Model gives the review of later developments in growth theory.

Theory of business cycles also took a new turn after the Keynesian revolution. The multiplier-acceleration principle gave a new vision into the dynamics of causality of cyclicality of economic activities. While the Keynesian neoclassicals dwelt on the real factors such as multiplier and investments in cyclicality of the economy, Friedman and Chicago School monetarists, however, emphasized the role of monetary factors and money supply growth in ups and downs in the economy. More recent analysis by Hyman Minsky, who was bred on both the Keynesian and Chicago traditions, examined the recessions of 1966, 1970, 1974–1975, 1979–1980, 1981–1982 and underscored the complexity of the phenomenon. "Analysis that builds on either the conventional Keynesian or the popular monetarist models cannot explain financial and economic instability" [3, p. 21]. Yet he emphasized the Fed's concern on inflation to have caused the recessions. "These three (1966, 1970, 1974–1975) near financial crises were triggered when Federal Reserve operations, undertaken in an effort to curb inflation, led to a run-up of interest rates. ... two additional episodes of financial trauma: in 1979–80 and in 1982–83, both followed an exercise designed by the Federal Reserve to curb inflation" [3, pp. 20–1]. Ironically, the worst recessions of 1974–1975, 1979–1980, and 1982–1983 and financial crises were contained and prevented from culminating into depression by the interventions of Federal Reserve and government by way lender-of-last-resort facility and deficit financing [3, p. 73].

The current crisis is much larger in magnitude and spread than the earlier ones but to a large extent analogous to those mini-crises. The cheap money policy from 2002 onward drove the record credit flow to the housing sector through the innovative vehicle of subprime debt securitization. The housing and real estate boom catapulted the economy into moderate growth range over 2% from the recessionary path that was a fallout of the dot-com bust of 2000. In 2005, the Fed began tightening interest rate on the concern of inflation. The policy continued till 2007. The interest rate as a tool of monetary control in the hands of central banks is a double-edged sword. While the rising interest rate brings pain from falling bond prices and higher credit cost but favors the savers, the falling interest rate triggers euphoria on rising bond prices and lower credit cost but hurts the savers. The Fed concern on inflation, reflected in its interest rate policy, continuing in 2006 and 2007 became most serious destabilizer of bond markets and became a precursor to recession. The experience was similar to that observed by Minsky in the earlier crises and recessions. Rising interest rates and slowing economy accelerated defaults in housing loan repayments, increasing foreclosures and busting the real estate market. The collapse of securities markets subprime debt created havoc among the holders comprising banks, insurance companies, and other financial institutions. The balance sheet implosion in financial system turned out to be record in history to cause the economy plunge in recession. Like in the earlier crises, the Fed liquidity as the lender-of-last-resort and government support from bailouts and deficit financing rescued the economy from the quicksand depression.

The upshot of the matter is that the Fed's low interest rate policy promotes the economic boom, but its premature concern on overheating of the economy germinates the seeds of its own destruction. The withdrawal effect of the reversal of the interest rate policy can be devastating depending upon the magnitude of reversal, stage of the economic boom, and sensitivity of the economy to the reversal. In the current crisis, the policy reversal did not affect the investment and consumption expenditure directly, but the withdrawal effect was large and threatening on the housing mortgage debt servicing segment which was very sensitive to such changes and could not bear the burden of such withdrawal effect. The subprime debt magnitude was very large and the borrowers had little capacity to bear the burden of higher debt servicing. The entire structure of newly built subprime debt portfolio that had penetrated globally into the balance sheets of banks collapsed like a pack of cards. The interest rate reversal was too large to trigger withdrawal effect of crisis proportion. The crisis could have been averted if the interest rate reversal was smaller than the subprime debt segment could bear. Or alternatively the size of subprime debt should not have been so large so the withdrawal effect would have had nationally damaging impact.

References

1. Keynes JM. The general theory of employment, interest and money. London: Macmillan and Co. Ltd.; 1961.
2. Solow Robert M. Growth theory: an exposition. New York: Oxford University Press; 2000.
3. Minsky HP. Stabilizing an unstable economy. New York: McGraw Hill; 2008.

Chapter 2
Subprime Debt Imbroglio: Risks–Rewards of Financial Sophistication

> Even apart from the instability due to speculation, there is the instability due to the characteristic of human nature that a large proportion of our positive activities depend on spontaneous optimism rather than on a mathematical expectation, whether moral or hedonistic or economic.
>
> John Maynard Keynes, *The General Theory of Employment, Interest and Money, 1936.*

Money, banking, and credit are in a constant evolutionary process. From coins and currency notes to digital money, from branch banking to universal banking, and later to Internet banking and now mobile phone banking, it is evolving fast with technology and innovation. The result is great convenience, lower cost, and instant service. Low-cost and high-speed digital money has been a great boon to the banking system and economy. While banking has taken great strides in technology, there has also been ongoing innovation on the credit side of banking. The subprime mortgage lending and its securitization were one such innovation intended to enlarge home ownership by directing credit toward tangible asset creation. Through the process of subprime lending and its securitization, a record amount of credit was channeled through the US and global banking, investment banking, and financial services industry to the housing and real estate sector from 2001 until the breakout of the crisis in 2008. Despite several safeguards, the system collapsed due to excessive exposure and a confluence of adverse economic trends.

If one has to describe the crisis in the shortest digital space, it would be as follows: the ingenuous method designed and engineered by the private investment banking industry to meet the basic need of housing for the millions of Americans, who would otherwise be deprived of this opportunity, by creating assets for the mutual benefit of all the stakeholders in the enterprise and the economy in general, through the invisible hand of the market, which failed to perform due to the growing mismatch in the risk–return matrix crossing the prudent threshold limit.

There are several aspects of the phenomenon of subprime debt securitization that need to be appreciated before looking at flaws in the system that made it vulnerable

S. Nayak, *The Global Financial Crisis: Genesis, Policy Response and Road Ahead*,
DOI 10.1007/978-81-322-0798-6_2, © Springer India 2013

to collapse. The goal of tapping the new segment of housing market was to be achieved without any support or incentive from the state. It was a pure market phenomenon driven by motive of financial gain secured by several innovative safeguards. The driving force without which the process would not have achieved the magnitude it did was the *Greenspan Put*. It refers to the low interest rate policy with successive cuts in interest rates that is favorable to the bond market in particular and financial markets and economy in general. The *Greenspan Put* assured automatic gains in valuation of fixed-income securities.

The Backdrop and Genesis of Securitization

The value of money in an economy is like that of blood in a body. Money is a vehicle through which economy transacts. Credit is a form of money through which assets are created; goods and services are produced, distributed, and consumed; and liabilities are met. The assets creation and consumption is a constant process in the economy facilitated by credit. Had it not been for credit created by the banking system, the process of asset creation as well as consumption would have been far slower than it is today. The burden of maintaining sustainability of credit cycle once the credit is granted lies with the borrower or debtor. The bank as a lender or creditor is in fact at the mercy of the borrower, while it is always the other way round until the credit is granted and used. Prompt servicing of credit by the debtors maintains the credit cycle. The default in servicing debt breaches the credit cycle. Credit involves risk, the business in which the banks are engaged day in and day out. The bankers can always deny credit for the fear of default. But if the credit denied is large, neither the bank nor the community benefits. The banks lose income, asset creation is halted, spending is deferred, and growth cycle is short-circuited. After the recent crisis, the fear of defaults had gripped the banks which were concerned more about credit quality than before. The credit was stand still and not flowing. It was the first thing to happen in recession and can aggravate recession. Fortunately, the Fed action pumped enough liquidity into the economy to revive the credit cycle in 2008–2009.

The process and development of financial intermediation in the continental Europe and the USA has taken different turns. The security-based lending has been traditionally a feature of American banking. In contrast, the European banking was loan based. The corporate debt securitization was not predominant in European banking. Securitization here means in conventional terms corporate debt incurred by way of issue of securities and not loans. The US banking intermediation was through a process of securitization and not loans. Securitization is more market-based phenomenon unlike loans which are not easily marketable. The predominance of loan-centric banking in Europe and also in all the emerging market economies and market-centric banking in the USA has different implication for banking operations as well as balance sheet management of the banks.

Firstly, risk rating and interest rate decisions for loans are taken by the banks in the light of externally determined market conditions. In the case of debt in the form of securities, the risk rating is done by an outside independent rating agency.

The decision on interest rate is a market derivative since there are several bidders for the securities. Secondly, the securities issues involve services of an investment banker who is an intermediary between the lenders and the borrower. No such intermediary exists in loan-based banking where the borrower approaches the bank directly. Thirdly, because of its market-centric approach, securitization is usually more economic for both borrowers and lenders. The borrowers get finance on much finer interest rates and other terms, while the lenders find it more economic and convenient as they do not have to engage in risk rating which is already done by an independent rating agency. This may be a problem as the lending banks often blindly follow the outside risk rating of the securities. It turned out to be the major problem in subprime mortgage crisis as the lending banks took outside risk ratings of the issuers for granted. Fourthly, loans until they are repaid continue to remain on the books of the lending banks, while securities are marketable. Resultantly, the asset side of loan-based banks is more rigid, but that of banks with securities can have more flexible debt portfolio due to its marketability. The market-oriented debt portfolio can be an advantage but at times drawback too. The flip side of the same is that the banks with securitized debt portfolio also run the risk of erosion in its credit quality due to greater turnover in its portfolio of marketable debt. Yet, because of being market-centric, securitization renders the debt portfolio of banks greater flexibility, which can give them an edge in terms of credit quality, but at times can also cause losses in mark-to-market valuations, as happened in the recent crisis.

A peculiar feature of US banking in contrast with its European counterparts is that the lending in US banking is dominated by securitized debt, while European banking is characterized by loans, cash credits, and overdrafts which are not securitized. However, the small individual loans are not initially securitized even in the USA, and they remain in the form of loans in the books of the banks. These small loans can be bundled together by the original lender and standardized them in the form of securities for selling them to other banks and also in the market. This is the process of securitization that was carried in the case of subprime mortgage loans. Further, over the years since 2001, it not only enlarged in size but also declined in quality, leaving larger number of secondary holders of securities containing higher risk which was masked by the credit rating. When the market enlarged in size and scope and grew to over trillions of dollars, it revealed its potential of destabilizing the entire banking system. The vulnerability of the banking system in the USA and abroad became clear and evident only when the first large casualty, Bear Stearns, became illiquid and had to be taken over by JPMorgan Chase in March 2008.

Financial Innovation: Mortgage Debt Securitization

The commercial banking, capital market, and investment banking sector in the USA have witnessed ever-growing innovation and sophistication in lending practices with the introduction of several new instruments and products. In line with its traditional practice of securitized lending in the banks, it evolved the new method transforming its nonsecuritized loan portfolios. It is this debt securitization or asset securitization, in vogue for last few decades and gained further momentum in the new millennium, that has been the subject of discussion, debate, and analysis and the center of focus of the current crisis. Debt securitization evolved in the 1990s. It is a process of structured financing which is a process of creating a structured financial product from the existing assets. The structured product has collateral as security and is readily marketable. Hence, they are also called collateralized debt obligations (CDO) or collateralized debt securities (CDS). The process of securitization involves the pooling of loans, debts, mortgages, receivables and repackaging them in asset-backed marketable homogenous securities of fixed denomination. The securities are rated, marketable, and regularly traded on the over-the-counter (OTC) markets providing liquidity to the instruments.

The advantages and drawbacks or hazards of securitization have to be viewed from the viewpoints of the issuers, investors, and the financial system. The benefits of securitization to the issuers is that it generates fresh resources on the sale of securitized debt from its portfolio, enables meeting capital adequacy norms, improves risk management, helps eliminate maturity mismatches, diversifies risk, and affords off-balance sheet financing. The benefits to investors are availability of marketable debt which is risk rated by independent rating agencies, better maturity matching and risk management, higher yield and lesser cost in acquiring ready-made debt portfolio, and flexibility in debt management. From the viewpoint of the financial system, the securitization provides wider distribution of pool of small loans or mortgages and recycles the resources of original small lending banks and financial institutions from bigger entities. Since the large size of securitized debt reduces the overall cost of intermediation, it improves the efficiency of the system.

Through financial innovation, the subprime mortgage loans emerged as a new loan and asset class and a new financial product to be held by banks and financial and investment institutions with better pricing for higher risk and collateralized lending. It also offered opportunity to lenders who prefer higher yield or return for extra risk and liquid instrument.

The process of rapid securitization of subprime mortgages allowed wider dispersal of these securities among banks and financial institutions which earlier did not have exposure to this segment of lending, namely, housing mortgages and subprime loans. It enabled the original mortgage lending institutions to procure quick refinance and thereby extend fresh loans to new borrowers. Without the securitization, this loan growth would not have been as phenomenal as it was. The availability of liquid OTC market for trading in these securities gave the investing institutions a measure of safety they needed to generate liquidity quickly in case of need.

A very important process critical in securitization that generated active institutional interest for investment in these securities and their trading was the rating and underwriting of these securities. If there was any weak link in the process of securitization, it was primarily in rating of these issues by the credit rating agencies (CRAs). The rating agencies seem to have given more weight to the credit rating of the originating banks issuing these securities than the riskiness in the collateral debt obligations (CDOs) represented by the pool of borrowers bunched into the securities.

Nor did the rating agencies have latest data on the leveraging and maturity mismatches by the originating institutions. The broader market risks of falling real estate prices, increase in rate of interest, and economic recession all increasing the default rate of the borrowers were also not reckoned with due weight. On all these scores, there appears to have been a systematic underestimation of the risk in rating these instruments.

Securitization applied some of the latest tools in security design and financial risk management. It was based on very intricate models and structures with innovative legal documentation and complex mathematical and statistical methods. It had incorporated all the legal, financial, and market safeguards to ensure the liquidity of the instruments. Yet, when defaults occurred, the market became illiquid due to opaque nature of instruments which masked their market risk. Inadequate information on the borrowers' debt servicing capabilities under stressed circumstances had made them vulnerable to the attack of illiquidity. The "Niagara effect," which is discussed later in this chapter, led to the collapse in prices of securities. Further, the crisis did not affect a portion of the market but encompassed the entire market in its fold emerging as the systemic risk.

Subprime Adjustable Rate Mortgage: Promoting Home Ownership

The subprime mortgage loans are those loans that do not fulfill credit risk criteria of prime mortgage loans. Home mortgages based on the credit rating criteria such as debt servicing-to-income ratio over 55% and mortgage loan-to-value ratio exceeding 85% are considered as subprime as the risk of delinquency in these loans is much higher. The traditional home mortgage loans, the loans to prime borrowers, are also only up to 40–50% of the home purchase price. By 2006, the subprime borrowers had debt equal to 95% of home purchase price with very little equity.

The development of securitization of subprime mortgage debt constituted a natural and positive step in the evolution in financial sophistication and engineering contributing to growth and efficiency of the financial system and promoting economic growth and economic and social equity. The benign instrument was aimed to spread the home ownership among lower sections of society and also give stimulus to economic growth through higher real estate and construction spending. The government measures such as tax breaks to homeowners, incentives to institutions in prioritizing loans to low-income owners, and guarantees for mortgages did create a favorable environment for growth in subprime securitization. It represented a unique market initiative upholding a social program for the benefit of all. It synchronized the profit motive of the private sector financial and real estate markets with the social objectives and good espoused by the government. It represented the win–win situation for the borrowers, lenders, builders, brokers, investment bankers, and also the economy and society.

The subprime mortgages again fall in two categories so far as the interest obligations are concerned. While the traditional loans were fixed rate mortgages (FRM), adjustable rate mortgages (ARM) with lower rates in the initial years and higher rates in the later years of mortgage became more popular. By 2003, adjustable rate mortgages of 866,000 far surpassed the figure of fixed rate mortgages of 780,000 in subprime loans. But what caused the phenomenal growth in subprime mortgage loans was the process of their securitization which enabled wider dispersal of loans that were earlier restricted only to the housing finance and mortgage banks, among other banks and financial institutions not only in the USA but also abroad. Until 2004, nearly nine million new homeowners were added due to this innovative means of financing the mortgages. The subprime mortgage is estimated to have helped nearly 5.3–6.2 million households to acquire houses with more than 1 million first-time homeowners. The young and minority households have been the major beneficiaries of this form of lending. The homeownership rate according to the US Census Bureau went up from 64.7% in 1995 to 68.8% in 2006. The Federal Reserve Survey of Consumer Finances showed the rise in homeownership in lower-income group tracts by 6% compared to 4% in higher-income tracts. In 1995, the size of the subprime loan market was estimated around $65 billion, but by 2007, subprime mortgages accounted for $1.3 trillion out of a total of $10 trillion in outstanding mortgages.

The major objective of subprime mortgage lending was to give opportunity to households who do not have standard credit history to own a house at the risk-based pricing of relatively higher rate of interest. The premium on subprime loans was on an average 2% higher than the interest rate on the prime mortgages during 1995–2004. The borrowers with credit score of B and C were treated as the subprime borrowers. The rapid growth in subprime mortgages was caused on account of a number of factors. The states promoted the homeownership through mortgages in low-income groups and minority communities. The interest in mortgage payments for a primary residence and one additional home qualified for tax deduction. The phase of low interest rates and rising home prices promoted cash-out refinancing by which the homeowner could get a new loan higher than the old loan and the difference in cash. During 1995–2004, nearly half of the subprime loan originations were for cash-out refinancing. The low interest rates and high liquidity among banks and financing institutions promoted aggressive competition among them for loan disbursals. The investment bankers worked on innovative securitization deals at rapid rate refinancing the originating institutions which could lend again. In addition to subprime loans, there were Alt-A borrowers who are lower than A and whose income is not verified and documented. And there were Jumbo loans which are above $400,000 but do not receive any refinance from the government agencies.

Pillars of Subprime Debt Securitization

The edifice of subprime mortgage securitization rested on three premises, namely, rising real estate prices, robust economy, and low interest rates. These three parameters provided a stable and strong base for the growth of subprime lending, its sustainability, and also financial viability. Instability in any one of the parameters was bound to shake the base undermining the stability of the edifice. Unfavorable change in all the three parameters was like a quake strong enough to shake the system to its collapse.

Apart from these macro factors, the subprime market flourished also on account of other micro factors which apparently provided several safeguards and features to improve the liquidity and security of the market. The fact that these safeguards and features also failed and collapsed in the wake of the growing imbalance in the market is another issue.

Firstly, the securitized debt market contained different issues, all of which were rated by the most reputed credit rating agencies. The ratings provided the benchmark for decisions by investment banks and other financial and investment institutions. The resources of the housing mortgage banks were limited to engage in unparalleled large lending. The securitization of mortgage debt, bunching and splicing the mortgages in different risk ratings, enabled them to recycle their portfolio and engage in further mortgage lending. This process of recycling through the tool of securitization enabled larger financing of housing sector not witnessed earlier. The commercial banks and financial and investment institutions which had liquidity but not expertise in housing mortgage could get exposure to the sector by investing in this debt. Collateralized mortgages and credit rating were adequate safeguards about the security. Higher rate of interest than available on conventional loans was an additional attraction. The secondary OTC market also gave liquidity to the securities not available in its traditional loan portfolio. And finally the instrument of credit default swaps (CDS) acted as an insurance against the institutional default.

In this way the securitized debt market, though complex in structure, documentation, and risk assessment, was simplified by the above features and safeguards and packaged as a lucrative, secured, safe, and liquid financial product, meeting the cherished objectives of a prudent banking. The investment bankers conducted the market making for active trading in securities, credit rating agencies provided the risk rating, and insurance companies and hedge funds built and operated the market for CDS. The *Greenspan Put* on interest rates, favorable macro factors of rising real estate prices, and high economic growth rendered the perfect climate for rapid growth in securitized mortgage debt during a long period of 2000–2007. The investment banking community was aggressive in selling the debt within the USA and abroad. The lending, therefore, achieved the international dimension.

By the end of 2007, all the three macro factors that formed the basis of strength and sustainability of the subprime debt market witnessed unfavorable trends. The decline in the real estate prices which began in 2007 became much sharper than expected earlier. The economy entered the phase of recession. At the same time, concerned by the fear of inflation, the Fed began its exercise of jacking up the interest rates. As discussed earlier the edifice of subprime mortgage securitization was also built on the intricate model containing several safeguards. It was built on providing elaborate link between the players, liquid trading platform, risk rating support, competitive pricing, adequate legal protection and buffer of insurance like CDS. Despite this intricate model and elaborate safeguards the system imploded.

The reason for this systemic collapse was that all the safeguards were based on the models that presume a level of probability of failure in a particular instrument. But when the systemic failure occurs the default is not limited to a few borrowers or a few instruments but pervades the entire market. When all the instruments become the victim of the crisis, the safeguards do not work. The subprime crisis was not crisis affecting a small percentage of its market or borrowers but encompassed its entirety. Further, because of the huge magnitude of the subprime market or what are called as the "toxic assets" and its penetration into the banking system in the USA and abroad, the crisis assumed very critical proportion in the USA and became global in nature.

Housing Collapse: The Crisis Trigger

The collapse of the housing market actually began in 2006. The interest rates were going up. The Fed in its zeal to combat imminent inflation lost sight of impending recession and more so of the damage it would do to the debt market in general and inverted pyramid of subprime debt market in particular. The Fed funds rate rose steadily from 1% in 2004 to reach a high of 5.25% by mid-2007. Considerable credit had already flown in financing homes in the earlier 5 years of mortgage securitization. The growth in demand for homes had tapered down in 2006. The signs of recession and higher interest rates had caused defaults to go up. The rise in the prices of houses halted, and the downward trend began in late 2006. The annualized defaults which had risen to the figure of 775,000 by the end of 2005 shot up to 1 million by the end of 2006. The pace of defaults rose to 1.5 million by mid-2007 [1, pp. 166–7]. This pushed the panic button and triggered a wave of selling of these mortgage debt securities.

Out of ten million home mortgages, one-sixth was in trouble of default with the face value of $2.75 trillion and equal to one-quarter of mortgage debt outstanding. Half of this, $1.25 trillion was subprime debt, another $1 trillion was Alt-A, and Jumbo ARMs accounted for the remaining $500 billion [1, p. 44]. The foreclosures which had increased by 80% in 2007 over the earlier year reaching a figure of 1.3 million rose to 2.3 million in 2008 and further to 2.8 million in 2009. In September 2009, nearly 14.4% of mortgages were delinquent or facing foreclosure with California and Florida accounting for 41% of the total. The delinquency rate in subprime loans was higher and reached 26.4%.[1]

The early signs of the financial crisis became visible in April, 2007 when the New Century Financial, which specialized in subprime mortgages, showed liquidity crunch and later filed for Chap. 11 bankruptcy protection. On July 30, 2007, two hedge funds of Bear Stearns, the top investment banking firm having large exposure in subprime debt, collapsed. The subprime debt market was getting deeper cracks, but not many knew the width and depth of the market. It was thought to be a localized

[1] Figures from Mortgage Bankers Association.

liquidity problem that could be resolved with the stronger institutions picking up the weak ones. The big names were not in yet. In October, the Citigroup, America's largest and most prestigious bank and one of the lifelines of the Wall Street and the USA, declared subprime debt-related losses of $3.1 billion. This was followed by disclosure by Merrill Lynch, legendary investment banker and citadel of Wall Street and American capitalism, of a much bigger figure of bad loans of $7.9 billion. Reckoning the gravity of the financial problem and continuing slump in the economy, the Fed started quickly reducing the Fed funds rate from 6.25% in August 2007 to 3.25% in January 2008, that is, nearly 50% cut in the cost of money and borrowing in less than 6 months.

While the Fed swung the first weapon in its armory to stem the subprime loan imbroglio culminating into a banking crisis, the government supplemented the Fed's efforts by pushing the Keynesian economic stimulus package of $150 billion through the Congress in January 2008 giving tax concessions to low- and middle-income families and incentives to business for investment. It encouraged the consumers spending grow, uplifting the slowing economy.

The gravity of the problem could be recognized in March 2008 when Bear Stearns, which was already struggling to keep afloat, finally drowned. Reckoning the implications of the failure of Bear Stearns, being one of the oldest and fifth largest investment banking institution on the Wall Street, on the banking system, the Fed in an uncharacteristic fashion opened its window of the lender of last resort and lent $30 billion to JPMorgan Chase for acquisition of Bear Stearns against the pledge of Bear Stearns' assets. This was the first such measure in the Fed's long history of 70 years. The crisis was temporarily resolved with the Fed helping the JP Morgan to take ailing Bear Stearns. By this time, it was knowledgeable among the banking and policy-making circles that the magnitude of the debt involved was much bigger than their earlier guesstimate. The G7 meeting in February 2008 which talked about the size of the subprime debt to be $400 billion turned out to be a gross underestimation. The IMF in March 2008 disclosed that the loan losses from the debt crisis which had spread globally could reach a figure of $1 trillion.

Despite the high magnitude of the write-offs by the banking system across the world crossing the estimate of a trillion dollar figure, the banking system weathered the crisis. But in August 2008, the disclosures by Freddie Mac and Fannie Mae about their provisioning rattled the markets again. The government and Fed's response was again more proactive. With the government's takeover of two big housing mortgage finance companies owning and guaranteeing nearly 50% of all housing mortgages of $10 trillion, yet another crash was averted until the Lehman Brothers, another large investment banker, filed for bankruptcy after the failed attempts for takeover by Bank of America and Barclays in September 2008. Here the Fed and government refused the bailout. With assets over $600 billion, Lehman Brother was playing on a dangerous leveraging ratio of 31 times. Wachovia and WaMu (Washington Mutual) were two more large banking institutions to go under precipitating a slide in the Dow below 9,000 mark and spreading contagion effect of the crisis to the European economies. Wachovia was taken over by the Wells Fargo Bank and WaMu by JP Morgan Chase.

In September 2008, the government initiated the proposal of massive and record $700 billion emergency package, to acquire mortgage-backed securities that had become illiquid causing this financial crisis, due to its magnitude and spread in the banking system was one of largest in the global history. This followed the earlier takeovers by the government or nationalization of the failing AIG by authorizing $85 billion line of credit from the Fed in exchange of 80% of its equity, marked a historical landmark in not only the US finance and economy but also the evolution the global economy and system. The collapse of Lehman Brother and takeover of Merrill Lynch by the Bank of America, two legendary investment banks, icons of the Wall Street, and torchbearers of American capitalism, triggering 500-point fall in Dow Jones reflected the worst financial crisis the USA was passing through since the banking crisis of the 1920s and the Great Depression that followed. These events demonstrated the fact that despite all the Keynesian tools and monetarist measures at its disposal, the US economy continued to be subject to recurrent damage by one of weakest spots of the capitalist system, its inherent cyclicality.

The US economy continued to remain vulnerable to the vicissitudes of investment and credit cycles. From 1987 Wall Street Crash to the current housing loan trauma, the American capitalism and the US economy has traversed through 1991 Savings and Loan Association crisis, 1994 Mexican Tequila, 1997 Asian Drama, 1998 Russian Roulette, 1999 hedge fund Long-Term Capital Management fiasco, and 2000 dot-com boom and bust. Since then, the dot-com bust, it took a long pause, and hence, the magnitude of the current burst was much larger and historically the biggest.

Financial security is like a boat floating on the sea of liquidity. Everybody wants the ride so long as it is afloat, but all desert it when it is sinking. The floating boat has many takers, but sinking boat has none. The market for securitized debt in housing went illiquid on the panic triggered by defaults. Like a sinking boat, it had no takers. The subprime debt crisis was no small crisis. The size of the market had grown to trillions of dollars. Resultantly, when the crisis broke out and crack in the ship could not be repaired quickly to avert further damage, in 6 months of its first symptom of the failure of Bear Stearns, and the crisis assumed the Titanic proportion.

Credit Derivatives and Credit Default Swaps

Like any other debt instrument from the viewpoint of an investor, MBS also face the risk inherent in the instrument. Although all the risks are actually embedded into the price of a security at the time of purchase, the market is not static and constant change in the parameters affecting the value of the security influences its trading price. In a fixed rate security, the interest rate risk represents the risk of loss in earning if the market interest rate goes up. The credit risk involves the possible default in payments by the issuer. Inability to sell the security without adversely affecting the price is the liquidity risk. And the prepayment risk is the risk of being paid prior to the maturity of the security. In the process of the natural development, innovation, and growing sophistication in the financial market to meet the requirements of several market participants to manage their risk profile, credit derivatives were designed and form a very big market helping risk management. The credit derivatives are financial contracts that enable the transfer of credit risk from one market participant to another at a price. They facilitate pricing and better distribution of credit risks among the financial market participants. A feature of the credit derivatives market is that they are negotiated and traded in OTC market.

Credit derivatives (CDs) are important financial engineering tool that facilitates unbundling and rebundling of various types of risks. The banks and financial institutions can realign their risk exposure in a much better way. The gains of issue and trading credit derivatives are better liquidity for the instruments and exposures, lower transaction cost for alteration in credit exposure or hedge, and facilitation in fulfilling regulatory compliances by altering exposures.

Since these products and instruments are of relatively recent origin, they are negotiated and traded on decentralized basis on over-the-counter market. They are not yet integrated into exchange-based markets, and hence, it is also difficult to get accurate and reliable data on the size and growth of the market.

Credit default swap (CDS) is a derivative instrument that was developed in the derivatives market in 1990s and traded regularly and aggressively in the derivatives OTC market. CDS is an instrument through which the holder of debt security buys risk protection against the defaults for a payment from the protection seller. In the CDs, the credit risk or exposure in fixed-income security is transferred by its holder to the seller of the swap or insurance. The payment to be made usually expressed in terms of basis points is called credit default spread. CDS is like an insurance against the defaults in debt securities, and spread is the premium to be paid for procuring the insurance. The market for CDS signals the changes in spreads from time to time. The spreads go on increasing with any adverse news or information about the institution whose securities are traded for swap. Although this credit default insurance market developed in 1990s, it grew very fast covering municipal bonds and corporate debt. Insurance companies, banks, and hedge funds which were the primary sellers of CDS enjoyed steady and growing flow of income during the flourishing economic times of 1990s. The CDS market later extended to structured finance instruments, such as collateralized debt obligations (CDOs) and mortgage-backed securities (MBS). After the growth of CDOs market in subprime debt securities, the trading in CDS also began in these securities. The investors in debt securities were very happy to receive risk-free incomes on payment of small spread on their interest income. After the initial transaction of a contract, CDS were traded at least 12–14 times among the institutions. The weakest feature of this market was that it grew into very large market in a short time, larger than other financial markets like the traditional equity, bond, and T bill markets, but was severely undercapitalized in relation both its volume as well as risk. Soros criticized the CDS when he said it is "like buying insurance on someone else's life and having license to kill." The market for CDS doubled in size every year since 2000 and grew rapidly from $900 in 2000 to $6 trillion in 2004 and was estimated to be around $45 trillion in 2007, three times bigger than NYSE market capitalization. The banks were the largest buyers and sellers of CDS. The leading ones were JPMorgan, Citigroup, Lehman Brothers, and Goldman Sachs.

American International Group (AIG), New York-based world's largest insurance company, declared largest loss in its history due to $11 billion write-off on its CDS holdings. It had $440 billion of CDS on its books and Lehman Brothers $700 billion. Top 25 banks were holding $13 trillion, the most active being JPMorgan Chase, Citibank, Bank of America, and Wachovia. No wonder Warren Buffett called them "financial instruments of mass destruction" and George Soros "Damocles sword" hanging over the financial system.

Indexed Credit Default Swaps (CDS)

The ingenuity and innovation of investment banking on Wall Street have no limits. Any new way of meeting the requirements of suppliers and users of capital with the intermediaries in between can pave way for a new instrument. The subprime debt securitization took shape and grew fast due to this demand–supply matrix in finance. While the MBS were the transferable instruments of debt obligations collateralized by the house properties of the borrowers, CDSs were derivative instruments in which the banks, investment banks, insurance companies, and hedge funds traded the risks of default. The banks and financial institutions needed to cover their risks from defaults; the insurance companies, investments banks, and hedge funds provided the cover for risks. The banks and institutions depended on the market prices of securities for the purpose of their valuation. The OTC market for these securities was also very active until the defaults increased by mid-2008. In order to make the valuations easier, the leading banks and investments banks in the CDS market developed the index for a basket of subprime residential mortgage-backed securities (RMBS) of ratings of six different credit qualities for different tranches. It became easier to trade as well as value RMBS. The trading in these indices gave huge profits to some investment banks. But the research on these indices later showed that they were not ideal for valuation. However, in the wake of the crisis and accounting requirement of mark-to-market valuation of securities and absence of market for every security, many banks used these indices for write-offs and marking down the portfolios of RMDS. The Bank of England report concluded that the index-based CDS valuations led to potential undervaluation of subprime obligations.[2]

Flaws in Risk Management and Collapse of Risk Trading

During the 1990s, trend toward growing sophistication and innovation in the financial markets accelerated. Several new instruments were developed to earn profits through arbitrage, or management or hedge of risks, by either owning and/or

[2] Bank of England, Financial Stability Report, Working Paper 23, 2008.

trading in risks. These derivative instruments revolved around the critical variable of risk. The critical element in the derivatives market is the time span that links present to the future. If everything remains stable from the present to future, the risk is zero and need not be covered. The financial environment is never stable and is on constant changing mode. The future markets offer instruments like call and put options, and futures which are the conventional products that enable the participants to hedge or trade risks at a price. However, the instruments are also used to speculate and profit. Both the hedgers and speculators are the users of these instruments. The counterparts of the users are the suppliers of these products who are also called book writers. The suppliers of these products or book writers are actually the risk-takers and traders. They are usually large institutions which price risks by using sophisticated mathematical and statistical tools and models and offer to undertake risks at a price. The derivatives market was primarily driven by the pricing quotes determined by the quants, mathematicians, statisticians, and physicists who used their advanced models for pricing the derivative products.

One of the very famous and widely used tools in options pricing is the Black–Scholes model. The financial institutions or investment banks offer these products for normal profits and not abnormal gains but can often result in abnormal losses or sometimes gains. So far as the users are concerned, one may say that only the hedgers may be permitted in the market but not the speculators because they distort the trend in the market. This is usually not true. Since the markets work on the principle of profit maximization and loss minimization, both the hedgers as well as speculators help in the process of price discovery. The speculators also run the risk of losing and will not bet unless they are sure of the price at which they are trading. But there are exceptions. The one-way market situation runs the risk of fueling pricing upward or downward due to excessive speculation. Hence, there is need for prudential regulation. The crisis can also emerge from volatile market and the collapse of Black–Scholes model or other models of pricing resulting in colossal losses. The collapse of Long-Term Capital Management in 1999 and AIG in 2008 exhibit blatant disasters from the failures and crises of derivatives markets which trade in risks. More detailed critical analysis of the quantitative finance and advanced financial models of pricing and resource allocation used by the financial community and their practical ineptitude in pricing financial products and decision making in financial exposures is covered in Chap. 13.

Accounting Fallacy That Triggered the Crisis: Mark-to-Market Versus Fair Valuation Accounting

One of the main causes for panic and crisis resulting from subprime debt defaults was the mark-to-market valuation accounting practice followed when the market for subprime RMBS crashed. As the prices of subprime securities faced the Niagara effect, the fall in the prices of securities was enormous. In many cases, the quotes were not available due to illiquid markets. This was the case for the majority of the subprime debt. Although the servicing of debt had stopped in many cases, the underlying securities were tangible, and despite the fall in the prices of houses, the debt was recoverable by foreclosure. The renegotiation of loans also could make them serviceable. Despite this fact, the write-offs were done at a very low prices and losses were magnified by undervaluing the portfolios on the basis of unusually low market quotes or prices. Lower valuations and write-offs had contagion effects.

When the markets went virtually illiquid, mark-to-market valuation accounting norm further worsened the impact on the credit market. When the market is dysfunctional or irrational under panic, mark-to-market rule should have been bypassed in favor of more practical and realistic valuation. Historical cost valuation based with discount for defaults would have mitigated the impact which huge write-offs created on the market and monetary implosion it triggered. Instead of very aggressive write-offs in valuation of debt securities, a more conservative approach in their valuation would have helped in preventing the creation of a huge black hole in the financial system. Since the securities were backed by tangible housing mortgages, the write-offs should have been limited at the most to the decline in the fair value of the houses. The crisis was, therefore, triggered by the accounting fallacy. If the market fails to give value due to liquidity collapse, the tangible assets cannot be written down to zero. The homeowners may have defaulted, but their mortgages were intact. This experience is a lesson to the accounting bodies to develop fair valuation methods in the case of a market collapse. This is not to suggest overvaluation of depreciated assets, but is to avoid gross undervaluation of safe tangible assets, which are temporarily illiquid. The subprime debt created huge inventory real estate that needed to be valued fairly to preclud exaggerated losses for the financial institutions that imploded the financial liquidity, money supply, and market capitalization of stocks and securities, valuation of real estate and eroded the consumer and investor confidence, finally leading to negative economic growth.

Interest Rate Shock: Tipping Point for the Crisis

Had it not been for the changeover of the charge at the Fed in February 2006 with Ben Bernanke taking over from Alan Greenspan after his longest and record stint with the Fed of over 18 years, the course of interest hike could have been different, and another scenario may have emerged. Undoubtedly, the concern on the inflation front was building up pressure on the Fed to raise rates. The rate of inflation was inching up from 1.6% in 2002, 2.3% in 2003, and 2.7% in 2004 to 3.4% in 2005. The Fed funds rate which had fallen from a high of 6.54% in July 2000 to the low of 0.98% in December 2003 rose to 4% in November 2005 and to a high of 5.26% in July 2007. This was a severe interest rate shock for the financial markets and more so for the bond markets. What was stressful for the financial system was sharp fall in the Fed funds rate first from 2000 to a low in 2003 and then a rise again till 2007. In the wake of the initial signs of the crisis, the Fed began lowering interest rate in the last quarter of 2007 from a high of 5.26% to a low of 1.81%

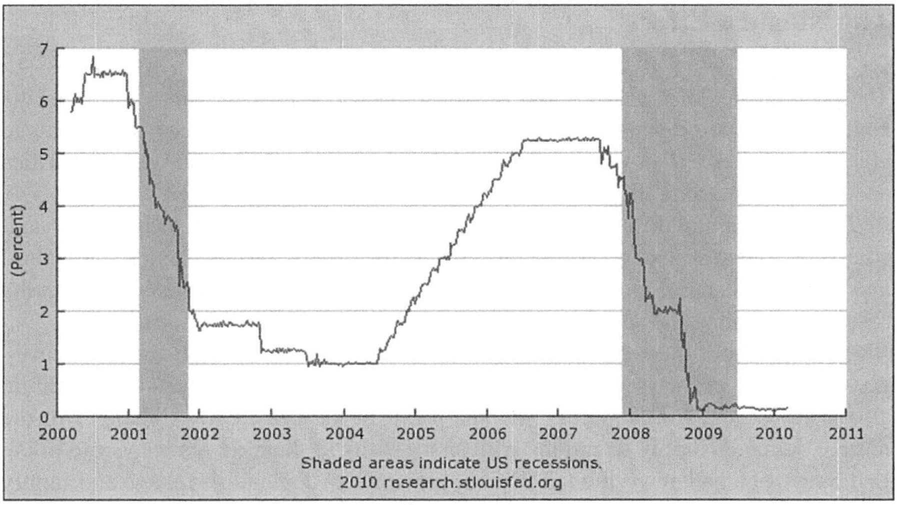

Fig. 2.1 Effective federal funds rate (FF). *Shaded areas* indicate US recessions. 2010 research.stlouisfed.org (Source: Board of Governors of the Federal Reserve System)

in September 2008 and below 1% since October 2008 reaching the lowest of 0.11% in January 2010. The Fed beginning to lower the rates in late 2007 was an afterthought. Much of the damage was already done by increasing rates from a low 1% in mid-2004 to 4% in mid late 2004 and rising to 5.26% in mid-2006. This 2-year, mid-2004 to mid-2006, increase of 4.26% had already done enough damage to erode the quality of portfolio of subprime debt held by all financial institutions. The system was on a tipping point of the crisis.

When the rates go on declining, it is most beneficial for the bond markets and also investment climate. But the phase of rising interest rates is financially painful. The falling bond prices throw the markets in disarray. What was more disconcerting was interest shock came in at the fag end of the peak of the real estate market and subprime debt revolution which were both beginning to slow down. A sharp V-shape movement in the Fed funds rate (Fig. 2.1) over the period of 7 years since 2000 until 2007 was too much of distress to the financial markets and more so to the newly developed and experimental market which was very sensitive to even small interest movements and whose magnitude had gone beyond one trillion dollars. It could have avalanche effect on the entire financial market which it did in 2008. The magnitude of the size of the market was a guessing game before the symptoms of the crisis manifested in the failure of Bear Stearns in 2007. By then, the damage was already done. The defaults and foreclosures were piling, and prices of subprime securities were plummeting both on defaults as well as rising interest rates. The rating agencies, which had given AAA or AA rating status to the debt, heavily downgraded the ratings. This turned out to be a death knell on the liquidity of the securities. The bonds became illiquid due to absence of buyers.

The Niagara Effect

The peculiarities of securities and financial markets and their vulnerability to the Niagara effect are discussed in greater detail in Chap. 13. Here we shall analyze how the Niagara Effect caused the crash in the prices of subprime debt securities and how they became illiquid.

The fundamental difference between the financial securities on the one hand and commodities and services on the other is that in the case of the latter sellers (suppliers) and buyers (users) are two different entities in their secondary markets, while in the case of the former, the sellers and buyers constantly switch their roles.

As news about the weakness in a security spreads, the demand for the security goes on falling even at lower and lower prices, while the supply goes on expanding also at lower and lower prices. The sharp fall in the price causes changes in the normal demand–supply equations with sharp shifts in their curves respect to price. In the case of a bad news, the fall in price precipitates demand shrinkage and supply expansion leading to a continuous fall in price until the exchange halts the trading with circuit breaker. There may be a situation of all sellers and no buyers, when trading halts, making the market illiquid. The subprime bond trading in the OTC market experienced the above situation and became illiquid. With no market quote available, the banks and institutions had to value the bonds at the last lowest quotations. This caused the balance sheet implosion of banks and institutions requiring write-off of losses as well as fresh liquidity to remain solvent.

Figure 2.2 shows D1, D2, D3, D4, and D5 demand curves and S1, S2, S3, S4, and S5 supply curves. The intersections of these demand and supply curves show several price positions. In a normal commodity market whenever there is a selling pressure arising from the rising supplies of goods, the supply curve falls down. It moves from initial S1 to S2 to S3 to S4 to S5. With the demand curve D1 remaining stable, the price of the commodity falls from P1 to X2 to X3 to X4 to X5. The price fall is demonstrated by line P1X5. This is the normal angular fall in the price. Similarly, when demand decreases from D1 to D5, the price falls from P1 to B5. The price fall is indicated by sloping line P1B5.

But the market for financial securities is different. Not only is it the secondary market for the existing stock of securities, but players in the market can be both on the demand as well as supply side depending upon the existing dynamics of the market and its future perspective which is also determined by the overall market view of all participants. This dual role of market participants makes the market more volatile in times of significant trend reversals. The market is, therefore, subject to wide up or down swings. The prices of securities are subject to wide fluctuations depending on the strength of the structure of the market represented by its demand–supply spectrum.

Whenever there is a selling pressure the market in the securities market, not only is supply increasing but demand also falls. The buyers on the demand–supply side either withdraw or also become sellers on supply side. Hence, supply rises and demand declines. When supply increases from X1 to X5, demand also shrinks from

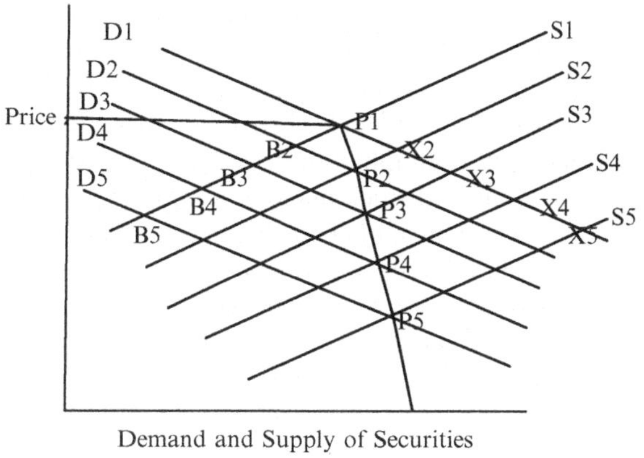

Fig. 2.2 Niagara effect. Demand and supply of securities

D1 to D2 to D3 to D4 and to D5. When the buyers also become sellers and sellers increase. Resultantly, the price falls not in angular fashion like P1 to X5 or P1 to B5 but crashes like the Niagara waterfall from P1 to P2 to P3 to P4 to P5. The price fall from P1 to P5 is the Niagara effect. In this event when the prices do not fall gradually but crash almost vertically, the effect is the Niagara effect resembling the waterfall at the Niagara River. The Niagara effect is most common in security prices than the prices of commodities and services. It contrasts the angular fall in prices in commodities from P1 to X5 or P1 to B5.

The price crashes due to lack of support from the supply side. Just as the Niagara River water flow takes a deep plunge when the land support to the flow of water drops vertically by causing a steep fall, the prices also crash in similar manner due lack of physical support from the supply side. This happens when the holders of securities are willing to unload quantities and sell them at any price available, while there is little or no demand for securities to keep the price afloat.

The prices of subprime debt securities experienced the Niagara effect due to lack of market making and support at lower levels due to its weak structure of demand–supply spectrum. The Niagara effect was also very common among the Internet, technology, and telecom stocks during the Y2K stock market crash also due to their weak structure demand–supply spectrum. The old economy stocks did not suffer the Niagara effect during 2000 stock market crash due to their relatively stronger structure of demand–supply spectrum.

Economic Crisis Causation

Economic or financial crisis does not occur as an all-pervasive phenomenon. It usually emerges in one sector and then encompasses the other and larger segments of the economy. Just as in the periods of economic boom, the virtuous cycle is set in motion by animal spirits of entrepreneurs and pervasive influence of the psychology of exuberance, the economic doom also begins with the vicious cycle culminating into a crisis. The vicious economic cycle usually begins with the germination of negative sentiments about the economy.

The speed and spread of crisis is inherently linked to interrelations of the first affected sector with the other sectors of the economy. During the 1929 crisis, both the real estate and stock markets were the focal points of the crisis. The stock market and real estate market crash that caused huge losses eroded the balance sheets of banks and brought the banking system to the brink of collapse. By 1933, 40% of the banking system was wiped out. This disastrous chain reaction of bank failures and resultant contraction of money supply by 30% affected all other businesses and economic activities. It was the banking crisis following the stock market crash and real estate crisis that finally culminated into the Great Depression.

During the current crisis, 1929–1930 repeat was precluded by the record bailout of the affected banks in the USA by the Federal Reserve and rescue and stimulus packages by the government. In 2008, half the battle was won by this one single measure of bailout and rescue package for bank and financial institutions. This could not happen in 1929. The economic thinking and policy dominated by *laissez-faire* economics, doctrine of balanced budget, and rules of gold standard could not permit the government intervention into economy to rescue the banking system. Nor was the Federal Reserve large and strong enough to provide relief to the ailing banks. The Great Depression could have been averted by the banking rescue restoring stability to the banking system followed by the budgetary deficit financing to pump prime the economy. The economic philosophy then had the faith in automaticity of the market mechanism to correct the economic disequilibrium. The technology of economic management was obsolete, and the new one discovered by Keynesian ideas had not yielded the political support for quite some time to discard the old rules and adopt unconventional policy which violated all old doctrines and dogmas of managing the economy. The 1930s experience has been a great lesson.

Each crisis has a different strain. The stock market crisis is different in its origin, scope, dimension, and contagion from the currency crisis. The banking crisis shows differently than the real estate crisis. If contained effectively none of these micro-sectoral crises can translate into a bigger economic crisis. But each has the potential on the measure of its size and scale and its linkages to culminate into broader macroeconomic crisis. A crisis is a sudden crash of the market forces, arising from the cumulation of creeping imbalance, which threatens the stability or momentum of the market in the concerned sector and the system affecting its normal functioning. The valuation losses of assets whose prices crash create the implosion of balance sheets of individuals, banks, institutions, and corporates which hold these so-called toxic assets. The balance sheets and central banks and governments also get imploded. At the macroeconomic level, it results in the liquidity crunch, lowering spending on consumption and investments by individuals and corporates. Falling sales and accumulating stocks cause cuts in production and layoffs in employments. This has the effect on reducing individual incomes, further causing negative multiplier effect on spending and income generation. The falling prices in real estate and stock market in addition to valuation losses from toxic assets also have negative wealth effect which further lowers spending for consumption and investment. In this situation, the continuing chain reaction in vicious economic cycle needs to be broken and short-circuited in order to ignite the recovery from self-igniting downturn.

The current financial crisis emerged from a peculiar method of financing of home mortgages in the USA. It could have been typically only US financial crisis, if the process through which its financing was done—the securitization—had been restricted to only US banks and financial institutions. It was not so because of the increasing integration of the financial markets of different countries under the phase of globalization for the last more than two and half decades. The securitized debt was held by several foreign banks and financial institutions and to such an extent that the exposure of banks of Iceland to this paper caused the banking and forex crisis in the country requiring IMF assistance of $2 billion to avert the collapse of the banking system and the bankruptcy of the Central Bank of Iceland.

The financial crisis is microeconomic, market-driven phenomenon. But it has macroeconomic ramifications. It affects the macroeconomic system through financial implosion. The first level of attack at the macro level is on the money supply and liquidity which incur severe crunch. The crisis has to be tackled both at the micro and macro levels. The restoration of liquidity, credit lines and levels, and money supply and credit availability at low cost through low interest policy is the first line of defense that has to be quickly adopted by the Fed, the central bank, and the controllers of money.

Free market capitalism often results in aggressive competition and cut throat, leading to bleeding in the concerned industry. The end result is the emergence of a duopoly or oligopoly which is bereft of true competitive spirit. In the heat of race for market share and business target, several imprudent and riskier decisions are taken. And when the boom starts petering out, the weaker units face the wrath of downturn. Although this is the normal pattern of capitalist development in industries, the banking industry remained immune to this trend due to several legislative and regulatory safeguards enacted after the banking crisis of 1929. The tendency toward aggressive competition in banking was preempted by the Fed by establishing several prudential norms and supervisory controls. Despite these structural contours, the subprime mortgage debt went unjudged and unregulated beyond the Fed's reckoning. The operations of investment banks were not as much within the purview of the Fed as of the commercial banks. After the repeal of the Glass–Steagall Act of 1933 which prevented the commercial banks from engaging in investment banking following the experience of banking crisis of 1929, investment banking operations and exposures of the subsidiaries of commercial banks started receiving financial support for leveraging from the holding company banks. Although the need for regulation of the subprime mortgage was recognized well ahead of crisis, the implementation was delayed and poor. "By May, 2005, the press was reporting that economists were warning about the risks of these new mortgages. In June of that year, Chairman Greenspan was talking about the 'froth' in the mortgage market and testified before the Joint Economic Committee that he was troubled by the surge in exotic mortgages. …Yet, in December, 2005, the regulators proposed guidelines to rein in some of the irresponsible lending. And we had to wait another 7 months, until September, 2006, before that guideline was finalized. Even then, even now, the regulators' response is incomplete" [2].

Apart from the general slowdown in the US economy which showed the signs in 2007, the devastating blow of the subprime crisis which showed its dimensions has been the major economic concern globally. While several macroeconomic measures comprising the fiscal stimulus, bailout packages, and relaxations in monetary policy combined with the microeconomic management steps to deal with the financial failures and individual mortgage foreclosures have been addressed to contain the crisis, it is still necessary now to have another dispassionate look at the anatomy of the financial crisis. This should enable us to have better perception of the whole crisis and adopt more targeted approach to deal with the crisis without dissipating action and energies diverted in all directions.

The current crisis can be referred to as recession, lack of consumer confidence, inadequate consumer spending, following the credit crisis that triggered stock market crash, investment slump, or liquidity crunch. These are actually all manifestations of the crisis. Since the root cause of the current problem is subprime housing mortgage crisis, it is desirable to look at the chronology of this securitized debt crisis. The recession had the potential of a deep depression. The genesis of the crisis lies in the housing market boom that preceded it. The economic buoyancy and the Fed's cheap money policy created and drove the real estate boom and subprime housing mortgage finance with its securitization, enabled the investment banks to sell these securities widely not only among the American banks but also European and Asian banks. The housing mortgage finance companies were thus able to recycle their debt and go on fresh lending spree. The securitization of mortgage debt and its globalization enabled the US housing finance companies to grant record credit for housing and sustain the real estate boom that also kept the overall economic growth rate in the USA high. The enormous growth in securitized housing debt was also facilitated by high leveraging by banks bordering imprudent and unhealthy levels in many banks which went illiquid and bankrupt after the crisis broke out.

Dot-Com Bust Versus Subprime Crisis

The subprime debt crisis and the tsunami of loss of financial wealth it caused globally make all the earlier emerging market crises look like small tidal waves which could be managed easily. The real estate and housing boom began in 2001 when dot-com boom had busted and left a big hole in the financial system. Luckily, the dot-com boom and bust was not very pervasive in its impact although it also caused the great Wall Street crash. Dow Jones tumbled from its high of 11,723 on January 14, 2000, to a low of 8,235 on September 21, 2001, and slumped further to a low of 7,286 on October 9, 2002. The Dow fell by 61%. The S&P slipped from 1,520 to 776, 49% fall. The collapse in the values of technology shares was much sharper with many stocks just wiped out and others facing values falling from 40 to 90%. Being the new industry whose growth was totally funded by equity, primarily from institutional investors, high net-worth individuals, and venture capital funds, the technology, Internet, and dot-com boom did not go into the balance sheets of either average American investors or banks. The technology stocks also formed a relatively small share in the US overall equity market capitalization. Billions were lost by venture capital, private equity and hedge funds, investment banks, and technology-savvy high net-worth investors. But mutual funds and average investors did suffer only the loss comparable with broad indices like S&P. The commercial banks did not face any brunt of the dot-com burst which remained a purely stock market phenomenon. The economic impact of the market crash was not devastating on the economy except for the technology sector. Nor was its recessionary impact pervasive to engulf the entire economy. And as the market valuations of the old economy stocks, which had gone down under the shock of technology valuation burst, revived, the overall economy showed the signs of quick recovery. This scenario contrasts the current crisis.

The worst and most sensitive aspect of the crisis was that this large volume of securitized mortgage debt had penetrated into the commercial banking system and not restricted only to investment and mortgage banks. The subprime mortgage debt had ballooned to a figure over one trillion dollars. The Y2K dot-com burst did not cause any banking crisis because the banking exposure to the equity investments was limited and venture capital funds and investment banks absorbed the shock. The subprime debt had penetrated the commercial banking system internationally. The current crisis, therefore, bears a great resembles to the 1929 banking crisis both in terms of leveraging as well as bank lending and exposure to stock market and real estate lending. History repeats itself. The mechanism of bank financing has undergone a remarkable innovation and sophistication since then.

In 1925 Florida real estate boom, the instrument known as "binders" was traded [3]. The binders were documents representing the right to buy the land at the stated price obtained by paying 10% of the purchase price and were traded. The binders gave the security of sale price and liquidity to the land seller and possibility of profit to the prospective buyers. They were a kind of options which became tradable and contributed to the speculative land price boom. New instruments create financial regeneration, promote liquidity, and attract larger investments. Mortgage-backed securitization also a financial innovation enabled mortgage-holding institutions to make their portfolio tradable and thereby generate financial resources for further deployment in new mortgages. This instrument of securitization of home mortgages became potent tool for large-scale financing and refinancing of home loans that generated one of the largest housing and real estate boom in the US history. Without the global commercial bank exposure in securitized home mortgages refinancing the original home mortgage banks, they would not have the adequate resources to finance 12 million new homes they did in 2001–2007. "At the peak of housing boom in 2006, the overseas investors owned nearly a third of all US mortgages" [1, pp. 86–7]. What was thought to be innovative funding technology that could also keep the growth momentum of the economy through its stimulus to investment in

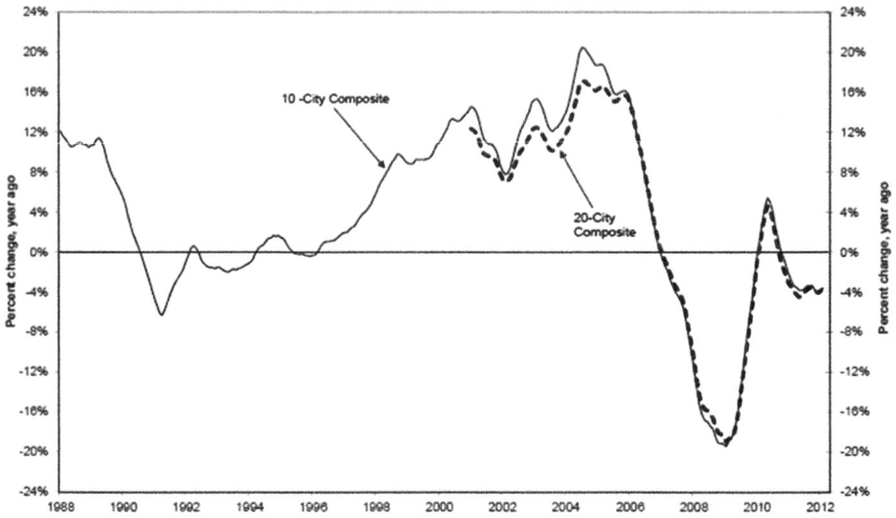

Fig. 2.3 S&P/Case-Shiller home price indices (Source: S&P Indices & Fiserv)

the real estate sector which offers high potential for overall economic growth became a financial nightmare and eventually undermined the stability of the USA and global financial system.

The subprime debt crisis also took toll of some of the oldest, leading, and most reputed investment banking firms that had played not only significant role in the growth of capitalism in the USA, but being at the cutting edge of technology and financial innovation and engineering, they were the torchbearers of the American capitalism and Wall Street culture. The failure of these firms vividly demonstrates how the financial engineering and innovation and creation of new financial markets can and do contribute to economic growth, but if carried to the extremes of risk-taking in terms of both degree and volume, due to the parametric dependence on favorable economic and financial factors as well as leveraging, such new developments can become instruments of financial wreck and chaos, when economic conditions begin to deteriorate (Fig. 2.3).

During the subprime crisis, the Dow Jones Industrial fell from the peak of 14,040 in July 2007 to a low of 7,392 in November 2008, a fall of 47%, and declined to a low of 6,440 in March 2009, a drop of 54% from the peak. This makes a sharp resemblance with the dot-com bust which caused the Dow Industrial to lose 61%. Unemployment which had increased from 5.7 million in 2000 to 7 million in 2007 rose sharply to 10 million in 2009. The unemployment rate rose from 4.5% in 2007 to 10% 2009. It was the fasted ever increase.

One of the biggest gains of subprime debt securitization is the wealth creation from the real estate of houses it built during this period. During 2001–2007, 12 million new homes were constructed with the annual figure going up from 1.6 million in 2001 to 1.9 million in 2005 and 2006.[3] On a rough reckoning of average valuation of $200,000, the value of this real estate is reckoned at $2.4 trillion, 15% of US GDP in 2009. This is one of strongest aspects of the whole phenomenon which needs to be weighed against tremendous losses it has caused. In a normal financial crisis, the losses are not recoverable since the assets disappear in value in thin air.

The GDP growth rate which had declined from 3.6% in 2004 to 2.1% in 2007 fell further to 0.4% in 2008 under the impact of the crisis. More serious was the GDP decline of 2.4% in 2009, the highest fall in the postwar history of the US economy. The last highest decline in GDP was 1.9% in 1982 after the savings and loan crisis. After the dot-com crisis, the GDP growth fell from 4.8% in 1999 to 4.1% in 2000. But the real effect was felt in 2001 when GDP growth fell by 3–1% in 2001. However, it never entered the negative territory which it did after the subprime crisis. The dot-com crisis was of a much smaller magnitude and less pronounced in its impact on the domestic as well as the global economy than the subprime crisis. The contagion effect of the subprime crisis on other countries and the global economy was also stronger. And how does the current crisis compare with the most severe crisis of 1930s? This is discussed in Chap. 6.

What Went Wrong?

It is time to have short summary of what went wrong and why the US economy unexpectedly and to everyone's surprise went into a deep morass after the long phase of robust growth?

The economic growth of 2002–2008 was fueled by low interest policy that fired and sustained the housing and real estate property boom. In the year 2007, the Fed started reversing the rate of interest on the concern of inflation. The Fed funds rate increasing from 2% in 2004 to 5.25% percent in 2006 was a shock to the economy that not only slowed the growth but triggered large-scale defaults in subprime debt mortgages. The OTC market in subprime debt securities collapsed, and their values plummeted causing a trillion losses in the banking system. The reverse and steep interest rate movement brought the crisis. The Fed and the government reacted using their monetary and fiscal tools. The Fed lowered interest rate from 5.25% in 2007 to near zero level in 2009 and injected record liquidity into the banking system, avoiding the systemic collapse. The government jacked up spending incurring record deficit to bring the economy back on the growth path.

The following factors can be identified as the major causal factors of the crisis:

1. *Interest rate shock*: The Fed went on continuously raising the Fed funds from 2% in mid-2004 to 5.25% until mid-2006 and kept stable at this high level thereafter until late 2007. Against the background of declining and low Fed funds rate from a high of 6.5% in 2000 to a low of 2% until mid-2004, the rising interest rate

[3] US Census Bureau, US Government, 2010.

came as a rude shock to the bond market and more particularly to the subprime debt market which was very interest sensitive. A large part of subprime debt securities market was adjustable or floating rate debt that raised the servicing burden of the mortgage borrowers. The rising interest rate had also adverse effect on the overall debt market, stock market, investment climate, consumer demand for credit, and the overall economy. The defaults on subprime debt went on increasing. The falling real estate prices due to recessionary trend in the economy further dampened the subprime debt market.

2. *Illiquid OTC market for subprime debt*: The subprime debt securities market was an OTC market without the clearing house mechanism and margin requirements. As the defaults in the subprime debt went on increasing, the market for the securities collapsed with the Niagara effect. The market eventually became illiquid with no buyers and only sellers.
3. *Excessive write-offs of subprime debt securities*: When the subprime debt market collapsed and price discovery mechanism failed, the valuation of these securities in the books of banks and financial institutions became a problem. With the large valuation losses, the write-offs of losses in the books of banks and financial institutions ballooned, threatening the accounting viability of the institutions. This happened despite the availability of tangible security of mortgages of the houses. When this fact is considered, the write-offs appeared to be magnified and overdone threatening the financial viability of the institutions.
4. *High leveraging*: Many large investment banks, banks and insurance companies with large exposures in subprime debt and also credit default swap (CDS) market were very heavily leveraged against huge exposures in the subprime debt portfolio and also liabilities arising from CDS exposures on large lines of credit from banks.
5. *Lehman Brothers collapse*: In a complex financial system with large institutions having counterparty exposures, the default of any one large institution can threaten the stability of the system. While the government bailout is option of the last resort, all the possibilities of market bailout by the competitors with the minimal support by the Fed and the Treasury need to be availed to avoid the failure of large institution due to its counterparty exposures and the huge cascading effect of its failure or bankruptcy. Lehman Brothers collapsed did have a cascading effect on other institutions which needed to be handled adequately.

Could the Crisis Be Averted?

It is easy to do postmortem, but three things seem to have perhaps avoided or delayed the crisis and also its impact. Although Bernanke had been the member of Fed Board even during Greenspan's tenure, a change in perception and stance which he took over from Greenspan in February 2006 was the first unsettling factor. The Fed remained insensitive to the possible impact of rising interest rates, may be due to lack of data of the size of the subprime market and its far-reaching effects. The interest rate hikes in 2004–2006 should have been moderated or avoided. The interest rate stability would have been much better. The rising interest rates sent the bond market in a tailspin creating ground for subprime valuation disaster. Further, the Fed and the Treasury should have prevented the Lehman Brothers from going bankrupt. The Lehman Brothers bankruptcy had a ratchet effect of the financial sector due to cross holdings and counterparty liabilities. This view is echoed by Robert Mundell, Nobel laureate economist and theoretical father of euro.[4] And thirdly, in the event of the crash or illiquidity in the subprime debt market, the valuation of subprime debt could have been higher than it was done on the sheer fact of being backed by the tangible security of real estate, avoiding the big accounting hole it created in the balance sheets of all financial institutions holding these securities. This would not have had such a devastating impact on the entire financial system and the economy. With the magnitude of the subprime debt market, which had no longer remained a small sectoral market but crossed a trillion dollar figure, it also carried a potential of devastating avalanche effect on the economy in the case of its crash or crisis.

References

1. Zandi M. Financial shock: a 360° look at the sub-prime mortgage implosion and how to avoid the next financial crisis. Upper Saddle River: Pearson Education Inc., Free Press; 2009.
2. Dodd C. Opening statement at the hearing on mortgage market turmoil: causes and consequences, US Senate Committee on Banking, Housing and Urban Affairs, March 22, 2007. In: Lewis M, editor. Panic: the story of modern financial insanity. New York: Penguin Books; 2008. p. 309.
3. Galbraith JK. The great crash 1929. England: Penguin Books Ltd.; 1975. p. 46–7.

[4] Mundell, Robert.

Chapter 3
Policy Response

> Arguments over the methods and the timing of government economic management can be severe. There is also a grave question, as yet unanswered, of whether the techniques of economic management now subject to discussion are sufficient to secure stability and growth of capitalism in face of all possible crises.
>
> John Kenneth Galbraith, *Economics and the Art of Controversy, 1955.*

Economic Wisdom and Political Vision

Human civilization over the centuries has witnessed a considerable change in how societies are governed. Greater part of history of human civilization covers government by monarchies. The functioning of parliamentary democracy, which is now ruling large portion of the world, has had relatively short life span. Far shorter is the record of totalitarian regimes established after revolutions through military power and armed struggle. In all these societies, from monarchies to democracies, contemporary knowledge of economics governed the policy making in the interest of society. Fiscal and monetary affairs were managed in a manner to balance the fiscal sustainability of the state against the societal interests. Learned men always advised the royalty on the right course of economic policy or fiscal stance. As economics developed as an independent body of social science, economists became the advisors to the policy makers. The affinity between economists and politicians has been a critical factor in most decisive moments in a country's destiny and also influencing the course of global development. Trust, courage and conviction, and vision of the political leadership determined its political survival from time to time. Such a synergistic partnership of economic wisdom and political traits has led to prosperity and equity at times, while the conventional wisdom and political myopia or obstinacy have also been the cause of economic doom and bankruptcy.

Economic wisdom is very difficult to be defined. What was economic wisdom in nineteenth century became a "conventional wisdom" in Galbraith's terms in the

S. Nayak, *The Global Financial Crisis: Genesis, Policy Response and Road Ahead*,
DOI 10.1007/978-81-322-0798-6_3, © Springer India 2013

depression years. Contemporary economic wisdom cannot remain as such if it is unable to grapple with the new economic realities and then becomes "conventional wisdom." Conventional wisdom can be a doom for the politicians and policy makers. Global economic history is replete with events of critical moments when failure to jettison conventional wisdom and adopt new path unleashed economic disasters. Balanced budget was an anachronism in 1930s. Roosevelt was the first and biggest Keynesian who shed the conventional wisdom of balanced budget and with the New Deal changed the course of USA as well as global economic history. Keynesianism turned global and economic depression slipped into history. Once forgotten seventeenth-century economist Adam Smith sprung up as the hero of wave of liberalization and globalization since the 1980s after being politically resurrected by Margaret Thatcher in UK and Ronald Reagan in the USA. Friedman's monetarism elbowed Keynesianism out of political caucus when stagflation and its dark economic fallout shook the ruling political system in the 1970s. Laffer curve and supply-side economics ruled in the era of increasing budget deficit reaching the record level in the Reagan era of the 1980s. Cheap money, soft dollar, rising trade deficit, fiscal budgetary surplus, and buoyant stock market in the Clinton era guided by Greenspan's monetary and Treasury's extraordinary fiscal managements led the economy into an unprecedented economic miracle of the 1990s. Economic theories developed in response to the imperative need to view and analyze pressing economic problems or phenomena differently and with new glasses due to the inadequacy of the existing body of knowledge and theories to grasp them.

Marxian economic thought, philosophy, and ideology emerged out of stark economic inequities of the times. If societies were equitable, Marxism or Communism may not have developed. What is equity? Is the right to property equity? For Marx, it is not, and equity stems without property. In contrast, in free societies including capitalist and neocapitalist societies, right to property is the fundamental pillar of equity. Can we have equitable societies with property rights? That is the challenge facing the modern welfare states. Economists, political philosophers, and policy makers are still grappling with this issue, and evolution of the state in theory and in reality is continuing.

Politically both 1929 crisis and subprime debt crisis of 2008 coincidentally show many commonalities and also some differences. Both the crises and their aftermath occurred in the Republican regimes. The presidential elections after the crises gave verdict to the Democratic candidates to deal with crises. Both Roosevelt then in 1933 and Obama now in 2009 faced daunting tasks ahead. When Roosevelt took over, the economy was in shambles. Inheriting the economy with 30% of GNP shaved off, farm prices down by 53%, 10,000 banks closed accounting for 40% of banking system, Dow Jones Industrial Average down by 74%, unemployment hitting record 23.4% with 12.8 million unemployed, money supply imploding by 30%, President Roosevelt had to face the rich–poor economy which no other president had faced in the USA and global history. It was the worst of the worst economic crises. The economy was close to what Marx had predicted as the turning point for the demise of capitalism and victory of communism. It needed either adopting the communist ideology or a total transformation in economic policy turning the conventional economic wisdom that ruled capitalism upside down. At this critical juncture, Keynes emerged as the great thinker and philosopher and Roosevelt as the courageous, sagacious, and visionary political practitioner, who saved capitalism by changing the rules of the game but preserving the ideals of democracy, freedom, and private property and thereby keeping totalitarianism and communism at bay. The recovery was slow but distinct, and unemployment was reduced to 9.7% only by 1941. The changes were so far reaching in building the foundation of reformed capitalism that never again did it give a way to the symptoms of depression until 2008. The crisis of 2008 in contrast was also an equally big crisis when it came into its full-blown proportion. But it was tamed in time with record micro- and macroeconomic measures with great finesse and speed involving global coordination. Another Great Depression was avoided.

Economic history is a great lesson and guide still in understanding the complex and critical economic problems and crises and also planning and devising measures to deal with them. It helps in more effective administration and management of the economy. Despite considerable sophistication in economic institutions, technological advance, information and data assimilation and management, regulatory apparatuses, and economic policy measures, the critical factors like human behavior and instincts that drive the economic decisions and develop patterns and trends have invariably remained relatively unchanged. Economics deals with laws of individual economic behavior and also of their groups and institutions. The basic laws are the same and universal, with minor variations in scope and degree in contemporary regions, cultures, and history.

In the 1930s when the legendary British economist John Maynard Keynes persuaded the then US President Roosevelt to initiate large government spending program through deficit financing, the economy responded and recovered from the bottom of depression, and Keynes emerged as the hero and savior of capitalism. Once again now Keynes and Keynesianism have come to the rescue of the capitalism. Although Keynesianism dominated the postwar US and global economic development and his rule book had to be referred again by the policy makers to deal with extreme and unconventional measures to tackle the current financial imbroglio gripping the US and global economy. Despite the miraculous postwar economic prosperity and sweeping institutional changes over the span of more than half a century to suit the brave new world, the Keynesian philosophy still remains intact undeterred by the ravages of time. The capitalism continues to suffer from the systemic cyclicality and needs government action in times major distress emanating from the swings of markets driven by the private sector. Unorthodox government intervention alone can save capitalism from its crisis. The theory of automatic correcting mechanism of capitalism is once again negated. The doctrines of market fundamentalism and smaller government which had resurfaced in the political philosophy in 1980s and dominated as Thatcherism in UK and Reaganism in USA are now put to rest. The new phase of globalization has no place for market fundamentalism and smaller government if it is to sustain without periodic hiccups. The recent experience also reinforces the view that the chariot of capitalism needs an accomplished charioteer (regulator) like Lord Krishna, the legendary last warrior, archer, commander, and philosopher with cosmic powers, who could rein the horses running wild distracted from the desired path. Prudential regulation is the only panacea for ensuring the chariot of capitalism and its financial system running on the safe and constructive path.

Quick Policy Response

The current economic crisis shows itself in two interrelated but separate aspects. In the analysis of the crisis as well as the evaluation of remedies to tackle them, both these economic problems need to be viewed differently. First is the banking crisis emanating from the securitized subprime mortgage debt meltdown and the collapse of the market for these securities and derivative products such as credit default swaps. The fact that many banks in the USA and other developed markets were and are over leveraged in their exposure to these products beyond the prudent norms risk managements is now evident. The magnitude of this financial black hole was far bigger than earlier fathomed. The second problem is the recessionary trend in the economy which got accentuated by the banking crisis.

The economic system would have fought the recession much more effectively if the banking system was stable and viable. The crumbling banking system is another blow which is aggravating recession. Two conventional barometers and drivers of the speed of growth of the US economy, car sales and house sales, were at their lowest levels. The banking industry, which traditionally pumps these sales, itself was in jeopardy. Weak consumer demand and dismal climate for investment were spinning the economy in a vicious circle economic contraction. In such circumstances, leave alone the market mechanism, but even the Federal Reserve's monetary policy of zero interest rate and large monetary injection could not usurp the economy. Only a large-scale government intervention into the economy could rescue the American capitalism for the second time since the Great Depression of the 1930s. With the global market capitalization disappearing to nearly half, record bank losses, rising unemployment, and dwindling output, the world was only a shade better than the first few years of Great Depression. The global economy did avoid the prolonged and harsher pain of depression, but it was already in its first phase. Today in a global village, with interlinked markets moving at the speed of light, the spread effects of crisis are much faster, sharper and volatile. The flip side of the same is that the recovery with action in right measure and direction can also be quick and more lasting.

Economic Policy Measures

The economic policy action taken to deal with the crisis since September 2008 when it first erupted by the Treasury Department of the US government and the Federal Reserve Bank from time to time has been quick, proactive, and decisive. These can be divided into:

1. Monetary policy support
   Monetary, liquidity, and banking measures from the Federal Reserve expanding money supply and lowering the rate of interest reducing the cost of money terms as the quantitative easing (QE).
2. Fiscal policy stimulus
   The budgetary measures of additional spending and tax cuts from the Federal government aimed to stimulate spending and economic growth. They can be classified into microeconomic measures relating to banking and financial institutions and broader macroeconomic action to influence the macro parameters.
3. Regulatory safeguards: legislative action on regulation of the financial system from the Congress.
   Apart from the monetary and fiscal measures that make a frontal attack on the crisis, the third weapon which is more crucial to prevent the recurrence of such crisis is the regulatory measures to ensure the prudential operation of the financial system with a fail-safe mechanism in place to avoid the recurrence of such crisis in future.

Macroeconomic Policy Action

The economic policy responses, both by the Fed and the Government, in terms of alacrity with which they were initiated as well as their magnitude in action have been commendable. It has probably averted major global crisis in recent years. The initiatives have been the judicious mix of both monetary and fiscal measures. The loan window of the Fed has not only pumped much needed liquidity of trillion dollars into the system following the record write-offs by the banks but also avoided a large bank failure which would have been too costly for the system. The financial history is replete with examples of the wreck a large bank failure can cause in the system and also as to how crisis-ridden bank can survive and grow with adequate dose of liquidity injection at crucial time. Even banks with negative net worth survive and grow on recapitalization and restructuring over a period. Citibank and other large US and multinational banks, which suffered heavily after the Latin American debt crisis in 1984, survived and grew after the Brady Plan and Bond Issue remedied the catastrophic probability.

Fortunately, the Great Depression has been an unforgettable lesson and a constant reminder evoking prompt, proactive, and decisive action in containing the economic crisis, emanating from the stock market and banking system. Due to the rise in the inflation rate caused by spiraling oil prices and increase in commodity prices, the Fed was unable to cut interest rates before the crisis. If it had done so, the crisis may have been averted. But its use of open market operations to avoid the liquidity squeeze gave the desired results after the crisis. The Fed injected liquidity in large doses by its open market operations of buying government securities as well as opening the fresh credit lines to meet the liquidity needs of troubled banks.

How Did the Fed Do It?

The Fed response to the crisis has been prompt, unconventional, unprecedented, decisive, and massive in its size and substance. It has avoided the greatest monetary implosion that would have crippled the US banking system and led the economy fast into deep recession. With the Fed's financial support, the banking failures culminating into a bigger banking crisis were avoided. The subprime loan securities of over one trillion dollars that turned bad and eroded the capital base and liquidity of the banking system could have caused the chain reaction of bank failures and collapse. This would have sucked the substantial liquidity from the system and led to monetary implosion, shrinking the money supply. The financial devastation, similar to one that took place in 1929–1933, was precluded. The Fed had to take a series of measures immediately after the crisis addressed to first to restore the stability of the financial system and then improve the system so that such crisis does not occur in future.

The Fed launched a six-pronged attack on the subprime debt crisis.

Firstly, through its traditional interest rate tool, the Fed moved fast to achieve the record reduction in interest rate. The Fed reduced its target Fed funds rate from 5.25% in 2007 to 4.25 in January 2008 and gradually to the target of 0.0–0.25% in December 2008 effectively starting the zero interest rate regime. The target of 0–0.25% Fed funds rate has been maintained till now, July 2012 (Fig. 3.1).

Secondly, as the lender of last resort, it opened its short-term loan window to support the ailing banks and institutions. The traditional rediscount window was opened for liberal short-term funding to banks, primary dealers, and institutions. This eliminated the immediate liquidity crunch faced by the troubled banks and institutions that may have led to their failures. This was the first line of attack that prevented banking failures snowballing into banking catastrophe.

Thirdly, Fed provided additional liquidity support directly to banks and also other financial intermediaries like money market mutual funds, investments banks, and insurance companies against the security of their troubled assets. Under the Term Asset-Backed Securities Loan Facility (TALF), the Fed gave loans to the financial market participants against the asset-backed securities (ABS) they held as the collaterals against home and commercial mortgages, car loans, credit card loans, and student and other small business and retail loans. It also funded money market mutual funds against their asset-backed commercial paper holdings. TALF was opened in March 2009 and closed in June 2010 with authorization of $200 billion out of which only $71 billion was used and the outstanding was reduced to $14 billion in May 2011. There wasn't a single credit loss and the program earned interest income of $1.2 billion which was remitted by the Fed to US Treasury.[1]

Fourthly, in its traditional open market operations, the Fed purchased massive amounts of longer-term securities from troubled banks and institutions to inject liquidity into the system. In November 2008, the Fed announced plans to purchase government-sponsored enterprise debt of $100 billion and mortgage-backed

[1] Federal Reserve Bank of New York, New York Fed 101:TALF.

Fig. 3.1 Federal funds rate (target rate) (Source: Federal Reserve Board)

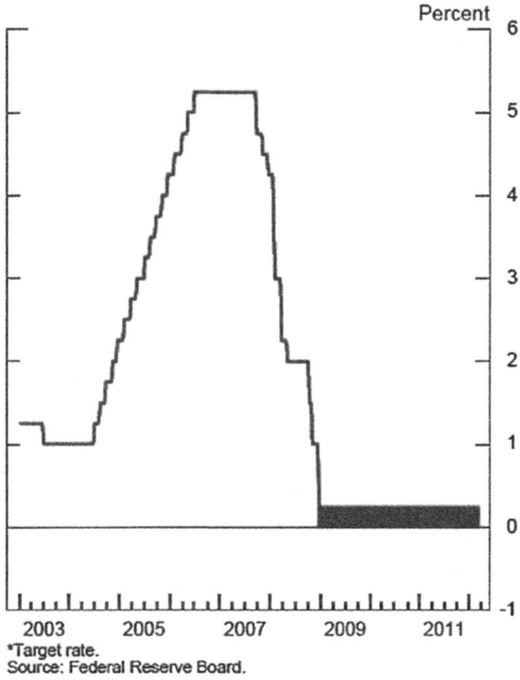

securities of $500 billion. In March 2009, the Fed announced the plans to purchase up to $300 billion of longer-term Treasury securities in addition to increasing its purchases of government-sponsored enterprise debt of $200 billion and mortgage-backed securities to $1.25 trillion. This $1.75 trillion injection of liquidity into money and credit markets by buying government and MBS paper averted market illiquidity crunch and more bank failures.

Fifthly, under the Term Auction Facility (TAF), the Fed auctioned term funds to depository institutions with full collateralization.

Sixthly, since the crisis was not isolated to the USA and had crossed the shores of the USA and affected the banks in other countries and their banking systems, they also faced the dollar crunch in their systems. The Fed provided the central bank (CB) dollar swap facilities to 14 foreign central banks to enable them to meet the demand for dollars by their banks. By the end of 2008, CB dollar swaps of $600 billion were outstanding primarily due to the dollar crunch abroad and strong demand of overseas banks to hold on to dollar balances in the wake of the crisis. These were unwound later. Amounts outstanding declined to less than $100 billion by June 2009, to less than $35 billion by October 2009, and to less than $1 billion by the time the program expired on February 1, 2010.

The result of the Fed action was instantaneous in avoiding further bank failures. This could not happen in 1929–1930. The Fed injected record liquidity into the economy by lending nearing $800 billion to the banks and other financial institutions.

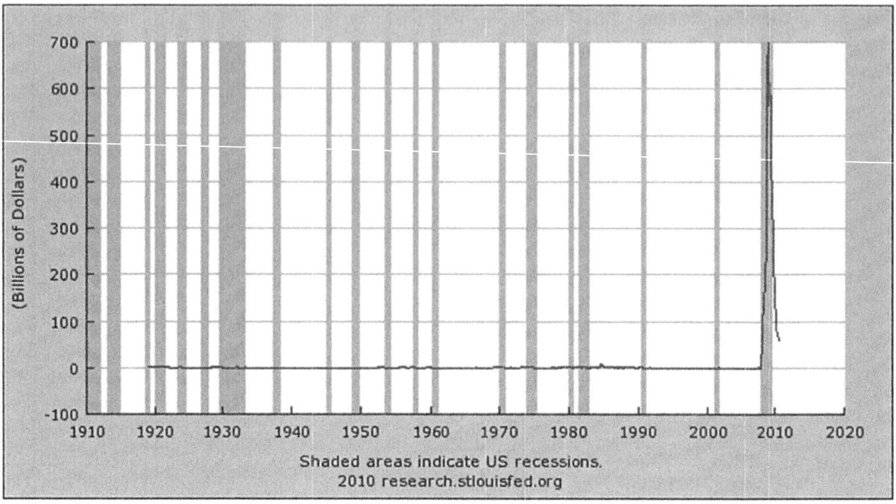

Fig. 3.2 Total borrowings of depository institutions from the federal reserve (BORROW). *Shaded areas* indicate US recessions. 2010 research.stiouisfed.org (Source: Board of Governors of the Federal Reserve System)

This accounted for 10% of M2 (currency in circulation + demand deposits + savings deposits + small denomination time deposits) of around $8 trillion. The Fed's support avoided the crisis causing monetary implosion or contraction. M2 growth which was 6.3% in 2007 continued to be high at 7.1% in 2008 and 7.6% in 2009.

Figure 3.2 below shows the Fed lending to the banking system over a century. The Fed lending to the banking system has always been very nominal. The banking system never wanted any extraordinary support from the Fed all these years. It was self-sustaining. It also demonstrates the strength and resiliency of the US banking system. The years 2008–2009 were extraordinary, and spike in the graph shows the sudden leapfrogging in Fed funding of the banking system. Never in the history of the Fed such a massive funding been ever provided to the banking system. It depicts the unprecedented blood transfusion into system conducted by the Fed to keep it alive and prevent it from collapsing. The banking system was on life support, and the Fed provided emergency oxygen and blood supply to the system to survive and sustain. The borrowings by the banks also returned to the normal levels once the system survived and began functioning normally. The graph shows the sharp drop in borrowing in the late 2009 after the crisis was blown over. Never had the US banking and financial system to depend on the funding support from the Fed of this magnitude in the last more than 100 years. Even in the worst years before the Fed's support to the banking system had never exceeded $10 billion compared to over $700 billion in the current crisis. This was an extraordinary crisis, even bigger than 1930s crisis in terms of its initial quake.

Although the banks' borrowings from the Fed went up by $800 billion, the monetary base (currency in circulation + deposits of banks with the Fed) surged to

$2,000 billion after the full-fledged Fed support by way of purchase of treasury and other securities from the banks by 2009. The total assets and liabilities of the Federal Reserve also went up from $900 billion to $2,100 billion over the same period.

Operation Bailout

Reckoning the implications of the failure of Bear Stearns in March 2008 on the banking system, the Fed in an uncharacteristic fashion opened its window of the lender of last resort open to the deposit-taking companies and lent $30 billion to JPMorgan Chase for agreeing to take over Bear Stearns. This was the first such large lending in the Fed's long history of 70 years. While the Fed swung the first weapon in its armory to stem the subprime loan imbroglio culminating into a banking crisis, the government supplemented the Fed's efforts by pushing the Keynesian economic stimulus package of $100 billion through the Congress. It encouraged the consumers spending grow, uplifting the slowing economy.

Looking to the gravity of the crisis, the US government moved swiftly in September 2008 to pass a bigger proposal of $700 billion emergency package to acquire mortgage-backed securities that have become illiquid causing this financial crisis. It turned out to be one of largest in the global history. This followed the earlier takeover by the government or nationalization of the failing AIG by authorizing $85 billion line of credit from the Fed in exchange of 80% of its equity. Despite the high magnitude of the write-offs by the banking system across the world crossing the estimate over a trillion dollar figure, the banking system weathered the crisis with the cushion of massive liquidity support from the Fed and other central banks. But it seemed that the end was not yet in sight. The disclosures by Freddie Mac and Fannie Mae about their provisioning rattled the financial markets again. The government and Fed's response was again more proactive. With the government takeover of Freddie Mac and Fannie Mae, two largest quasi-governmental housing mortgage finance companies owning and guaranteeing nearly 50% of all housing mortgages of $10 trillion, marking it a historical landmark in not only the US finance and economy but also the evolution the global economy and system, yet another crash was averted.

Fiscal Stimulus Packages

The democratic response to the financial crisis and worsening recession in the economy typically reemphasizes the Keynesian philosophy in restoring the financial stability and economic recovery. President Obama's $825 billion stimulus package and $350 billion financial stability plan were aimed to accelerate spending and reequip the financial system to resume its speed of lending. Both the size of the state intervention and its direction were aimed to attack twin evils of near financial collapse and aggravating recession. The fiscal support of this $1.18 trillion was sizeable enough to tackle history's worst economic ill. In a situation of financial crisis, growing unemployment, declining stock market, and negative business expectations when private sector delays spending, lending, and risk-taking, three critical elements of economic growth, only the state spending and risk-taking can jump-start the economy. The government's dual plan was the most optimum strategy to galvanize the private sector that could then set the economic juggernaut back in growth momentum. The financial stability plan provided for stress test for the banks for their bailout which would preempt bank failures.

American Recovery and Reinvestment Act

The economic crisis coincided the last year of the Republican presidential term. In October 2008, the Congress passed the Emergency Economic Stabilization Act (EESA) with the specific goal of stabilizing the nation's financial system and preventing catastrophic collapse allocating $700 billion. Although there was bipartisan approach to tackle the crisis, the election of the Democratic president in 2008 gave the usual ideological touch to the stimulus package. The most pressing need for the new government was to get the stimulus package approved by the Congress. American Recovery and Reinvestment Act was signed by the President Obama in February 2009 and passed by the Congress in March 2009 to provide a package of targeted investments and tax cuts to jump-start the economy and create millions of jobs. The act authorized the budgetary support of $825 billion to jump-start the economy and create and support 3–4 million jobs. It comprised tax cuts of $275 billion to boost consumption expenditure and extra government expenditure of $550 billion targeted in priority investment areas. The expenditure was targeted to the modernization of infrastructure of roads, bridges, transit, and waterways; renewable domestic energy; education; health care; science and technology; and protection of vital government services and labor rehabilitation.

Troubled Assets Recovery Plan (TARP)

In addition to the emergency measures taken by the Federal Reserve to bail out banks and financial institutions by providing them lines of credit to avoid their illiquidity and insolvency, the Treasury came out with another massive funding of $350 billion under TARP for the rescue of the weakening banking system. This was the single most critical measure that avoided bank failures and banking crisis. It stalled the repeat of 1930s when following the stock market crash and property boom burst, the bank failures spread like wildfire, imploding the entire banking system. The situation was worst at the bottom of the crisis in 1933. The current crisis skipped the widespread banking crisis due to timely action by the Fed and the Treasury in avoiding bank failures culminating into a full-fledged financial meltdown like 1930s.

In addition, the public–private fund for the rehabilitation of the banking and financial system was provided to combine private equity and financial investment along with the Government financial support to be as large as $1.5–$2 trillion. This was a formidable measure. Driven quickly at the right speed and with sizeable magnitude and judicious direction, the Fund can act as the pacemaker of the country's banking system driving it back on its racing tracks. The heartbeat of the banking system had slowdown, thwarting the quick economic recovery. The new financial stability plan acted as a pacemaker of the system, bringing heartbeats of the credit system to its normal growth level.

The stimulus package consisted of government spending and tax reliefs. While the former was aimed to generate more employment and income that would multiply its effects, the latter would trigger consumer spending and corporate investment. The package must ensure maximum multiplier effects on employment and growth. Complementing these two fiscal initiatives, the Fed continued its cheap money policy with low interest rate and ample liquidity. The twin fiscal plans were ably complemented by the Fed's monetary policy. It injected record liquidity into the system and in the weak banks to preclude liquidity crunch in the system and also cash starved banks. Money was cheapest with Fed funds rate of record low blow of 0.25%. Extra money and cheaper money were intended to stimulate consumer credit demand, consumer spending, working capital demand from businesses, small and big, and also long-term corporate investment.

In times of weak consumer confidence and uncertain and shaky investment climate, the potency of monetary policy is undermined. It can be only realized when the economy starts ticking. While the Fed's low interest rates can stimulate consumer demand to some extent, the more important element for rebound in income and employment growth is buoyancy of corporate investment spending. It would be preposterous to expect a spurt in corporate investment under the conditions of lower or negative cash flows and rates of return. Even zero interest regimes do not evoke investment when macroenvironment is fraught with uncertainty and bleak prospect of growth. More than a decade, long and protracted Japanese economic stagnation is a clear case in point. The monetary policy can, therefore, ignite growth only when the fiscal stimulus reveals its impact on the economy.

Micromanagement: Tackling Corporate and Banking Failures

The market economy is more efficient than regulated one. Yet the handicaps from which the market economy suffers are asymmetry of information and psychology of euphoria and panic. Over the last year or so, the macromanagement of the economy in the USA despite the recurrent financial crises has been commendable in containing their ripple effects. Despite the most proactive macromanagement, the micromanagement has been weak and is the issuc that needs to be addressed. The corporate failures are a part of the market economy, and if the pain of failures is to be avoided, the market economy has to institute a prudent and effective supervisory framework which deters market excesses without curbing enterprise and initiative. We have seen earlier how financial markets are different from other markets. The failure of an industrial corporate is not as damaging to the economy as the failure of a bank or financial institutions. Hence, the existing supervisory and regulatory structure needs to be tighter for banks and financial institutions. It also raises the issue of "too big to fail." Whether the banks should be allowed to be too big to be a systemic risk? Or whether they can be subject to special supervisory and regulatory provisions to make them less vulnerable to failures? We have seen the Niagara effect which the banks and financial paper can cause. The case for special attention to the big in banking and finance becomes stronger. The norms for provisioning of weak assets and capital adequacy need to be reviewed.

Yet another aspect of banking which actually exaggerated the crisis was the mark to market valuation norm. The panic reaction in the market about defaults caused Niagara effect on prices actually undervaluing the securities due their inherent strength of a mortgage of property. Hence, micromanagement can also be improved by changing some accounting norms like mark-to-market valuation every quarter. The solution to this issue can be to switch over to average pricing over a period rather than a single-date pricing for valuation. This would eliminate the insolvency problem when the firm is actually not insolvent on the basis of average pricing. In line with this, the liquidity problem also needs to be resolved with the infusion of fresh funds which the Fed has done quite admirably. The crisis would not have assumed the proportion it did if the valuation norms were more realistic than the mark to market influenced by market panic.

The governments and central banks in Europe, Japan, and China took similar measures to infuse much needed liquidity into the system and support some of the large banking institutions adversely affected by the crisis. It shows coordinated action taken globally to deal with this extraordinary problem now affecting the global financial system and threatening its stability.

Specter of Protectionism

In times of global recession, if protectionism raises its ugly head as it did in 1930s, it wouldn't be long before the global economy plunges into morass of depression. Any attempt toward protectionism needs to be strictly thwarted by the global leadership. Any flavor of protectionism, like "buy American," in stimulus packages would have set in a wave of reactionary protectionism far worse to the global economy. Protectionism is the worst enemy of development and can intensify the recession more quickly like it did in the 1930s when the global trade shrunk to half. In 1930, reacting to sharp fall prices farm products and their rising stocks import tariff of 40% was imposed under *Smoot–Hawley Tariff Act*. This caused the chain reaction and retaliatory measures that were worst in global economic history, leading to contraction of world trade. The coordinated effort in G20 meetings avoided this phase in the current crisis.

Falling Oil Prices: Great Stimulus

Another factor that spelt a blow on the global economy on the eve of the crisis was the relentless spurt in oil prices that squeezed the households and consumer spending. The drop from the high of $147 per barrel in July 2008 to $32 in December 2008 was a great respite and helped the US and global economic recovery. This downtrend in the market would favor the economy globally and generate the flow of resources to individuals and corporates for higher consumption, savings, and investment. In fact, low oil prices would offer a smooth gear for the fundamentally sound economy to put its financial superstructure in order. But the oil prices firmed up again in 2009–2011 and crossed again $100 per barrel mark, undermining the recovery process in the global world.

G-20 Agenda: Quick Stimulus and More Effective Regulation

In a globalized world, no country is insulated from the US economy. Despite its declining dominance over time, the USA still accounts for a quarter of the global GDP and therefore has significant influence on the behavior, growth, and stability of the global economy. On account of the magnitude and severity of the US financial crisis, every country is affected depending upon its economic, financial, trade, and investment links with the USA and rest of the world. The US administration and the Federal Reserve have acted in dealing with this crisis with great alacrity and proactivity to avoid the economy slipping into severe recession arising from credit crunch and illiquidity and lower spending. Had it not been for the other central banks like the European Central Bank and the Bank of England also following suit with the reduction in their interest rates and infusion of additional liquidity, the Eurozone would have felt much sharper adverse impact of the crisis. In addition to the European governments announcing the fiscal stimulus packages, China unfolded massive $877 billion which seems very large and relatively bigger than the USA, looking to the size of the Chinese economy. The fight against the crisis has been global (Fig. 3.3).

G-20 meeting in Washington in 2009 was reminiscent of the Bretton Woods meeting held in 1944 that created the postwar global financial architecture. Dramatic changes in structure and growth in global economic and financial flows have brought pressure on the system which has now become archaic. Technological advance and financial sophistication have substantially outgrown the institutional setups and supervisory capabilities. The crisis is a reflection of these institutional lacunae and underscores the imperative need for institutional and regulatory reforms. The G-20 meeting endorses this understanding and reality and reinforces the need to common consensus and joint and coordinated approach and action in resolving the crisis. In its agenda for action, the G-20 has agreed on immediate measures comprising fiscal stimulus and monetary relaxation to reinstate the global economy on a sustainable

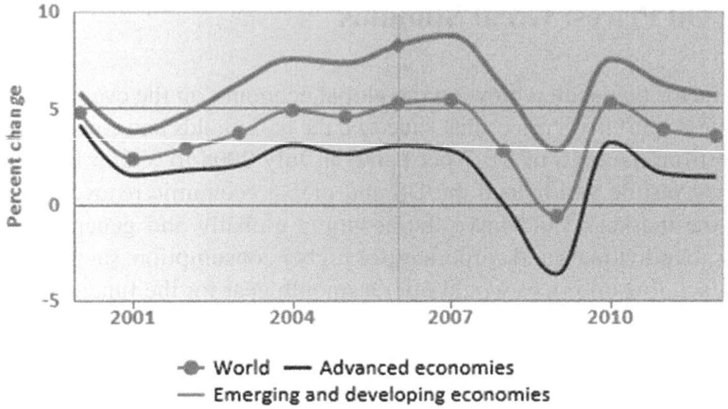

Fig. 3.3 Global aggregates: real GDP (percent change) (Source: IMF economic outlook, Graphs by Knoema beta)

growth path and institutional and regulatory reforms to avoid the recurrence of such crisis in future. Looking to the experience of protectionism, the countries have also shown consensus in desisting from falling into the destructive trap of protectionism.

Over the last three decades, the policies of liberalization and globalization have brought dramatic changes in the structure of global economy. The size, pattern, and trend of global trade and investment flows have altered dramatically. It is not surprising to see these changes causing far-reaching movements in financial flows globally. Light-speed technology has revolutionized information and data flows remodeling the market mechanism. Financial sophistication and growth of derivatives and futures markets have gone beyond the traditional framework of regulatory arms and tools. The twentieth-century institutional apparatus overseeing the rapidly growing and fast-changing system remained archaic. The current financial crisis manifests the systemic failure unable to cope with the speed and dynamics of cyclicality of markets and institutional inadequacies and loopholes in dealing with risk management. The gravity of the financial crisis is leading the global economy into a dangerous terrain of severe and protracted recession unless the prompt and effective globally coordinated action is taken. The first meeting of G-20 was held in Washington, DC, in November 2008, the second in London in April 2009, and the third at Pittsburg in September 2009. It is commendable that US president called this meeting of 20 nations which account for 90% of global economy and 75% of global population. There was need to have consensus and coordinated action plan.

The crisis has to be perceived from both the short-term as well as long-term perspectives. Invariably, the management of the crisis in order to be effective and lasting has also to comprise some short-term quick fixes and also the long-term policy and institutional changes and reforms that avoid its recurrence in future. The G-20 agenda for plan of action exactly did this. The proactivity with which all the nations unanimously endorsed the future course of action overcoming the minor differences they may have had about the details and operationalities was remarkable.

The G-20 recommended the coordinated action on two fronts. The economic stimulus package was aimed to pull the global economy from slipping into recession and to direct it onto the sustainable growth path. The institutional and regulatory reforms were intended to effectively regulate the fast-changing twenty-first-century financial system to suit new requirements and avoid the recurrence of this crisis in future. The study of Great Depression of 1930s shows that financial crisis led to bank failures and credit contraction. The wave of protectionism that followed became anti-growth and exacerbated the recession that culminated into deep depression.

The G-20 plan of action was targeted to avoid the chronology of 1930s. All the nations have agreed to follow low interest and easy credit monetary policy. It would inject much needed liquidity into the system suffering from the crunch. The Federal Reserve already infused the record liquidity nearing $2 trillion followed by the European Central Bank and Bank of England. The credit markets world over were becoming more restrictive and losing their velocity. In such times, easy credit from the central banks would regenerate the credit lending cycle which had slowed down considerably. The monetary action needs to be supplemented by the vigorous fiscal boost. The fiscal stimulus package was intended to raise spending and revive consumer and investor confidence. With the fiscal and bailout packages crossing $1 trillion and liquidity injection by the Fed totaled a figure close to 1/6th of the US GNP and large enough to reflate the economy in 2009.

While the adverse events are behind us, it is imperative to improve the transparency and regulatory requirements suited to the new and fast-changing financial world. The G-20 has agreed to reform the regulatory structure to bring operations of cross-border institutions which currently remain outside any supervisory framework. There is the need to also to render better and more transparent market mechanism to several new products like credit default swaps (CDS) which magnified the current crisis. It was felt that the efforts to create more prudential and wider regulation should stifle the free markets and initiative for innovation. And most importantly, the developed nations, and more particularly the USA, agreed to not resort to and fall into the destructive trap of protectionism. The emerging market economies were assured of the same support from the developed world.

The objective of G-20 is to reform the global financial architecture to meet the needs and demands of twenty-first century. G-20 meeting at Pittsburg decided to increase the resources of the IMF so as to avoid the spread of the crisis to the emerging market economies. The resources of the IMF have been trebled. The members contributed $500 billion, a renewed and expanded IMF New Arrangements to Borrow (NAB). The IMF made special drawing rights (SDR) allocations of $283 billion in total, more than $100 billion of which would supplement emerging market and developing countries' existing reserve assets. Resources would be raised from the sale of IMF gold consistent with the IMF's new income model, and funds from internal and other sources would more than double the Fund's medium-term concessional lending capacity. In the light of the growing importance of the emerging market economies, their share in the quotas was to be raised in 2011.

An important decision at the meeting was the unanimous opinion that "Major failures of regulation and supervision, plus reckless and irresponsible risk-taking by banks and other financial institutions, created dangerous financial fragilities that contributed significantly to the current crisis."[2] The leaders, therefore, agreed to create a better, more comprehensive and effective mechanism for supervision and regulation of over-the-counter (OTC) derivatives, securitization markets, credit rating agencies, and hedge funds. The Financial Stability Board (FSB), which also includes the major emerging markets, was established in London in order to coordinate and monitor the progress in strengthening financial regulation.

Financial Reform (Dodd–Frank) Act and the Volcker Rule

The US financial system is already subject to not any less regulatory oversight from different agencies than any other country in the world. The popular belief within the USA and outside that American capitalism is free for all business environments with minimal regulation and bureaucracy is not well founded. More so in banking and financial services industry which is subject to regulation at the federal level by the Federal Reserve, Comptroller of Currency, and Deposit Insurance Corporation Act and at the state level by the department of banking.

Large and structural institutional changes in a society have to occur over a long periods usually spanning over half a century if the system shows inadequacies of dealing with the hopes and aspirations of people which are embedded in goals government wants to achieve and direction of the private economy driven by the market forces within the prevalent regulatory ambience.

The National Commission on the crisis after hearings and study observed, "In April 2010, the Subcommittee held four hearings examining four root causes of the financial crisis. Using case studies detailed in thousands of pages of documents released at the hearings, the Subcommittee presented and examined evidence showing how high risk lending by U.S. financial institutions; regulatory failures; inflated credit ratings; and high risk, poor quality financial products designed and sold by some investment banks, contributed to the financial crisis."[3]

The financial reform bill was to address the above issues pointed by the commission and work toward strengthening the regulatory mechanism. It is most comprehensive piece of legislation since the New Deal that aims to plug several areas of financial indiscretion emanating from the repeal of Glass–Steagall in 1999 and also fast growth and growing sophistication of the financial system and markets not earlier covered by the oversight. The bill is aimed at not only preventing the recurrence of the banking and financial crisis but also providing a fail-safe mechanism in the case-banking failures that prevents jeopardizing the banking system.

---

[2] Leaders' Statement: Pittsburgh Summit, September 24–25, 2009.

[3] The Financial Crisis Inquiry Report: *Final Report of the National Commission on the Causes of the Financial Crisis in the United States, January 2011.*

The repeal of the Glass–Steagall was biological necessity of globalization, growing integration of the global financial markets, and advent and growth of universal banking. The US banks and financial institutions would have been at considerable disadvantage vis-a-vis their international counterparts. What was missing was the regulatory aspect of the new universal banks. After the repeal of the Glass–Steagall Act, holding company vehicle was extensively used by the banks and investments banks to take heavy exposure to products and instruments that would not be possible for a bank or deposit-taking company. The large part of the exposure was also passed to the banks through the securitization. In addition to large exposure, the quality of debt was not very sound, since it was subprime debt facing high solvency, servicing, liquidity, and price risks. Rising interest rates, slowing economy, and increasing unemployment translated all risks into reality in a vicious circle of market collapse. The rest is history.

Dodd–Frank Wall Street Reform and Consumer Protection Act, the financial services law and financial overhaul legislation, passed in 2010 gave the federal regulators greater powers to deal with 2008-like situation in future. It has now given the powers to authorities to seize large financial holding companies that are on the verge of bankruptcy. The main aim of the bill is also to avoid the repeat of this phenomenon and has addressed this issue by providing several safeguards. It has suggested several tighter regulatory measures to ensure greater stability of the financial system with more increased degree of accountability and transparency and end the "too big to fail" situations in future and public rescue of such institutions. The *Volcker rule* prevents the deposit-taking institutions from proprietary trading and restricts their investment in private equity and hedge funds up to 3% of the bank's Tier 1 capital. One of the key areas of weakness that contributed to the crisis was ratings to subprime debt given by the reputed rating agencies. The bill also aims to regulate the operations of credit rating agencies

The foremost requirement has been the capital adequacy of the holding company. During the last decade, banks and financial institutions were using the subsidiarization route to bypass the capital adequacy norms for riskier and leveraged exposures. This route has been plugged by providing capital adequacy for holding companies. The missing regulatory link in the new age of universal banking has now been installed.

The bill provides wide powers to authorities to prevent the abuse of financial illiteracy of clients by the financial institutions and protect the consumers from unfair financial practices. The Bureau of Consumer Financial Protection has been proposed covering mortgages, credit card debt, and other products to avoid the abuse of consumer financial illiteracy for unfair gains.

The derivatives, weapons of mass destruction, need to be moved over from the OTC markets to the exchange-based clearing house markets that would eliminate the counterparty risks, market failures having the domino effect, and also regulate leveraging and provide more transparent trading. This would minimize the speculative element of the derivatives market which are destabilizing for the entire financial market in the case of failures and crises.

Quantitative Easing 2 (QE 2)

When the interest rates are near zero level, there is nothing that can be done by the central bank on the interest rate front. If the economy fails to respond, it means that it is in typical nonresponsive state which is known as the "liquidity trap." The only way the central bank work in trying a further stimulus is by increasing the liquidity in the economy. As a conventional measure to infuse or suck the liquidity in the economy, the central bank uses its open market operations. It involves the central bank buying short-term government securities from banks and institutions and increased liquidity or selling the securities to contract liquidity. The Federal Market Operations Committee (FMOC) comprising 12 members holds 8 regular scheduled meetings in a year that "reviews the economic and financial conditions, determines the appropriate stance of monetary policy, and assesses the risks to its long run goals of price stability and sustainable economic growth." The meeting, among other monetary options, determines the quantum and direction of the Fed's open market operations strategy in government securities to influence the liquidity in the economy.

While the Fed funds rate is the shortest interest rates used by the banks for their overnight borrowings and lending, the medium- and longer-term interest rates are governed by the yield rates on the longer-dated government securities. These rates are the benchmark for the interest rates prevailing in the commercial banking and financial markets. It will be seen from Fig. 3.2 that although the Fed funds rates and short-term rates crashed after QE1 in 2008, the decline in the yield rates on the long-dated government securities was not steep. This raised the yield spread. It can be seen that the spread between 30-year government bond and the Fed funds which was as low as 0.5% in 2007 and 1% in 2008 gradually rose to 4.15% in mid-2011. This "operation twist" is undertaken finally to reduce the long-term interest rates and the interest rate structure in commercial banking and private sector. The objective is to stimulate consumer spending and mortgage and business borrowings. The QE is not restricted to the purchase of the government securities but encompasses the private sector financial assets. This is intended to inject liquidity directly in hands of private institutions in addition to banks. The "operation twist" in QE2 reduced the long-term yield rates by causing a rise in the prices of bonds. The lower long-term interest rates reduced the mortgage rates and private banking lending rates. While rising asset prices has wealth effect stimulating consumption and spending, higher liquidity with banks enables them to promote lending (Fig. 3.4).

After the crisis until mid-2010, the Fed purchased treasury notes, MBS, and other private paper worth $1.3 trillion. This could be referred to as the QE1 (quantitative easing1). The Fed balance sheet during this period went up from $800 billion to $2.1 trillion. When the economy was recovering from the GDP decline of 2.4% in 2009 to a positive territory in 2010, it was thought desirable to give second round of monetary injection in order to sustain the recovery. In November 2010, the Fed announced the plan of monetary expansion with the program of purchase of long-dated government debt from the private sector of $600 billion. This was called

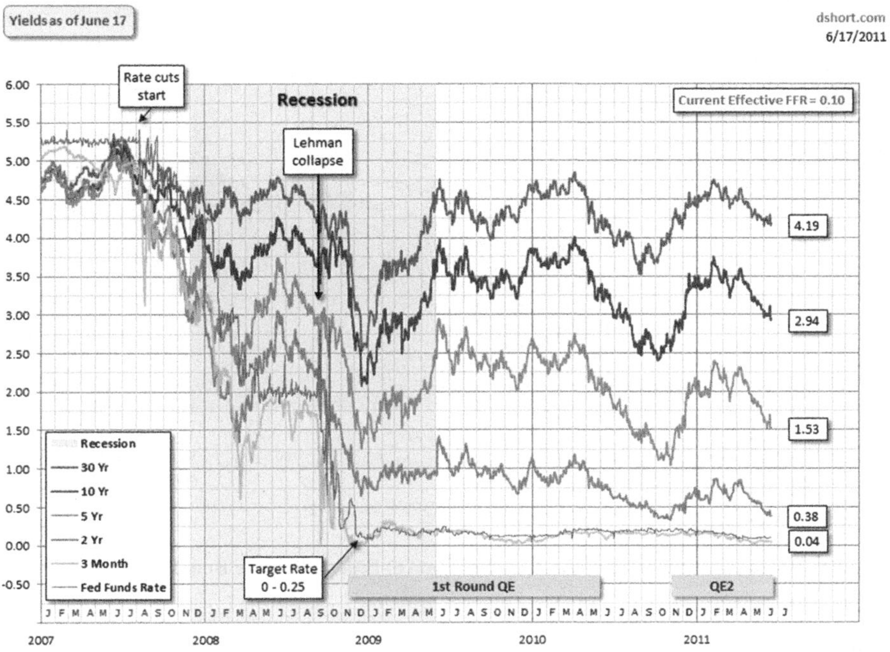

Fig. 3.4 Daily treasury yields since 2007 and the effective federal funds rate

QE 2. Also launched was the program of operation twist where the Fed planned to buy long-dated securities with maturities of 6–30 years and sell those with maturities of less than 3 years, reextending the average maturity of Fed's own portfolio and also reducing yield curve spread between the long-dated and short-dated government securities. On the fourth anniversary of the crisis in September 2012, the Fed announced QE3 of $400 billion involving plan for purchase of MBS (mortgage-backed securities) of $40 billion every month and also signaled that the zero interest rate policy will continue till 2015. Bernanke Put was thus extended by one more year from earlier 2014 (Fig. 3.5).

The impact of the two QEs on the Fed balance sheet is shown in Fig. 3.1. The size of the Fed balance sheet has gone up from $800 billion in 2008 to $2.9 trillion in 2012.

Central Banks and Financial Regulators: Countervailing Force Against Market Abnormality

The central banks can act as a strong countervailing force in the financial and forex markets but not in stock and commodity markets, which remain entirely the domain of private individuals and institutions. It is this absence of countervailing intervention

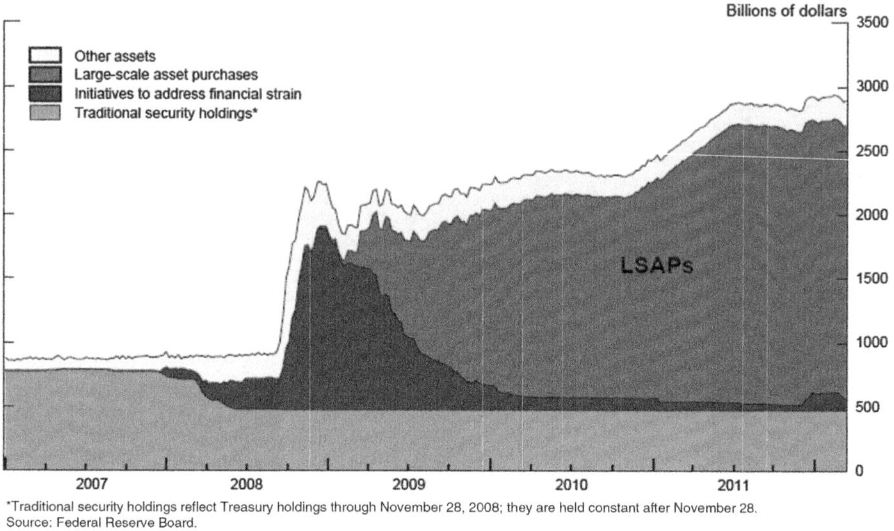

Fig. 3.5 Federal reserve balance sheet, assets (Source: Federal Reserve Board)

that makes the stock and commodity markets more susceptible to wide fluctuations. Markets are gripped more by either greed or panic in their extremities. The central bank or government intervention into the stock and commodity markets is an anathema of the free markets and also unconventional in economic policy matters. But the recent trend of massive losses in stock prices across the globe after the crisis has underscored the imperative need for the first ever coordinated action at the global level by the governments or government agencies to intervene also in the stock markets. The past events have been the interplay of markets versus governments. One is reminded of the concept of "countervailing power" propounded by one of the most outstanding American economists, John Kenneth Galbraith in his popular book, "American Capitalism." The changing complexion and character of capitalism needs a new policy to deal with unprecedented problems. The new policy needs to act as a strong countervailing force and more as a deterrent. It would then create an impact on its very existence and work even without any action. It would turn crisis and panic into opportunity. The values in the markets are sought to be captured at bottom of the crisis wherein lies the opportunity. In such stock market conditions dominated by pessimism, the even normal profit expectations get seriously dampened by negativity. Profit expectation guided by long-term projections get altered by market pessimism, halting large project investments. The state of the stock market has a serious impact on dampening the investment climate and delaying the actual outlays. With the slump in investment, the recession gets momentum and runs into a vicious circle.

Conventionally, markets can be better regulated by the external independent bodies like SEC. Yet the recent trend of the growing size and operations of the sovereign wealth funds is a pointer to the emerging influence of the central banking and government power of forex-rich countries in the global stock and commodity markets. Further, the growing size and influence of hedge funds and footloose money floating in the offshore markets beyond the control of any central bank or regulatory authority need a countercheck of larger magnitude than imagined earlier from the governments. If this is the trend, is it not the time also to evolve the fail-safe mechanism for markets? And it can be initiated only by the governments. Would it amount to nationalization of some banks and corporates? Would it be passive government investments in private enterprises? Would it be bringing government nominees on the boards of listed companies? Would it be a new face of American capitalism with a socialistic lipstick? All these perceptions are a matter of dogma. And in times of economic crisis, dogmatism can be the biggest enemy of economic wisdom and pragmatism. Historical events and economic calamities have been the witness to economic shortsightedness and political inertia.

Keynes on Slump and Management of Economic Cycles

In times of recession or slump caused by the financial crisis, it is imperative that government steps in to give fiscal stimulus to the economy. The fiscal stimulus comprises step-up in government expenditure and tax concessions both of which are aimed to substitute the deficiency in aggregate demand caused by the hole in the balance sheets of households, businesses, banks, and governments and liquidity crunch created by the crisis. The restoration of aggregate demand to the pre-slump level is aimed to restore economic growth by external stimulus or pump priming when the internal, autonomous, or private sector, the household and industry, fails to respond to bring about economic recovery. The originator of this policy, Keynes, has brought about succinctly the rationale for this policy and also highlighted the reasons for weak private investment response to the low interest rate policy. "When once the recovery has been started, the manner in which it feeds on itself and cumulates is obvious. But during the downward phase, when both fixed capital and stocks of materials are for the time being redundant and working-capital is being reduced, the schedule of marginal efficiency of capital (expected rate return on fresh capital investment) may fall so low that it can scarcely be corrected, so as to secure a satisfactory rate of new investment, by any practical reduction in the rate on interest. (The economy faces the liquidity trap with inelasticity of investment to the interest rates at its lowest or even zero level.) Due to the Thus with markets organized and influenced as they are at present, the market estimation of the marginal efficiency of capital may suffer such enormously wide fluctuations that it cannot be sufficiently offset by corresponding fluctuations in the rate of interest. Moreover, the corresponding movements in the stock-market may, as we have seen above, depress the propensity to consume just when it is most needed. In conditions of *laissez-faire* the avoidance of wide fluctuations in employment may, therefore, prove impossible without a far-reaching change in the psychology of investment markets such as there is no reason to expect. I conclude that the duty of ordering the current volume of investment cannot safely be left in private hands. …whilst for the reasons given above the slump cannot be prevented by a low rate of interest (due to liquidity trap and interest insensitivity of new investment), nevertheless the boom can be avoided by a high rate on interest. There is, indeed, force in the argument that a high rate interest is much more effective against a boom than a low rate of interest against a slump" [1, p. 320, the words in brackets are mine].

Despite the fact that more than 70 years have passed since Keynes wrote this in the *General Theory,* the institutions have changed, *laissez-faire* has been abandoned, management of economy is more in the control of the state, the basic human and private institutional urges, instincts, and tendencies that govern the private behavior have not changed in the free world. The greed and fear and short-term or myopic irrationality have continued their strong hold on the basic economic parameters of consumption and investment, two most critical elements in the growth of any economy. The economy consists of a wide matrix of decisions on consumption and investment which move in one way in normal times but go haywire and adopt confusing and contrary patterns in times of crisis and panic.

Keynes's concept of marginal efficiency of capital is actually the prospective rate of return on fresh capital investment. It is now popularly known as the internal rate of return (IRR) using discounted cash flows (DCF) forming the fundamental principle of capital budgeting decisions in the modern theories of finance and investment and what investment science and analysts refer to as the earning per share (EPS) or earnings forecast.[4] The pessimistic projections and overoptimistic forecasts of earnings in slump and boom, respectively, are a bane that exacerbate these cycles and make the state intervention imperative to curb these hyperactive behaviors. At the same time, it is essential to keep the animal spirits, which are the driving force of investment, alive. It would be counterproductive if the boom is checked at a stage when the goose is still giving the golden eggs.

The situation in a slump is different. A boom is fueled by positive sentiments governed by positive information about future such as expectation of financial gain. When the gains are realized over short time and repeated over a longer period, it turns into euphoria that turn future expectations more irrational and unrealistic, overpowering the reasonable, more realistic, and lower expectations. This state which Greenspan called *irrational exuberance* is bound to get dashed when the results turn out considerably short of expectations. Keynes referred to this phenomenon as the "*misguided state of expectations*" [1, p. 322]. When the reality fails to meet the misguided expectations, irrational exuberance blows over and the reversal starts. It first impacts on the stock market where the long and buy positions are unwinded and covered by short and sell positions. This reversal of sentiments and long positions continues longer depending upon how much is the gap between the expectation and reality and how big is the long position. When the reversal takes place and continues for a longer period, the positive sentiment turns into negative one.

[4] Keynes is the first economist who used the discounted cash flow method, which is now common in the subjects of financial management and investments. It related the computation of rate of return on capital with the time value of money.

The expectation is not the gain but avoidance of loss. The bear cycles begins with panic and rush for profit booking or loss minimization.

So long as the expectations are negative, it is difficult to find the lowering of interest rate to have any impact on investment decisions. The economic recession which lasted in Japan for more a decade and could not end despite zero interest rate policy is a starkly evidence of the impotency of rate of interest as a weapon to tackle the slump. The recent recovery in the US and global economy is also slow despite the near zero interest rates in the developed world and shows that the expectations have yet to cross the threshold of interest rates. Unfortunately, as positive sentiments in a boom phase get cumulated, so do the negative ones during slump. While the boom is welcome until it turns counterproductive resulting in inflation, the slump is damaging in all its effect. The objective of economic policy is to promote growth with stability. The boom can continue so long as it is does not harm price stability. The slump is unwelcome and is not desired for long except for a temporary period for cooling off the overheated economy. The tactic or strategy of managing the economy is to tame the boom before it bursts and stall the slump in its short run. Keynes describes this more precisely as the *essence of prudent economic management and recession proof economic system* in his *General Theory*. "*The right remedy for the trade cycle is not to be found in abolishing booms and thus keeping us permanently in a semi-slump; but in abolishing slumps and thus keeping us permanently in a quasi-boom*" [1, p. 322].

Metaphysics of Money and Markets

The recent global financial drama typically illustrates the market psyche in times of economic distress. The behavior of markets is shaped by not only news and information but also the perception of participants reacting to such information. The degree of optimism or pessimism with which the participants respond to factual information varies. In the market conditions bordering extremes, the tendency is to view the future with either euphoria or panic. In such conditions, participants respond more to instant information than to distant information. This behavioral psychology manifesting in commonly found *trend reinforcing nature of the market movements* gets severely amplified in times of market extremities. Both the bull and bear phases show the tendency to exaggerate their trends until they are corrected by the reverse forces. Such inherent dynamics of the volatility of markets are regularly evident not only in stock markets but also in other financial, forex, and commodity markets when the environment in the market is influenced by events that are likely to cause significant changes in demand/supply matrix.

As the events unfolded in 2008, more and more disclosures surfaced. And as more facts and information flowed into the markets, they continued to tumble further. The information from the market players, viz., corporates, banks, financial, and investment institutions, was primarily negative. The market regulators, like SECs and the central banks, and governments were the only hope giving the news of either takeovers, liquidity infusion, or regulations controlling the panic selling, bull unloading, and short positions in the markets. These measures afforded some positive dimensions to the market perspective.

Before the stock markets could be brought to its rational senses, the virus of panic had spread from the stock markets to banks. The money, credit, and liquidity are the lifeblood of not only business and economy but day-to-day economic activities. Money is an idea, a product of central banks and commercial banks. It is an IOU (I Owe You). It is a liability, a promise. We all exchange these paper or digital liabilities of the Fed and other banks day in and day out in our economic activities. Since money is a liability or a promise, it survives and thrives on confidence and trust and is destroyed by fear. Mistrust and suspicion breed fear of loss, and fear triggers panic. It can disrupt the normal economic activities. First target of the wave of illiquidity was the legendary US investment banks. Then it hit US commercial banks. It didn't dissipate or isolate there but spread to the European and Japanese banks. Growing suspicion killed the liquidity of money. Money was frozen. It had lost its velocity. The credit among the banks had come to a standstill. Resultantly, more banks were getting illiquid. More banks were declining credit to business and individuals. And normal economic activities were beginning to freeze.

Money losing its velocity is a sure way to recession. Although the current financial crisis is reminiscent of Great Depression, the global economy was now on the brink of a deep recession. Historical experience, economic wisdom, institutional adaptability, legislative and regulatory safeguards, and finally political pragmatism, and quick and globally coordinated action succeeded to nip the crisis in its bud, the crisis that typically triggers downward vicious economic cycle capable of culminating in depression over a long stretch of 2–3 years. What has happened in 2008–2009 in terms of policy responses from the central banks and governments could not have been achieved in 1930s even over several years. Whereas the human sentiments and animal spirits that drive the markets are getting more accentuated with greater materialism and financial sophistication in the twenty-first century, the technology in economic policy and management has also been far more advanced and proactive than before to deal with the current crisis. The specter of depression could not haunt the markets and spread panic that could worsen the environment further. So long as the consumer spending and investment outlays remain lackluster and need pickup, the economy can be revitalized only with government action.

Keynesianism, Friedman's Monetarism, and Turns in Monetary Policy

The rate of interest is the toll for the bridge of present to future. The money or credit is the instrument through which you pass the bridge to future. Not only is it time related but the toll earned or paid is in terms of percentage. It is a price, but since the price is related to time, it is expressed as percentage per annum. "It is the price to part with liquidity." Keynes revolutionized the interest rate theory by divorcing it from the classical theory, which maintained that it was a real economic phenomenon determined by supply of savings and demand for savings for investment. Keynes treated interest rate as purely monetary phenomenon determined by the demand for money and supply of money. He wove a novel, impressive and realistic "liquidity preference" theory of interest rate. This new and fresh approach to interest rate changed forever the conduct of monetary policy by the central banks. Money is an intrinsic element and variable in all economies and an institution over which the central banks have the monopoly of control. Looking to the interest rates through the monetary glasses gave a new vision in monetary and economic management. Keynes did not want to complicate the General Theory by also bringing savings into the interest determination. Since the savings are the one of the origins of money, it was impractical to ignore its role in interest rate determination. The difference between the savings and money is that the savings are a flow, while money is a stock. The savings constitute money, but money need not constitute savings. The central and commercial banking institution collectively creates money supply. The central bank provides currency for transactions, payments, spending, saving, borrowing, lending, and holding. The monetary theory of the classical economists was expressed in the Irving Fisher's famous quantity theory equation, $MV=PT$ (M—money supply, V—transaction velocity of circulation of money, P—price level, T—volume of transactions). Since money is stock and is used for transactions, spending and incomes which are flows, money has a transaction or real income and nominal income velocity of circulation.

Further, as money supply cannot be higher or lower than what people want to hold, if money supply is higher than the demand for money, the velocity of money will fall and/or income and/or prices will go up. Alternatively, if money supply is lower than the demand, the velocity of money will rise and/or incomes and/or prices will fall. The classicists never related supply of money and demand to the interest rates which was Keynes's discovery.

When you add commercial banking institutions to the central banking function of providing currency, you get another component of money supply which can be in multiples of original bank deposits emanating from savings. It is here we have a component of money supply, viz., bank deposits, a part of which is created by the banking system. Hence, money supply need not always be equivalent to savings but also comes from bank-created deposits, and demand and supply of this component of money supply as well aggregate money supply (currency + bank deposits) are related to the rate of interest rate. This was the crux of the Keynes's theory of rate of interest. Despite the scourge of monetarism, the Keynes's theory of interest rate remains even toady vindicated and more so in the light of the more dominant use of tool of interest rate as a tool of monetary control over the last three decades.

The decades of 1950s and 1960s were dominated by Keynesianism and stable financial environment. Unable to tackle quickly with the problem of stagflation which sprung up in 1970s, the monetarism came to dominate the economic policy. Milton Friedman, the father of postwar monetarism, denounced Keynesianism and worked on the optimum quantity of money. Friedman's monetary theory pronounced that an economy needs an optimum quantity of money to achieve growth and full employment. He established the direct relationship between the money supply and its growth with the macroeconomic aggregates like GDP, employment, and prices. He advocated steady growth in money supply to achieve growth without inflation but cautioned that any attempt to reduce the natural rate unemployment in the economy would result in inflation. His theory and empirical work on monetary history of the USA termed as monetarism prescribed monetary targeting as the instrument of policy by the central bank for growth without inflation.

During the 1970s when the US economy faced the new economic problem of stagflation, Friedman's monetarism was practiced by the Fed to treat the bizarre phenomenon of coexistence of low growth and high inflation. In the early 1980s, the focus shifted from the target money supply to the target interest rate. The Fed abandoned setting M1 targets in 1987 and M2 targets in 1992. The famous Volcker monetary regime of high interest rates broke the back of inflation and strengthened the weakening dollar in the forex markets. Growth suffered, unemployment increased, but inflation was conquered forever. The Greenspan regime 1987–2002 saw the most frequent use of the Fed funds rate for monetary control. It was also an era of cheap money which produced sustained economic growth, lower unemployment, price stability, and budgetary surplus. It also resulted in record asset price inflation, especially in the stock market and housing and real estate.

During the Second World War, Fed had pegged the interest rates at low to finance war. This policy of low pegged rate continued until early 1950s was getting criticism for being "an engine of inflation." Although pegging of interest rates low was abandoned in 1951, the acceleration in money supply grows in the second half of the 1960s. Rising inflation again became a concern. At this point, Friedman was recommending jettisoning Keynesianism and deficit financing in favor of policy of a steady growth in money supply. In the early 1970s, the Fed turned away from the interest rate targeting to money supply targeting in order to have better control over money supply. Monetarism was in its heyday and was practiced by the Fed vigorously. In 1975, the Congress directed the Federal Reserve to formulate the quantitative objectives as the explicit targets and Humphrey–Hawkins legislation of 1978 required the Federal Reserve to report these targets to Congress in advance and later on its success or failure in achieving them. The era of Paul Volcker beginning in 1979 marked a turning point in the implementation of monetary targeting. Volcker announced that there will change in the operating procedure of monitoring the target growth. With the operation of targets for nonborrowed reserves of banks with the Fed, money supply growth was controlled. The Fed first started targeting M1 growth but shifted to M2 growth targets in mid-1980s after gaining the empirical evidence of the stability of velocity of M2 compared to relatively volatile M1 velocity. During the late 1980s, the relationship between the money supply growth, whether M1 or M2, and nominal GDP became less and less reliable. The decade of 1980s was marked with financial liberalization, innovation, and globalization that changed the structure and functioning of the financial markets. Unstable relationship between money supply growth and macroeconomic aggregates like GDP, prices, and interest rates observed during the 1980s in the USA and other developed nations led to the abandonment of monetary targeting as the monetary policy tool. The shift was to the short-term interest rates. The interest rate target became the key tool of monetary policy in monetary management.

Some Fallacies on Interest Rate Policy: Zero Interest Rates, Money Traps, and Interest Rate Illusion

Interest Rate Illusion

The movement of interest rate is subject to an interesting common psychological perception or delusion. Keynes coined the term "money illusion" to describe how people perceive the changes in their money wages with delusion or ignorance about the real purchasing power of money. The interest rate illusion arises due to the common ignorance about the effect of a uniform 0.25% change in the interest rate at different interest rate levels. The common perception about the uniform changes in interest rate is delusional. A uniform 0.25% rise or decline in interest rate at different levels does not have the same effect technically or arithmetically, but the common perception or delusion about 0.25% change is usually the same. The technical, mature financial and sophisticated market reaction is, therefore, diluted by interest rate illusion suffered by the commonality.

Zero Interest Rate Policy

Following the high interest rate policy of Volcker era in the early 1980s when the Fed funds rate reached the peak of 20% in January 1980, the rate began to decline and reached the low of 5.875% in August 1986. Under the Greenspan regime which began after the October 1987 stock market crash, the Fed funds rate started rising and reached the peak of 9.75% in February 1989. Thereafter, the phase of falling interest rates began which continued until September 1992 when Fed funds rate reached a low of 3%. The rate was rising along with the stock market boom during 1993–2000, reaching a high of 6.5% in May 2000. The Fed rate was consistently lowered after the dot-com bust to a low of 1.25% in November 2002 and to lowest of 1% in June 2003. Since then on the Fed's concern on inflation, the rate began its upward journey again to 2.25% in 2004, 4.25% in 2005, and 5.25% in 2006. The worry about recession in 2007 and early signs of subprime debt defaults led the Fed again to lower Fed rate to 1% in October 2008 when the crisis broke out. The rate was lowered to 0–0.25% target in December 2008.

The Fed decision to adopt zero interest policy came as a surprise due to both theoretical premise and recent practical experience of such policy. The theoretical argument against the policy emanates from its impotency in boosting investment due its interest inelasticity in times of recession. Unless the signs of recession peter out and economic turnaround becomes sustainable and stronger, the business expectations, which are a driving force of investment, cannot turn sufficiently positive. Even zero interest rate cannot spur investment when the expectations of future economic and business activity are grim. Keynes expressed his conviction about the impotency of monetary policy and more particularly low interest policy in boosting private investment and why the government should intervene by offsetting expenditure program. "I expect to see the State, which is in a position to calculate the marginal efficiency capital goods (internal rate of return) on long views and on the basis of the general social advantage, taking an ever greater responsibility for directly organizing investment; since it seems likely that the fluctuations in the market estimation of the marginal efficiency of capital of different types of capital, calculated on the I have described above (discounted cash flow method), will be too great to be offset by any practicable changes in the rate of interest" [1, p. 164, the terms in brackets are mine].[5]

Keynes had repeatedly emphasized that the role of government expenditure was to pump prime the economy and improve business expectations which determine private investments. It is only raising private investment that would collectively with government expenditure raise aggregate income, output, and employment. He was also skeptical about the quick improvement in private business expectations due to the dominant psychological influence of the downturn. "There is no clear evidence from experience that the investment policy which is socially advantageous coincides with that which is most profitable. It needs more intelligence to defeat the forces of time and our ignorance of the future than to beat the gun" [1, p. 157]. The short-term expectations of business tend to dominate the investment decisions than the long-term rates of return. In the context of this phenomenon of delay in the recovery and in which interest rate cannot play any positive role, Keynes advocates continuing government support to the economy till the business confidence driven by animal spirits revives and generates private investment. By October 2010 although the US economy succeeded in taking a sharp U-turn from recessionary trend, growth rate is still faltering and unemployment numbers have yet to show positive improvement, " a large proportion of our positive activities depend on spontaneous optimism rather than on a mathematical expectation, whether moral or hedonistic or economic. ...our decisions...can only be taken as a result of animal spirits-of a spontaneous urge to action rather than inaction, and not as the outcome of a weighted average of quantitative benefits multiplied by quantitative probabilities" [1, p. 161].

While the impotency of low interest rate policy is one issue, another more serious impending problem with such policy is the hazardous reverse journey. The slide to zero or near zero interest rate is a pleasurable journey for the borrowers and bond holders, but not to the savers who would receive very low return for their act, forgoing or sacrificing consumption and retaining their wealth in deposits and bonds which are less risky. What is of critical importance in the zero interest rate policy is

[5] They are commonly used in modern theory of finance and investment now but were first introduced by Keynes in his General Theory.

the return journey. The most devastating effect of the return journey from zero interest phase is on the bond market which undergoes a bearish influence due to the falling bond prices caused by the rising yields. It erodes the value in bond portfolio. While the individual investors suffer the negative wealth effect, the institutional investors have to face fall in the market value of their bond portfolios. The bond market crash affecting the valuations of bond portfolios of institutions which have to be marked to market is bound to have strong bearish impact on the financial markets. The return journey of zero interest rate policy is fraught with bond market crash.

Reference

1. Keynes JM. The general theory of employment, interest and money. London: Macmillan and Co. Ltd.; 1961.

Chapter 4
Why Is the Economy Not Taking-Off?

> Rising output and rising incomes will suffer a setback sooner or later if the quantity of money is rigidly fixed. Some people seem to infer from this (Quantity Theory of Money) that output and income can be raised by increasing the quantity of money. But this is like trying to get fat by buying a larger belt. In the United States today your belt is plenty big enough for your belly. It is a most misleading thing to stress the quantity of money, which is only a limiting factor, rather than the volume of expenditure, which is the operative factor.
>
> John Maynard Keynes, *An Open Letter to President Roosevelt, The New York Times, December 31, 1933.*

Monetary Mechanics

Since the outbreak of the crisis in September 2008, the Fed has finished two rounds of quantitative expansion and launched the QE 3 in September 2012. It has added \$1.9 trillion to money supply over 3 years and will inject \$400 billion more over a year. Money supply, M2, has gone up from \$7.4 trillion in January 2008 to \$10 trillion in August 2012, i.e., by 35% over four and half years and average annual growth of 7.8%. Over the earlier decade 1998–2008, the M2 grew from \$4.4 to \$7.4 trillion, at the average annual growth of 7%. The roaring 1990s saw M2 rising from \$3.2 to \$4.6 trillion, a lower average annual growth of 4.4%.

In spite of such mammoth monetary expansion and near-zero interest rates, the economy has not responded with the buoyancy which it should have. To understand this sluggish response, one must go into the monetary mechanics and ascertain how QEs have percolated down into the different channels in the monetary structure of the economy to influence vital economic parameters such as investment, consumption, output, and employment. From the viewpoint of the monetary aggregates and policy, the issue has been examined in economic literature and experience from the Keynesian as well as Friedmanian angles. Although the Friedman's analysis of direct effect of money supply on output and employment in normal times known as monetarism became prominent in 1970s, it lost its relevance later. Since 1980s,

S. Nayak, *The Global Financial Crisis: Genesis, Policy Response and Road Ahead*,
DOI 10.1007/978-81-322-0798-6_4,

Table 4.1 Dynamics of money

	C		M1		M2		M2–M1		Ex Rs	Vm2	Vm1
		%		%		%		%			
(In $ billion)											
1990	223		798		3,163		2,365		1	1.8	7.1
2000	524	(13.5)	1,140	(4.2)	4,633	(4.6)	3,493	(4.8)	2	2	8.9
2008	757	(5.5)	1,370	(2.5)	7,451	(7.6)	6,081	(9.2)	1.6	1.8	10
2012	1,060	(8.9)	2,400	(16.7)	10,123	(8)	7,723	(6)	1,477	1.6	6.9

Data Source: FRED, Economic Research, Federal Reserve Bank of St. Louis
C = currency in circulation, M1 = C + demand deposits, M2 = M1 + savings and small time deposits
M2 – M1 = savings and small time deposits
Ex Rs = excess reserves of banks with the Federal Reserve
Vm1 = nominal GDP/M1, Vm2 = nominal GDP/M2

interest rate emerged as more important tool of monetary impact, and Keynes' analysis via interest rate again became preeminent. Further, in times of recession, the Keynesian perception is more relevant and dominates in understanding of the influence of monetary measures. Apart from this macro angle of money supply and economy, it is essential to also examine microstructure of money supply. Money supply is defined in many ways and gauged by different measures. To understand the impact of money supply on macroeconomic parameters, one must first ascertain the impact of monetary expansion on different components or constituents of money. Money can be most narrowly defined as currency in circulation and as widely defined to include not only demand, savings, and time deposits of banks but also deposits of nonbanking financial institutions, money market funds. Another important component of money is credit. Expansion in money supply without credit growth is like pumping the air into leaking balloon.

Where is the money going? The money is still sitting tight in the Fed in the form of excess reserves of banks with the Fed. The bank lending has not increased as desired. The monetary base is getting bloated, but money supply is not growing fast. What has grown is the demand deposits of banks and excess reserves of banks with the Fed. Table 4.1 shows the growth in different components of money since 1990 over the last more than two decades.

If we see currency M1 and M2 since the crisis, we find that growth has been more in M1 than in M2. Compared to the growth of M1 of 2.5% in 2000–2008, the growth since the crisis in 2008–2012 has been record as 16.7%. The growth is in demand deposits of banks and excess reserves of banks with the Fed which have gone up from mere $1.6 billion in 2008 to a record figure $1,477 billion in 2012 (Fig. 4.1). Out of the QEs of $1.9 trillion, $1.48 billion is with the Fed as reserves of banks. Money is yet to move into the productive channels of the economy. The credit growth has not gained momentum. Bank credit before the crisis in 2008 had reached the high of $9.5 trillion. This level was crossed in February 2012 indicating the slow growth in credit demand as well as delivery. The commercial paper (CP) issues are worst affected because of the fear of holding securities. The CPs outstanding

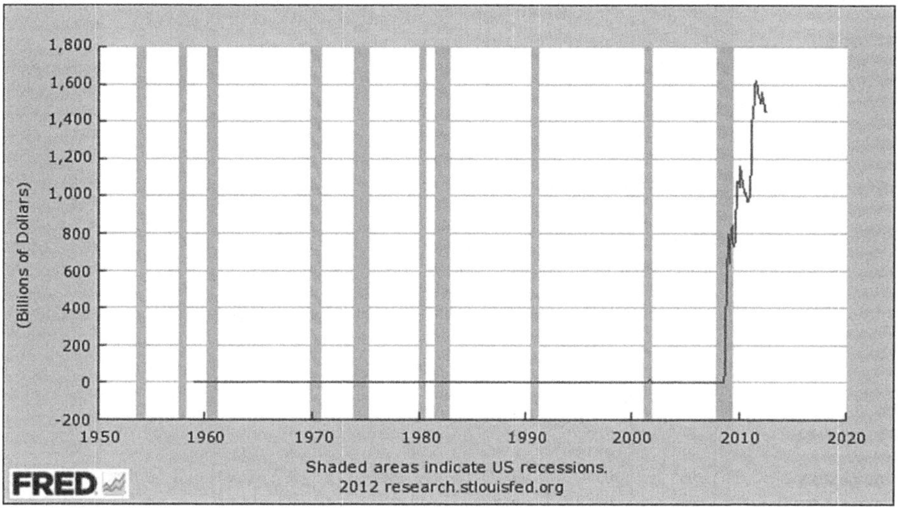

Fig. 4.1 Excess reserves of depository institutions (Excresns). *Shaded areas* indicate US recessions. 2012 research.stiouisfed.org (Source: Board of Governors of the Federal Reserve System)

came down after the crisis from $2.2 trillion in 2007 to a low of $916 billion in 2012. It has yet to reach its precrisis level. M2–M1, which show the savings and small time deposits of banks, have grown at 6% in 2008–2012 compared to 9.2% in 2000–2008. The growth in money supply is totally concentrated in the excess reserves of banks with the Fed. Unless it percolates down to credit growth and into more commercial paper, the recovery will be sluggish.

The velocity of money is still at record lows. The velocity of money, M2, is the ratio of GDP to M2. It shows how many times money, $ in form of M2, moves in a year to create GDP. During the 1990s, the Vm2 went up from 1.8 to a high of 2.1 before the dot-com crisis (Fig. 4.2). It dropped sharply after the crisis and to the level below 1.6, the lowest since 1965. Vm1 has shown more dramatic drop from 10 in 2008 to 6.9 in 2012. The velocity money is yet to move up even after more than 3 years of antirecession fiscal and monetary nutrition.

Never in the history has the Fed given the lending support to the banking industry to the extent it has done after the crisis. The banking industry has never approached the Fed for major financial support. Until 2008, all the banking crises which the economy faced were managed by the government deposit insurance corporation, through mergers and acquisitions in the industry and government support to the extent of $153 billion. There was hardly any Fed support in the crisis. In postdepression history, the Fed has been managing money supply and its cost, but was never a large financier to the banking industry $1.5 trillion in 2009 and to $2.5 trillion in September 2012 constituting 25% of money supply, M2. Huge monetary expansion has yet to translate into credit and accelerate the production cycle and promote growth.

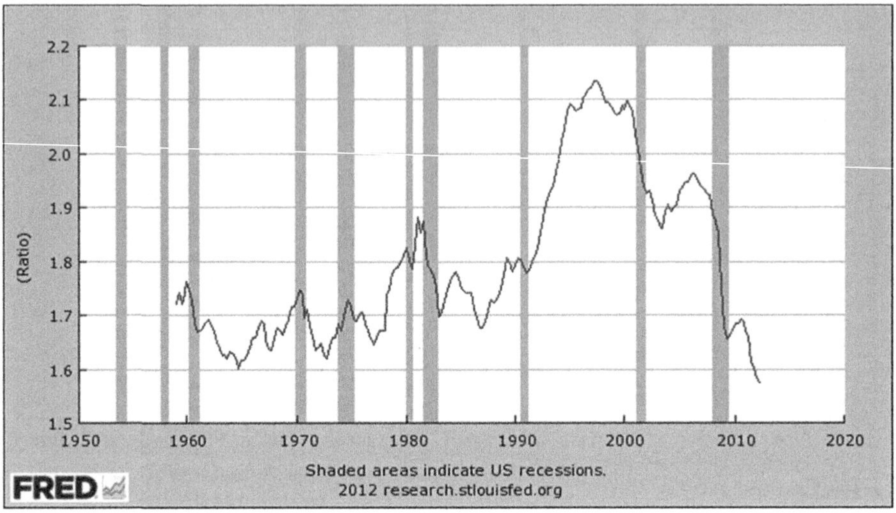

Fig. 4.2 Velocity of M2 money stock (M2V). *Shaded areas* indicate US recessions. 2012 research. stiouisfed.org (Source: Federal Reserve Bank of St. Louis)

Sluggish Investment

One of the main reasons why the economy still to gain vigorous growth momentum and employment is not growing at the rate it should have is that investment has not picked up except in few consumer-oriented sectors not on the considerations of profitability but because sheer uncertainty of the overhang of Euro crisis which still needs to be resolved (Fig. 4.3). Until the Euro crisis comes to its logical and financially viable solution, the investment climate in the USA is likely to be somewhat lackluster. While the ECB, Germany, and IMF have to be large contributors in the financial involvement, China, Japan, and OPEC also need to give assistance to avoid the backlash of Eurozone recession on their economies. The USA has its own fiscal cliff to manage and can hardly afford to extend any finance. It can extend support in kind by exporting goods, including agricultural products, and swapping them against the Eurozone's holdings of US government securities.

The corporate America has been resilient and shown healthy growth. The sectoral and corporate changes are a part of the economic changes and capitalistic system. That is what capitalistic system does to corporate on its knees. The industrial or sectoral changes follow the technological progress and pull of consumer demand. The market rules and capitalism are ruthless. Market-driven capitalism does not spare the lax, nonresponsive, incompetent, and inefficient corporate for long. The economic Darwinism is the driving force of optimal capitalism. The declining and dying sectors suffer and wither. The rising and growing sectors perform and attract capital. In this constantly changing industrial and service sector space, the proactive, perceptive, dynamic, and financially efficient corporates overtake the ones which are not. Yet, the overall results of the corporate sector give the sense

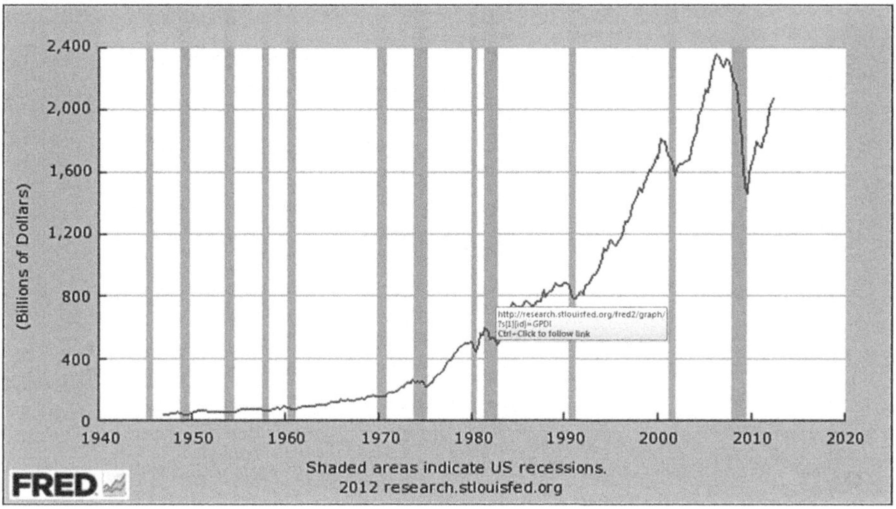

Fig. 4.3 Gross private domestic investment (GPDI). *Shaded areas* indicate US recessions. 2012 research.stlouisfed.org (Source: U.S. Department of Commerce: Bureau of Economic Analysis)

of where the economy is moving. In this context, the corporate performance has shown progress. The post-tax profits of corporate (Fig. 4.4) are growing. Under the impact of the decline in GDP in 2009, the corporate profits had shown a sharp dip. The revival of the economy in 2010 has added buoyancy to the corporate performance. Record-low interest rates and record rise in government expenditure have rejuvenated the corporate America. The stock market has gone up with Dow showing the rise from 10,000 to 13,000, 30% rise. Yet, the corporate America has not been unrolling its capital expenditure program. This is reflected in the record cash pile up by companies and record liquidity status of banks. The nonfinancial corporations held cash of $1.24 trillion at the end of 2011. Apple, Microsoft, Cisco, Google, and Pfizer held 22% of the total. Nearly 57% of American corporate cash was held abroad.[1] Until this cash moves in the economic cycle from the current financial cycle, the economy would not take sustainable spin for growth.

Infrastructure: The Growth Driver

The housing and real estate sector has been the driver of the US economy. One of the major handicaps of the current recovery is that the crisis was the result of the borrower's payment defaults in the housing sector that not only led to the collapse

[1] Moody's Investor Service, March 14, 2012.

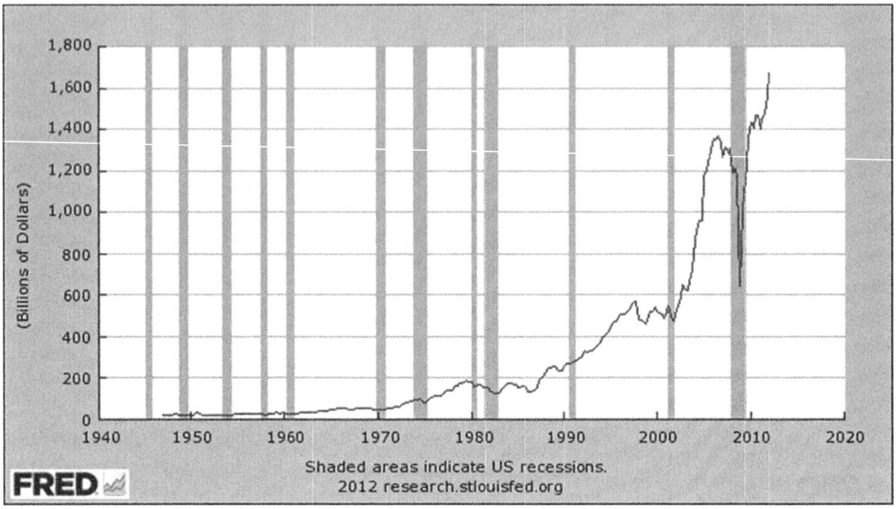

Fig. 4.4 Corporate profit after tax (CP). *Shaded areas* indicate US recessions. 2012 research. stlouisfed.org (Source: U.S. Department of Commerce: Bureau of Economic Analysis)

in housing prices, but the avalanche of foreclosures created a huge overhang of stock of housing units. This overhang of houses has hampered the new construction activity which can attract fresh investment and generate employment. The backlog of housing stock is so large that there is less scope for new house construction except in areas and towns where the earlier boom had not reached or could not reach. Until this unsold housing stock is reduced sharply, new housing construction would not begin in a big way to give boost to employment and growth in the economy. The housing sales plummeted from the peak of housing boom at 1.28 million units to an all time low 323,000 in 2010. The new home sales have to pick up to 600,000 units to generate investment and employment in this sector.

Since the housing and real estate sector will continue a laggard and fail to be the driver of growth for a few more years to come, the other sectors have to take the lead to be the engine of growth. While the service and technology sectors comprising several industries offer the right potential in the light of the demand pulls as well as supply and endowment factors, the sector which is in urgent need of refurbishment and offers large employment potential is the infrastructure. Instead of leaving it entirely to the forces of markets, there is a need in the current environment to engage in public–private partnership in this sector. This unorthodox venture could act as the sustainable accelerator of growth in the current uncertain environment.

One of the major reasons for slow growth in employment is that over the years, the employment intensity of government expenditure has gone down due to the technological change as well as the shift in the composition of government expenditure. In early stage of capitalist development, government expenditure on infrastructure was relatively large contributing to fast growth in employment. Although the infrastructure is not in short supply as it was in the early days of industrialization, a large stock of infrastructure is in need of refurbishment and modernization. Now is the opportune time to allocate resources in this sector which will yield quick results in employment generation.

Chapter 5
Eurosclerosis: Causation and Control

Euro and Eurozone Management: Lessons from Greek Tragedy

> It is astonishing what foolish things one can temporarily believe if one thinks too long alone, particularly in economics (along with other moral sciences), where it is impossible to bring one's ideas to a conclusive test either formal or experimental.
>
> Keynes, John Maynard, *The General Theory of Employment, Interest and Money, 1936.*

Economists get elated but also most concerned when their models become tools of economic policy administered by governments and operated by bureaucrats and professional economists. Every model has its a priori setting and conditions, and if reality does not resemble the model, as it does in most cases, only ingenuity and dexterity of the policymakers can make it adapt for its purpose. Yet, this is not always the case. More often than not, the model fails due to either lapses of realism or overzealous actualization. Yet, despite these concerns, great economic truths and ideas have transformed the world with all the infirmities in dealing with reality.

The upshot of the matter is that the great economic truths have changed the reality for the good of the future. Adam Smith's model of invisible hand of market was resurrected in the political economy by Margaret Thatcher in the UK and Ronald Reagan in the USA in the early 1980s after the downfall of the Bretton Woods era of fixed and stable financial markets to usher into a new era of liberalization, privatization, and growth with globalization. David Ricardo's model of comparative cost advantage succeeded in transforming Gunnar Myrdal's Asian Drama into Asian Miracle much as he had dreamt. John Maynard Keynes's model of deficit financing found its first experimentation in Franklin Roosevelt's New Deal that lifted the American capitalism from the morass of deep depression and transformed it into new welfare capitalism. Translating the economic truths into policy that go against the conventional wisdom demands tremendous political vision and audacity which the great leaders have showed from time to time. While Mikhail Gorbachev in the USSR paved the way for totally abandoning the communism to be replaced by the new capitalist model, Deng Ziuo Peng retained communism but reoriented and reinvented the Chinese economy with radical reforms toward privatization, foreign

S. Nayak, *The Global Financial Crisis: Genesis, Policy Response and Road Ahead*,
DOI 10.1007/978-81-322-0798-6_5,

investment, and private property. These economies enjoyed unprecedented economic progress and growth. In India, Rajiv Gandhi set the Indian economy free on the path of liberalization and reform.

The road to economic success is not always sweet but is sometimes also beset with hardships and failures. The economic reforms, liberalization, and globalization did bring quick economic gains sometimes at the costs of recurrent crises emanating from the excesses of markets and compulsions of some policy goal. If the global free trade raised the growth rate of the global economy, it also created a huge imbalance of overhang of liquid assets and savings in some countries vis-a-vis the borrowings of others. The philosophy of deficit financing instead of being an instrument of sustainable growth degenerated into a tool for achieving political goals producing uneven and deleterious results.

When Mundell formulated his theory of optimum currency area in 1961, he had Western Europe which had formed a common market to be its ideal region for a single currency. The continent of Europe is fragmented into smaller geographic regions by different languages, cultures, climates, natural bounties, and ecosystems, besides political parties and systems. With so much of diversity in their economies and political systems, it was very hard to believe that the region will ever have a common currency. Yet, despite their differences, the European nations were determined to go slowly but steadily toward the goal of a single currency. After setting the European Union in 1993 with headquarters in Brussels, the next milestone then was the common currency. The formation of the European Central Bank in 1998 headquartered in Frankfurt paved way for the introduction of common currency, the euro on January 1, 1999. The Germans and French gave up their national pride in favor of the euro abandoning deutschemark and franc. Great Britain, Denmark, and Sweden did not heed the call and retained their currencies, pound and kroner, as symbols of their monetary sovereignty and national economic stature. The euro coins and banknotes were introduced for circulation on January 1, 2002. In 2011, euro was used as currency by 23 European countries with the population of 320 million, out of which 17 are the members of European Union. Over a short period of a decade, the euro has emerged as the second largest reserve asset and traded currency after dollar. Difference between euro currency and dollar notes is that euro currency notes are also available in denominations of 200 and 500 euros. By October 2006, the euro became the world's single largest currency in circulation with euros 610 billion at $800 billion (then exchange rate between euro and dollar) surpassing the greenbacks (dollar notes) in circulation.

Strong Euro and Worsening BoP

Apart from the savings in conversion cost of 23 currencies of different countries which is the primary economic gain of common currency, the euro brought several economic advantages from the wider scale of its single currency operations and uniformity in monetary standard and accounting across the Eurozone. Yet, one of the most critical problems of common currency with different political and national entities, in addition to the one of fiscal independence, lies in the accommodation of their different balance of payments positions. If a nation within the common currency zone faces the balance of payments problem, it does not have an exchange rate measure as a remedy for its problem as it would have had if it had its own currency. Individual nations can continue to pursue their own fiscal policy with their budgets, but the monetary policy is controlled by the European Central Bank (ECB). Individual countries also continue to maintain their BoP accounts and exchange reserves. But the country facing BoP deficit cannot correct it through exchange rate mechanism but has to finance it through borrowings or pursue tighter fiscal policy to slow growth and reduce BoP deficit, unless the Eurozone itself is in the BoP problem.

If all or majority of the Eurozone countries faced the BoP deficits, though of different degrees, the falling euro (depreciation of euro) in the foreign exchange market would remedy their problem. The dilemma is that Eurozone comprises countries with different BoP structure, status, and trends. While the strongest nation in Eurozone, Germany, is an export and a BoP surplus nation, the others are in moderate to worse condition in their BoP position. The exchange rate of euro becomes double-edged sword. If the euro appreciates to reduce the German surplus in BoP, the other countries suffer as their BoP deficit worsens. And if euro depreciates, the BoP deficit countries can correct their BoP deficits, while Germany faces bigger BoP surplus. The former scenario is worse than the latter, and current euro crisis is a blowout of the former phenomenon. The strengthening of the euro against dollar during 2002–2008 was a matter of internal concern to Eurozone. Even if the euro had remained stable and not appreciated the way it did, the euro crisis would not emerge as Greece, Portugal, and Spain would not have suffered the BoP deterioration they faced during 2004–2008.

The euro crisis has its origin in the year 2002 when the euro began strengthening against the dollar. Although the appreciation of euro could be tolerated by Germany because of its export and BoP surplus, it was not very conducive to the other BoP deficit nations which faced the problems promoting their exports and curbing imports. The exchange rate of euro against the dollar, which had reached lowest of \$0.8565 in 2001 per euro, was strengthening later. It rose steadily to \$1.35 in 2005 and further to high of \$1.58 in 2008, 76% appreciation since the low of 2001. Such a high degree of strengthening had severally damaging effect for BoP deficit nations. In fact, it created a BoP problem for nations like Greece which until 2002 did not face any major BoP deficit. Hence, the Greek problem has been largely the making of euro. The strengthening of euro during 2002–2008 except for some depreciation in 2005 was harming the Eurozone BoP deficit nations like Greece, Portugal, and Spain and the Greece most (Fig. 5.1).

One of the factors behind the rise of Euro has been the interest rate policy pursued by the European Central Bank (ECB). While the overnight interest rate of ECB remained at 2% through 2004–2005, it began to rise in 2006 and reached 4% by 2007.

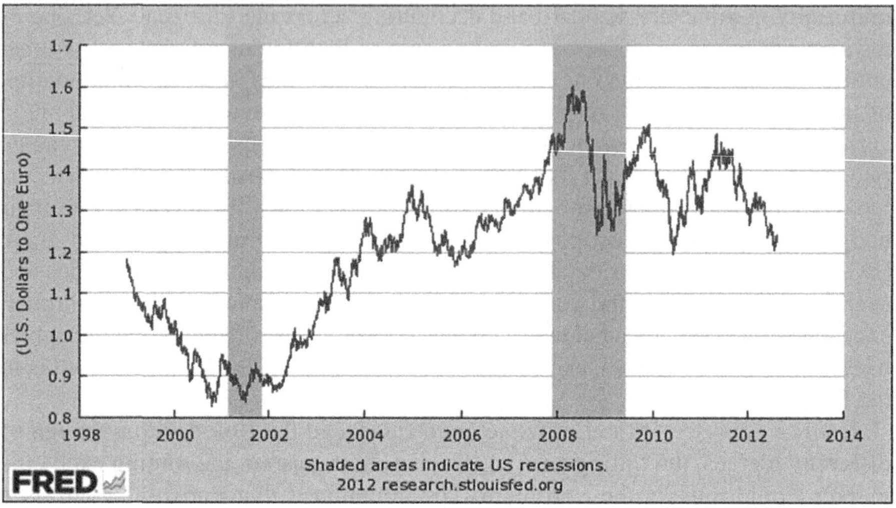

Fig. 5.1 U.S/Euro foreign exchange rate (DEXUSEU). *Shaded areas* indicate US recessions. 2012 research .stlouisfed.org (Source: Board of Governors of the Federal Reserve System)

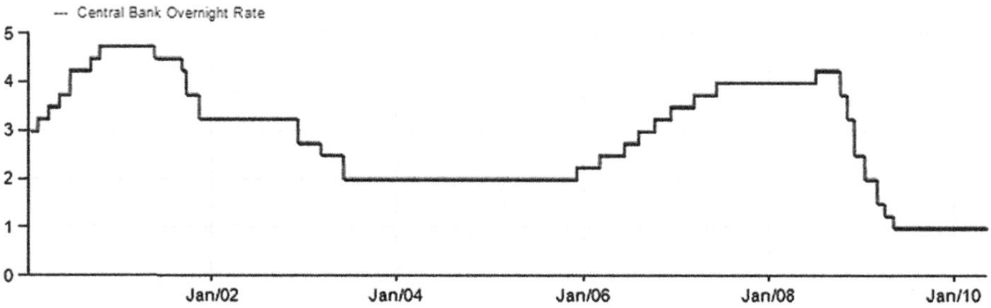

Fig. 5.2 Euro area interest rate (Source: European Central Bank)

Looking to the overall Eurozone requirements such an increase in the interest rate was devastating on the weaker economies, especially those dependent on exports. This brought a severe adverse BoP problem for Greece, Portugal, and Spain whose current account deficit rose from 6 to 14% of GDP, 7.6 to 10%, and 5 to 10%, respectively, during 2004–2008. In contrast, the Eurozone turned from current account surplus of 0.7% of GDP to a marginal deficit of 1.6%. Greece had to continue borrowing in the international market to fund its BoP deficit.

On the budgetary front, it faced rising government expenditure but falling tax revenue despite the sustained growth in its economy. The failure to raise the tax revenue resulted in persistently higher borrowings which triggered current crisis (Fig. 5.2).

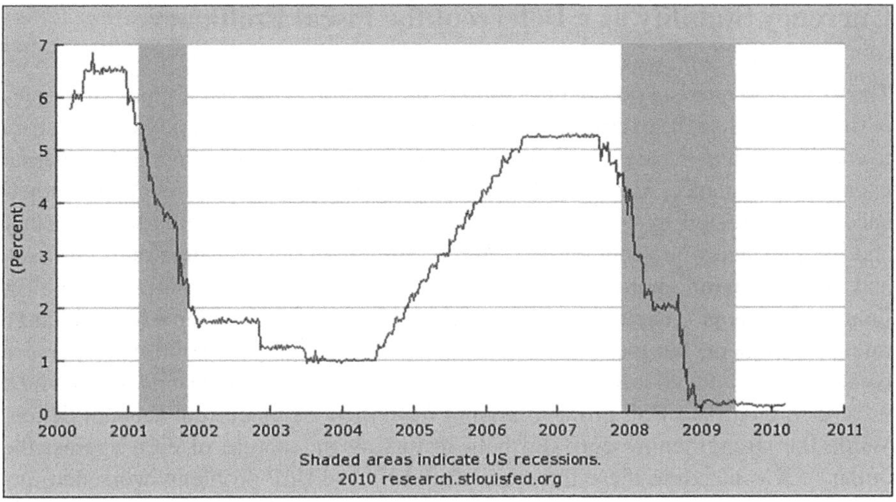

Fig. 5.3 Effective federal funds rate (FF). *Shaded areas* indicate US recessions. 2010 research.stlouisfed.org (Source: Board of Governors of the Federal Reserve System)

Greece had an excellent investment rate of 22%, GDP growth between 4.5 and 5%, inflation at 3%, and unemployment rate of natives at 6% until 2007 when its economic woes began. The adversity of the strengthening of the euro was further aggravated by the global crisis and recession (Fig. 5.3).

During 2004–2007, the strongest member and pillar of euro, Germany, enjoyed the BoP surplus on current account which went up from 4.7% of GDP to 7.5%. The euro is the first experiment of a common currency with different political entities. One of the ingredients for its success is the financial support from the strong member like Germany to the weak member like Greece until the weak economy recovers from the flights of the common currency. If Greece was not the member of Eurozone, the Greek drachma would have depreciated by about 50% and let the economy adjust to new exchange rate relationship with rest of the world. The members of Eurozone do not have these options. Hence, financial support from ECB and Germany with domestic program to reduce budgetary deficit is the only solution. Since, in addition to strong euro, fiscal profligacy by Greece also compounded its problem, domestic fiscal adjustment with ECB financing could alone save Greece from economic downturn and avoid the breakup of euro.

The Greek crisis can be followed by the ones in Ireland and Portugal, and the potential targets and land mine include Spain and even Italy. If their fiscal and BoP balances are not quickly managed to resolve the potential hazards, the Eurozone is in the danger of disintegration and collapse giving another jolt to the global economy. The Eurozonc economic management has to be now more comprehensive and sensitive than before focused on both fiscal deficit and current account deficit reduction.

Currency Stability as a Deterrent for Fiscal Profligacy

The exchange rate is a powerful economic tool of correcting economic imbalances or disequilibria. If the exchange rate is held fixed by the monetary authority, restrictive monetary and fiscal policies have to undertake the task of adjusting the external payments imbalance. Under the flexible or floating exchange rates, these imbalances are corrected by currency depreciation or appreciation, while the monetary and fiscal policies pursue their own course. But when the exchange rates are fixed and macroeconomic policies are not adjusted to disequilibria, a perfect recipe for financial crisis is created. The Eurozone did not function under fixed exchange rate environment, but the rate movements, although it gave flexibility euro, were worse and detrimental to some nation, especially Greece, Portugal, and Spain which were facing chronic BoP problem arising from their rising current account deficit. While the strengthening euro did help in raising the stature of euro against the dollar, it was bleeding these three economies whose BoP problems worsened further. The stable exchange rate of euro would have been a great advantage to these nations, but the adverse behavior of euro, its strengthening in the forex markets, was a great blow to these economies. The euro crisis was simmering in this environment and finally blew out first in Greece and later in Spain. The Greek crisis is the beginning of a much bigger economic destabilization which can still be avoided.

Economically, Germany is the strong force and center of the Eurozone which comprises several economies which are weak on their fiscal and BoP status as well as their growth potential. Eurozone is a conglomerate of some strong, some not so strong, and some weak economies. This economic union has facilitated unrestricted trade and factor mobility. While the common currency, euro, and common monetary and exchange rate policy bind and unify these economies, being separate political entities, their fiscal policies can divide them. It is this fiscal divide that has brought the Eurozone in the crisis zone.

After the formation of the Eurozone, the weak economies failed to observe the fiscal as well as BoP discipline. As a part of the economic union and common currency and exchange rate, the weak economies did not face the pressure of their BoP deficits which they used to earlier as individual countries with their own currency which was subject to destabilization. The prospect of their currency depreciation acted as a strong deterrent against both the BoP as well as fiscal profligacy. The BoP imbalance was earlier corrected first by fiscal and monetary restraint and, if it did not work, later through currency depreciation. Preunification weak economies treated BoP imbalance with concern. Under the Eurozone, individual country's BoP deficit was not a concern so long as the overall Eurozone BoP was in order. The individual country's BoP deficit was met by credit from Eurozone banking system or outside and/or from European Central Bank (ECB) which managed the money supply of euro and the price of euro in terms of its interest rate and exchange rate.

So long as the Eurozone BoP remained in surplus and forex reserves of ECB remained comfortable, the BoP disequilibrium or deficit of an individual country did not pose any problem to the country. It was this level of false sense of comfort which led all the BoP deficit countries to borrow more to meet their BoP deficits without any measure to correct them. Since both the monetary policy and exchange rate management were the prerogative of the ECB, the only policy tool which the individual countries had to correct their BoP deficits was the moderate fiscal policy. In contrast, the borrowings for BoP financing and escalating government expenditure enlarged the fiscal deficits of these nations.

Dilemma of Common Currency in Pluralistic Community

The Greek tragedy reflects this inherent weakness, flaw, or contradiction in the institution of euro which is a single currency with common central banking and monetary for countries which still have different fiscal budgets and policy. Although the common currency extended tremendous economic and financial benefits to the member countries, the prevalence of independent fiscal budgets underscored the imperative need for harmonization of fiscal budgets and policies. The fiscal budget and policy is a much stronger political prerogative than monetary policy. The political parties in democratic system with periodic elections want to have full control over fiscal policy with the electoral votes in mind. No government wants to entertain politically unpopular fiscal budget and policy when the election is in sight however financially detrimental it may be in the long run. Hence, fiscal harmonization, which is an indispensable element of the stability of the common currency, cannot be undermined. Although it is difficult to have perfect fiscal harmonization in the light of the political imponderables, it is desirable to monitor the fiscal imperatives of different member States and prevent the occurrence of Greek like fiscal extreme in advance.

In this phenomenon of fiscal profligacy of weak economies, the ECB had an important role to balance the demands and constraints on both the strong and weak economies within the Eurozone in order to maintain the stability of the weak economy, thereby strengthening the Eurozone. We now come to critical element of ECB monetary policy and course it should have followed. The price of euro is the most critical element influencing the global economy as well as the individual economies in the Eurozone. The euro interest rate and exchange rate were most important factors that determined the monetary and financial developments and to a large extent the damage in the Eurozone.

Part II
Evolutionary Economics: A Systemic View

Chapter 6
Benign Neglect of Dollar: The Bretton Woods and Its Demise

The shortcomings of economics are not original error but uncorrected obsolescence

John Kenneth Galbraith, *The Affluent Society, 1958.*

In order to understand the present financial crisis in a longer perspective, it is essential to look at and realize the systemic changes both in the USA and the global economy over the last century. The postwar economic prosperity presented a sharp contrast to the economic devastation of the earlier period of two world wars. Against this backdrop, the new global economic and monetary system was built at the Bretton Woods summit in New Hampshire in 1944, where financial experts, economists, and policy makers from all nations had gathered to create a framework for establishing a new global economic order for sustained and broad-based economic growth based on mutually advantageous trade and investments and stable international monetary system. The new system based on cooperation and accommodation, rather than hostility, conflict, retaliatory politics, and economic policies emanating primarily from political and economic rivalries, paved the way for uninterrupted economic progress for more than two and a half decades until 1971. This era of economic growth and tranquility of the 1950s and 1960s could not be sustained further by the Bretton Woods Framework. By the beginning of the 1970s, the postwar global economic architecture was showing the signs of weakness under the stress of demands for sustainable global growth and its more equitable sharing among the nations.

The Bretton Woods global financial architecture was linked to gold stocks of the USA with the dollar convertible into gold only for the central bankers. The upper limit to the liquidity, which the USA could create for rest of the world to grow, was imposed by the value of its gold stocks. The fixed exchange rates ruled an implicit discipline on the USA in creating dollars for the rest of the world by spending and investing more abroad than it received. The continuing enlarging of the US BoP deficits was ballooning the overhang of US liquid liabilities with the foreign central banks. The dollar was weakening in the forex market. The central bankers were losing gold to the private holders as they sold gold in the open market to keep the

S. Nayak, *The Global Financial Crisis: Genesis, Policy Response and Road Ahead*,
DOI 10.1007/978-81-322-0798-6_6, © Springer India 2013

gold price in the free market from rising above the official level of $35 an ounce. This impasse was finally resolved in the historic decision in August 1971 when President Nixon freed dollar from its monetary link with gold. The age of gold standard came to a dramatic end. No longer could gold rule the economic destiny of nations and the global financial system. The global money entered the new era of gold free system of fiat money with floating exchange rates.

The current global financial crisis with its epicenter in the USA and Europe offers the right time to retrospect and introspect on the current global economic and financial architecture and its weak spots that have triggered this crisis. For the post-war baby boomers, it is an experience, though short lived, they have never gone through compared to the 1930s depression which extended over 10 long years.

It is not that there have not been economic calamities much serious than the current one. Several developing economies now known as the emerging market economies have been subject to abysmal poverty, malnutrition, inequality, disguised unemployment, hyperinflation, and currency and forex crises. Some of these problems have been the perennial features of these societies in which their development strategy could not make any significant headway. The others have been the result of the theoretical model-based misguided strategies which could not cope up with local economic milieu perpetuating the old problem or resulting in fresh economic ills.

Even developed economies have their own share of economic malaise which recurrently raises its head in the form of recession, rising unemployment, or creeping inflation or currency depreciation. These phenomena are thought to be a feature of a mature capitalistic economy. Despite the advances in economic theory and sophistication in economic policy, the goals of near full employment and zero inflation have not been achievable on sustainable and enduring basis in the mature capitalistic economies. And intractable ills of poverty and malnutrition continue to haunt millions in the developing economies.

Notwithstanding this ongoing economic firefighting, it was beyond any one's expectation or imagination that the powerhouse of the global economy could ever be on fire. Keynesianism provided economic policy tools to battle with recession and banish the phenomenon of economic cycles that used to repeatedly haunt the capitalistic economies and erode their secular growth potential. In the age of Keynesianism, economic cycles were thought to be defunct. Although moderate economic downswing called recession did show up occasionally, it has invariably been overpowered by quick policy action that ensured soft landing of the economy and gradual recovery.

Monetarism rendered better understanding of the impact of cost of money and other measures of controlling money supply on demand and supply of money and other vital macroeconomic economic parameters. The monetary and inflation targeting emerged as the standard strategy of monetary management with frequent use of Fed funds rate as its lever. The system of floating exchange rates, which is in vogue since 1975 replacing the earlier Bretton Woods arrangement of fixed and adjustable rates set up in 1945 with the IMF overseeing the global monetary arrangement, worked as the critical safety valve adjusting the excessive pressures of international payments on the monetary and economic systems. The floating exchange rates opened the new gate for higher economic growth through larger volumes of trade and investments.

Evolution of Global Economy: The Bretton Woods Architecture

The gold standard is the earliest organized international monetary system. Although gold and silver served as money in the form of coins for a much longer period in history, the gold standard as the system of determining exchange rates between different countries and settling payments among them has a much shorter history. During this short period of about two centuries until its collapse on the onset of the First World War in 1914, the standard did render considerable monetary stability and paved way for economic prosperity.

Under this standard, the value of currency units of each country was expressed in terms of their gold content in physical terms. This determined the gold price in each currency and also the exchange rates among the currencies. The gold price and exchange rates remained fixed over time because the central banks issuing the coins and currency guaranteed their conversion into gold at the stated price. The deficit or surplus in the balance of payments caused the gold to flow from the deficit country to the surplus country. Because of this feature of gold flows between the countries, the system was also known as gold price–specie flow.

Although an international monetary system is based on its economic viability sustained by the markets, in times of stress it survives and grows only on the element of cooperation and accommodation among countries. Since the countries honored to convert their currencies into gold, payments differences between the countries were settled in gold flow, while the exchange rates between them remained fixed. The central banks also linked their money supplies to the level of their gold stocks. The deficit country lost gold and contracted its money supply, while the surplus country gained gold and expanded its money supply. Implicit in these rules of gold standard was the automaticity in economic adjustment mechanism of economies. Due to monetary contraction in the deficit country, the demand, output, income, and prices fell, while they rose in the surplus country. This brought exports and imports of two countries back into equilibrium. Despite its simplicity and automaticity, the gold standard could not cope up with the demands of governments. The onset of the Keynesian revolution which had demolished two pillars of economic philosophy that guided the prewar governments of free society, viz., the doctrines of laissez-faire and balanced budget, also found the third pillar, the gold standard anachronistic.

In addition to providing the fail-safe mechanism to the capitalistic societies ensuring their sustained growth in the post-1930s depression era, Keynes' influence was also evident on the building up of the postwar monetary system which led to the abandonment of gold standard and formation of IMF (International Monetary Fund) and the World Bank (International Bank for Reconstruction and Development) with the gold-based dollar-centric flexible exchange-rated system of fixed but periodically adjustable exchange rates. Although Keynes had proposed to have the new international monetary system divorced from gold, it was probably not thought pragmatic to dislodge gold entirely from the monetary system especially in the light of large gold stocks held by the Federal Reserve and other European central banks.

Era of Stable Financial and Trade Milieu

Ravages of deep and long economic depression of the 1930s followed by the destruction caused by Second World War had underscored the need for global cooperation in economic and political matters. The collapse of gold standard as the anchor of the monetary system, emergence of fluctuating exchange rates, and growing protectionism posed a great threat to international trade and financial stability. One of the most outstanding achievements of the Bretton Woods meeting in 1944 was the creation of the institutional framework that would set up firm financial infrastructure and oversee the development of a stable global financial, trade, and investment environment. It became the anchor of global monetary system since 1945.

During the interwar period (1914–1945), global economy suffered some of the biggest blows. In addition to the destruction caused by two wars, the economies suffered from the Great Depression. International monetary system was nonexistent with countries abandoning gold standard and exchange rates freely fluctuating. International trade was at a low ebb with countries engaged in retaliatory game of trade restrictions. Uncertainties in economies and international trade and volatility in exchange rates undermined the climate for in cross border investments. Global economic and financial environment was in need of new structure.

With the gold standard abandoned and losing its validity in the age of Keynesianism, there was a need to create a new system. The gold standard did provide stable exchange rates but exchange rates became too sticky and rigid, and countries did not want to devalue the currencies in terms of its gold value for the apprehension of loss of national prestige. The most striking case in history was that of Britain when it returned to gold standard in 1927. In spite of Keynes' advice to return to gold standard at a lower parity by reducing the gold content of pound and increasing the official price of gold, Winston Churchill, then finance minister, went against the sound and logical advice and pegged the pound at its prewar parity of $4.86 with a view to restore the pound sterling to its earlier glory. The consequences were economically disastrous. The decision pushed the British economy into a tailspin. The stock market crash of 1929 and depression in the USA further worsened the global economy.

The exchange rates needed to be more flexible in the new system. Yet another weakness of the gold standard was that the international liquidity required to finance global balance of payments from international trade, investment, and money transfers remained restricted by the supply of gold from gold mines. The global economic growth was limited by the discoveries and production of gold and, therefore, externally determined and not within the control of the central banks of major economic powers. This was an antithesis to Keynesianism. The supply of global liquidity needed to be within the control of the central banks.

The most critical element on which monetary system survives, lives, runs, and prospers is public confidence. Historically, gold shaped monetary world and guided the economic behavior of many economies and global economy for centuries.

But the system was not equitable. It gave a bonanza to the gold-producing nations and worked to detriment of the countries not producing gold. Gold could not meet pressures of demands from global economic development and had to give way to a new system.

Keynes was in favor of abandoning the gold from the system. He had proposed the creation of a new international money called "Bancor" and a global central bank. This proposal was not acceptable to the USA. Not only the political and economic supremacy of the USA dominated the discussion in 1944 at the Bretton Woods, New Hampshire, where the representatives of nations met to create new economic order, but the factor that weighed against the creation of the new international money was the size and value of US gold stocks. In 1944, US gold stocks of 21,678 tones (now valued at around $670 billion) accounted for 80% of the total value of monetary gold of all the central banks. It was still a formidable strength in the global economic system looking to the scarcity value of gold and general attachment to the metal worldwide. By retaining gold at center of the system, the USA could capitalize on its strength for another two and a half decades. Gold continued to have international appeal, liquidity, and scarcity value. It was, therefore, thought politically and economically expedient not to totally abandon gold from the new system. The gold reserves of $42 billion were a formidable figure in 1944 in global economic and financial context. It gave leverage to the USA to operate the system for about two to three decades without any serious systemic disturbance. The USA could print dollars and supply global liquidity without worrying about its gold stocks.

The new Bretton Woods system was not rigid as the gold standard. Although the currency values were expressed in terms of gold content and the US dollar gold price of $35 per ounce of gold formed the basis for the structure of fixed exchange rates parities of all currencies, the rates were required to be changed in times of serious BoP problem. The US dollar established its strength by making dollar convertible into gold at the price of $35 per ounce to all central banks but not private entities. The US president also passed an executive order in April 1933 confiscating the private gold and prohibiting its residents from holding gold. The Bretton Woods established the dollar standard with gold as its anchor.

Benign Neglect of Dollar: Bretton Woods Drill

The emergence of the US dollar as the global currency in the postwar period marked the beginning of a new financial era in the world economy. While it endowed several economic benefits to the USA, it also placed constraints in the operation of its monetary policy. The USA had to look at its balance of payments not only from its own national angle but also perceive its international implications. Despite this handicap monetary management by the Federal Reserve under the Bretton Woods, financial architecture was solely guided by the domestic economic goals of economic growth and price stability. The USA did not use its monetary and fiscal policy tools for its balance of payments and dollar exchange rate management. This economic strategy was called the policy of "benign neglect" of dollar [1].[1] The macroeconomic policy was aimed primarily at domestic objectives of growth, employment, and price stability. The USA did not impose any restrictions on trade and capital movements, nor did it target any change in the parity of US dollar. The postwar Bretton Woods system was guided by the passive policy by the USA for its balance of payments and dollar exchange rate management [2].

The three main postulates of the policy were:

1. "The macro-economic policies (monetary, fiscal policies, demand management) should be guided by domestic policy objectives-employment, price stability, growth – and should not be used to influence the balance of payments.
2. The US should not try to improve the balance of payments by measures of control, such as import restrictions, export subsidies, capital export controls, 'buy American' policies and the like
3. The US should not try to devalue the dollar, but leave it to other countries to change the par value of their currency, thereby changing the exchange value of the dollar" [3].

The crux of the policy of "benign neglect" was that the USA should pursue a passive balance of payments policy, which meant that the USA should neither use demand management policy nor devalue its currency for adjusting its balance of payments deficits. It also suggested that the adjustment in the US balance of payments deficit was the responsibility of its major trading partners requiring more expansionary policies in their economies and/or revaluation of their currencies. Since the US dollar constituted the core of the global monetary system, the burden of adjustment in the BoP fell on the other nations.

Gold–Money Rift, Collapse of Bretton Woods: Obsolescence of "Benign Neglect"

Gold-centric dollar-based standard enabled the global economic system to have stable economic growth during the 1950s and 1960s. By 1971, gold was ready to be demonetized from the international monetary system because of the pressure of market forces. Although dollar was not convertible into gold for private holders, it was for the central banks. This necessitated the USA monitoring the gold price in the bullion market and keeping it from rising above $35 as it would amount to a devaluation of US dollar. In times of greater pressure on gold price, the USA also involved other European central banks to form a gold pool to collectively offer gold stocks in the market to keep the gold price stable at $35.

[1] Prof. Gottfried Haberler was the chief architect of the theoretical exposition of this policy which he developed with Thomas Willett. But it was also simultaneously but independently put forward by Lawrence Krause.

The fixed exchange rates system which pursued managed flexibility continued for nearly two and a half decades before showing signs of cracking under the pressure of increasing buildup of overhang of the US dollar liabilities to other central banks which began exceeding the value US gold stocks. The market took it as the weakness of the dollar and speculated on the increase in the price of gold by the USA. The rising demand for gold in the international market compared to its supply brought pressure on the market price of gold. The central banks of gold pool countries were liquidating their gold stocks to supply in the market to keep the gold price stable at $35.

The system benefited three nations. The USA which incurred deficits on the capital account financed it through treasury bills held by the foreign central banks. It could loan and invest dollars abroad when warranted by its trade surpluses and still finance it without the pressure on the dollar exchange rate through its treasury bills. Japan and Germany rebuilt from the war ravages could emerged as the export led growth economies and models in the development experience, possible only with the support of undervalued currencies fixed for a long time. Any revaluation of D-Mark or yen during the 1960s would have thrown their growth model awry with the speed to prosperity invariably slowing down. Revaluation of D-Mark and yen would have also meant devaluation of the US dollar although it could have been achieved by Japan and Germany by reducing gold content of their currencies.

The policy of benign neglect was based on the premise of the fixed gold price and adequate margin of the US gold stocks over its short-term liabilities to other central banks so that it would preserve the market strength and confidence in the US dollar. While the USA faced trade and current account surplus in its BoP until the late 1960s, the only way it could meet the demand for international liquidity was through a deficit in its overall BoP. This meant the USA incurring deficit in its capital account of BoP to meet the global requirements of liquidity, mainly dollar. In the early 1960s, the global economy faced the problem of “dollar shortage” because of the demand for dollars far exceeded the US BoP deficits that generated limited liquidity for global economy. The USA continued to meet the global demand for dollars through grants, aid, and loans to other nations from its budgetary allocations. During the 1950s and 1960s, the US budget provided for capital export to meet global demand for dollars. The system worked and was sustained by the continuing surplus in the US trade account. Declining US trade surplus in the 1960s posed a threat to the system. The sizable trade surplus of $6.83 billion in 1964 shrank to meager $0.62 billion in 1968 and a trade deficit of $2.84 billion in 1971. The “dollar-shortage” problem of the early 1960s turned into the problem of “dollar glut” by the late 1960s. In the perception of the markets, the strength of dollar lay in value of US gold stocks. In 1945 the size of gold stocks was $24 billion at the price of $35 per ounce of gold. The gold stocks of the USA reduced to $16 billion in 1962 and further to $12 billion in 1967. The rising BoP deficit raised the external short-term liquid liabilities of the USA held by the foreign central banks to $36 billion, raising doubts about the convertibility of dollar into gold at the fixed price of $35 an ounce and weakened the confidence in dollar. It created the gold–money rift [4].[2]

1971 Dollar Crisis: A Global Systemic Problem

Firstly, one has to distinguish between disequilibrium of the world monetary system reflected in the "dollar problem" and structural disequilibrium in the US economy that causes persistent deficit in its balance of payments. In the early 1960s, the "dollar problem" was not the US balance of payments problem, but was a revelation of a growing weakness in the "gold–dollar standard" which the Bretton Woods system created. "The hope that by strengthening our (the U.S) balance of payments we would restore confidence in the dollar, increase the willingness of foreign central banks to hold dollar reserves, and create a favorable climate for international monetary co-operation has proved to be unrealizable. Although our balance of payments has become strong, gold losses have increased owing to substantial central bank conversion of dollar into gold. The balance of payments is strong but the dollar remains weak. This must seem paradoxical to those who have maintained that the dollar problem was a balance of payments problem and that as soon as this country's international payments were brought into balance all would be well" [5, pp. 215–216]. Elaborating this distinction, Despres writes, "…it is gold rather than the dollar whose use as international money is artificial and contrived. The resulting and quite unnecessary tyranny of gold is increasingly preventing the dollar from performing fully and effectively its appropriate role as international money. Further worsening of this situation will have highly adverse economic consequences, here as well as abroad. We were mistaken from the beginning in regard to the defense of dollar as a balance of payments problem …. As was previously pointed out, annual deficits of perhaps two billion dollars would be normal under a healthily functioning international monetary system, less than this over a prolonged period would have undesirable deflationary effects on the world economy…. Deficits of three or four billion dollars for a few years are trivial by any fundamentally meaningful criterion for an economy of the size of the United States; it is only in relation to gold that the deficits have not been trivial. In treating the problem as a balance of payments problem, we have not, in fact, been defending the dollar. Instead, we have been engaged in attempting to defend the contrived role of gold as international money at the expense of the dollar" [5, p. 218].

Since its formation, the stability of Bretton Woods's system remained anchored to the value of gold stocks of the USA that rendered a degree of confidence to the dollar. The liquid dollar liabilities held by the foreign central banks were lower than the value of US gold stocks. This positive margin of safety between the US gold stocks and liquid dollar liabilities held by foreign central banks was getting eroded

[2] Professor Brahmananda predicted the imminent collapse of gold–dollar standard in 1969 when he analyzed the growing rift between US external liquid liabilities and value of its gold stocks potentially rocking monetary system.

as the USA was supplying dollars through deficit in capital account of its BoP to meet global demand for international liquidity which was primarily dollars. The amount of US BoP deficit of $3–4 billion was trivial in relation to its gold stocks even in the early 1960s.

By the mid-1960s when the "negative convertibility guarantee margin" (value of US gold stocks—US short-term liquid liabilities held by the foreign central banks) started, mounting the dollar problem no longer remained the balance of payments problem of the USA but the world monetary concern. The disequilibrium in the world monetary system was reflected in growing size of the US external dollar liabilities on shrinking foundation of gold. This situation exacerbated by the middle of the 1960s when the dollar crisis emerged. The solution to the problem lied definitely not in correcting deficit the US balance of payments but in increasing the official price of gold (devaluing the US dollar) sufficiently to create adequate positive "convertibility guarantee margin." The suggestion in this regard was made by a group of economists in the early 1960s. The gold hawks were advocating increase in the official price of gold to restore the stability in the system and confidence in dollar. The most prominent among them were Sir Roy Harrod, Prof. Jacques Rueff, and Prof. Michael Heilperin, who advocated the gold price revaluation from $35 an ounce to $70. However, they had different standpoints. Harrod wanted gold–dollar exchange standard to be reinforced by rise in the price of gold, while Rueff and Heilperin desired revaluation of gold to revert to the old-styled classical gold standard with the stricter monetary and fiscal discipline. The devaluation of the US dollar was necessitated not so much by any structural disequilibrium on its balance of payments, as it was by the special responsibility assigned to it as the main reserve center for the world monetary system. However, devaluation of a currency is often related to national prestige. In this process, devaluation is delayed, often jeopardizing the larger interests of national economy as well as global monetary system.

Although in the early 1960s the dollar problem was mainly the problem of confidence in the dollar convertibility, it began to turn into the US external payments deficit problem by the late 1960s, and the latter naturally intensified and aggravated the former one. For correcting the adverse balance of payments trend arising out of its domestic disequilibrium, the devaluation of the US dollar was not an appropriate measure, since US dollar served as the world money and exchange rate of dollar was a matter more related to the equilibrium of the world monetary system than the US balance of payment equilibrium. It is here that the third tenet of policy of "benign neglect" involving nondevaluation of the US dollar but revaluation of currencies of surplus nations fits in correctly.

Divergent Trade Propensities

When surplus countries undertake the burden of adjustment by revaluing their undervalued currencies and thereby face a slowdown in their export expansion and overall economic growth, the USA could impose upon it an equal degree of financial discipline by controlling its expansionary monetary and fiscal policies. It is argued that US economy is not as foreign trade oriented as some of the Western European economies are. Imports of the USA constituted only 5% of its GNP. Nevertheless, despite its average propensity to import of 5%, its average income elasticity of imports almost doubled from 0.9 during 1950–1964 to 1.8 during 1965–1971, and the marginal propensity to import also doubled from 4.5 to 9%.[3] The marginal propensity to import of the USA was almost double its average propensity to import of the USA. Slower economic growth that reduces growth in imports would also have a substantial impact on the exports of relatively smaller European nations and Japan and would have corrected their exports surpluses.

Strong case for the USA pursuing less expansionary policy than that followed by the European nations and Japan was supported by a study made by Houthhakker and Magee in relation to income elasticities in world trade [6]. "Johnson showed that if trade is initially balance in two country model, if prices are constant and if income grown is same in both countries, then the trade balance between them can still change through time if their respective income elasticities of demand for the others' exports differ. In this case the country with higher income elasticity of demand for imports will face rapid import growth than export growth, a deterioration in its trade balance and eventually pressure on its exchange rate" [6, p. 111].

The disparities in income elasticities in foreign trade of the major industrial nations made these countries suffer from perpetual surpluses or deficits in their trade balances with equal income growth and stable relative prices. West Germany, Japan, Italy, and Canada which faced higher income elasticity of demand for their exports than their income elasticity of demand for imports would face perpetual surpluses in trade balance, while the UK, the USA, and France facing exactly the opposite condition on income elasticity of demand for their exports and imports would face perpetual deficit in their trade account, if both group of countries grow at the same rate and relative prices in their economies remain unchanged. The study suggested that the USA should pursue less expansionary policies than its trading partners in order to avoid the emergence of perpetual deficit in its trade account. It validates the rationale behind the use of demand management policies for external balance.

The study covering the period of 1951–1966 recorded income elasticity of demand for imports of the USA of 1.51 in contrast with the rest of the world's income elasticity of demand for US exports of 0.99. The UK also faced similar elasticities which were 1.66 and 0.86. Italy and France faced similar elasticities, but with smaller divergence. The elasticities for Italy were 2.19 and 2.95 and for France 1.66 and 1.53. Contrasting this, the elasticities for Japan and West Germany were exactly opposite. The elasticities for Japan were 1.23 and 3.55 and for West Germany 1.8 and 2.08 [6, p. 113]. These divergent income elasticities of imports and exports among the major countries created structural trade deficits and surpluses.

The Bretton Woods exchange rate arrangements were such that kept the yen and D-Mark undervalued despite their trade surpluses and continued to enlarge their export surpluses. Japan and West Germany enjoyed high growth rates driven by

---

[3] Bank for International Settlement, Forty Second Annual Report, 1971–1972, Basle, June, 1972, p. 6.

their sustained exports growth supported by their undervalued currencies. China is now pursuing similar policies under a different regime of floating exchange rates but with fixed, stable, and undervalued yuan. The model of China's growth is similar to Japanese and West German growth model of the 1950s and 1960s.

Moving to Fiat Money

In the second half of the 1960s, the US government expenditure was increasing on account of several welfare measures as well as war in Vietnam. Taxes were not raised to reduce budget deficit. US export surplus was declining. Inflation rate had reached 6% which was high by the standard of postwar prosperity. The speculation in the currency markets against dollar led to increase in the market price of gold above $35 level. The USA, France, and other European countries formed gold pool to sell gold in the market to stabilize the market price at the official level. The loss of gold from the central bankers was so much that the gold pool was abandoned and two-tier gold price system was followed. The official price remained at $35 level for all central bank transactions, and market price was allowed to go up. Despite this, the speculation and shorting of dollars in the forex markets continued.

The signs of weakness of dollar in the currency markets and increasing pressure on the market price of gold, which was pegged by the USA and other European nations by selling their gold into the open market, were clear signals for the reform of the Bretton Woods gold–dollar standard. The three plausible alternatives were available. First, devalue dollar by increasing the official gold price from $35 per ounce to either $70 or much higher level, and perpetuate the gold–dollar standard for couple of decades more before which another devaluation of dollar in terms of its gold price would be necessary. Second, establish new international monetary unit like the SDR (Special Drawing Right) earlier created by the IMF, with the IMF assuming the powers of the global central bank. This was similar to Keynes' suggestion for International Clearing Union (ICU) with Bancor to be the new global currency. The third option was to demonetize gold from the international monetary system by delinking dollar from gold and allow exchange rates to float in the currency markets. It involved the USA revoking the convertibility of dollar into gold for the central banks and also the official price of gold.

In August 1971, President Nixon took the bold and historic decision to end this market impasse by demonetizing dollar and delinked it from gold by closing its gold window at the Treasury. The major currencies were realigned at the Smithsonian Institute in December 1971 in which dollar was devalued by 8.75% by raising its gold price from $35 to $38 and other currencies revaluing their currencies. Moving away from gold standard to fiat money in international monetary system was a great step. A sharp weakening of dollar would have meant market unacceptability to the idea of fiat money. Fortunately, dollar migrated from gold-based convertible currency to fiat currency in relatively stable manner due to the step-by-step approach by the Treasury and the other central banks to ensure the soft landing of dollar.

While the currency markets stabilized for a while, there was renewed pressure on dollar and pound. The pound began floating in June 1972, and dollar was devalued again by 10% in March 1973 to $42.22. Since then dollar and all other currencies began floating in the forex markets. The global monetary system moved from the fixed exchange rates and gold standard to floating exchange rates and fiat dollar standard without much market disruption and any crisis. The step-by-step experiment of migration from gold convertible dollar to floating exchange rates succeeded.

The 1971 dollar crisis was the result of the gold–money rift [4]. The dollar liquidity which generated inflation had eroded the purchasing power of dollar. Through the Marshall Plan of $14 billion, accounting for 8% of the US GDP then, the USA rebuilt the Europe and Japan from the destruction of productive capacities caused by the war. The favorable exchange rates of 4.5 DM and 360 yen vis-a-vis US dollar opened a new vista for their growth through exports and supply of cheaper goods to the USA. This pattern of growth between the USA and Germany–Japan continued till the mid-1960s. With the USSR and China not trading much in the global economy, there was no further scope for the USA to import more from its trading partners and lower inflation. The developing economies primarily exported raw material and minerals. The pressure on prices was building up, and cumulative US BoP deficit over the years also could not go beyond the threshold of value of gold stocks. The lease which the gold-based dollar system had given for a sustainable international monetary system was getting over. The system had reached the point of inflection for collapse. The estimate of revaluation of gold required by the rise consumer price index in the USA between 1945 and 1971 gave a figure of $84 per ounce of gold. Instead revaluing the gold, it was economically wiser to demonetize gold which Keynes had suggested in 1944.

The lesson from this crisis as was from 1929 crash is that excess liquidity always creates and builds up pressure against the prices which are artificially pegged by the central banks or other authorities. And when the overhang of liquidity cannot be adequately redressed, the point of inflection creates the crisis or implosion through the market forces. The crisis is market reaction at a point of inflection of eliminating the imbalance in the system. This is a constant seesaw between the market and the regulator. The regulator can always stop the growth spiral by an early measure. If it is too early, it saps the growth potential. To know the right time to regulate the growth spiral is a difficult task, as difficult as predicting the stock market.

Decade of Economic Uncertainty and Stagflation

The decade of 1970s presented a sharp contrast to the earlier two decades of stability and growth in the global economy. Both decades of the 1950s and 1960s witnessed high economic growth with price stability. The GDP growth in the two decades was 4.5 and 4.4% per annum with the lowest annual rates of inflation of 2 and 2.4%, respectively. The floating exchange rates were a new system to be tested in the global currency markets. The era of stability came to close with the exit of fixed exchange rates system. While new floating exchange rates created a climate of uncertainty that haunted the global financial and currency markets, the global economy was also passing through an unusual economic malaise of stagflation. Before the financial and currency markets could absorb the dollar shock, in 1974 OPEC nations assaulted the markets with oil shock by quadrupling the oil prices from $3 per barrel to $12. The economic consequences of the oil shock were wide, deep, and far reaching. It sent global payments balances into a tailspin. The cost-push effect on prices and inflation became globally irreversible. The decline in output and incomes in the oil-importing nations exacerbated stagflation. When the output and incomes declined, prices continued to rise under the effect of cost-push influences. The stagnation was further coupled with the BoP problem due to higher import bill. Both the domestic and external economies of the oil-importing nations were shattered.

American capitalism was once again under attack. The malady of stagflation and weakening dollar took a heavy toll on the economy. The inflation was a new malaise of capitalism which Schumpeter had predicted could bring its downfall because of the bureaucracy taking over the power by establishing rationing and controls.[4] The fact that American capitalism did go through this phase in 1971 forcing the Republican President Nixon to adopt wage-price controls vindicated the hypothesis of Schumpeter. But his prophecy ended here. The wage-price controls were short lived and did not last long. Keynesianism was skirted to be taken over by monetarism in took over. At each point of its serious crisis, capitalism has shown tremendous adaptability not only to overcome the crisis but also to pave fresh way for its new phase of growth. In the 1980s, it had to migrate into the new philosophy of growth called globalization with economic reforms.

References

1. Krause LB. A passive balance of payments strategy for the US, Brookings papers on economic analysis, No. 2, Washington, DC; 1970.
2. Haberler G, Willett TA. Strategy for US balance of payments. Washington, DC: American Enterprise Institute; 1971.
3. Haberler G. US balance of payments policy and the international monetary system. In: Schultz W, editor. Convertibility, multilateralism and freedom. World economic policy in the seventies, essays in honor of Reinhard Kamitz. Wein/New York: Springer; 1972. p. 177–8.
4. Brahmananda PR. Gold-money rift. Bombay: Vora Publications; 1969.
5. Despres E, Meier GM. A proposal for strengthening the dollar. In: International economic reform – collected papers of Emile Despres. New York: Oxford University Press; 1973.
6. Houthhakker HS, Magee SP. Income and price elasticities in world trade. Rev Econ Stat. 1969;LI(2):111–25.

---

[4] Schumpeter, Joseph, *The March into Socialism*, Address before the Annual Meeting of American Economic Association, at New York, December 30, 1949.

Chapter 7
Enter the Globalization: A Paradigm Shift

> 7000 plus *languages and hundreds of disciplines of study, but thoughts, emotions, motivations and ideals remain the same across the tiny fragments of time and space*

The phenomenon of globalization is not new to the world economy. The global economic history is replete with the regimes of restrictive trade practices of different orders. The trade between nations in pre-seventeenth century was primarily motivated to acquire new goods, which were not available within a nation and whose acquisition did not adversely affect domestic production and employment. All the ancient oceanic expeditions sponsored by the royalties for either explorations of new lands or hitherto inaccessible regions known for their wealth and prosperity were aimed primarily to secure new commodities and also precious metals such as gold and silver not easily sourced in the known regions. The trade in competitive products which hurt national production and employment was curbed and not encouraged. It was an era of regimented and restricted trade.

This scenario changed with the advent of first articulate and comprehensive expression of economic phenomena and their underlying laws by Adam Smith in his book, The Wealth of Nations in 1776, and this was followed by David Ricardo in his book Principles of the Political Economy in 1817, both of which laid out the clear and logical foundations of the economic benefits and gains from the free trade. Monarchies across the Europe gave the political support to free trade despite the opposition from the vested interests. The regime of free trade that ensued for nearly two centuries (the seventeenth and the eighteenth) was a phase of globalization although it was limited by the state of contemporary technology in transport and communication than prevalent. Twenty-first-century globalization is driven and accelerated by the unstoppable waves of advances in transport, computer, and Internet and telecom technology. Even the retrograde fivefold increase in crude oil price to $100 per barrel in 2008 could not tame the speed of globalization.

The fragmentation of the global economy between 1914 and 1945 and the devastation it caused further compounded by the Great Depression are stark reminders of the misery from deglobalization. The period characterized military fight and territorial

S. Nayak, *The Global Financial Crisis: Genesis, Policy Response and Road Ahead*, DOI 10.1007/978-81-322-0798-6_7, © Springer India 2013

aggression for political and economic supremacy causing massive loss of life and property unprecedented in human history. The postwar world moved slowly thereafter from the era of confrontation to the era of cooperation.

Globalization represents a paradigm shift in the phase of evolution and development of the global economy. The postwar global economic development and stability was the outcome of the policy of global monetary and economic cooperation and trio of institutions, the IMF (International Monetary Fund), the World Bank (International Bank for Reconstruction and Development), and the GATT (General Agreement on Trade and Tariff), that ensured implementation of the new policy. The IMF instituted and supervised operation of fixed but adjustable exchange rates and provided financial support to countries to meet their temporary balance of payments problems. The World Bank provided long-term capital to countries affected by the Second World War for their reconstruction and growth and for the development of the less developed countries. The GATT provided the framework for the promotion of free trade among nations by removal of tariff and nontariff barriers. This global economic institutional structure played a crucial role shaping developments that brought sustained growth and stability in the global economy for two and half decades until the beginning of 1990s. In contrast to the interwar period characterized by economic instability and turmoil manifest in depression, hyperinflation, trade wars and hostility, boom and bust cycles, exchange instability, and growing economic isolationism instead of cooperation, the postwar period demonstrated the gains of economic wisdom and political pragmatism. The United Nations avoided another global war or conflict although the period was punctuated by some temporary as well as some prolonged military conflicts in different regions.

Global economic developments are both governed and constrained by contemporary economic thinking and policy. The conventional wisdom, historically accepted and established body of economic thinking and policy, and institutions built and supported by it survive so long as it continues to solve the contemporary economic problems and helps in attaining economic goals without much economic and social distress and turmoil.

Globalization is not a quick-fix magic formula that will uniformly bring positive results in all countries. The economic, social, and political conditions across the borders are too diverse and intricate to be left to magic of indiscriminate globalization. We have countries ranging from the poorest of the poor landlocked economies in Africa, small island economies, and resource-rich poor nations to large continental economies like India, China, Russia, and Brazil. The rich nations like the USA and Japan offer contrasting features in nearly all aspects except the consumerism. The two nations at the Far East and the Far West ends separated by all other nations of the world reflect one of the oldest and youngest of the global economies. The contrast continues in their geographical size, natural resource endowments, culture, social structure, and lifestyle. What unite these two large economies are capital, technology, trade, consumerism, and growing service orientation. In fact these common denominators are vehicles of globalization sweeping across the globe into the nations in different degrees of freedom.

Foreign Aid and Trade for Development

In the early 1950s with Keynesianism operating in the developed world in full swing, the earliest development models for the LDCs (less developed countries) highlighted the role of foreign aid and trade in promoting growth. If the LDCs were short of capital, the developed nations could provide concessional aid to these countries to finance their development plans. With the World Bank in place for such purpose, the emphasis was more on multilateral aid. The bilateral foreign aid came under criticism for being tied and also reduced due to the budgetary constraint of the rich nations. The routing of aid through multilateral channels like the World Bank became more popular and efficient. However, this route also suffered from resource limitations since the major funding sources of subsidized loans and aid continued to be the budgetary allocations from the rich nations which could not increase their share due to their own budgetary and tax constraints. In 1969, the Pearson Commission Report on International Development recommended the target for the transfer of resources from the industrialized nations to developing nations in the form of official aid to be 0.7% of their GDP. "The actual experience was, however, disappointing with percentage share declining from 0.53% in the early 1960s to a low of 0.32% in 1976. The absolute amount of official aid, however, doubled to $18 billion over 10 years in 1978. The share official aid in resource transfer declined from 52% in 1969 to 38% in 1975, while that of non concessional flows increased from 48 to 62%" [1, p. 28]. Simultaneously, the efforts were on also to promote foreign trade as the engine of growth among the developing economies under the auspices of UNCTAD (United Nations Conference on Trade and Development) led by Raul Prebisch, Chilean economists who propounded the theory of secular deterioration of the terms of trade of developing nations. Prof. Gunnar Myrdal, a Nobel laureate in economics, provided the theoretical basis and model and a case for Asian development through foreign trade in his most perceptive, deep, and scholarly study and book, the Asian Drama. The economic miracle which Asia experienced in 1990s was in fact the vision and dream of Myrdal. In 1960s and 1970s foreign trade could not usher growth and development in developing nations due to the prevalence of several barriers to trade and inadequate foreign investment to promote export-oriented industries. Asia had to wait till 1990s for its export-oriented growth model to be experimented under the philosophy of globalization.

Sovereign Debt Crisis and Brady Bonds

With aid and trade not cutting much ice with development in 1970s, there was a need to try another alternative. In 1973 oil crisis hit the developing world hardest with the biggest transfer of resources to the oil-exporting nations. Not only was the economic growth halted globally due to the quadrupling of crude oil prices from $3 to $12 per barrel, but the global economy faced the grave threat of plunging into severe recession. The oil-importing developing nations were devastated. During 1973–1980 the

OPEC countries enjoyed the current surpluses of $330 billion, against the current deficits of industrial oil-importing nations of $157 billion and of developing nations of $195 billion. The international organizations like IMF and World Bank did not possess the resources needed to finance the BoP deficits of the oil-importing nations. At this juncture, it was the eurodollar market which stepped in quickly to recycle the surpluses of the oil-exporting nations for financing the BoP deficits of oil-importing nations. The international banking system of eurodollars saved the global economy from slipping into deep recession following the first oil crisis in 1974 and also the second one in 1979 when oil price went up from $16 to $40 per barrel. The oil crisis ushered an era of commercial borrowings for the developing nations.

The tempo of commercial borrowings from the private international banking system rose substantially since 1974. The eurocurrency market also rose at a breathtaking rate. The international borrowings in the form of eurocurrency credits and eurobond issues (excluding foreign bond issues) increased from $42 billion in 1976 to $366 billion in 1985. The total lending in the eurocurrency market in the form of publicized eurocurrency bank credit and international bond issues reached a massive sum $592 billion during 1973–1980. Compared to this, the IMF's new lending commitments and other use of fund resources during the same period amounted to SDRs 36 billion ($42 billion). The IMF's flow of credit was mere 7% of total medium- and long-term lending in the eurocurrency markets. The fund was too rigid in responding to rapidly changing world monetary environment and also did not have adequate resources.

Not only did the private and public sector institutions from different countries borrow in the eurocurrency market to fund their projects of expansion, diversifications, and modernization, but the governments of different nations raised sovereign debt as a source of their budgetary and balance of payments support. The increasing recourse to the eurocurrency lending by the oil-importing LDCs changed the volume, composition and maturity structure of their external debt, and the burden of debt servicing. The outstanding external public debt of non-oil LDC's in 1979 of $250 billion was twice the amount in 1975 and three times the level in 1973. The external public debt of all LDC's soared to $580 billion in 1980. As a proportion of their GNP, the external public debt of all oil-importing LDC's rose from 13% in 1974 to 17.3% in 1980. In 1979, the share of private sources of financing in the external outstanding debt of the LDCs went up to 50% from 33% in 1973. The share of commercial banks in total private credit to LDCs rose to 80%. The ratio of external debt of non-oil LDCs to their exports of goods and services reached 80% in 1979 from 70% in 1973. The ratio of external debt to GDP for non-oil LDCs increased from 14 to 19% during the same period. The shift from the official to private source also resulted in shorter maturities and higher interest rates than in the official loans. This further added to the debt servicing burden of the LDCs. The debt servicing payments of non-oil LDCs rose by four times since 1973, i.e., from $10 billion in 1973 to $42 billion in 1980.

The commercial borrowings were primarily in dollars and on floating interest rates based on Libor (London Interbank Offer Rate) which moved in tandem with interest rates in the US money markets. So long as the Fed funds rate was low in the USA, the debt servicing burden of the borrowers also remained moderate. But raging inflation in the late 1970s was the major economic problem faced by the USA requiring measures to control prices. The rising oil prices had stoked cost-push inflation.

In order to tackle inflation, the Fed began the monetary tightening by hiking interest rates in 1979. The Fed funds rate rose from 10% in 1979 to the record level of 19% in 1981. The Libor for the US dollar reached the record level at 21%. This unexpectedly high level of interest rate had crippling effect on the developing nation with large external debt. The debt servicing ratios of several heavily indebted nations went beyond the cautionary level of 20% of export earnings. Several nations of Latin America, Africa, and Eastern Europe defaulted on external payments.

A series of factors were responsible for this setback. Some of the Latin American countries like Brazil, Mexico, Argentina, and Venezuela were borrowing in the market very heavily. These countries borrowed in some cases beyond their foreign exchange requirements and used the eurocurrency markets as a generalized funding source for government budgets. The sound norms and prudent limits of debt servicing were thrown overboard. The foreign currency finance was used in projects irrespective of their contribution to the balance of payments. Resultantly, following the second hike in oil prices in 1979–1980, the balance of payments situation worsened making servicing of their external debt very difficult. Added to that was the rising interest rate in the market in 1980 reaching the record level that raised the interest burden substantially. The pressure of higher debt servicing finally created defaults in 1982 requiring loan rescheduling.

The magnitude of the exposure of the US banks to the LDCs and primarily the Latin American countries, and the possibility of payment defaults threatened the stability of the US banking system raising the fears of the banking collapse. "At the end of 1982, the nine major U.S. banks had lent out over 287% of their capital to the developing countries" [2]. In order to redress the crisis, the Citicorp, the biggest lender to the Latin American borrowers, took the lead of writing off the loan losses from its free reserves in 1987. The other US banks followed suit and averted the onset of major banking crisis since the 1930s. This was followed by the Brady Plan of debt reduction and rescheduling in 1989 that defused the debt crisis and gave a long-term solution to the debt servicing and BoP problems of the borrowing nations by issuing the 30-year zero-coupon par value Brady Bonds of the record amount of $175 billion. The LDC debt crisis of 1980s was a big setback to the development effort as the debt model of development stood discredited and needed a better replacement. It also opened up a fresh debate on the right model for future development of the developing nations [1, p. 31]. The commercial debt model lay disgraced by the excessive and reckless use of debt and its onerous servicing impact.

The Setting for Globalization: 3W (Washington-World Bank-Wall Street) Policy Model

With the foreign aid, trade, and debt testing their chemistry in promoting growth in the less developed countries for three decades in the postwar world period, it was imperative to develop a new economic model and policy for global development. The unsettling economic experience of 1970s warranted a fresh initiative in this direction. The philosophy of globalization as the development strategy in the post-Bretton Woods floating exchange rate era owes its origin to the ideas of the think tank in Treasury Department in Washington, World Bank economists, and Wall Street gurus. The 3W (Washington-World Bank-Wall Street) model is also known as the Washington Consensus as the future strategy for global development beginning in 1980s with the emphasis on the equity capital and investment in development. Despite considerable theoretical work on the role of risk capital in the form of foreign direct and portfolio investment acting as a catalyst in growth in developing nations, this form of financing never dominated the earlier development models. Further, the emphasis on this new channel for transfer of resources fell perfectly in line with the overall philosophy of economic liberalization and globalization centering on the removal of restrictions on foreign trade and investments. One of the predominant reasons for globalization was the economic environment in the mature industrial nations which were beset with excess capacity, high cost of production due to high labor cost, recession, and lackluster state of effective demand. With the declining rate of return on capital in these economies, the surplus savings and investible resources awaited more lucrative deployment.

The search for new channel for transfer of resources was backed by the developments in investment theory and the empirical results advocating diversification of investment portfolio on higher investment frontier giving higher returns with lower risk. Markowitz's theory of investment diversification, although published in 1952, found increasing acceptance among large institutional investors in the late 1970s [3].[1] In 1979 the Labor Department which hitherto restricted equity investments by institutional investors like pension funds permitted equity investment on the logic of risk diversification. This paved the way of large equity investments by pension funds revitalizing the stock market. The principle of investment diversification internationally gave a logical place for portfolio investment the globalization model. The return on capital in developing nations was much higher than in industrial countries. The portfolio investment by institutional investors, like pension funds and mutual funds, and insurance companies into the equity in the emerging markets was a win-win situation for both the group of nations. The foreign direct investment by multinational companies also became the centerpiece of globalization complementing the portfolio investment from the institutions.

The new economic policy of economic liberalization, privatization, and globalization involving removal of barriers to foreign trade and capital movements, deregulation of domestic industrial, trade and banking and financial sectors, and privatization of government owned companies, developed by the ideologues in 3W (Washington-World Bank-Wall Street) constituted the new strategy for global development since 1980s.[2] The change was not cosmetic. It dawned a new era of resource

[1] It gives an excellent account of the application and impact of Markowitz's theory and tools of measuring risk on fund and investment management in the USA during the period.

[2] John Williamson coined the term Washington Consensus giving articulation to the new reform policy in the emerging markets. See John Williamson [4].

transfer to the emerging market economies that changed the development philosophy and established as the central feature of globalization.

Globalization: Smith-Ricardo-Keynes (SRK) Model

The philosophy of globalization which began its journey with the emergence floating exchange rates in 1975 gained the theoretical articulation and real momentum only in the early 1980s. The 3W think tank gave theoretical shape and strategy for adoption in both the developed world and emerging market economies and even the communist countries. The philosophical structure of globalization is built on the economic logic containing the theories of three great British economists, Adam Smith (1776), David Ricardo (1817), and John Maynard Keynes (1936).[3] While the 3W model explains the main postulates of globalization in terms of the coverage, character, mechanism, and degree of strategy of economic reforms, it is necessary to discuss the underlying theoretical base and its importance and significance. The SRK (Smith-Ricardo-Keynes) model forms the theoretical base of superstructure of the policy of economic reforms and philosophy of globalization.

Let us start with Adam Smith. The father of economic science in his magnum opus examining the causes of the Wealth of Nations laid some eternal economic laws. In a society protecting and nurturing individualism, freedom of enterprise, and right to property, free markets can achieve the best of societal good with private gain. In fact the invisible hand of the market will transform the race for private gain into social good. This model does not fit into the Marxian theory or communist ideology which does not recognize individualism, freedom of enterprise, and right to property, the three fundamentals of the market economy. The market is the source of profit, inequality, and unjust society according to communist ideology which has the tool of central planning, replacing markets for signals, and bureaucracy executing the market operations. The economic, political, and military race between the USA and USSR reflected the economic efficiency of both ideologies and economic systems.

David Ricardo, British economist and author of the Principles of Political Economy, the founder of the comparative cost theory, laid the logical foundation for advocacy of free trade. None of the earlier economists had given the idea of comparative cost or opportunity cost which is the true measure of gains from trade. His theory led to the end of mercantilism which restricted trade and began a new era of freer trade in 1846 comparable to the current era of globalization. At no time in history did Ricardo's principle of comparative costs work so extensively as it is today under globalization. The gains from large-scale operation of his law have increased global trade by 200% in the last two decades and raised the global economic growth, raised the living standards in the emerging markets, and established the phase of lowest level of inflation.

[3] The years refer to the year of publication of their works propounding new theories.

Keynes becomes a part of the globalization model when we carry his General Theory and its policy outcomes in the international context. The spending is what spurs economic growth is the central theme of the General Theory. If growth slows down or enters negative territory, monetary measures can be taken to spur spending, consumption, and investment spending. If the recession or stagnation is stubborn, monetary measures may not have any effect on spending. In this scenario the government has to spend through deficit financing to spur growth. In the domestic context, deficit financing is the only sure recipe for recovery from recession. But in the international context, sustained global economic growth is possible only when the most dominant economy, the USA, incurs deficit in its BoP which spurs global growth. The US spending for imports, foreign investment, and lending through its BoP deficit promotes the global growth. The US BoP deficit is, therefore, critical to global growth just as deficit financing is an essential recipe for averting recession in the domestic economy.

The Bretton Woods system functioned under fixed exchange rates, dollar value tied to gold and BoP financing by the USA and IMF. The USA could not incur large BoP deficit because of the constraint of dollar convertibility into gold with its fixed gold reserves of $10 billion at $35 per an ounce of gold. The post-Bretton Woods floating exchange rate system in 1975 freed the dollar from bondage of gold. The dollar became a fiat currency, and its strength depended on its demand and supply in the international market determined by its BoP flows. The dollar not only has continued to be the major international currency in floating exchange regime which has functioned and survived over last three decades but has been the centerpiece in the financing of globalization ensuring its success. The strength of the dollar has been determined by the dominance of the USA in the global economy, global trade, and investment pattern and flows, its ability to keep its capital market vibrant through its technological advance keeping the rate of return on capital from declining, and its price stability and structure and level of real interest rates (the current near-zero interest rates reflect an extraordinary situation where the Fed has deliberately kept the interest rates lowest to initiate economic recovery). The foregoing factors have continued to maintain the dollar as the global currency. In this structure of global economic and monetary balance, the Keynesian law applied in the international context advocates the US BoP deficits for sustained global growth. The US growth would spill over to other countries through its BoP deficits. Any attempt by the USA to curb its BoP deficit would have adverse impact on global growth. It can continue to incur its BoP deficit so long as it does not have large unemployment or inflation in rest of the world. Keynes going international forms the third ideological pillar of globalization along with Smith and Ricardo.

The MOT Revolution

If one has to identify crucial factors that have been both the precursor as well as the accelerator of globalization, three institutions that have also been common denominators in industrial revolution in the nineteenth century stand out with distinction.

The institutions of money, organization, and technology (MOT) developed to an extent since the early 1980s to discard the national borders and go global. The MOT revolution of more than two and half decades marks a distinct driving force of globalization. The national governments of all countries have bent their economic and foreign policies to the dictates of the MOT revolution. It has broken the iron curtain, ended the cold war, and broken the USSR, and also bent China in its ideology. It has staged the transition of communism in the erstwhile USSR and east Europe into democratic societies with freedom of choice, private property, and free markets. It has made China bow to the wave and take U-turn on its ideology of economic growth driven by the spirit of private enterprise, private property, and the magic of free market mechanism. China has accepted the wave of MOT revolution ending its long isolationism to be a partner in global growth. It has accepted free markets and private property and given vent to its enormous resource potential under the MOT inflow to achieve double-digit growth and an economical miracle. Gorbachev in the USSR and Deng Xiaoping in China have been the architects of this change. A significant counterpart in inducing this historic change was the lead taken and diplomacy initiated by Ronald Reagan.

The modern money is neither coins nor paper currency. It is digital money. It is not immobile but can travel throughout the world at the speed of light. Technologically or virtually it is impossible to limit the global mobility of money. However, realistically several countries, especially the emerging market economies, through the regulations of their central banks limit inflow and outflow of money from their economies because of the nascent nature of their money and capital markets in the global context. Nevertheless, in most developed economies money moves freely without any regulations on their cross border movements and faster now due to the digital technology. Yet each central bank has its regulations on their national banks, which are institutions dealing in money. These relate to cash reserve and capital requirements for banks that accept and lend money. Without these regulations the central banks would find it difficult to ensure the safety and security of money, since in addition to the central banks which issue money in the form of coins and currency, the commercial banks create more money through its process of accepting and lending money. The currency component of money supply in the USA was only 10% in 2009. Apart from these nationally regulated money of different countries, the offshore banking centers are several island economies which allow banks to accept money with minimal cash reserve and capital requirements. Over the last two and half decades of globalization, the offshore money, which was earlier known as the eurodollar deposits or eurocurrency deposits, known and popularly referred to as the "shadow banking system", has grown at a phenomenal rate. The BIS estimated the size of this international banking system at $27 trillion in 2008.

Money abhors national borders. So does business organization. The organizations have global ambitions to capture new markets, improve supply chain management, outsource from other nations, reallocate production facilities, and finally achieve economies of much broader scale of markets, production, and marketing. The corporate organization with limited liability and transferability of equity ownership on the stock markets has revolutionized the business development and economic growth and prosperity across the world. Even the communist regimes abandoned their totalitarian economic model of production in favor of the corporate model of stock market liquidity. The corporate organizations are no longer regional or national, but are global with global markets and global production sites.

So is technology. In an open and interconnected world, the technology can transfer fast to advantage of endowments which any country can offer. Notwithstanding the patent protection technologies are growing and spreading fast on development of legal alternatives. Internet and telecom technology itself has made knowledge and information accessible to all at fast speed, with tremendous ease, at the least and affordable cost, and at easy storage and retrieval. Technology is also moving with capital. With global capital most mobile in the last two decades, technology is moving faster from county to country with capital. MOT is becoming global at a fast rate.

Gresham's Law in Reverse Gear

Not only is money traveling more internationally in search opportunities, it is also influencing its quality. Unlike the Gresham's law under which bad money drove good money out of circulation, today good money is driving out bad money. The Gresham's law stated that when good and bad currencies are both in circulation, the bad money will drive the good money out of circulation. The story about the Gresham's law goes like this. In the sixteenth century Queen Elizabeth I asked Sir Thomas Gresham, financial agent of English Crown in Antwerp, to explain what was happening to shilling. During the regime of Henry VIII, although he inherited a fortune from his father Henry VII of pounds 1,250,000 (current value of 375 million pounds), a prosperous economy and surplus Treasury, his wars, and dynastic ambition in Europe with stagnant revenues caused inflation draining his treasury. He had to turn to Parliament for money, grants of subsidies to finance war. To solve kingdom's financial problem by reducing the treasury cost, the currency was debased during 1526–1539 by reducing the silver content of shilling coins. Actually if the silver content had been reduced by the extent of inflation, he would been logical and right in bringing the intrinsic metal value of shilling to its true price over time. However, the old coins were still in circulation. When the old and debased coins were both in circulation, it was normal financial instinct for people to hoard the old coins and dispense with the new coins for transactions. With this, the debased coins drove the old, more valuable coins out of circulation. Gresham gave a report to the Queen explaining why bad money is driving good money out of circulation. Gresham's law became a popular in economics of money. The story has relevance even today in democracies which run fiat paper currencies. All the economies are experience inflation of different degrees. Hence, paper money gets automatically debased by the extent of inflation. Modern democracies face the same economic and financial problems of governance which the monarchs experienced in ruling their kingdoms.

Not only is money traveling now more and faster internationally in search opportunities, but it also gets influenced by its quality. Unlike the Gresham's under which bad money drove good money out of circulation, today good money is driving out bad money. The US dollar is strong internationally due to less erosion in its purchasing power over the last century compared to other currencies. Whereas the Gresham's law operated in the world of precious metal-based coins, in today's world of the fiat paper currencies, it is the reverse gear. The strong and good money is now driving out the weak and bad currencies and monies in the global as well as many national economies. The so-called dollarization has occurred in several weak emerging market economies of Panama, El Salvador, and Ecuador, where dollar is a legal tender and the national monies have failed in their useful function of stable money. The dollar is also used in Nicaragua, Uruguay, Belize, Bahamas, Zimbabwe, Haiti, Liberia, Lebanon, Vietnam, and Cambodia along with their local currencies as a legal tender. There are several other countries where dollar notes are unofficially used and circulated.

The currency is a prerogative of the central banks. The central banking acts give them the monopoly or the sole right of notes issue. The central banks want to keep the control of currency which they issue for circulation within its own jurisdiction and its own national borders. The Currency Acts of most countries do not permit the export of their currencies in large quantity to foreign countries. Yet good, strong, and widely accepted currencies are usually in demand also outside the countries of their issue and find their way in foreign countries despite legal restriction on such movement. Some governments have agreed to the dual-currency use. Demand creates its own supply. Good money abhors national borders and travels across counties. Good money also drives bad money out of circulation.

Technology has changed the character of money. For transactions, digital money, i.e., credit and debit cards, is fast replacing the currency globally. The proportion of currency in the money supply is increasingly declining. Digital money is handled by the commercial banks, while the currency is issued by the central banks. The former works for profit, while the latter does not. The digital money has now become global eliminating the need for holding foreign currencies or travelers checks.

Economic Compulsions of Globalization: Genesis

Even metaphorically the world is not flat although it may seem to be flattening under the influence of globalization. In fact its diversity is so immense, and its economic, social, cultural, and political surfaces are so uneven that one needs to take a flight of fantasy to even metaphorically say that the world is flat. Despite the heroic human efforts, the world will continue to offer its distinctive heterogeneity and contrasting disparity. The natural and geographical identities of different regions are so peculiar that they are known from their underlying features. In addition to nature the world is divided by the political boundaries of nation states. If one looks at the wealth of the nations, the levels of economic prosperity or privation offer a sight which is far from being flat. Under the compulsive influence of the MOT (money, organization, and technology) revolution, the world is unleashing its economic growth potential in a pattern far different from the past to level the regional economic disparities. The policy responses of the nation states and the global community have been such to unleash the forces of MOT revolution and not to suppress them. What we have witnessed in the last more than two and half decades is globalization that has reduced the disparities between the nations but has at the same time widened the economic inequalities within nearly all nations. Despite the wider sharing of the benefits of globalization, intranational economic disparities have increased. This is paradoxical but is now corroborated by facts and figures.

The bigger economies are for the first time in history willing to engage in higher volume of trade and investment in order to share their prosperity with other smaller and growing economies, instead of remaining large islands in isolationism. This phase of growth in the global economy has been the second most important turn in the postwar development of the global economy. Both the technology and economic compulsions have helped carve this new phase known as the globalization. Bringing different national economies closer through the removal of restriction on their economic exchanges and thereby allowing all to grow at faster pace, lower economic hardships, better efficiency, and more equitable sharing of their gains has been the goal and meaning of globalization.

The economic compulsions of globalization arise from a number of economic factors:

1. The capital accumulation in the mature capitalistic nations such as the USA, UK, Germany, Japan, and France resulted in decline in the rates of return on capital in their economies to low and stagnating levels.
2. With lower and limited scope for further capital accumulation and investment and slower consumption growth, main impulses of economic growth in the developed economies lost their thrust.
3. The low return on capital and absence of technological innovation made the mature capitalistic nations more prone to recession primarily due to investment drought.
4. Several large commodity and other industries had reached excess capacities and had to cut output due to higher costs despite reaping economies of large scale.
5. The comparative cost differentials in several relatively labor-intensive industries widened between the developed and the emerging market economies.
6. The capital-labor ratio between these two groups of economies continued to widen.
7. Declining rate of return on capital and higher and rising wages in the developed economies raised the comparative advantage in several commodities in favor of the emerging market economies.
8. Lower return on capital and lackluster stock market in the developed economies and higher return on capital and buoyant stock markets in the emerging market economies highlighted the growing mismatch between the demand for and supply of capital between them.
9. This growing mismatch between the two groups of economies underscored the imperative need for the transfer of private capital from the developed to the emerging market economies.

10. The massive transfer of private equity and debt capital involved raising the overall rate of return on global capital.
11. The capital transfer process also meant transfer of technology for creation of output capacities in the emerging markets in industries in which they could have comparative advantage.
12. Technology became an overriding consideration in speedier globalization. Rapid growth and advances in technology and inability to retain monopoly in innovations and new inventions necessitated reaching wider markets through globalization.
13. The developed economies could import low-cost and price products and drive export-led growth in the emerging markets and keep the inflation rate down in their economies.
14. The emerging market economies could drive their growth on import of foreign private capital and technology and exports of goods and services.
15. In effect globalization meant freeing restrictions on trade and capital movement between the developed world and the emerging market economies to achieve higher growth and lower inflation in both the economies, and more efficient allocation and higher return on global capital and resources.

Financing Globalization

The structural change in the US economy towards trade deficit since 1970s from its earlier export surplus status is a change that is not only irreversible but a feature of a mature capitalistic economy. If the US economy had enjoyed export surplus, there would have been ongoing shortage of dollars which the USA would have had to export to the rest of the world to meet its trade deficit. Autonomous export of private capital would have prevented the dollar shortage. In comparison to the trade deficit counterbalanced by autonomous private capital inflow into the economy, the effect on money supply would be the same. However, from the point of view of the global economy and the USA being about 40% its GNP, the US trade deficit is more growth producing for the global economy than the export surplus. The US trade deficit has opened up several growth centers in the exporting nations.

The policy of globalization strongly entrenched in free trade and capital flows has over the years brought a strong pressure on the US economy towards rising trade deficit. The US trade deficit in the heyday of globalization jumped from $111 billion in 1990 to $836 billion in 2006.

In the 1950s and 1960s, the US trade propensities showed the propensity to diverge. In contrast to the rest of world's income elasticity of demand for US exports of 0.99, the US income elasticity of imports was 1.51.[4] "The recent study by IMF measuring price and income elasticities of US imports and exports during 1986–2006 shows a much wider gap between the income elasticities of US imports and

[4] Houthakker and Magee, op.cit., p. 113.

exports. The estimates show the respective elasticities at 1.86 and 0.76, a gap of 1.1, which is double the earlier estimate of 0.5 of 1950s and 1960s.[5] The IMF estimates also vindicates the theory that the conundrum of US trade deficit is deciphered by the Keynesian spending or absorption propensities in the US" [1, p. 44]. The US current account deficit is financed by the foreign central banks holding the US T bills. This is the core around which philosophy of globalization revolves. The US balance of payments policy has entered the phase of "*benign neglect II*" dominated by the Keynesian principle of deficit financing. Now, it is not budget deficit, but it is balance of payments deficit. Keynes has gone international. His principle of deficit financing is now applied to open international economy.

The private spending and investments abroad create current account and balance of payments (BoP) deficit of the USA, which is financed by the flow of public savings of rest of the world into the US T bill. The central banks of BoP surplus emerging markets like China, Russia, South Korea, India, and developed nations of Germany and Japan finance the US private spending and investments. Any disturbance either in spending and investment from the USA or the T bill financing of the US BoP deficit is likely to slow the process of globalization and growth of global economy. So long as the rest of the world's demand for dollar is larger than the US BoP deficit, the central banks of the rest of the world would continue invest the surplus liquidity into the US T bills, and dollar would not weaken in the global currency market. But when the US BoP deficit becomes largest than the rest of the world's demand for dollar, the dollar would continue to weaken and central banks would move away from the US T bill investment. The US current account deficit would not be problem for the USA, so long as it helps in reducing the rate of inflation without causing the problem of unemployment. The US deficit would also be sustainable if the emerging market economies have enough surplus capacities to export goods to the USA without inflation. The current surplus capacities in goods imported by the USA do not warrant any worry also on this score. The process of globalization has continued on sustainable basis in this fashion for the last two and half decades. The current global crisis has to some extent slowed the growth and globalization. The theoretical and practical aspects of financing globalization are discussed in detail in Chap. 8.

References

1. Nayak SS. Globalization and the Indian economy – roadmap to convertible rupee. London/New York: Routledge; 2008.
2. Sachs J. Making the Brady plan work. Foreign Aff. 1989;68(3):91.
3. Bernstein PL. Against the Gods – the remarkable story of risk. New York: Wiley; 1996. p. 247–55.
4. Williamson J, editor. Latin American adjustment: how much has happened. Washington, DC: Institute for International Economics; 1990.

[5] IMF, *World Economic Outlook – Spillovers and Cycles in the Global Economy*, Chapter 3, Exchange Rates and the Adjustment of External Imbalances, Table 3.2, April, 2007.

Chapter 8
Great Crash and Depression: Last Economic Apocalypse: A Relook

> The right remedy for the trade cycle is not to be found in abolishing booms and thus keeping us permanently in a semi-slump; but in abolishing slumps and thus keeping us permanently in a quasi-boom.
>
> John Maynard Keynes, *The General Theory of Employment, Interest and Money, 1936.*

Birth of Capitalism *sans* Economic Insecurity: Fail-Safe Capitalism

Unlike the economic devastation of the Second World War that was motivated primarily by the political rivalry and territorial ambitions, the economic misery of the Great Depression was not a man-made crisis. It was an institutional crisis. The Great Depression was caused by the stress from inadequacy of contemporary institutional framework to deal with the heat and exuberance of growth euphoria and attendant risks. It was a market reaction resulting from the pressure of exuberance of high which the economic and financial institutional and structure failed to cope up with. The prevalent institutional framework possessed neither the potential to assume economic aspirations of people at the height of boom nor the resiliency to guarantee protection from risks emanating from the exuberance of boom and growth fueled by the animal spirits. To a large extent, the current crisis is analogous with crisis of 1930s except that it occurred despite tremendous institutional and regulatory sophistication and safeguards created in the last more than half a century. The amount of legislation on economic and financial affairs and the degree of its refinements that had gone into no doubt created a feeling to everyone's belief that the system possessed the fail-safe mechanism. The crisis did occur, not unwarned though, when the greed of growth and prosperity could not be tamed by the market's assessment of risks and remained beyond contours of the prevalent regulatory framework. The sophisticated financial market products and practices had far outgrown the regulatory apparatus

S. Nayak, *The Global Financial Crisis: Genesis, Policy Response and Road Ahead*,
DOI 10.1007/978-81-322-0798-6_8,

that could restrain it. The deployment of financial resources unleashed by such a fast growth in financial engineering and product sophistication that neither the regulatory system nor the participating banks and institutions could reckon risks was involved. The failure lied in inadequate judgment or quantitative measure of risk which enlarged like a balloon with the confluence of adverse developments. The market mechanism failed without adequate and timely warnings. Finally, it is the frenzy of animal spirits and the system's capability to deal with it which is of crucial importance. The fact that the current crisis did not culminate bigger and larger economic calamity is due to the extent to which the system was adept in responding to it and alacrity with which the US Treasury and the Fed reacted in global coherence.

The Great Depression made the biggest difference to the functionality of capitalism. The economic philosophy on which old-fashioned capitalism functioned was obsolete and could not cope with the worst crisis it had ever confronted. The system needed a revamp, and its logical foundation a change. John Maynard Keynes, Cambridge economist and author of *The General Theory of Money, Income and Employment (1936)* that revolutionized economic theory and prescription, was advocating the change which did not carry majority support in 1930s among not only the political leadership in Britain but also economists. In the USA, Roosevelt followed Keynes' advice on pump priming and deficit financing immediately after he was elected as the President in 1933. Keynes gave new prescription against the collapse of capitalism and proved Marx wrong in his prophecy to emerge as the hero and savior of capitalism. He gave continuity to capitalism by rescuing it from its path of self-destruction once in 1930s. Now is the second time.

The predepression capitalism was devoid of any element of economic security and contained maximum financial and economic vulnerability. The bank deposits were not insured. Illiquid and failing banks could not receive adequate and timely support from the Federal Reserve. There was no social safety net for the unemployed. Looking to the risks inherent in the equity investment in stock market, there was no agency overseeing the functioning of the market and its participants and protection of investor interest. The *laissez-faire* economics advocated no intervention by the government in the downward slide of the economy, which was supposed to be self-correcting. The cyclical behavior of the economy, the inherent behavioral feature of capitalism caused by the free play of competitive markets forces in the economy, was not to be disturbed by government intervention. Such a play of capitalism was used to incur severe economic and social costs by way of bankruptcies and unemployment. Such a face of capitalism without economic security was most vulnerable to attack by economic depression as was experienced in 1930s. It was cowboy capitalism.

Roosevelt's revolutionary legislative package popularly known as the New Deal gave a new face to American capitalism which became a standard model for emulation by other European countries. The transformation of the economy into capitalism with economic security, the fail-safe capitalism, permitted sustained growth in the economy for more than seven decades without any severe and protracted economic misery. With its transformation, American capitalism survived many mini crises which have been overcome to bring the economy back on the track of growth and prosperity. The events of September 2008, however, were too overwhelming to be overtaken by the conventional measures. The edifice of capitalism under the influence of globalization was becoming vulnerable to the shocks from within the system. The situation needed unconventional measures to deal with the new problem. The problem of financial implosion causing a huge hole in the financial system needed to be redressed afresh in order to restore its financial viability and lift the economy from slipping into economic morass.

The 1920s Economic Boom: Golden Age of Prosperity

Despite considerable research and study, the Great Crash of 1929 and 1930s Great Depression still remain an enigma with no unanimity of opinion among economists, researchers, and analysts as to the precise cause of the crisis that was global and continued for a prolonged period nearing a decade. Was it an aberration or a normal cyclical development of the capitalist system? Was it caused by excess capacity or under consumption? Was it the result of vanishing investment opportunities? Did the stock market crash trigger depression? Was the banking crisis and resultant monetary implosion its main cause? Did the weak Federal Reserve fail to respond? To what extent did the prevalent system of gold standard share the blame for the crisis? Was it then the systemic crisis? These are some of the questions which naturally spring up when we think about the dismal era.

A number of studies have been made to analyze the crisis and its causality. Although they show a number of institutional factors and regulatory aspects or their absence to have precipitated the crisis, there seems to be consensus among the economists that the Great Depression was the worst phase of the business or economic cycles that are a peculiarity of the capitalism and, therefore, a market phenomenon.

A precursor to the crash was the economic boom that was taking shape in 1924. The decade of 1920s was one of the most prosperous decades in America's economic history. Only such possible comparison in later years is that of the roaring 1990s. The economic boom of 1990s was more technology driven with microelectronic, telecom, and software revolution, while 1920s was an era of high growth led and sustained primarily by automobile revolution and oil rush. Both the booms ended with the stock market crash. The dot-com bust of 2000 was, however, neither of the magnitude of 1929 crash nor as enduring and far reaching in its effect on the economy.

The economic boom of 1920s was fueled by remarkable growth in wide range of industries such as automobile, steel, aircrafts, aviation and airlines, electricity, chemicals, and oil. It was also an era of great entrepreneurial resurgence in

America. The giant corporations in several industries were developed in this era under the entrepreneurial spirit, drive, and direction of American entrepreneurs and industrialists. Henry Ford's Ford Motors, William Durant's General Motors, John D Rockefeller's Standard Oil, Du Pont's Du Pont, Thomas Edison's General Electric, Charles Schwab's Bethlehem Steel, and David Sarnoff's Radio Corporation of America were all in the forefront of the new industrial era. America was at the center of innovation in automobile, radio, electrical equipment, oil and chemicals, and iron and steel. While the industrial entrepreneurs built new products and capacities, the financial men were also equally ingenious in building institutions, products, and services that allowed the mobilization of resources of millions of households for industrial and business growth. It was the age of creation of the investment bankers at the Wall Street, and prominent among them were J P Morgan, Goldman and Sachs, Lehman brothers, Merrill Lynch, and Paul Warburg.

During 1920s, the production and employment in America was high and rising. The index of industrial production rose by 70%, GNP by 40%, and per capita income by 30% in 1922–1928. These 7 years of economic growth are often described as the golden age of prosperity. The automobile output increased from 4.3 million in 1926 to 5.4 million in 1929. In comparison new car registrations were 5.7 million in 1953. Henry Ford's immortal T Model was on the rising curve of popularity. The prices of automobiles fell from $2,120 to $800 after Ford introduced Model T. The car population reached 23 million with 3.5 million trucks. One in five American owned a car. "Like railroads too, the automobile drastically reconfigured the American landscape and its demographics" [1]. The most critical element that supported the auto growth and created a new way of life was the State and Federal government funding for creation of network of roads and highways connecting all towns with more than 50,000 population that helped development of satellite towns and suburban areas around the big cities and metropolises.

On the financial side, the monetary policy during this period was also favorable to innovation, economic growth, and boom. Inflation during and after the World War I, which ended in 1918, had reached high level requiring the Fed to raise interest rates. The rediscount rate was gradually raised from 4% in 1919 to 7% in 1920. However, quick recovery in industrial production and decline in inflation rate thereafter led to the Fed reducing the rate to 4.5% by the end of 1921.

Along with the stock market euphoria, the Great Depression was also preceded by the housing and real estate boom. Until the World War I, most of the houses in the USA were bought from own saving and borrowings from friends and relatives. This changed in 1920s when mortgages were available but up to the period of 5 years. In fact the housing boom was financed by the sharp rise in mortgage lending during 1920s. It was similar to the spurt in subprime mortgages in 2001–2007. When housing boom burst, the mortgage foreclosures mounted from about 100,000 in 1927 to a quarter million in 1933.

The great real estate boom was more pronounced in Florida and more particularly in Miami and other beach and coastal locations. Had it not been for the worst hurricane that hit Miami in the autumn of 1926, the boom which petered out in 1928 would have lasted longer. An instrument which played an important role in promoting huge speculative investment in land in Florida was the "binders." "Such is the genius of capitalism that where a real demand exists it does not go unfulfilled. In all great speculative orgies, devices have appeared to enable the speculator so to concentrate on his business. In the Florida boom, the trading was in 'binders'. Not the land but the right to buy the land at a stated price was traded. This right to buy – which was obtained by a down payment of 10% of the purchase price – could be sold. It thus conferred on the speculators the full benefit of the increase in values" [2, p. 46]. This instrument raised the speculative demand for land and pushed up land prices at faster rate. It was like margin trading in land.

The international circumstances were favorable to the USA. Britain returned to the gold standard in 1925 against the advice of Keynes at the pre-World War I exchange rate of $4.86 per pound to regain its financial supremacy or hegemony. This decision has now been seen in retrospect and on research as one of greatest errors of judgment in economic history. The British pound was clearly overvalued at this exchange rate, and consequences became visible soon. Britain began to face heavy trade deficit and lost gold heavily to the USA in its effort to maintain its exchange parity. Stressed by the exchange crisis, heads of the central banks of England, Germany, and France made a pilgrimage in the USA to urge the Federal Reserve to follow easy money policy and reduce interest rates. The Federal Reserve obliged by reducing the rediscount rate from 4 to 3.5% in the spring of 1927.

Stock Market Boom: 1920s

The stock market is thought to be the fair-weather cock of economy. It renders direction in which the economy is moving. Yet at times the stock market can turn irrational and be either overly optimistic or pessimistic. These mood swings of the market usually occur at its extremes and are in fact a reflection of the human behavior of greed and panic in times when its expectational risk-return matrix becomes uncontrollably irrational and unreliable for decisions about future. This is typical of all boom–bust market phenomena since the great Tulip mania attacking the Dutch golden age in 1637 until the more recent 1929 Great Crash, 1987 crash, or Y2K dot-com boom–bust. The subprime debt crisis is no different than these earlier crisis in terms of excessive or even extravagant financial exposures on the buildup expectations that depart more and more from prudence, rationality, and reality. The reversal of expectations by any economic or even noneconomic factor is enough to burst the bubble causing financial and monetary implosion. Consequently, drastic contraction of money supply and liquidity sets in motion serious deflationary forces in the economy.

The golden age prosperity of 1920s also led the stock market boom and bull market at the Wall Street. The securities prices began to rise rapidly in the last 6 months of 1924. Dow Jones Industrial Average shot up from a low of 64 in 1921 to the high of 381 in 1929, an increase of 495% in 8 years, an average annual return of 62%. The volume of shares traded at NYSE marched up from 162 million in 1921 to a record 573 million in 1927. Darling of the market General Motors was quoting at $187, ten times earnings. Du Pont went up from $310 to $525, Radio Corporation from $85 to $420, Montgomery Ward from $117 to $440, and Wright Aeronautic from $69 to $289 during the year. The volume of shares traded on the New York Stock Exchange jumped further from 573 million in 1927 to record 920 million in 1928. The market was undoubtedly fueled by large increase in margin business [2, p. 45]. The cheap credit was one of factors that fueled the stock market speculation on heavy leveraging with small margins in the last phase of the boom. This is the year in which the "irrational exuberance" was building up that was to be the precursor to the crash.

The stock market boom in 1920s was reflected in the volume of margin trading. The brokers' loans—loans collateralized by the securities purchased on margin—which were from $1 to 1.5 billion in the early 1920s increased to $2.5 billion in early 1926, to $3.5 billion in 1927, and to a record $6 billion by the end of 1928. While the risk-free rate—gilt edged rate—was 5%, the call money rate and rate on margin money for securities shot up to 12%. At this rate even the corporates were tempted to lend their surplus funds to the Wall Street. The New York banks borrowed money from the Federal Reserve at 5% and lent it in the call money market at 12% [2, pp. 48–50]. The stock market had reached its highest level in the boom.

The Great Crash of 1929

The cheap money policy encouraged 1920s economic boom. As is often the case, market frenzy can fizzle out only with some regulatory action or monetary policy measure like interest rate hike. The increase in interest rate in most cases triggers the crisis in the market built on irrational expectations not realizable in performance.

On October 23, 1929, Wednesday, a sharp sell off in automobile stocks sent the wave of selling and liquidation in motion. Dow dropped 20 points with 6.4 million shares traded. By October end Dow slumped to 273 from the high of 381, a fall of 28%. All the gains of the year were wiped out. The relentless decline and one way trend in the market continued with Dow going below 200 level on November 13, 1929, a further 48% drop.

In order to stabilize the markets, the Fed cut the interest rate from 5 to 4.5%. There were some gains in December and January 1930. The Fed cut rate by 0.5 to 4% and from 3.5 to 3% in May 1930, and again to 2.5%. The stock market temporarily recovered reacting to the sharp cuts in interest rates with Dow rebounding to 294 in 1930. However, the market could not stand in wake of continuing bad

Fig. 8.1 The Great Crash 1929 and after

economic news and dropped to a low of 117 in 1931 and further to the lowest level of 41 in 1932, 89% drop from the high of 1929 (Fig. 8.1).

Although stock market was overheated, nobody anticipated the crash. After Herbert Hoover was elected with a landslide victory as the President in 1928, he was concerned about the growing tide of stock market and probably had a premonition of crash. However, the market reacted and rallied with the victory boom. Despite his conviction about the market behavior, he could not do anything to tame the market for the fear of letting the booming economy come to a halt.

Prominent economists and advisers to governments could not correctly judge the fall of the market. Irving Fisher, America's legendary economist from Yale University, who developed index numbers and equation of the quantity theory of money, and also a great investor in the stock market, also missed the right judgment on the stock market boom. Being a bull and resisting selling his holdings, he incurred severe losses due to huge margin calls during the crash. Although he could not predict the crash, after the crash he foresaw and warned about Great Depression ahead. His solution, however, remained restricted to his own confines of quantity theory. He advocated new discoveries of gold and increasing gold production so that the Fed could expand money supply to avert depression. In contrast Keynes suggested government spending through deficit financing that would also expand money supply. Keynes was also a seasoned investor trading in currencies, stocks, bonds, and commodities. He was managing the funds of his College at Cambridge, Provincial Insurance Company, and National Mutual. He lost more money in 1937 Wall Street crash than in 1929 [3, pp. 417–8, 565].

The public memory is short and this is more true of markets. The cyclicality of the economic system and its behavior is the inherent feature of capitalism. Although the downward swing of the economy has been halted with more proactive fiscal and monetary policy measures and much better institutional framework for the functioning of the financial system and its regulation, the periodic ups and downs in the economy and more so in the financial and capital markets have not been eliminated. The stock markets, being the most liquid markets trading in the bits of ownership of risk capital, have traditionally been the most sensitive institution in the economic system. Any change in an economy having influence on business is rapidly sensed by the stock markets first. In fact markets are rather more anticipatory and do not wait even for the evidence of change. Driven by the expectations, the markets move quickly on anticipation of change. As the collective voice of buyers and sellers of risk capital in different industries, business, and services, the stock markets give the signals of millions of participants about the future. The markets are not predictive but they are signals, perspective of the millions on the available information and future expectations. As to the question what caused the crash, there is no firm answer.

"No one was responsible for the great Wall Street crash. No one engineered the speculation that preceded it. Both were the product of the free choice and decisions of thousands of individuals" [3, p. 28]. This was an era of total free markets with little regulatory oversight. The Securities and Exchange Commission (SEC) did not exist in 1929 to regulate the stock markets and their participants.

Political Reaction to the Great Crash: Measures in Desperation

The Great Crash of 1929 shook the foundations of American capitalism and the political faith in the ideology as the only way toward continuing economic prosperity. The realization that the capitalism needs several safeguards, fail-safe mechanisms, safety nets, and support system from the State for its revitalization did not go very easily with the polity. The conventional wisdom of *laissez-fairism*, balanced budget, and gold standard was so dominant and widely entrenched not only among the politicians but also general public, that any idea for a drastic change was a political suicide and needed political audacity due to the overwhelming compulsion of public education on the issue.

A wrong diagnosis of an illness can result in wrong prescription. In the wake of declining production and prices, one of the ways to arrest the declining trend is to eliminate the threat from imports and give protection to domestic production of farm and industrial products through restrictions on trade such as quotas and tariffs on imports. In the orthodox diagnosis, it was a remedy which in reality turned out to be worse in global context. In Keynesian analysis, it was a most retrograde move.

The cause of declining output and prices was not competition from imports but inadequate domestic demand and expenditure. One such wrong measure was the *Smoot–Hawley Tariff Act* passed in 1930. It imposed 40% tariff on imports, intended to promote demand for American products in the country and reduce unemployment. It was another misconceived and shortsighted policy act non-Ricardian and anti-Keynesian, which further worsened the global depression and postponed the chances of early global recovery. When the US imports accounted for 6% of GDP in 1930, there was no logic in imposing this tariff which was to have very little impact in increasing aggregate demand in the USA. On contrary it triggered retaliatory measures from the other nations reducing the volume of global trade. By 1932 the global trade declined to two-third the level in 1929. The *Smoot–Hawley Act* was a measure taken in desperation. In 1932, in order to raise the government finances, another anti-Keynesian measure was adopted that further dampened the private spending, lowering aggregate demand, and tightening the grip of depression. The maximum income tax rate was raised from 25 to 63%, when exactly opposite should have happened to release income for higher spending among individuals and families. The logic was that to spend more government needed more money which it intended to raise by increasing the tax rate on the rich. It was like adding fuel to the fire in the midst of thick depression. It also demonstrates how frantic the polity was to tackle depression.

Renowned Cambridge economist John Maynard Keynes was the messiah that spread the message of change to save the capitalism from its ultimate devastation. The institution of capitalism needed much broader and deeper regulatory framework to avoid it from running again on to its devastating course and damaging the financial and economic fabric of society. Only when President Roosevelt came to power in 1933, he mustered political courage to undertake a comprehensive overhaul of American capitalism passing several legislations, setting up comprehensive regulatory institutional framework for banking and stock market, which were the main focal points of the crisis, and concerning government spending for economic and social infrastructure, welfare, and security.

President Roosevelt's first 100 days were historic in passing several legislation beginning an era active and potent government intervention in the economy undertaking the commitment to revive the economy on the strength of government spending and not leave it in the private hands. The new era of American capitalism ushered in to establishing the fail-safe mechanism for the system making it depression free.

Great Crash and Monetary Implosion

While the 1929 stock market crisis was the starting point or a trigger for the downward spiral of economic activities in the USA, the crisis spread to other sectors and engulfed them at a much faster pace rather than being repelled by or contained by the other sectors, mainly the banking sector. When the banks failed due to liquidity crisis, the Federal Reserve could not provide adequate finance or credit to the failing banks due to its relatively limited reserve position. In fact the hard line in the *laissez-faire* saw failing of the weak banks as sign of system emerging stronger. This misconception triggered a chain reaction of bank failures.

As the banking crisis worsened in the USA between 1929 and 1933, 10,500 banks closed, nearly 40% of the banking system. The commercial bank deposits fell by $18 billion, 42%. M1 fell by 33% from $24 billion to $19 billion [4]. The currency in circulation was in severe short supply. Apart from this there was considerable decline in the velocity of bank money, i.e., the demand deposits which together brought a severe deflationary impact on business and economy. At this juncture when bank deposits and money supply shrank, the Fed could have entered into open-market operations purchasing securities and injecting liquidity into the system. This did not happen due to some members thinking that additional liquidity would again go into speculative activities in stock market and real estate and others believing that monetary policy was ineffective to stem depression. Further, the world was still on gold standard with the central banks defending currency convertibility into gold at fixed price. In Britain, the declining gold reserves of Bank of England forced her to abandon the gold standard in September 1931. This resulted in the run on dollar, since the dollar had continued to remain on gold standard and preserved the dollar convertibility into gold. In 6 weeks, the USA lost gold of $700 million to Europe. Under the gold standard, the drain of gold further constrained the ability of the Fed to purchase securities in the market when Fed actually sold securities to maintain the gold-liabilities margin. It was the *Glass–Steagall Act* of 1932 which finally allowed the Fed to issue paper currency against the government bonds. Although the demand for currency by public was met, the continuing drain of gold to other countries was threatening the gold reserve position of the Fed.

Onset of Great Depression

The roaring growth of 1920s was beginning to recede in August 1929, 2 months before the stock market crash. The stock market crashed on October 24, but it was on Black Tuesday, October 29 that the investors incurred record losses. The sales and production had begun declining much earlier, and stock piles of goods were mounting to the level three times the year earlier. Despite the sharp cut in interest rate from 6 to 4% in February 1930, the economy continued its downslide. The worst was the spate of run on banks leading to failures that created panic. The money supply contracted contributing to economic gloom. The GNP fell by 9% and unemployment increased from 3.2 to 9% in 1930. With no major action taken to fight depression in 1931, economy further declined by 9% and unemployment rose to 16%.

Although a declining sector in the early 1920s, the agriculture still formed one of the lead sectors of the economy providing 25% employment. The agriculture constituted 8% Of GNP, and 25% of farm production was exported. Automobiles and tractors had revolutionized farming raising its productivity bringing the sector into overproduction. Resultantly, when recession set in 1930 and spread to Europe, both the domestic and export demand for farm products declined causing the crash in food prices.

The depression brought as much or more suffering in the agriculture or farm sector in the rural areas than the industrial sector in the urban areas. In 1930 about 44% of the American population was rural. Nearly 57 million people lived on farms or towns dependent on agriculture and 31 million were farmers. The agriculture offered the perfect canvass for the Adam Smith's free market, and free market did prevail for farm products during the predepression period. As the stock market crash of 1929 and the banking crisis spread to the other sectors through the implosion of demand for industrial and farm products, their prices also began to crash. So sharp was the decline in the prices of farm products that in 1932 prices were 53% lower than in 1929. In 1932, the GNP fell further by 13.4% and unemployment rose to 23.6%. With bank failures and monetary contraction leading to deep depression, the industrial stocks lost 80% of their value in 1930.

Gold Standard and Depression

Yet another institutional factor that contributed to the depression was the system of gold standard. It restricted the central banks from pursuing expansionary policy in the wake of falling growth and rising unemployment and deflation. There was an overall systemic deflationary influence due to limited output and supplies of gold to the central banks of the USA, Britain, France, and Germany. "The Depression was not even inevitable in 1929. Had the policy makers been able to free themselves from the straight jacket of the gold standard, they could have instituted counter cyclical policies. But without that change, the rule of gold standard mandated deflation" [5]. In his study on the Great Depression, Temin identified four factors in the USA that contributed to the deflationary tendency in the economy to culminate into full-fledged depression. They are the 1929 stock market crash, the *Smoot–Hawley tariff Act* of 1930, the banking crisis that followed, and the worldwide collapse of the commodity prices. These factors offer a mix of institutional inadequacies and outdatedness and also weaknesses of the free unregulated market mechanism. They collectively contributed to the Great Depression. Galbraith and Shiller have examined the effect of the great stock market crash. Dornbusch and Fischer have studied the impact of tariff. Friedman and Schwartz have researched the banking collapse of 1930, and Kindelberger has identified the impact of fall in commodity prices. Despite the ambivalence on the causality of these factors in depression, Temin emphasizes that restrictive monetary and fiscal policy under the compulsions of the rules of the gold standard and balanced budget to be most important factor responsible for prolonged depression. This is also empirically proven by Bernanke's research that found the countries that abandoned the gold standard did not feel the higher gravity of depression and recovered early [6].

The decision to revert to gold standard by Winston Churchill, who was the Chancellor of Exchequer of Britain, in 1925 at prewar parity of $4.866 was a disaster. It was an "economic hara-kiri." Harry Johnson described it as "an act of blind traditionalism." Galbraith called it "the most decisively damaging action involving money in modern times." Severe economic downturn and falling gold stocks led finally to the Britain abandoning the gold standard in September 1931 and constituting the Sterling Area, a regional currency arrangement to clear the payments from countries dealing with Britain in pound sterling. Roosevelt after assuming power in 1933 paved the way for the USA abandoning gold standard which was resisted earlier by Hoover. The commodity prices had fallen to such a low level that only abandonment of gold standard, devaluation of dollar, and increase in the price of gold could reverse deflationary prices and start recovery. This was required to be combined with low interest policy and public works program. "Keynes advocated for both the Great Britain and the United States a policy of devaluation combined with public works and lower long term interest rates" [6, p. 38]. The USA possessed 42.5% of monetary gold stocks of the world. By 1933 21 countries including the USA, France, Italy, and Germany followed suit in abandoning the gold standard. Yet, nearly 46 countries imposed tariffs and quotas to conserve gold and currency reserve [6, p. 15]. The world economy had entered the worst phase of retaliatory economic policies that shrank the world trade and further accentuated the domestic deflationary forces in all the economies.

Bernanke's treatise on Great Depression conclusively proves with econometric analysis of very extensive data base covering large number of factors that the deficiency of aggregate demand which persisted for so long a number of years was caused by contraction of money supply which in turn was the result of the improper institutional framework of gold standard, inadequacies in Federal Reserve System, and bank failures that reduced the overall banking deposit base [6, pp. 5–37]. The banking panics and wave bank failures which affected just above half the number that existed were a great shock to the financial system. "...the number of banks operating at the end of 1933 was just above the half in 1929. The banks that survived experienced heavy losses" [6, p. 44]. Friedman and Schwartz also made detailed documentation and study of the impact of contraction of deposit base leading to credit squeeze and contraction of money supply and its impact on output. Before 1931 the export surplus countries like the USA and France, which were gaining gold, sterilized the gold flows and did not allow their natural expansionary impact on money supply under gold standard to happen [6, p. 156]. "Our most important finding is the confirmation of the view that monetary forces played an important role in the world depression both in early and later stages" [6, p. 156]. Fortunately, when the current crisis struck, Ben Bernanke was at the helm of affairs at the Fed, which controls the US financial aggregates.

Income Inequalities and Deficiency of Demand

The inequality of wealth and income in the 1920s was not only increasing with general economic prosperity but also threatening to tread into the level where it could result in insufficient aggregate demand to sustain growth further. One of the real causes of depression is also the growing inequality of incomes. "Between 1920 and 1929, per capita disposable income of all Americans rose by 9%, but the top 1%

of the income recipients enjoyed a whopping 75% increase in disposable income. The share of disposable income going to the top 1% jumped from 12% in 1920 to 19% in 1929. Here in stark statistics was one of the principal causes of the Great Depression" [6, p. 38]. Equally bad or worse was the distribution of wealth. Nearly 80% of the families—some 21.5 million households had no savings. The 2.3% families controlled two-thirds of America's savings, and top 0.5% of Americans in 1929 owned 32.4% of all net wealth of individuals. One of the reasons for growing inequalities was that the productivity was growing at a much faster rate than the wages. Between 1923 and 1929, the labor productivity went up by 32%, but wages rose by only 8%. The corporate profits went up by 62% and dividends by 65%.

Both Marx and Keynes identified growing income inequalities as one of the weaknesses of capitalism that would lead to its collapse. Keynes introduced the concept of propensity to consume, a relationship between individual consumption and income, and pointed out that since the rich have low propensity to consume than the poor, growing inequality of incomes would reduce the growth of effective demand in the economy. The resultant deficiency of aggregate demand would be one of the causes of depression, he argued.

The New Deal: Roosevelt's 100 Days of Silent Revolution: American Capitalism Under Reform

The biggest differences in dealing with depression came from the perception of the US President about the crisis and the measures taken to combat the same. President Herbert Hoover despite the best intention could not come out of the classical economic thought and conventional wisdom to overcome depression. In the light of deflationary pressures, sharp fall in investments and corporate incomes, falling consumption, massive erosion in farm incomes due falling commodity prices, and record unemployment, Hoover blamed the crisis on the trouble in Europe. He held the war reparations of Germany, abandonment of gold standard by Britain, and formation of the sterling bloc that affected the US farm exports to be responsible for the worsening crisis. With this mind set, he could only deal with problem in a limited manner and was also firm on the US adherence to gold standard [7]. This resulted in continuation of deflationary monetary policy by the Federal Reserve.

The focus of all nations was on conserving the gold reserves, the exact error which Adam Smith and Ricardo had warned against. Nation's wealth does not lie in its gold reserves but in its tempo of generating national output and income. But in the pre-Keynesian world, this perception was rare. Only Keynes' *General Theory* changed that perception and view of the functioning of an economy and its main growth drivers. Retaliatory tariff policy further accentuated depression. At this stage it was imperative to have international cooperation in abandoning gold standard and moving to a more functional and equitable international monetary system, agreeing on withdrawing all tariff restrictions and promoting expansionary fiscal monetary policy without constraint of balanced budget.

Beginning in 1933 Roosevelt mounted a heavy attack on the ills of the economy and ushered a new era of massive government intervention through new legislations that resurrected the falling market economy. It provided ample financial support to farmers, industrial units, corporates, and households to rejuvenate the economy, and increased government expenditure through several infrastructure projects to generate more employment. The Keynesian theory and its political agenda in the American form of the New Deal not only transformed the American *laissez-faire* economy rendering it a fresh lease of life but also permanently changed the character of the economy, where the government assumed and retained responsibility for proactive role and action in the guidance and regulation of its course. Economy was no longer left to the mercy of the *laissez-faire* market mechanism, nor was economic and social welfare left to the mercy of the free market economy. If the market failure took heavy toll on welfare of the society, government stepped in time and in right measure redressing the heavy and unpalatable imbalance in the economy.

The New Deal under President Roosevelt increased the role of government and public spending to revive the economy, provided unemployment insurance, established Securities Exchange Commission to regulate the stock market, and extended deposit insurance to mitigate suffering of small depositors in bank failures. All this took America on the brave new path of progress, prosperity, and welfare. Roosevelt was working assiduously giving the right shape to this historic task of burying the edifice of *laissez-faire* that was to be the doom of capitalism worldwide in 1930s and architecting and building the new crisis proof economic infrastructure capable of weathering the vicissitudes of cyclical, free market dominated economy. "His top priority was to use this moment of political, sociological, ideological disruption to accomplish reforms that he had thought well before the Great Depression came along were necessary to make modern American life viable. Single word that sums up. Social Security Act. Unmistakably the touchstone and core of everything he wanted to accomplish: take the risk out of old age, mortgage lending, securities trading–or at least reduce the risk in all these sectors; and to make American life across the board for individuals and institutions more predictable and less susceptible to these wild ups and downs that had been characteristic of the American economy since the early nineteenth century, since the United States had entered the early industrial revolution era. He got a lot of that accomplished" [8].

The legislative and regulatory reforms Roosevelt introduced after he took power as the President in January 1933 were unprecedented, historic, broad based, and far reaching in their effect. The most important piece of legislation which restored stability and order to the banking system was the *Emergency Banking Relief Act (1933)* to reorganize and reopen failed banks. It also gave the powers to the President to declare national emergency and has absolute control over the national finance and foreign exchange. It permitted the treasury to take control of and operate any bank, by a takeover or nationalization. It put moratorium on debts of all banks. It also gave far reaching powers to the Federal Reserve convert all the US debt obligations into cash at 90% of its apparent value, unsecured loans to member banks at 1% over the discount rate, and secured loans against government securities for 90 days. Within a few days of the Act, nearly 500 banks reopened, and two-third of the banking system started operating. This single legislation restored the US banking system from its total collapse.

Yet another revolutionary step by Roosevelt was to end the gold standard in 1933 by stopping the convertibility of dollars into gold by the Federal Reserve and nationalizing the private gold holdings at a price of $20.67 per an ounce of gold. The government received $300 million of gold coins and $470 million of gold certificates from private holdings. In 1934, the gold price was raised to $35 per an ounce. This increased the balance sheet size of the Fed by 69% and enabled it to expand money supply so very necessary to promote economic recovery. The conventional wisdom had for long time resisted this move which was indispensable for economic recovery.

The Great Crash of 1929 had taken heavy toll of the banking system. The banks were blamed for their large involvement in stock market investments, lending margin money to brokers and investors, and underwriting of the new issues. The involvement of banks with investment banking activity was frown upon by the regulators. This resulted in the passing of another piece of legislation, *the Glass–Steagall Act (1933),* as a part of the New Deal. The Act was responsible for separation of investment banking from commercial banking. *The Glass–Steagall Act* created a regulatory barrier between commercial banking and investment banking and prevented the commercial banks from lending or underwriting for stock market investments and thereby deterred the excessive speculation in stocks. It limited the involvement of commercial banks in lending for investment banking and stock market related activities.

The Act was repealed in 1999 in the light of emergence and growth of universal banking in Europe. The US banks could not engage in investment banking activity, while the large European banks could. This placed the large US banks to disadvantage against their European competitors. The lobbying by the US financial services industry finally resulted in the repeal of the *Glass–Steagall Act* that enabled the US banks a level playing field in the international arena. The subprime debt crisis, however, raised doubts over the wisdom of the repeal of *Glass–Steagall Act.*

The most reassuring measure for the banking system was the creation of the *Federal Deposit Insurance Corporation* insuring the deposits of banks against the bank failures. *Homeowners Refinancing Act (1933)* provided low interest loans and mortgage assistance or refinancing to homeowners for homes facing foreclosures. The assistance covered nearly 29% of urban homes. *National Industrial Recovery Act (1933)* allowed $3.3 billion to be spent for the construction of public works to create employment and purchasing power and revive the American industry. *The Securities Act (1933)* sought to protect investor interests by requiring material information about the securities offered to public for sale. This Act led to the legislation of another landmark step in the financial industry, viz., *Securities Exchange Commission Act (1934),* and a significant move to set up Securities and Exchange Commission, a federal agency, for the oversight of the securities markets and enforcement of the securities laws.

Two more steps which relate to the housing, housing finance, and home mortgage industry were *National Housing Act (1933)* which created Federal Housing

Administration (FHA) and Federal Savings and Loan Insurance Corporation to promote home ownership and housing industry. The Congress also authorized the creation of the *Agricultural Adjustment Administration* and the *Farm Credit Administration* to provide credit to farmers, avoid foreclosures of farm loans, and support farm prices. *The Federal Emergency Relief Administration, the National Recovery Administration, the Public Works Administration, the Tennessee Valley Authority, and the Civilian Conservation Corps* were intended to create jobs, generate incomes and spending to revive overall demand for farm and industrial products, and thereby induce new investments.

All these measures produced significant impact in lowering the GDP decline to 2.1% in 1933 although unemployment rose marginally to 24.9%. The economy turned around in 1934 with the GNP growth of 7.7% and unemployment lowering to 21.7%. Although GNP continued to grow, the reduction in unemployment rate was slower. By 1937 unemployment rate had fallen to 14.3%. The GDP at current prices which had fallen from $104 billion in 1929 to the low of $56 billion in 1933 began gradually rising in 1934, but to cross $100 billion mark again only in 1940. While it took 11 years for the USA to reach the predepression GDP of $100 billion, the recovery of Dow Industrial was much prolonged, and the predepression level was reached only in 1954, 25 years to reach back to 386.

The political sagacity and economic magnanimity which President Roosevelt displayed in advocating and passing the New Deal have hardly any parallel in history. The reform of American capitalism was so deep rooted and broad based that the system not only survived any minor economic hiccups but paved safe and steady path of economic progress until 2008. The New Deal is now completing the three quarters of a century without leaving any of its institutional structure obsolete. It was a formidable effort based on the Keynesian philosophy. The institutional arrangements of the New Deal have been far reaching in its provision of welfare as well as the regulation of the excesses of capitalism. The New Deal architecture has not only survived the test of time but also has steered the American capitalism across the vicissitudes of economic fluctuations and impacts of social transformation, political changes, and technological advances.

The current crisis has a different underpinning. It concerns the overgrowth, sophistication, and tremendous synthesis and transition in financial markets arising from structural changes in the economy in the new age of globalization and imperatives of urges of the growth dynamics of capitalism. These aspects will be discussed later.

Although Roosevelt reformed the capitalism through several legislative changes and built a new edifice which was broader and stronger in withstanding shocks, there is wide belief that more government spending was needed to hasten the recovery which was slow and prolonged till 1937 when the economy suffered another relapse. "Roosevelt's New Deal achieved long-lasting improvements in the US banking system and transport infrastructure, but the amount of 'stimulus' was actually quite small. Keynes attacked President's National Recovery Act of 1933 for putting reforms before recovery, and reckoned (in 1934) that loan-financed spending $4.8 billion a year (amounting to close to $76.5 billion today), or 11% of US national income was needed to set America firmly on the road to recovery" [9].

Budget Deficit, Depression, and Economic Revival

The conservative philosophy of *laissez-faire* and balanced budget dominated the economic policy and governance throughout the 1920s both in the USA and also the Europe. Except for the large budget deficit in the USA in 1918 and 1919 to the tune of $9 billion and $13 billion, incurred primarily to finance World War I, the government finances returned to surplus later. These deficits were large in absolute terms as well as in relation to GDP and were nearly two-thirds of the government expenditure. During the 1920s, the budget surpluses ranged between $500 million and 900 million with record surplus of $1.1 billion in 1927. The stock market crash and depression did not much change the budget status in 1929 and 1930 with the continuing surpluses of $734 million and $738 million. It shows how wrong was the understanding about behavior of an economy, its main growth drivers, and what should be the policy to overcome economic downturn. It was a pre-Keynesian era. During 1931–1933, the GDP declined in current dollars from $104 billion by the one-third and in constant dollars by the one-fifth. The effect on employment was most devastating. The unemployment of 1.6 million in 1929 constituting 3.25% of the labor force peaked at 12.1 million, nearly a quarter of the labor force in 1932. The interest in effect of Keynes' ideas to tackle depression and the influence of the Keynesian philosophy seem to have grown gradually from 1932. A marginal budget deficit of $462 million in 1931 turned into deficit of $2.7 billion in 1933. The deficit rose sharply to $3.5 billion, 5.4% of GDP in 1934, and to $4.3 billion, 5.1% of GDP and half of government expenditure in 1936. The government expenditure during the period increased two-and-half times. Contrasting the *laissez-faire* philosophy, the size of the government in the economy also rose from mere 3% on the eve of depression in 1929 to 10% in 1936. The decline in GDP which began in 1931 was reversed in 1934 when the economy grew by 10%. By 1936 the economy reached its 1929 real GDP level. Although the downswing in the economy halted in 1934 and it reverted to its growth path, it took much longer to restore unemployment figure at a respectable level.

When the capitalist world was reeling under the pressure of severe depression and rising unemployment in the early 1930s, one country in Europe was well ahead in fighting record joblessness. When Nazis came to power in Germany in 1933, Hitler had perhaps fully grasped the new economic ideas of Keynes and their implication for fighting unemployment. With his socialistic leanings, he was quick in understanding and implementing Keynes' concept much before Britain did. He started huge government spending programs through large-scale public borrowings for building roads, railways, canals, and land development schemes and even subsidizing the private sector to promote investment. The famous Autobahn project was initiated in this period. By 1936 when Britain and America were still struggling with the unemployment rate of 15% or more, the problem almost disappeared in Germany. Within 3–4 years of Hitler's policies masterminded by his Finance Minister Herr Schat, nearly six million jobless got jobs. Germany followed the policy of deficit financing, and it was this Keynesian policy which was the single most determining factor behind Hitler's popularity [10, 11]. The evidence of German experience clearly demonstrates how, in matters of economic policy, conventional wisdom and political dogmatism can be a big roadblock toward progress and openness to new ideas, and exercising political expediency and pragmatism can pave smooth path to economic prosperity. When rest of the capitalist world still suffered from the prangs of depression, Germany was far ahead with near full employment, rising output and wages.

Another development that speeded up the German economic progress during the depression years was Hitler's plan to replicate the US automobile revolution of 1920s by making Volkswagen the Model T of Germany. The automobile revolution was in the forefront of the US economic boom. It was Henry Ford's T Model that reduced the price of car from $850 in 1909 to $260 in 1920s transforming the car market from luxury to utility and ushered new phase of economic boom in the USA.

Stock Market Crash and Banking Crisis: Then and Now

How does the current crisis differ from the Great Depression? The stock market crash of 1929 was a catastrophic event that preceded the onset of depression. The crash also coincided with the real estate burst. Since the banks had heavily financed both highly leveraged land and stock speculation, the real estate and stock market collapse triggered a wave of bank failures. The Keynesian Revolution had not arrived. The political ideology was strongly entrenched with the economic philosophy of balanced budget and *laissez-fairism* and gold standard. With the unshakable political faith in these twin doctrines, the takeover or support of failing banks was unthinkable. "Let the weak, inefficient, unviable, and overexposed banks fail." That was the motto of traditional capitalism and market fundamentalism. The Federal Reserve System created in 1913 was a fledgling quasi-public institution, also weaker in size, legislative powers, and control in the context of the size of the banking system. The state-wise regulation of banking was also another hurdle in ushering uniform and decisive supportive action to avert bank failures. The authorities could not cope with the disastrous consequences of *laissez-fairism* or limited Fed intervention in bank failures due to the institutional inadequacies. "In 1929, 659 banks failed a fair number after the crash. In 1930, 1,352 went under and in 1931, 2,294. … By the end of 1933, nearly half of all the nation's banks had disappeared" [12, pp. 232, 240].

In 1933, Roosevelt suspended the gold standard which had brought uncontrollable monetary expansion in the USA in the 1920s, as it was the gold-gaining country under gold standard with fixed exchange rates. The European nations which were losing gold experienced monetary contraction. He also extensively reformed the Federal Reserve System giving it greater powers to deal with extraordinary banking crisis. Federal Deposit Insurance Corporation (FDIC) was created and capitalized by the Treasury and Federal Reserve Banks. "The anarchy of uncontrolled banking had been brought to an end not by the Federal Reserve System but by the FDIC" [12, p. 240].

Fig. 8.2 2008 crisis and stock market crash (Source: Yahoo Finance)

The current financial crisis bears considerable degree of resemblance with 1929 crisis. Due to several systemic improvements in banking system, the banking crisis was averted, but both the crises were triggered by the real estate fall and banking failures. The difference is that the current crisis did not emanate from the stock market crash as did 1929 crisis, and the stock market went into a bearish phase in 2008 following the news of events of the subprime crisis. The stock market was not overvalued at the peak of its boom, as it was in 1929. The subprime loan delinquency was the main trigger for the current crisis which was diffused by the prompt and decisive action from the government and the Fed. The blowout of a full-scale banking crisis was averted (Fig. 8.2).

In 1929, Dow Jones Industrial fell by 48% from its high, rebounded by 48% in 1930, but fell again in 1931 by 60%, and further 64% in 1932. The Dow Jones lost 89% from its high of 381 in 1929 to 41 in 1932. Both the dot-com as well as the subprime crises did not have such a sharp and prolonged adverse impact on the stock market. But if the 1 year fall in both crises are considered, they are comparable in their shock. Dow Jones Industrial lost 61% in a year in the dot-com crisis and 47% in the subprime crisis.

The subprime took a heavy toll on the banking system although it was not allowed to have a snowballing effect like in 1930. Three largest and oldest investment banks, Bear Sterns, Lehman Brothers, and Merrill Lynch, disappeared from the banking scene of America. Other large institutions like AIG, Freddie Mac, and Fannie Mae survived with government support. The commercial and investment banks like City Group, Bank of America, UBS, Morgan Stanley, and Deutsch Bank were affected. Wachovia merged with Wells Fargo Bank, and Washington Mutual was taken over by JP Morgan Chase. The full-fledged banking crisis type of 1930 was avoided due to timely support from the Fed.

After the stock market crisis of 1929, the GDP fell by 8.6% in 1930, 6.6% in 1931, and 13.1% in 1932. The rise in unemployment was much sharper. From a low of 3.2% in 1929, it rose sharply to 9% in 1930, 16% in 1931, and 23.4% in 1932.

But the GDP fall and unemployment rise were arrested by the Roosevelt's New Deal in 1933. The GDP fell by only 1.3%. Since then, the economy recovered under the impact of the New Deal and reverted to positive growth path with the GDP growth of 10.9, 8.9, 13, and 5.5% during 1934–1937. The subprime crisis did have the potential of the depression of equal magnitude if not worse. The GDP declined by 2.4% in 2009 and unemployment crossed 10% and stock market fell by 47%. Yet the situation improved in 2010 due the unprecedented monetary and fiscal support in the USA and on the global scale.

References

1. Klein M. Rainbow's end: the crash of 1929. New York: Oxford University Press; 2001. p. 33.
2. Galbraith JK. The great crash 1929. Harmondsworth: Penguin Books; 1954.
3. Skidelsky R. John Maynard Keynes: 1883–1946, economist, philosopher, statesman. New York: Penguin Books; 2003.
4. Wells DR. The federal reserve system: a history. Jefferson: McFarland & Company, Inc.; 2004. p. 51.
5. Temin P. Lessons from the great depression. Cambridge, MA: MIT Press; 1989. p. 34.
6. Bernanke B. The essays on great depression. Princeton: Princeton University Press; 2000.
7. Rosen EA. Roosevelt, the great depression and the economics of recovery. Charlottesville: University of Virginia Press; 2005. p. 8.
8. Kennedy D. Freedom from fear: the American people in depression and war, 1929–1945 (The Oxford history of the United States). Oxford University Press, New York; 1999. http://www.econtalk.org/archives/2010/08/kennedy_on_the.html.
9. Skidelsky R. Keynes: the return of the master. London: Allen Lane; 2009. p. 70.
10. Stewart M. Keynes and after. England: Penguin Books Ltd.; 1972. p. 174–5.
11. Galbraith JK. The coming of J M Keynes. In: Money: whence it came, where it went. New York: Bantam Book; 1976. p. 274–5.
12. Galbraith JK. Money: whence it came, where it went. New York: Bantam Book; 1975.

Part III
Structural Gaps

Chapter 9
Metamorphosis of American Capitalism

> It is told that such are the aerodynamics and wing-loading of the bumblebee that, in principle, it cannot fly. It does, and the knowledge it defies the august authority of Isaac Newton and Orville Wright must keep the bee in constant fear of a crack-up. The bumblebee is a successful but an insecure insect.
>
> John Kenneth Galbraith, *American Capitalism: The Concept of Countervailing Power, 1952.*

American Economic Psyche: Adaptive and Resilient

Does capitalism have an inherent instinct or tendency that contributes to its periodic bouts of instability? Are there any infirmities which need to be streamlined to get the system on its sustainable growth path sans crisis? One of the biggest jolts and setbacks which the system and philosophy of capitalism received was during 1930s experience. Since then the system and the philosophy have adapted to sustain its development and continue as the best-suited organization to contribute to economic growth and stability. For nearly seven decades, the American capitalism, despite the few temporary hiccups, survived and strengthened under the pressure of tremendous technological, societal, and ideological changes across the USA and the globe. The crisis emanating from the subprime debt problem leads us to have fresh look at the system's efficiency and identify its lacunae to build a stronger and more responsive institution with more effective fail-safe mechanism and avoid the distress from crisis. A prosperous nation cannot sustain without an adaptive and resilient economic philosophy. To understand the psyche of the affluent American society, one must understand the building blocks of social and economic thought and structure and its evolution and influence in shaping the policies that create institutions driving its growth.

Wealth creation is the end of all pursuits of societies. Different civilizations, over different times under varying political systems, have all endeavored to create wealth for sustained periods for the well-being of their habitants. From monarchies to democracies on the one end and to communist regimes on the other, societies have

S. Nayak, *The Global Financial Crisis: Genesis, Policy Response and Road Ahead*,
DOI 10.1007/978-81-322-0798-6_9, © Springer India 2013

been struggling to vindicate their philosophies as the panacea for the well-being of human race. Over time, economic events and phenomena have turned the philosophies, on both the ends of ideologies, topsy-turvy. Civilizations that stopped creating wealth stagnated, decayed, or just survived. Either the economic philosophies were anachronistic and needed reformation or the sheer gross mismanagement of resources brought the societies to their brink. The Greek, Roman, and Egyptian civilizations prospered, reached their pinnacle, declined, and collapsed on becoming economically bankrupt. The Spanish, French, Dutch, and British empires reached their zeniths and nadirs. Empires growing on territorial acquisitions and annexations did not last long. Europe broke up into linguistic states, colonies gained independence, and monarchies embraced either democracy or were overthrown after revolutions by communist ideologies under totalitarianism.

One of the most decisive moments of the twentieth century through the ongoing Cold War between the capitalist and communist blocs has been the fall of Berlin Wall in November 1989, the epitome of dividing ideologies competing to show their superiority. The conquest of communism in Europe, Russia, and China by the forces of American capitalism marked a new era for the global economy and political order. It proved beyond doubt the victory of pragmatism of capitalism over the idealism and dogmatism of communism. The long experiment with communism, which began with the Russian Revolution in 1914 and later spread to China in 1949, came to an end on both economic and moral failures. While the economic inefficiency brought the communism to its bankruptcy, it also showed miserable record on the moral fronts of human freedom and dignity.

It is not that the early capitalism although theoretically presented as the best practical ideology actually functioned as the flawless or most practical ideology in experience. In fact both the feudalism and capitalism had their fair share of inequities which were so rampant in some countries of Europe that the ideology of communism developed as an alternative on the important fundamental issue of right to private property. Yet as communism degenerated, the capitalism with democracy reformed in so many ways to curb its inimical characteristics. Despite the benign metamorphosis of America capitalism over decades, it is still not devoid of its elements of imperfection. It undergoes a constant process of pulls and pressures, and adjustments between personal free will and freedom, and public good.

The capitalism is a system that works on the three principles: markets, money, and gains. In all economic spheres, the free will is expressed through the markets. The individual efforts work toward personal gains. And all economic entities work through markets for their own economic gains. The link between these two elements of markets and gains is money or capital. The ideal system of capitalism is where all its three elements, markets, gains, and money, work toward public good. The State has the responsibility to ensure the efficient working of these three forces in coherence toward growth and stability. The State has to keep the institutions of oversight and regulation in place to ensure orderly working of the three elements. The failure of the system can occur or emerge from any one or more of these parameters. In fact all the crises which capitalism has experienced over last three decades of globalization involved weaknesses on all the three fronts. The markets do provide an ongoing mechanism of price discovery and liquidity, but in times of crisis, they have failed to determine right prices and give adequate liquidity. The individual or institutional human endeavor for gains has got sidetracked into irrational zone instead of being on rational behavioral path. The human rationality was overtaken by excessive greed. And money intended to create assets and earn adequate return have failed to generate it. These infirmities exist in the very system on its periphery. Companies fail and file for bankruptcy, individuals incur losses, assets fail to create output or give returns, and money lent is beyond recovery. These are the normal adjustments in a system or costs that are borne by the system.

The crisis occurs when these infirmities are of a magnitude so large that it jeopardizes the system. The economic system is usually on autopilot. Yet, there has to be ongoing monitoring of any infirmity going beyond its normal limits. The crisis normally occurs as a confluence of several factors which is usually not anticipated to happen. The entire superstructure of derivatives markets and exposures is based on this low probability of a confluence of adverse factors, the tail factor. The crisis is, therefore, a tail event, which all the market men, bankers, corporates, regulators, and even government expect to have low probability in normal times. It is, therefore, a known systemic risk. It was not a black swan. Though not predictable on its exact occurrence and magnitude, it was an event which was becoming more probable than before as the time passed and adverse factors in the environment emerged. Information about the buildup of pressures in the system and the risks attached to them is of crucial importance. This information is usually available with the regulators and the major market participants. Not all have access to or is aware of it. That is what makes the crisis unpredictable.

American capitalism is adapting under its systemic stress. During the current crisis, it pumped enough financial adrenaline in its fight or flight response and came out triumphantly resolving the crisis. The Fed, SEC, and government used the most potent weapons in their armory to dissolve housing loan-borne financial meltdown. America abandoned *laissez-faire* economics in 1930s to overcome depression. Keynesian fiscal policy and cohesive Fed direction regulating the growth of money supply and its cost (rate of interest) paved the way for post war prosperity. Despite all the institutional and legislative changes about the fiscal budget and the monetary, banking, and financial system, the basic principles of capitalism of free market mechanism remained intact. In fact the Reagan–Thatcher era gave greater thrust on the magic and goodness of market and smaller government. The institutional arrangement could not have tackled the current crisis which went beyond its jurisdiction. The financial markets that developed have overgrown the current regulatory framework and set up. The market including derivatives market stretched out a little too far and went beyond prudent self-restraint.

The *Laissez-Faire* Capitalism

The word capitalism is often associated with labor exploitation, growing inequalities, society with the affluence, opulence, and ostentation of the rich on the one hand, and misery and privation of the poor on the other. It is thought to be an economy of large and oppressive monopolies, run and driven by big and strong finance capitalists. This may have been the picture of capitalism of the nineteenth century in the early stages of its growth and development.

The first phase of Britain's industrial revolution covered the period of 1780s to 1840s. The rate of capital formation until 1815 was barely 7% of GDP and did go up to 10% by 1840s under the impact of the industrial investments [1, p. 53]. The industrial growth was powered by the steam engine, coal, and iron industries followed by the cotton and woolen industries. Britain being the homeland of industrial revolution did get an advantage in early and speedier growth due to the fact that the discoveries could be translated into commercial production capacities due to cheap and adequate availability of the main energy source, the king coal. The railways and steam shipping expanded the markets and global trade at much faster pace. The colonies provided larger markets for manufactured goods in return for the tropical agricultural products.

The second phase of industrial revolution covered the period of 1840s to 1895 and was led by mining, transportation, shipbuilding, engineering, iron and steel, and building. Britain was again on the forefront of the global economy in the middle of nineteenth century with two-third of output of coal, half of iron, five-seventh of steel, half of cotton cloth, and 40% of hardware [1, p. 96].

By the early 1890s, Britain was losing its status as the leading industrial power to the USA and Germany which emerged as the largest producers of steel. Declining growth in demand from colonies, competition from other industrial nations and lack of growing domestic market led to the declining profitability and growth of British industries.

What was coal to Britain in industrial revolution in eighteenth and nineteenth century was oil to the USA in its industrial progress in the nineteenth and twentieth centuries. Coal and textiles fired the Britain's industrial revolution, while the other industries followed the lead from them. In the USA the automobile and oil industries were the engines of overall industrial development.

Industrial revolution was the precursor to the evolution and development of capitalism. Under the influence of industrial revolution, societies moved from the feudal land-based agrarian states to the capital-driven industrial states with mass production of consumer goods and city-dominated culture. The institution of capitalism also took deep roots into the democratic system of governing societies and flourished during the industrial revolution in 1850s. The corporate form of organization with limited liability and separation management from ownership and transferability of ownership rights turned out to be biggest organizational vehicle that facilitated and promoted the inventions and innovations into large-scale applications. It also democratized the ownership of capital and entrusted management of enterprises with the professionals succeeding the innovative founder entrepreneurs, and thereby sustained the perpetuity of corporates. Other institutions such as banking and capital markets lubricated the engines of industrial societies and ensured faster progress. The stock market facilitated industrial growth and strengthening of capitalism. In free and democratic societies, freedom of choice of enterprise, right to property, and free markets came to be established as the foundations of the industrial and commercial structure that came to be known as the capitalism.

Combined with the belief in free market mechanism, yet another feature and principle of nineteenth century capitalism was the policy of government non interference into the economic activities and dynamics of economy and balanced government budget. Known as the *laissez-faire* policy, it served as the strong and abiding faith of capitalism and flourished to accomplish the industrial revolution. It looks so preposterous now with the experience of the Great Depression and post-war economic prosperity, but the balanced budget formed the fundamental principle of government concerning what it should and should not do with respect to economy and state finances. So much was the public antipathy and opinion against the larger government role in societies even after the birth of communism as an alternate ideology in 1848, that even the liberals in the free and democratic societies could only advocate anything against it only at the cost of severe public backlash. So long as the societies were free from any deep economic malady which was automatically corrected over time, the *laissez-faire* economics survived without any challenge, and balanced budget was the golden rule of government finance and Lakshman Rekha not to be crossed into the dangerous territory of deficit finance.

The free market fundamentalism of *laissez-faire* economics drew its intellectual foundation from Say's law of markets and Adam Smith's thesis of the invisible hand of the market. Keynes's theory established that the structural disequilibrium of capitalist economy arising from the basic inadequacy of aggregate demand cannot be corrected by the market and would require the state intervention by increasing government expenditure. Say's law that the supply will create its own demand even in deep depression to correct the disequilibrium and restore normalcy failed to work. Keynes's demonstration of the root cause of depression, the failure of market dynamics to reduce the unemployment, and his remedy marked the intellectual repeal of Say's Law. Although this aspect of the market fundamentalism was abandoned to make the capitalism more resilient by empowering the State with rights to have larger share in the economy and to vary budgetary deficit to neutralize the adverse effects slump in market demand for consumption and investment, Adam Smith's invisible hand was also not free from the practical flaws. Adam Smith, the father of economics and the author of the most celebrated first treatise on economics science titled *The Wealth of Nations* written in 1776, wrote, "and by directing that industry in such a manner as its produce may be of the greatest value, he (employer) intends only his own gain, and he is in this, as in many other cases, led by an invisible hand to promote an end which was no part of his intention" [2]. The competition for individual profit produces public good because of efficient use of resources. This being true Adam Smith himself qualified that noncompetitive practices or monopolies would not be socially beneficial. The competitive model of Adam Smith is very rare in reality. Every new industry through its initial stage of growth is non-competitive and so is it when it reaches the stage of maturity. "Both adversity and prosperity work alike to reduce the number of firms in an industry" [3]. The adversity forces the weaker ones to merge to avoid losses, while the prosperity entices smaller ones to merge to reap profits. The competitive model requires all units of insignificant power but uniform business acumen and rationality. Yet business acumen and rationality are not widely and abundantly distributed. The economics science thrives on scarcity and inequality, and not on abundance and homogeneity. The market which Adam Smith imagined in his treatise is not the market today. Although competitive spirit abounds, the homogeneity is a scarcity. Today, market is kaleidoscopic. It is not only more complex but constantly adapts to changing technology, which in turn affects ethos of consumer. The Internet technology has given a new dimension to the functioning of the market. It has bridged the information gap, in terms of time, space, cost, and quality that existed earlier about the market. The market information today, due to Internet, is instant, real time, transparent, and inexpensive. Resultantly, the dynamics of markets has changed dramatically to be more efficient and more consumer friendly.

The institution of market is also affected by the teaching and practice of management science, the most recent science which also uses economics, finance, accounting, mathematics, and other branches of physical and social sciences to develop tools and theorems to improve businesses in their management. The management science and schools have given a new dimension to the dynamics of businesses in the twentieth century. This is the contribution of science and academics to business and is actually a gift of free societies for its betterment. One of the strongest elements of *laissez-fairism* that cannot be banished or abolished is freedom. Despite all its other ideas which have been obsolescent, the freedom is its core and cannot be jettisoned. Renowned economist Frederick A Hayek, one of the staunchest opponents of communism and votary of freedom, brings out his arguments against state planning in *Road to Serfdom*.[1] Even in the postdepression era of the dominance of Keynesianism globally, *laissez-faire* capitalism still has its supporters and advocates now known as the market fundamentalists. In addition to Hayek, belonging to the Austrian School, Milton Friedman of Chicago School is also an ardent advocate and believer of free markets and state nonintervention.

The Fall of *Laissez-Faire* Model: Noncompetitive Market Reality

Tremendous gains of old-fashioned *laissez-faire* capitalism from nineteenth century industrial revolution and economic growth and progress did not necessarily warrant its unequivocal support as an economic or political ideology, due to its adverse impact on the long-term and ever changing structure and dynamics of the economy. Adam Smith's competitive economy was far from reality. The distribution of wealth, income, and economic power in the society was getting more and more unequal. "In 1929, 200 corporations controlled nearly half of all American industry. The $81 billion in assets held by these corporations represented 49% of all corporate wealth in the nation and 22% of all national wealth. … And by 1932, 600 American corporations owned 65% of the nation's industry" [4, p. 37]. The growth of corporate enterprise, imperatives of technology for large-scale production and capital intensity of production, was

[1] Hayek, Frederick A., *Road to Serfdom*, George Routledge & Sons, London, 1944.

changing the Adam Smith's simplistic competitive model of the industry into large oligopolistic structure with the entities enjoying power against their smaller competitors and other stake holders such as suppliers, workers and consumers, and even minority shareholders. The booming twenties also showed large number of mergers. "...between 1919 and 1928 some 1,200 mergers involving the disappearance of over 6,000 independent enterprises had been registered" [4, p. 38].

The emergence of noncompetitive market reality of industries in contrast to the competitive market model is another flaw which the market fundamentalists fail to acknowledge. This brings us back to the argument that the *laissez-faire* model is more unrealistic, and the State has to step in to regulate monopolies and restrictive practices. In this respect American Capitalism was much ahead having passed the Sherman Antitrust Act in as back as in 1890. Derived from the English common law reckoning the wickedness of monopoly, the Sherman Act prohibited combinations in restraint of trade and made it a misdemeanor to monopolize or attempt to monopolize any interstate or foreign commerce. In its constant and ongoing battle against the emergence of monopoly, the Clayton and Federal Trade Commission Acts in 1914 prohibited price discrimination, and Celler–Kefauver Anti-Merger Act prohibited mergers between firms which might promote monopoly.

Birth of American Welfare Capitalism: New Deal—Antidepression and Communism Pill

The fact that the American capitalism has brought remarkable economic, scientific, and technological progress through the twentieth century into the new millennium which has no parallel in global history, surpassing other nations and also alternative ideology, mainly communism, has to be reckoned to a large degree as the success of its institutional framework. Apart from the natural bounty of land, and being the new territory and the last continent of human habitation, all other economic factors such as size of capital, its accumulation, labor productivity, technology, innovative, and entrepreneurial spirit are the products of the basic institutional framework described as capitalism. While the institution of capitalism itself has undergone a radical change since the Great Depression in the USA and other developed nations, the basic principles of right to private property, freedom of choice, and free market mechanism have remained the driving forces of the wheels of capitalism. Yet there are a number of market developments as well as the institutional safeguards from the government that have changed the character of capitalism. This metamorphosis of American capitalism has increased its resilience to conventional destabilizing forces to which it was subject in the prewar period. But at the same time, its vulnerability to the newer forms instabilities and fluctuations has also increased.

After the President Roosevelt rescuing the capitalism from its collapse and rebuilding it with several new institutional creations fundamental to securing the true philosophy of capitalism based on the Keynesian wisdom, and abandoning both Communism as well as *laissez-fairism,* the postwar period of global peace and cooperation offered the true testing ground for the success of this new institution. While the State rebuilt the edifice of capitalism to offer to society the platform for achieving sustained economic growth and distributive equity secured by the fundamental principles of freedom and private property, both the private institutions and the State constantly acted and reacted with each other to slowly adapt the content and the power of structure of capitalism. To curb the abuse of economic power by large corporations through formation of cartels, mergers, and acquisitions, creation of monopolies, and use of discriminatory practices, the Sherman Antitrust Act of 1890 was further amended in 1914 by Clayton Act. In spite of being subject to criticism from the market fundamentalists, the Antitrust Act nipped in bud tendencies that over a long period tended to create inadequacy of effective demand, main cause of prolonged depression.

After the Great Depression of 1930s, the Keynesian theory and its economic agenda in America in the form of New Deal transformed the traditional American *laissez-faire* economy into a state-sustained capitalism, giving it a new lease of life, and permanently changing character of the economy. The government assumed and retained responsibility for a proactive role and action in the guidance and regulation of its course. Economy was no longer left to the mercy of the *laissez-faire* market mechanism nor was economic and social welfare left to the mercy of the free market economy. If the market failure took heavy toll on welfare of the society, government stepped in time and took right measures redressing this heavy and unpalatable imbalance. New Deal under President Roosevelt increased the role of government and public spending to revive the economy, provided unemployment insurance, established Securities Exchange Commission to regulate the stock market, extended deposit insurance to mitigate suffering of small depositors in bank failures, and set up Antitrust Commission to control the use of economic power by the large corporations. All this took America on the brave new path of progress, prosperity, and welfare in the 1950s.

The end of Second World War saw America emerging as the super power, economically rich, militarily strong, and one of the oldest, largest, and most mature democracy. Both Germany and Japan rose from the devastation of the war as sphinxes on economic and technological aid from America and joined the rank of the richest nations in the world surpassing the other European economies. Newly independent developing nations charted their course of economic progress for elimination of poverty under their own left or right leaning ideologies. World Bank, IMF, and GATT determined the rules of the new game to promote more equitable trade, direct economic assistance to the poor nations, maintain orderly global payments mechanism, and ensure stable exchange rate arrangement and thereby sustain economic growth with price stability. The US dollar played the supreme role of the global currency elbowing gold gradually out of the global monetary system. America reached the economic zenith and affluence, unprecedented in human history. The share of the USA in global GDP took major jump since the industrial revolution in 1850 when it was 8% and steadily rose for a century to the peak of 26% in 1950.[2]

[2] Madison, Angus, Contours of World Economy, 1–2030 AD.,Oxford University Press, London, 2007.

Despite the decline in the share of the USA in global GDP in the last half a decade to 22% in 2000, American capitalism has managed to survive the world's largest and strongest economy in size and influence.

From the east to the west, the shades of concepts of capitalism and socialism undergo a radical change. Theoretically, capitalism and socialism in their purest forms are distinguished by three underlying principles, ownership of means of production, operation of market mechanism, and personal freedom. Socialism entails public or state ownership of means of production, control of market mechanism through centralized planning, and control of personal freedom of choice.

Private ownership of means of production, free play of market mechanism, and safeguard of personal liberty and freedom have been the cornerstones of capitalism. From this polarity, countries have established and evolved the institution of capitalism or socialism in varying shades. In the twentieth century, several older civilizations being independent from the colonial regime consciously adopted a shade of socialism contrasting the one in erstwhile USSR, Eastern Europe, and China. The biggest such exercise was in India, the world's largest democracy that enshrined in its constitution formation of a republic with socialistic pattern of society having private ownership of means of production along with the state enterprises, market mechanism along with planning and regulation, and personal freedom. With India's cooperative structure permitting common ownership of means of production, Indian economic institutions remained far ahead of time.

The *Countervailing Power* Under Capitalism

The early experience of Keynesian capitalism under postwar prosperity also showed the emergence of *countervailing power* [3]. When large corporations grew at a fast rate enjoying handsome returns on capital, rewarding shareholders well and plowing back profits for growth, the other stakeholders like labor and consumer also mustered their power to have their fair share. The labor unions and consumer activism sprung up as new forces check mating the might of the large corporates. So much was the power of unions and also the giant companies that the US Presidents Kennedy and Nixon had to urge both the managements and unions not to raise wages and prices to curb the wage–price spiral that had become uncontrollable in 1960s and 1970s.

The institution of capitalism was adapted under the influence of countervailing power of consumers and unions, and technological imperatives and new practices, under the development of management science through business schools that changed the rules of the game and evolved the corporates into major societal institutions that looked after and cared for also other stakeholders such as employees, suppliers, and consumers in addition to their owners.

Despite the power of few large corporations to engage in manipulative pricing, restrictive output policy, and cartel arrangements, the experience has not shown any industry major to have engaged in behavior detrimental to the interest of consumers. This change has also occurred due the influence of management science on the corporate behavior. The economic model of a corporation was still traditional, static, and primarily driven by the goal of profit maximization. This underwent a dramatic change. In a dynamic setting with ever changing costs, technology, productivity, demand conditions, consumer tastes and preferences, and competitive scenario, and also cost and structure of financing, the corporates aim at rising growth in turnover and market share. This goal could result in some sacrifice in profits in the short run. But the companies try to offset that by some saving due to cost cutting or technology upgrade or productivity gains, rather than price increases. Further in many new industries, the costs are declining with output growth. The U-shaped cost curves of theoretical microeconomic model of production are out of line with the reality. The costs are not so much curved but are declining over most of the phase of output capacity and tend to flatten near the full capacity. The rising half of U curve is prevalent only in the full employment conditions. Additionally, the technology has been so much of an overriding factor to lower the cost curve and eliminate the right half of the U cost curve. Over the last two and half decades of globalization, there has been such a large global expansion in output capacities that right half of the U cost curve has been totally eliminated.

The upshot of the matter is that capitalism has not resulted in any rampant or large-scale use of cartels, price manipulation, and market fragmentation and restriction as monopolistic practices. In most of the industries, prices have fallen. In others they have gone up due to higher material or commodity prices and fuel costs. The industry experience is not a testimony to theoretical abuses of corporates under capitalism. The oversight by the Federal Trade Commission with legislative powers from the State has been an effective and efficient deterrent to monopolistic power abuses.

The early postwar industrial growth brought a sea change in the market structure in several industries. Economics science has developed along with economic institutions and their issues and problems. Microeconomics studied the behavior of industrial enterprises and capitalism at the microlevel, and macroeconomics examined the systemic functioning and influence of capitalism. The perfectly competitive model did not face trial of reality test in many industries. Economists unhappy and frustrated with outdated competitive model and monopoly structure that failed to fit the realism in industry struggled to reformulate microeconomics in a manner Keynes had redrawn macroeconomics. This time it was not only the Cambridge in Britain but also the Cambridge in America, the MIT, which took the lead in resolving the riddle of market structure and dynamics of an industry and develop theory much closer to reality. Joan Robinson in Cambridge and Edward Chamberlain in MIT both brought out at the same time in 1933 but independently the theory of non-perfect competition. While the former titled it as the Theory of Imperfect Competition, the latter named it as the Theory of Monopolistic Competition. New economic theories help passing new legislations. The majority of New Deal legislations that emanated from Keynes's philosophy were welfare oriented. The new theories of monopolistic and oligopolistic competition which were more realistic expression of market structure in industries in fact helped the business and industry to defend their practices in the court of law and in the eyes of Department of Justice. Monopolies have more destructive power than oligopolies. Oligopolies are not as iniquitous as monopolies. Mergers that promote monopolies are likely to be socially harmful, but mergers among oligopolies are more benign.

Each new industry which developed under industrial revolution evolved in its own way, primarily based on the technological nature of the industry. The access to technology remained a big barrier to entry. But as the industries expanded, the number of units within the industry also went on increasing fast. At one stage when the output and supply exceeded the demand, heavier competition among large number of enterprise led to price cutting, leaving inefficient and weak units to be taken over either closing down or merging with the big units. This process of industrial attrition led to a stage where a few large players dominated the industry. It may be duopoly of two large players like Coke and Pepsi or oligopoly as in automobile, telecom, consumer electronics, and other such industries where a few large corporates capture the major market and the determine the trends. In automobile Ford, GM, Chrysler, Toyota, and Honda share the majority of the vehicle market. In the telecom, Verizon, Sprint, AT&T, and T Mobile are the major players, while in the consumer electronics, Sony, LG, Samsung, Panasonic, and Phillips are. In computers HP, Dell, Apple, Toshiba, and Acer share the major market.

The shape of American capitalism has been molded by its antitrust legislations and the verdicts in its court cases. Yet one single critical element which survives and in fact rules all the legal and market developments in the American business is the famous Darwin's principle of the survival of the fittest. The market and industry developments that have shaped American capitalism are a distinct market reaction to all the important provisions of its antitrust acts. It was inevitable for large corporations to find their businesses entering more in the realm of law than in economics. The contribution of these legislations has been that they have worked as the watch dog and therefore been a strong deterrent to the formation of the worst forms of monopolies.

Paradox of Affluent Society: Social Imbalance

Another glaring example of the negation of the principle of automaticity of *laissez-faire* and need for the state action is the phenomenon of "private affluence and public squalor" that emerged as the by-product of break neck industrial growth racing to meet the growing demand for goods of mass consumption. In 1958 John Kenneth Galbraith, Harvard Professor of Economics, former US Ambassador to India, close adviser of President John F Kennedy, prolific writer with inimitable style, and perceptive eye for subtle structural changes, in his popular and world famous book, the *Affluent Society,* brought out an economic symphony of the functioning of the wealthy American society and what was still wrong with it. Galbraith articulated very subtly but in a forthright manner the great lacunae in the post New Deal US economic structure that changed the course of policy managing the economy and political system as a modern welfare state.

Economic affluence generated by the institution of market mechanism did raise material consumption and welfare of those who were participants in the institution, but not of those who were on the periphery of the market mechanism or the market rejects or market nonparticipants. Secondly, market-driven production machine of capitalism accelerated faster by the advertising, not only excessively expanded the quantum of production but also altered the character of pattern of production from simple utilitarian to strikingly ostentatious. Thirdly, growing private consumption needed to be supported by several public services. More food and grocery consumption means more litter and need for bigger garbage disposal, waste management, and water and air purification. Expanding car ownership demands wider and better highways, roads and flyovers, and parking spaces. Water and air also take their toll, and pollution that degrades these necessities of life requires more government spending on ecological improvement.

Private consumption of material goods creates public bads that needed to be tackled. It required proportionate increase in supply of public goods and services to make private consumption enjoyable or possible without any discomfort to others and society. Economic affluence also requires several other social services to be strengthened. Advertisement motivated private consumption supported by the GDP obsessed growth creates a great social imbalance between the private goods and public goods that needs to be redressed. This cycle of growth degrades the intended welfare gains from private consumption.

The growing mismatch between the supply of private goods by the market economy and the demand for public goods supplied by the government was later redressed by the government in 1960s by spending heavily on the public infrastructure. This problem is now very acute in the emerging market economies, which are growing at a very high rate but are not able to increase the infrastructure facilities at the same pace creating bottlenecks. Capitalism is not an immutable law of nature although it is based on the fundamental principles of moral philosophy of freedom, individualism, and equity. Its institutional structure does need a periodic adjustment to restore its vitality.

The Cold War and Military–Industrial Complex

The most celebrated theoretical exposition of this phenomenon of emergence and growth of military–industrial complex in the Cold War era was given by Galbraith in his book, "The New Industrial State" in 1967. Galbraith explained how under the pressure of Cold War the character of industrial structure in maturing American capitalism underwent a change and adapted the functioning of the market mechanism as well as the corporate–state relationship, breaking a new ground requiring new approach to understand the economic reality of industrial America. The old theoretical model of capitalism remained incapable of grasping the reality.

Both in macro- and micro perspectives from the legislative angle in the USA, the institutional structure of American Welfare Capitalism in 1960s, the heyday of American industrial supremacy, presented a strong and resilient edifice in the service of maximum public good. On the global political front, America was engaged in the Cold War which it could not fight without the technological support from the corporate America. Communism being the number one enemy of the capitalist system, the Cold War with the communist bloc raised expenditure for military, defense, and space programs with large high technology contracts to private industries. Arms and space race with the USSR, the Communist State with its own government machinery, could not be fought by the State without the active cooperation and support from the private corporations. With the technology achieving overriding importance in large corporations, the traditional entrepreneurs were replaced by technocrats and *technostructure*. Among the leading and giant corporations of outstanding entrepreneurs and industrialists, Rockefeller and Ford were the only families that continued to lead their corporations. The indispensable military–industry nexus also adapted the structure of large corporates and their working. High technology and heavy capital base which modern large corporations needed could not be left to the whims the ebb and flow of market demand. In such a complex setting and environment, the corporates instead of reacting to the markets wanted to have control over them, through elaborate planning and publicity, in price, output, and new product decisions. Planning became an integral part corporate functions and a critical aspect of business development and operation. And corporates received continuing financial support from the State for the supply of advanced technology products. Galbraith described this development in the USA as the birth and growth of *military–industrial complex* finding it closely similar to the Soviet industrial planning process [5]. The phenomenon of Industry–State cooperation although new to the American economy has been the driving force of Japanese industrial growth in the postwar period, and the large Japanese corporations worked in active cooperation and coordination of MITI (Ministry of International Trade and Industry) which provides the vision of where the economy should be progressing.

Once again after its crisis of 1930s and rescue by the State under Keynesianism, American capitalism under the imperatives of challenge from its ideological opponent, the communist bloc led by the Soviet Union, had to engage in the arms and space race. The State involvement in the economy went beyond probably what Keynes would have imagined on account of the race for supremacy in military power with Soviet Union triggered by nuclear technology. It was, therefore, not surprising that after the Cold War ended in 1991, and Soviet Union accepted its defeat in military as well as economic fronts vis-a-vis the American economy and broke up, the new strategy of downsizing the government with Reagan and Thatcher began. Arms race was the big burden on both the superpowers. Economic policy and economic institutions are the result of not only pure economic factors but also political ideologies, influences, and beliefs of regional, national, and international levels. It is a political economy. The American capitalism as we see today is the end result of all such influences. The fact that it survived one cataclysm of depression in 1930s and another long battle with communism from 1960s to 1980s is true test of its supremacy, resiliency, efficiency, and finally its social acceptability.

The capitalism underwent a change over the late nineteenth and twentieth centuries as it turned into a more mature stage with the industrial era reaching its pinnacle. All the inequities of traditional model of capitalism moderated in the postdepression era. The inequalities were not oppressive, fruits of industrialization reached larger section of labor, and monopolies were tamed by legislative restrictions on abuse of economic power to the detriment of society. From industrial capitalism, the USA is moving to service-based society which thrives on information, research, and human skills. The postindustrial service society represents the evolution of capitalism to a mature state with abundant stock of capital which sustains high labor cost. The capital is cheap because of its abundance, but labor cost is high due to its high productivity associated with its capital input and its relative scarcity.

Since then the polity in the USA and European nations has been so circumspect that it has given it suitable legislative adjustments and refinements, while capitalism adapts on its own by the forces of market, competitive or otherwise, in order to keep it in line with public aspirations and consensus. Finally, the institution of capitalism functions within the institution of democracy and the constitutions of the free world countries resting on the three ideals or pillars of capitalism. These ideals, the freedom of choice, right to property, and right to work of choice, are enshrined in the constitutions of all the countries of the free world. Every successive government since the New Deal has been mindful of these obligations to their people, and has created new legislations to meet the same old obligation, and protect the rights, welfare, and security of their countrymen whenever market developments under the pressure of private greed came to jeopardize these sacred ideals. Be it the right to have gainful employment of choice, or the right to choose a product or service, or the right to property. Even in today's world, these rights, though so well protected by law, are often indirectly encroached upon by the market developments. The capitalism supports free market for consumer welfare, and new legislation emerge and are passed whenever market excesses encroach upon and trample consume interest. The current crisis is the biggest case now of market excesses jeopardizing the stability of not only the US financial system but also the global economy.

In the golden age of infinite abundance, the economic problem of achieving growth and full employment would hardly exist. Nor would there be competition for existence, sustenance, and growth. In such a world, if only goods can be freely obtained and consumed, and bads would not be available, then it would make the society free of conflict. Work will only be passion and leisure will take more time. But in the practical world of scarcity, society has to evolve institutions which can sustain attainment of the maximum with the minimum of the limited available. That is what economics and economic policy is all about.

Culture of Contentment

After successfully overcoming the collapse of dollar in 1971, problem of stagflation in mid- and late 1970s, American capitalism rebounded in 1980s with the new economic philosophy of globalization, liberalization, and reforms. Hands free approach to economic and financial regulation promoted the domination of free play of unhindered market forces. Resurgence in American industry, high economic growth, buoyant stock market, booming real estate sector, and low inflation flushed the economy with dopamine producing a wave of contentment. American capitalism entered the new phase, the culture of contentment [6]. This new phase of capitalism represented several positive developments. But it also underlined a number of negative or adverse factors and states to which Galbraith alluded. Galbraith's stress and thesis was his very articulate expression of the changing character of American capitalism and its underlying contradiction not very apparent from its glossy economic achievements. He dwelt on the simmering stress of growing maladjustment between public good and private bliss, beneath the shinny veneer of affluence, prosperity, and contentment. He drew more on the negative connotation of the new culture of capitalism and sought measures to redress the weakness failing which he predicted the capitalism was in for another bout of crisis. And the crisis did occur in 2008 like the prognostication of many other critics of the shape which American capitalism had taken in the globalization phase.

The culture of contentment propounds a theory that the majority of the contented section of population who also form the majority interests in the elections and political power are beginning to ignore the interests of minorities and poor. In the area of corporate affairs and financial sector, also the culture of contentment is reflected in euthanasia of shareholder power, dominance of managerial power, plethora of mergers and acquisitions and leveraged buyouts, and commitment to deregulation and *laissez-faire* and free markets. In spite of the roaring growth in the 1980s and 1990s, the income inequalities in the USA continued to rise. The Gini index, which measures the degree of and change in inequality, for the USA went up from 39.7 in 1967 to 46.9 in 2005, showing 18% increase in income inequality reflecting the weakening structure of American capitalism which Galbraith theorized.[3]

The recent crisis in fact validates his thesis to which he addressed in 1992, 16 years before the event. The form which crisis takes varies with time. What is important and crucial is the inherent contradiction which, when reaches the blow out stage and proportion, triggers the crisis. In the late 1950s, when he wrote his famous book, *The Affluent Society*, he portrayed similar problem of American capitalism of the conflict between the achievements of the market economy and the obligation of the State to ensure larger social welfare. The problem of providing adequate social and public infrastructure was largely resolved after growing awareness of this schism among political authorities.

Although on the welfare front American capitalism has shown progress and more so in the light of the recent health care reform which has enlarged the cover of medical care to larger population which cannot afford, the growing income and wealth inequality, on the one hand, and enlarging fiscal deficit and public debt, on the other, raise serious issues about sustainability of government finances.

---

[3] US Bureau of Census, 2006.

Powerhouse of American Capitalism: The Wall Street

If American capitalism survived and missed the crisis in the last two decades of the twentieth century in the era of globalization, it is due to the industrial resurgence which took place in this period efficiently channeled by its capital market. While the industry improved its efficiency under the impact of global competition and improved the shareholder's returns, the burgeoning middle class actively participated in the capital market either directly or through the vehicle of mutual funds, pension funds, and other modes of equity investment.

The stock market has been the harbinger of capitalism and capitalistic growth model. As a market for stocks of uniform equity ownership interests, it provides ongoing mechanism for liquidity and valuation of these financial instruments which are now, with digital technology, held in the random space in hard disks. The elimination of jamming paper traffic in this market has been a great boon to the growth, speed, cost, security, efficiency, and transparency of this market. As a bridge between the savers and users of risk capital, it circulates the lifeblood of economy, the finance capital, to nourish the growth of investment, the most critical element of economic growth. It rewards the efficient, judicious, and lucrative user of capital and punishes the lousy and mediocre. In this process it directs the flow the precious risk capital of savers in productive enterprises that keeps the institution of capitalism vibrant and away from decaying. Although the capital formation is fixed and cannot be liquidated, the investors have got the option of liquidating their investment by selling their stake to other willing investors. By providing liquidity to investments without disturbing the capital assets which generate output, services, and income through the ongoing buying and selling of stakes of ownership, it facilitates and contributes to the process of capital formation and addition of new capital stocks more productive than the existing ones in the economy. The community benefits by addition to the capital stock, and investors benefit by exchanging its ownership when needed. Keynes described this feature of stock markets as "Investments which are 'fixed' for the community are thus made 'liquid' for the individual".[4]

Despite these boons it also suffers from a bane, which is the flaw of all market mechanisms and of suffering from extreme volatility out of temporary or short-term bouts of irrationality. Since it deals with the value of a bit of equity or risk capital in an enterprise, it sets its eyes on future and gives its discounted judgment on its present value. Hence, they call the stock market a barometer or weathercock of future. The modern stock markets are equipped with the state-of-the-art hardware and software technology which was few decades back the floorshow and telephone markets. Today's markets are global, instant, and real time. The information capture as well as information decay is fast and adds to continuing volatility in the valuations of securities done by the market. Keynes again is critical of this malign element of the market and observes, "Of the maxims of orthodox finance none, surely, is more antisocial than the fetish of liquidity, the doctrine that is a positive virtue on the part

[4] Keynes, John Maynard, The General Theory, op. cit., p. 153.

of investment institutions to concentrate their resources upon holding of 'liquid' securities. It forgets that there is no such thing as liquidity of investment for the community as a whole. The social object of skilled investment should be to defeat the dark forces of time and ignorance which envelop our future. The actual, private object of most skilled investment today is 'to beat the gun', as the Americans so well express it, to outwit the crowd, and to pass the bad, or depreciating, half-crown to the other fellow." Written 74 years back, it explains the crux of the postwar stock market crises and more particularly the current crisis of subprime debt securities backed by housing assets.

Capital market has been the powerhouse of American capitalism and US economy since its early industrial revolution in eighteenth century. The satellites of the capital in addition to the individual household investors are also the institutional investors like pension fund, mutual fund, insurance companies, hedge funds, venture capital and private equity funds, banks, and other financial institutions. These on the one end of the market supply financial resources in effect giving energy to the market. The corporates and government are on the other end of the market using their resources. The stock markets, broking firm, and investment banks are the agencies in the institutional framework of the capital market that keep it ticking all the time. The SEC is an independent agency that oversees the functioning of the market to ensure that everyone follows the rule book laid down by it. The Federal Reserve manages the issue of government paper in the capital market and also controls money supply, through banks and financial institutions. It also controls and regulates the cost of money which is represented in the rate of interest, inflation rate, and exchange rate of dollar. In addition it oversees the banking intuitions to ensure safe and fair conduct and financial viability. While the SEC is primarily a supervisory body, the Fed in addition being a supervisory institution is a policy-making institution responsible for managing money supply and its cost, which have formidable influence functioning and behavior of the economy. Its primary goal is to sustain growth and price stability in the economy and achieve near full employment.

New York Stock Exchange (NYSE), the world's largest stock exchange, has $17 trillion market capitalization handling the annual volume of stock turnover and daily turnover of transactions of $120 billion. NASDAQ (National Association of Securities Dealers Automated Quotations), the world's second largest stock exchange with 2,711 listings, had market capitalization of $4.5 trillion in January, 2011. The nerve center of American capitalism, billions of eyeballs across the globe with video and audio networks constantly watch the play of the market from 9.30 AM eastern time till 4 PM. Despite wire connected with most advanced digital technology being used to process buy and sell orders from billions of players within the country and outside, it still continues to have trading floor with brokers, punters haggling for prices and volumes with show hand signs. Many other countries have dispensed with the trading floors and have become a quiet computerized and Internet trading machines where you cannot see the physical action, emotion, and sentiment. But on the NYSE at the Wall Street, you can watch the animal spirits of the market. You can watch surprises, frustrations, and triumphant spirits on the faces of the participants. Unlike the NYSE, the NASDAQ which started functioning in 1971 later became the world's first electronic exchange and popular as the major trading platform for the technology stocks.

The US market capitalization experienced unprecedented boom under sustained economic prosperity during the decade of 1990s. The market capitalization of US equities which had marginally risen from $2.8 trillion in 1988 to $3 trillion in 1990 leapfrogged to the record of $16.6 trillion in 1999, accounting for 178% of GDP. The market was ripe for correction. The Y2K dot-com crisis reduced the market capitalization to a low of $11 trillion in 2002. It rose later to $17 trillion in 2011, 100% of GDP.

Democratization of Stock Market and Equity Ownership

What changed the character of American capitalism in the 1980s is the trend of increasing retail investor participation in the stock market. It marked a new development that altered the functioning of traditional capitalism and gave it modern technology savvy touch. Equity ownership penetrated into households of majority of American households. In addition to the rising direct participation in the stock market, a larger number of investors became stake holders in the equity of corporate America through pension funds, mutual funds, and insurance companies. The institutional holding in the equity of corporations rose sharply.

The 1987 stock market crash shook the investor confidence again with new and potential investors being more hesitant, risk averse, shying away from the market, and reverting to the safer option of saving deposits and treasury bonds. Although this was the usual investor response following the crash, the recovery that followed was unusual. Underlying the quiet and lackluster milieu, a gradual but enduring trend was emerging primarily motivated by a series of policy changes and market developments.

The most significant new development that became very popular in the capital market in the 1980s was the LBOs (leveraged buy outs). But it did exactly the opposite of the wave of equity investment in 1990s. LBO was an important vehicle of buying out companies from public ownership, delisting and restructuring them and then selling them at huge profits. The vehicle totally denied the original shareholders the right to gain advantage from their restructured company. The wealth creation was amassed by a wealthy few than the large majority of individual shareholders. LBOs was the fashion of the Wall Street in 1980s, and it did very little to spread wealth among the larger body of shareholders. It short circuited the process of wealth creation and bypassed minority shareholders. LBO game climaxed with $33 billion RJR Nabisco deal in 1989.

Pension funds were not too far behind in the wave of equity investment that enlarged indirectly small ownership of large and upcoming corporates. Public employees of municipals and state governments had their retirement money and pension funds traditionally invested in bonds and deposits earning fixed incomes. By late 1970s there was a gradual shift in the investment policy of pension funds of public employees, which are much larger than the size of several private mutual funds and even private pension funds. Until 1979, the so-called prudent man rule did not permit investment by pension funds in equity which were considered as risky investment. In 1979 the Department of Labor clarified the concept of prudence and permitted investment in equity which were treated as risky provided they were a part of diversified portfolio strategy. It was this landmark judgment that paved the way for pension funds, endowment funds, and trusts investing in listed equities. Peter Drucker called it "*Unseen Revolution of Pension Fund Socialism in America*." Investment of a small percentage of pension funds in equity made a significant impact on the character of trading, holding pattern, and values of equities. The trend was reinforced by the exemplary record of several public and university pension funds showing huge appreciation above the market indices.

Capital gains tax cuts encouraged retail investment in equity and boosted the stock market. Traditionally, it has never been on the agenda of democrats. In fact democrats have always opposed the capital gains tax cut terming it as a measure of enriching the rich at the cost of the poor. It has always been the bastion of the republicans who have been the market friendly party. Changing character of the capital market changed the politics of affinity to the market among the democrats. By the early 1990s, the direct or indirect ownership of shares was spreading fast to the large middle class and organized labor and formed a strong voting group which cannot be ignored but could in fact be exploited for power. Clinton's bold step in proposing the capital gains tax cut pulled the rug from the republican's feet and added to his popularity index. The stock market received the record boost. The decade of 1990s witnessed one of the most vigorous bullish phase in the US stock market history. American capitalism at end of the stock market boom of 1990s represented large degree of corporate democratization.

The equity market rewarded the long-term investors well. During the great bull markets of 1980s and 1990s, the sources of annual return on stocks generated for each decade were similar. Dividend yield contributed 4% to each decade's return, and earnings growth was about 10%. But the price–earnings ratio rose by 110% in 1980s and another 100% in 1990s. "Those stock returns, averaging 17% annually, reached the highest levels, for the longest period, in the entire 200 year history of the US stock market" [7]. In these two decades, the equity ownership spread widely into households giving the US stock market a broader base. "America has become a society of equity investors. The number of household owning equities has increased more than threefold since the early 1980s. In 2005 nearly 57 million US households, half of all households, owned stocks directly, or through mutual funds".[5] The survey showed 91 million individual investors with the median age of 51 years and median household income of $65,000 owned equity. Their median household equity assets were $65,000 out of median household financial assets of $125,000. American capitalism established a broad-based ownership among the households across the country.

[5] Investment Company Institute, Equity Ownership in America, 2005, p. 1.

Institutional Investors: Dominant Monitors of Corporates

In addition to the rising direct investment of the US households into the stock market in equity, their investments through the vehicles of pension funds, mutual funds, and 401 K and IRA accounts have risen very sharply. These investments are through several institutional investors. The institutional ownership of equity went up from 10% in 1950 to 40% in 1980. The decade of 1990s witnessed a further sharp rise in the institutional investments in equity. The total assets of all institutional investors rose from $9.7 trillion in 1990 to $27.5 trillion in 2004. Their equity investments increased from $1.7 trillion to $9.4 trillion during the same period with their share in total equity of listed American companies rising from 53 to 66%; mutual funds held 28%, while pension funds, 26%. The largest 300 institutional money managers held $7.5 trillion, 56% of US market capitalization of $13.2 trillion in 2004 [8]. The large US corporations are technically owned and held by the US institutional investors. Such large institutional stake technically investing public money under pension plans, 401 K, insurance, and mutual funds runs across the cross section of American companies from high tech stores like Microsoft to retail stores like Macys and makes the American business democratized in terms of its ownership and also the profits of these corporations. The institutional ownership in Microsoft, Intel is 65%, Google 82%, Apple 73%, AT&T 56%, Verizon 57%, Delta 86%, GE 51%, Ford 58%, Exxon 49%, Pfizer 71%, P&G 58%, Wal-Mart 36%, Macys 91% Citibank 35%, and Bank of America 51%.[6]

This development has had a tremendous influence on the stock market. The investment portfolios of households are managed by thousands of professional fund managers. The market behavior is dominated by the decisions and actions of large and leading institutional investors who collectively manage individual investments. The structure of American capitalism has changed and is governed by the collective voice of large institutional investors who control individual savings. The institutional investors constantly monitor the performance of the corporates and safeguard the interest of their client investors. This keeps the corporate America on its toes. The research by the institutional investors on corporate financials, their performance, their earnings guidance, market behavior, interest rate scenario, economic variables, and all other parameters affecting investments and wealth portfolio of clients adds a valuable input in the system.

New Liberal Democrat: Non-Keynesian Economic Boom

President Clinton began his term in 1994 with a new vista in democratic economic policy. Democrats have traditionally been thriving on liberal policies which are welfare oriented and pro-labor and pro-middle class and not pro-rich, pro-industry,

[6] The figures relate to August, 2010.

and pro-stock market, which remained the bastion of republicans. Clinton maintained this stance throughout his election campaign. Critical of income tax and capital gains tax cuts benefiting the rich, cut in welfare spending affecting the poor, he advocated tax increase for the rich, higher welfare spending for the poor and distanced himself from the Wall Street. He had been a fierce critic of the republican trickle-down economics.

The scenario changed after Clinton's election as the President. Clinton inherited the economy gripped by recession, unemployment of 7%, rising prices, high budget deficit of $200 billion, and lackluster stock market with Dow stagnating at 3,000. It was the perfect environment for adopting the conventional Keynesian remedy to reflate the economy by lifting investment by the bootstrap through budgetary spending. Clinton could have easily fallen in this policy trap looking to his liberal orientation and the influence of his London School days in his perception of economic problems. His primary target was the reduction of budget deficit by raising the income tax rate on the high income brackets affecting the rich. The second target was reduction in interest rate to stimulate investment and growth rate. Guided by the low interest rate regime of Greenspan and the technological revolution, the economy ushered an unprecedented boom. The Non-Keynesian prescription of cheap money policy did the trick and turned record and chronic budget deficit into miraculous surplus. During Clinton's tenure, Dow tripled benefiting 200 million Americans, mutual fund holders.

Age of Universal Banking—Repeal of Glass–Steagall Act: A Calculated Risk

Among the New Deal legislations, the most outstanding that have been foundation of welfare capitalism, providing it with an enduring strength and stability, are the Glass–Steagall Act and Social Security Act. Of these two pieces of historic legislations, the Glass–Steagall Act of 1933 has been of overriding importance to the financial system in curbing the repeat of the mistakes of 1929 stock market frenzy and collapse. After the Great Crash of 1929, when the blame game began, the first to come in the firing range were the banks which had lent very heavily for stock market investments including underwriting of new issues. As a part of the series of measures which the government took to remedy the crisis and avoid its recurrence, the Glass–Steagall Act was passed in 1933 by the Congress which separated the commercial banking and investment banking and created a firewall between the two activities in order to eliminate the possibility of lending depositors money for stock market investment and underwriting. As a result of this Act, the large commercial banks like Citibank, Chase Manhattan, Bank of America, American Express, and Wells Fargo could not undertake investment banking and broking and other capital market activities. The development gave rise to the growth of investment banks such as Goldman Sachs, Lehman Brothers, Merrill Lynch, JP Morgan, and Morgan Stanley which did not have any banking affiliates. The commercial banking and investment banking businesses developed as two separate businesses without common ownership and management interest. For 66 years until its repeal in 1999, the Glass–Steagall did provide safeguard against the crisis emanating from the excessive bank credit to sensitive financial sector areas such as securities business.

In the early 1980s, financial deregulation and globalization changed the climate and perspective on the ball game and entire gamut of banking and financial operations and activities. Not only banks and other financial services corporations expanded their operations globally but the concept of universal banking gained roots and increasing support for achieving higher efficiency, cost-effectiveness, and better viability. The European countries like the UK, Germany, France, and Netherland did not have stiff regulations for banks banning them from entering into investment-related activities. This placed the American banks at disadvantage against their European counterparts. The lending business was also getting increasingly securitized globally with the traditional loan business of banks shrinking and restricted to individuals and small business. The big banks needed accessibility in the securities business in order to keep their assets growing with their deposit liabilities and retain lucrative profit margins. The banking industry and lobby had been pleading for a change permitting it to cover a wider canvass of financial services and be more competitive. Finally, in order to keep abreast with this changing character of banking and financial services business, the Glass–Steagall Act was repealed in 1999. The lacunae in the brave new world of financial markets were the absence of fresh regulatory mechanism directed to both reckon the growth of the new system and its direction and momentum and also, in times of need, curb its advance on undesirable and potentially riskier and destabilizing path. The weak spot in the American capitalism reappeared in the wake of the pressures of demands for higher growth in banking and financial services industry.

The Challenge of Crisis of Capitalism

One of the features of capitalism which gives it a great enduring strength and sustainability is its adaptive nature. Like skin which gets constantly renewed, shedding the old and dyeing cells by the fresh ones, the capital stock that depreciates is replaced by the new capital production, which keeps the growth momentum of gigantic machine of capitalism. Innovations and new markets add to this capital stock and further invigorate the engine of capitalism. American capitalism has been in the constant process of adaptation emanating from the disequilibria it causes by the drive and spirit of the market economy, and the consequent state reactions which correct them by adapting the rules of the game. At the every stage of its crisis, the problem either takes a new dimension or represents the same old riddle in new form.

The crisis of capitalism can arise from one or more causes according to Schumpeter: excess production and excess capacity, falling consumption and savings glut, declining rate profit and vanishing investment opportunities, obsolescence of entrepreneurship, bureaucratization of capitalism, and lack of innovation. Inadequacy of effective demand which Keynes identified as the root cause of depression which if not treated in time could lead to collapse of capitalism. The Great Depression was the biggest crisis which capitalism faced in its history and could cause its collapse.

Decaying capitalism is characterized by a state when it loses its vitality and fails to renew its capital stock, suffers from obsolescence of capital and technology, lacks innovative spirits, and fails to expand its markets. These are the symptoms of decaying capitalism. In fact they are the manifestations of stagnating or declining industrial or postindustrial society, whether capitalist or socialist. Marx identified this decaying of capitalism when it reaches a very mature stage to be caused by the rate of profit declining below the rate of interest caused by absence of innovation and stagnant markets resulting from inequalities in incomes and wealth. Writing in 1867, much before the Keynes' General Theory which appeared in 1937, Marx was already a Keynesian in identifying the inadequate aggregate demand and its cause being high income inequality paving way for decay and collapse of capitalism. Unfortunately, events proved wrong not only about the dynamics of capitalism but more so about decay and collapse of communism which he could have never imagined or may have had thoughts and apprehended about but never forewarned in his writings. The history of events of the last two and half decades in the communist regimes and world is a testimony that vindicates this hypothesis. It is ironic that Marx's prophecy that the disequilibrium in capitalism would lead to take over by communism and its spread across the world did not work. His analysis of decay of capitalism in fact proved to be the right analysis that destroyed communism. The irony is that it is not a matter of fate, but it is the failure of communism as an institution and philosophy to adapt as did capitalism in its constant effort in shaping societies to be equitable. The failure of communism lies in continuing its system as autocratic, bureaucratic, and totalitarian in its functioning and its resistance to adapt to achieve its goal of establishing egalitarian society. The bureaucracy and autocracy thrived to create instead an economic machine that generated shortages and became technologically obsolete and financially unviable.

What is the dynamics of financial or economic crisis in capitalism? In an open economy, three important components that drive economic growth are investment, consumption, and exports. Exports are externally determined but can be the engine of growth as it has been in China and other Asian tigers and much earlier in Germany and Japan. Domestically induced growth stems primarily from the size of private investments and hence is the importance of animal spirits in determining the growth momentum of an economy. While consumption and exports do not have much relation to future, investment is entirely linked to future. Since investment is focused on the future, the expectations play a crucial role in decision making about investments.

Keynes in fact believed that, in their extremities, the markets remain in the grip of sentimental overdrives dominating rather than being governed by rationality. He explained in the *General Theory* how prospective rate of return is overstretched at the peak of the boom and causes crash when the expectations are not met. Similarly, at the bottom of recession, the rate of return expectations is more pessimistic than realistic and, therefore, fails to revive investment. The market mispricing of returns and risks is the bane of unfettered market mechanism that makes it vulnerable to crash and crisis. The prudential market regulation is the anchor of constructive capitalism and is indispensable if it is not to degenerate into casino capitalism. One is tempted again to rehash here the famous quote of Keynes on markets and capitalism, "Speculators may do no harm as bubbles on a steady stream of enterprise. But the position is serious when enterprise becomes the bubble on a whirlpool of speculation".[7]

References

1. Hobsbawm E. Industry and empire: the birth of the industrial revolution. New York: The New Press; 1999.
2. Smith A. The wealth of nations. New York: Bantam Dell; 2003. p. 572, Originally published in 1776.
3. Galbraith JK. American capitalism: the concept of countervailing power. Harmondsworth: Penguin Books Ltd.; 1952. p. 48.
4. McElvaine RS. The great depression: America, 1929–1941, times books. New York: Random House, Inc.; 1993.
5. Galbraith JK. The new industrial state. Boston: Houghton Mifflin Company; 1967.
6. Galbraith JK. The culture of contentment. Boston: Houghton Mifflin Company; 1992.
7. Bogle JC. Commonsense on mutual funds. John Wiley & Sons, Hoboken, New Jersey; 1999. p. 104.
8. Bogle JC. The battle for the soul of capitalism. New Haven: Yale University Press; 2005. p. 73–5.

[7] Keynes, John Maynard, op.cit., p.159.

Chapter 10
Downfall of Communism: God That Failed

> I have no concern with any economic criticisms of the communist system; I cannot inquire into whether the abolition of private property is expedient or advantageous. But I am able to recognize that the psychological premises on which the system is based are an untenable illusion. In abolishing private property we deprive the human love of aggression of one of its instruments... but we have in no way altered the differences in power and influence which are misused by aggressiveness.
>
> Sigmund Freud.

Marx: Vision of Manifesto and Premise of Communism

As one of the most outstanding political scientist basing his theory of evolution of society and the role of state on dialectic materialism and materialistic interpretation of history, Karl Marx stands as the tallest one providing the logical foundation and basis for an alternative political and economic model for an egalitarian society. He not only condemned the capitalistic or feudal societies for their inaptitude for developing into more equitable societies but also prognosticated their eventual demise due to their own inherent contradiction. His work, *Das Capital: Critique of Political Economy*, published in 1867 illustrated the working of a capitalist society and described how it would fail in evolving into an ideal economic and political ideology.

While the theory of Marxism inspired several political leaders across the world in executing regime change, following the death of Marx in 1883, the success of revolutions never touched the mature capitalist nations which he had predicted to be the first targets of his ideology. In the eighteenth century, technical inventions and industrial revolution, mass scale production, and capital accumulation gave rise to a system of economic relations in the society that is known as capitalism. Marx's prognosis about the demise of capitalism was based on two postulates. First, he postulated that capitalism would stagnate wage levels and accentuate inequality of

S. Nayak, *The Global Financial Crisis: Genesis, Policy Response and Road Ahead*,

DOI 10.1007/978-81-322-0798-6_10,

incomes and wealth. While this would stagnate consumption demand, the declining rate profit on investment would retard investment growth. Both would draw the aggregate demand down, leading to declining production and rising unemployment in a vicious cycle of depression. In Keynesian terms, lower propensity to consume resulting from the inequality in incomes would result in deficiency of demand further causing unemployment. In this analysis of capitalistic system, both Marx and Keynes make the same prognosis. But their methods of dealing with the problem of depression and unemployment arising from deficiency of aggregate demand in the economy differ.

Marxism is a political ideology that is based on principle of communal ownership of means of production. The economic theory of Marxism brings out the inequities in the working of capitalism arising from class division and inequality of income and wealth. Since the prevalent institutional structure supports the class relations, and payments for services and goods upheld by the legal and judicial institutions invoked by the state, Marx advocated the class conflict and revolution to establish new order. Marxism is, therefore, an economic theory and political strategy for acquisition of political power to change legal foundation of capitalism and adopt an alternative legislative structure that upholds the ideals of communism. In some countries, change may come through democracy and peaceful change by voting and universal suffrage. "The French revolution abolished feudal property in favor of bourgeois property.... The theory of the communism may be summed up in the single sentence: Abolition of private property... Capital is not a personal property it is a social property" [1, pp. 52–3]. That was the fundamental principle of communism which Marx aimed the states to abide by. Writing the Manifesto in 1848, Marx expected the communist revolution to first occur in France or England or Germany which were on the forefront in industrial revolution and emerging as fast growing industrial economies and evolving as capitalist systems.

The fundamental problem of capitalism when it reaches its critical stage of collapse, as is highlighted by Marx in his brilliant critical analysis in *Das Capital*, is the secular decline in the rate of profit on capital below the real rate of interest. When the stock of capital is high and technological innovation or advances do not yield return higher than the real rate of interest, the process of capital accumulation stops, investment falls, income reduces, consumption drops, output is reduced, employment falls, and the economy enters the vicious circle of depression, Keynes's deficiency of demand causing economic contraction. This is a typical phenomenon of decaying capitalism and its eventual collapse not experienced since 1930s.

The Communist manifesto, however, did not elaborate on how its economic system would move ahead after the buildup of a new order based on new economic laws and new rules of material exchange of goods and services, devoid of market and market pricing mechanism which determines all prices for commodities and services and also factors of production in the game of communism. Manifesto was much before Marx came out with his theory about development and collapse of capitalism in *Das Capital.* It only hinted at the alternative model of command economy which involves centralized decision making about investment, saving, production, and consumption overtaking the function of invisible but enlightened hand of market mechanism which is guided under capitalism by profit motive for production on the supply side and consumer fancy and satisfaction on the demand side.

The practicability and long-run viability of communism rested on two important pillars: absence of private property rights and centralized investment and consumption allocation. The first tenet eliminates incentive for hard work and innovation. The second mechanism which overtakes decentralized market mechanism is fraught with several practical imponderables resulting in wrong decisions and waste. The breakup and demise of communism in USSR on economic fronts clearly vindicates the economic failures of these two main ideas in the apparatus of communism.

The mammoth machine of communist economy remained technologically obsolete except for space and defense technology, and could not cope up with shortages of consumer products and their low quality. The resource pressure in the economy resulted in repressed inflation, long queues and waiting period for consumer goods and rationing. It created technologically lagging shortage economy with strong but unresponsive bureaucracy. The collapse of the system was imminent. The difference between the command economy and market economy is that the former is centralized, the latter is decentralized. The former is slow in adjusting to the demand–supply imbalances, while the latter is quick and fast. The market price is the indicator to which trade and production respond in the market economy. In the command economy, the market price signal is absent. The command economy often signals wrong allocation of resources for output and consumption. The discretionary bureaucratic decision making is not more efficient than market price directions.

The communism failed in regard to both the private property rights and the command economy claim of establishing much better, efficient, adaptable, and egalitarian society, which Marx and others dreamt about. The institution of communism is far complex a system to be established and further more intricate and extremely elaborate for its functionalities. It is not a plausible alternative but a Utopian dream and that too may not deliver results for sapping the individual freedom, initiative, and innovative spirit. No other principle or system nurtures initiative, effort, commitment, spirit of discovery, and innovation as freedom of choice, individualism, and right to private property. These ingredients form the basis of human ingenuity that adds to the capital stock, improves its productivity, and paves way to economic progress. They are not the ingredients of communism, and the experience of more than half century now testifies that these societies can survive until they reach their decay through stagnation, inflation, and erosion of capital, but they cannot progress economically and technologically as the adaptive capitalism can. The disaggregated market determines what will be consumed and hence produced, how much, and at what price. These decisions are centralized in communism leading to errors, waste, and noncommittal system of economic delivery leading to erosion of capital stock and its obsolescence.

It was not possible to predispose the future course of communism at the end of the Second World War. Although an ally of the capitalistic world against the common enemy of Nazism, the USSR had yet to traverse a longer path to prove its supremacy as a military as well as economic power against its rival America. At the end of the War America established its lead in nuclear technology with the success in Atom bomb. But the Korean War of 1950–1953 resulted in its breakup into North and South ruled by communist and capitalist ideologies, respectively. America faced the psychological defeat against communism and Russia. Russia was also growing faster in the 1950s to lead in space programs and also in its economic status. The man-on-the-moon mission of President Kennedy was in fact aimed to lift the public spirit and project the image of America as technologically superior to Russia after the Russians succeeded in being the first to send Yuri Gagarin in space in 1961. In the 1960s, the battleground shifted to Vietnam where America fought war against communism aided and supported by China. The cold war against Russia was also in full swing. The prolonged Vietnam war was getting costlier for America not only in terms of casualties and economic losses but also in terms of its domestic and international image. Public debate about the war and peace and budget deficit was raging in America. The Nixon–Kissinger diplomacy with China finally drew the curtain on the long ideological battle with communism and ended the costly war.

Demise of Communism

Until the popular understanding and rise of the philosophy of communism in 1848 with Marx's work, the emerging industrial societies were market oriented and driven by capital accumulation rather than earlier land-based economies and hence began to be called capitalistic to distinguish them from land-based feudal societies. In the market economies, the price mechanism describes how incomes are distributed and resources allocated into different uses and products. The production and supply responds to demand. The demand is governed by income distribution and taste and preferences of consumers. The consumer is the king and supreme and dictates the resource use of the community. In contrast, the communism discards the market signals. The market is subverted to the central planning board which decides what the community wants, the prices, and quantity, and not the market.

Although the communism for its ideology as well as its system of discarding the markets by central planning was subject to criticism, the Soviet bloc and China were making progress and experimenting with the ideology and testing its success in promoting higher human welfare. The collapse of the Soviet bloc and China's U-turn in ideology have proved the communist ideology to be a failure in sustaining the community growth and welfare. It has negated two important hypotheses which formed the basis of the claim that communism was a better ideology than capitalism for maximum societal welfare.

Firstly, it was argued that surplus value accruing to the state can be better distributed among society and also used by the state for accumulating capital and improving its productivity. This was supposed to increase the productive capacity of the economy much better than the capitalistic society and also create better income distribution. In reality, after the experimentation of working of two generations in the system in the USSR and Eastern Europe, the results showed worsening capital stock, lower productivity of labor, lack of innovation and technological stagnation and obsolescence, and non-motivated labor. The state appropriation of surplus value did not add value either to capital stock or to national wealth. "Already in the late 1970s and early 1980s we began to feel that the economy was failing and beginning to slip back. The individual's interest in working productively had been undermined. The economy was holding back scientific and technical progress. The country found itself in a state of progressive depression" [2, p. 103].

Secondly, the command economy failed to fill and adjust the gaps of mismatches in supplies and demand for goods and services and failed to improve the quality of products. Both the shortages and surpluses in commodities became a common feature, with the central planning body taking time in removing the mismatches quickly. With the nonexistence of the market signals of prices, the mismatches were not adjusted quickly and persisted longer. In the market economy, these mismatches are quickly reflected in prices, and profit motive works faster in eliminating the mismatches. The subversion of market mechanism did not improve the efficiency in resource utilization. "What came to light through *glasnost* about our past confirmed inexorably and brutally that a system created according to the rules of tyranny and totalitarianism (not of the market mechanism) could no longer be tolerated, not simply from the moral point of view but also from the point of view of the country's basic economic and social interests" [2, p. 102, The words in bracket are mine].

On these two fundamental principles, capitalism scored victory over communism. The private ownership of means of production is vital in enlarging the capital stock of society and improving its productivity. The institution of markets needs to be used, preserved, and improved to give efficient price mechanism and allocation of resources. Free choice to consumers can only guide the economy into right direction. "The economic reform has rendered irreversible the transition to a market economy on the basis of a variety of forms of property" [2, p. 101].

Collapse of USSR: Transition Under *Perestroika and Glasnost*

The failure of communism in erstwhile USSR and Eastern Europe has been a systemic failure both at the micro- and macroeconomic levels. At the micro level, the system failed to provide better alternative than the market. There were both shortages in goods and services which were in demand and glut in goods which were not in demand. The production mechanism did not match the actual demand. The goods and services lacked variety, quality, and innovation. As the shortages developed, price controls and rationing became imperative. Repressed inflation became rampant. The black markets and smuggling thrived. At the micro level, the system failed due to the nonexistence or absence of the market mechanism. The macroeconomic picture manifested the failure to grow at a sustainable rate. The rate of investment fell below the capital replacement levels, and resources were also too scarce to finance even at a low rate. Moreover, outdated technology eroded the productivity of capital and labor. The economy was left with outdated and eroding capital stock. The end result was economic stagnation due to low investment, resource crunch, and obsolescence.

As the chief architect of the transition of USSR from communism to democratic market-oriented private-cum-state enterprise economy, the former President Mikhail Gorbachev, a maverick Soviet politician and a great global leader, introduced the policy of *glasnost* (openness) and *perestroika* (restructuring) as the means of peacefully reforming the communist state into more open democratic and market-oriented society. He candidly and forcefully argued his thesis, "I have never, not once, regretted the fact that I was the initiator of a sharp turn in the life our country. What came to light through *glasnost* about our past confirmed inexorably and brutally that a system created according to the rules of tyranny and totalitarianism could no longer be tolerated, not simply from the moral point of view of the country's basic economic and social interests. It had already led the country into a dead end and brought it to the brink of an abyss. And it was kept in place by force, lies, social apathy, and also with the assistance of artificial injections, which squandered resources and weakened potential for the future. Had we preserved the old regime for a few more years there would have been every reason to speak of the end of history for our great state. Already in the late 1970s and early 1980s we began to feel that the economy was failing and beginning to slip back. The individual's interest in working productively had been undermined. The economy was holding back scientific and technical progress. The country found itself in a state of progressive depression" [2, pp. 102–3].

Mikhail Gorbachev guided the collapsing Soviet economy in its transition from the brink of bankruptcy of totalitarian regime to a more stable democratic and market-oriented economy. The Stalinist model of command economy with totalitarianism was showing the signs of weakening and unable to hold its sustainable growth-oriented economic structure. The strategy of cold war with the USA which took shape in the Stalinist regime had incurred heavy cost on the economy. The arms and space race between the USSR and USA proved expensive and wasteful to both but more so to the Soviet Union. Additionally, outdated technology, low productivity, and mismatch in demand–supply in mass consumer goods due to faulty centralized planning left the economy with piles of low-quality products along with shortages in others. The presence of price controls created long queues and waiting periods. The economy was crippled under pressure of repressed inflation.

Marx theorized the socialist economy to be free from the vicissitudes of business cycles of the capitalist economy and grow faster on account of higher investment of the surplus value accruing to the state that goes as rent and profit to the propertied class under capitalism. Actually, the surplus value was not generating sustainable growth but, on the contrary, eroding the decadent capital. Gorbachev foresaw the impending disaster and collapse of the structure. After assuming power in 1990, he showed an extraordinary courage to come out criticizing the outdated and dogmatic model of communism that was failing to give results.

"So why was *Perestroika* necessary? The previous theoretical and practical model of socialism (the Stalinist totalitarian bureaucratic system) which had been imposed on the country for many decades turned out to be bankrupt.... What came to light through *glasnost* about our past confirmed inexorably and brutally that a system created according to the rules of tyranny and totalitarianism could no longer be tolerated, not simply from the moral point of view but also from the point of view of the country's basic economic and social interests. It had already led the country to a dead end and brought it to the brink of an abyss.... The monopoly of power by one party is being replaced by pluralism. *Glasnost* and freedom of speech have already become an indispensable feature of public life. The economic reform has rendered irreversible the transition to market economy on the basis of variety of forms of proper" [2, pp. 101–3]. The dissolution of the Soviet Union, the USSR, and demise of communism in 1991 following the failed coup by the conservatives who were opposed to Gobarchev's policy of freedom and reform marked a new era in the resurgence of capitalism and global ideological convergence.

Free Market Capitalism Versus Central Planning

Free markets or planning is no longer a debatable point in economic policy. In the prewar period, the advent of communism pursuing the Marxist economic philosophy and the theoretical criticism of free market for its gradual culmination into monopolies and restrictive trade practices had opened the doors of concept of state planning subverting the free market for social good. The idea of central planning did possess many attributes which the free market could not have. It could have much larger and longer view of the market which the free market comprising large number of diverse participants could not have. Yet supplanting the free market by planning was totalitarian and proved to be an utter failure. The collapse of the Soviet Union and adoption of the institutions of free markets and private property by the erstwhile communist China were the final proof of the failure of central planning devoid of market mechanism.

The institution of free market triumphed over communism and central planning. The market represents freedom of choice. It characterizes economic democracy. The argument of market antagonists is that the market does not represent true economic democracy since it represents only haves and not have-nots. It is an economic democracy with an entry barrier. That, however, does not negate the hypothesis that the market is more efficient mechanism of resource allocation than other systems that suppress it. In the early days of experiment in communism, the economic science as well as computing technology was not as advanced as it is today. Even with the use of advanced mathematical and complex models and super computer technology, the central planning could not and will not be as efficient as the market. In comparing the market mechanism with the central planning, one can think of a robot and a human being. The planning system is robotic, driven by its intricate design of inputs it can sense, while the markets are like humans and belong to humans with their constant interaction. Once we replace the market mechanism with the central planning, the pattern of goods produced is thought to be in the best interests of society irrespective of their choices. And if pricing mechanism is not operative, there would be mismatches in demand and supply. If these mismatches are to be eliminated, in times of shortages, the output will be forced on people as quotas irrespective of their choice; in times of overproduction, there will be continuing glut of goods. If the pricing mechanism is allowed to operate, it means that the central planning board would get constant feedback on market reaction and mismatches to adapt the future pattern of output. Such a constant feedback-based output adaptation means central decisions which under free market mechanism would have been disaggregated. This method of constant and automatic feedback mechanism and constant adjustments in output volume, quality, and diversity of product range in a single commodity is possible only with free markets and its pricing mechanism. Nothing can be more efficient than the market. Top-down decision making by central planning is undoubtedly inefficient even in today's information world and supercomputer technology. The bottom-up disaggregated decisions of free markets and pricing mechanism offer more efficient and faster adaptive mechanism. This thesis is now widely accepted the world over and more so in the former as well as current so-called communist regimes, which are now not ideologically dogmatic and have adopted free markets pricing and abandoned central planning. The issue of haves and have-nots in the market has to be separately dealt in the context of the state policy.

The supremacy in efficiency of free markets and price mechanism in allocation of resources of the community in guiding pattern of output of goods and services to the maximum satisfaction of societal needs and requirements goes undisputed in modern societies and has now universal acceptance in the light of former communist Eastern bloc and USSR having totally abandoned their model and adopted free market and capitalist philosophy in economic management under perestroika and glasnosts. Even China, despite still adhering to the communism in principle only, embraced the free markets, private property rights, and capitalist ideology to achieve modernization and record economic growth preventing social unrest and political destabilization. This philosophy of free markets, which has been the matter of study among economists, other social scientists, and philosophers, is not a subject of controversy any more. The financial markets and mechanisms whose behavior, structure, and dynamics have been the target of considerable debate and criticism, and that too not only because of its occasional failures in rationally guiding the economy but due to its continuing total dysfunction from time to time causing devastating impact and irreparable damage to the real economies. One of the biggest drawbacks of markets, as has been proven historically and more experienced in recent times, is its cyclicality that runs the risk of systemic collapse when it reaches its extremities. In order to avert the distress caused by these cyclical failures, it is necessary to device fail-safe mechanism which avoids severe crisis.

Schumpeter's Creative Destruction: The Seed of Growth of Capitalism and Fall of Communism

At every stage of evolution of capitalism, the structure of capitalism and its institutions and sectors undergo a sharp change. Some institutions and sectors just decline and disappear, while those that can adapt quickly restructure and evolve to play their purposeful and more productive role in the newly evolving system. They not only adapt to changes but also mold the shape of evolution and be a part of it. This is a constant process of innovation, Schumpeter's "creative destruction." The process of creative destruction, the phrase coined by Joseph A. Schumpeter, was also discussed by Marx who described it as the living force of capitalism. Schumpeter, an Austrian economist, who was also its Finance Minister during its days of hyperinflation in 1920s and later a Professor at the Harvard University in 1935, was one of the most outstanding contemporary economists who reviewed Marx, his writings and ideology in the light of the changes in societies, technology, and institutions of capitalism and democracy in the twentieth century, and the actual experience of communism in his classic book, *Capitalism, Socialism and Democracy* in 1942.

Marx prophesied, "The bourgeoisie (capitalism) cannot exist without constantly revolutionizing the instruments of production, and thereby the relations of production, and with them the whole relations of society.... The constant revolutionizing of production, uninterrupted disturbance of all social conditions, everlasting uncertainty and agitation distinguish the bourgeois epoch from all earlier ones" [1, p. 38]. Capitalism evolves and grows on seeking larger markets, rising production, mass consumption, and lower prices. It sustains on seeking newer markets, newer products, newer equipments, and methods of production. Capitalism regenerates itself through this process of constant renewal, renovation, and innovation. Schumpeter calls it the process of "creative destruction," which he did actually derive from Marx's thesis of evolution of capitalism and demise also brought out clearly in the Manifesto. "The conditions of bourgeoisie society are too narrow to comprise the wealth created by them. And how does the bourgeoisie get over this crises? On the one hand by enforced destruction of a mass of productive forces; on the other, by the conquest of new markets, and by the more thorough exploitation of the old ones. That is to say, by paving the way for more extensive and more destructive crises, and by diminishing the means whereby crises are prevented" [1, p. 42].

Creative destruction is the rejuvenating process of capitalism which prevents it from decaying, degenerating, and finally collapsing if not regenerated in time. Schumpeter describes it as "The essential point to grasp is that in dealing with capitalism we are dealing with an evolutionary process.... Capitalism is by nature a form or method of economic change and not only never is but never can be stationary.... The fundamental impulse that sets and keeps the capitalist engine in motion comes from new consumers' goods, the new methods of production or transportation, the new markets, the new forms of industrial organization that capitalist enterprise creates. ...the process of industrial mutation -if I may use that biological term- that incessantly destroying the old one, incessantly creating a new one. This process of Creative Destruction is the essential fact about capitalism. It is what capitalism lives in and what every capitalist concern has got to live in" [3].

The discovery of steam engine; use of coal, coal-run railways and ships; invention of electricity, bulbs, and power-driven machines; invention of automobile and telephone; discovery of oil and atomic energy; and invention of airplanes, television, computers, Internet, wireless communication, and mobile phones have all been the major discoveries, and their commercial applications churned by the institution of capitalism, have been the milestones that have revolutionized the economic life from time to time. So long has been the track covered by the capitalism over the last 200 years from the dawn of the industrial society. At every stage the capitalism has moved forward with creative destruction. Under capitalism the private enterprise drives the wave of creative destruction. If this process slows, it will manifest the symptoms of stagnating or decaying capitalism. With the orderly and regular onset of this wave of creative destructions, capitalism demonstrates its vibrancy and resilience. One of the primary reasons of the breakup of the USSR and collapse of communism in Europe and Russia was the stagnation in this process with the resultant decay of its capital stock unable to move the economy forward. The secret of survival of Chinese communism and its unprecedented and record growth lies in its abandoning the path of state ownership of capital under the leadership of Deng in 1980 and adopting state–private–foreign capital-driven creative destruction rebuilding the economy. The transformation of Shanghai into a world-class metropolis in less than a decade with 18 million population is a shining example of creative destruction unparalleled globally.

One of most critical cornerstones of capitalism is freedom. The second is private property. And the third is democracy. These constituents have enabled American capitalism to survive a series of crises it faced from time to time and emerge stronger after adaptation. These are the genes that determine the DNA of American capitalism. The DNA of communism lacks freedom and democracy that allow the system to adapt in times of crisis and decay and move on to the progressive path. The USSR collapsed, but China took hint of this disease which claims communism and adapted at the right moment and in quick succession to pursue on the path of diluting communism to private ownership with state capitalism, a new breed of capitalism within the framework of socialism. It did not permit democracy and also freedom in large measure, but allowed private property and imported technology to keep its economic machine updated supplying goods in plenty. It also became less autocratic and bureaucratic and promoted decentralization in its pattern of economic growth. Despite its success in preventing its downfall and engineering growth and economic prosperity through pragmatic adaptation of its dogmatic ideology, which the USSR could not achieve, it still remains way behind in freedom and democracy.

References

1. Marx K, Engels F. The communist manifesto. London: Verso; 1998.
2. Gorbachev M. The August coup – the truth and the lessons. New York: Harper Collier Publishers; 1991.
3. Schumpeter JA. Capitalism, socialism and democracy. London: George Allen & Unwin; 1976. p. 82–3.

Chapter 11
Structural Shifts

> To believe as many American economists do that empirical economics begins and ends with time-series analysis, is to ignore a lot of valuable information that cannot be put into so convenient a form. I include the sort of information that is encapsulated in the qualitative inferences made by expert observers, as well as direct knowledge of the functioning of economic institutions. Skepticism is always in order, of course. Insiders are sometimes the slaves of silly ideas. But we are so well off for evidence that we can afford to ignore everything but time series of prices and quantities.
>
> Robert M. Solow, *Growth Theory: An Exposition, 2000*

Backdrop: The Setting

The current crisis is as much a global crisis as was the Great Depression. It emerged initially as the subprime debt crisis but soon snowballed into a global financial and economic meltdown. The financial crises invariably cause monetary implosion whose magnitude depends on the size and coverage of the crisis. The financial implosion is the result of financial losses arising from sharp drop in prices of securities or assets. In the case of forex crisis, the losses arise from sharp drop in exchange rates which is later exacerbated by the capital flight. Working at the accounting and monetary aspects at the microlevel, the financial implosion at macrolevel produces insidious monetary contraction and economic slump. The first attack of the financial crisis is on money supply and liquidity. It happened after the Great Crash of 1929, Black Friday in October 1987, Asian Crisis of 1997, Long-Term Capital Management failure in 1999, and dot-com bust in Y2K. All these crises resulted in financial implosion and carried devastating potential that was quickly diffused except in 1929. In 1929, the monetary contraction was much bigger due to failure of banks affecting nearly half of the banking system. The financial implosion leading to monetary contraction is sure way toward much deeper malady of depression. All the crises in recent years, including the current biggest of them, have averted their culmination

S. Nayak, *The Global Financial Crisis: Genesis, Policy Response and Road Ahead*,
DOI 10.1007/978-81-322-0798-6_11,

into depression signs although they have all caused recessions of various magnitude and longevity.

Systemic Context

Any major economic crisis has its systemic roots. So has the current one. In this way, we can approach the problem not in its visible manifestation but go deeper into its root cause. The deeper analysis of the current global crisis needs the study of several systemic changes. The changes in trends, institutions, and policies at several levels:

1. The structural change in the composition, pattern, and dynamics of the global economy induced by a new phase of global economic policy for growth
2. The ideological change that has brought institutional changes on both sides of the iron curtain: the demise of communism and rise of capitalism in the erstwhile communist world and metamorphosis of capitalism in the USA
3. The dynamics of the US economy and analysis of its growth drivers
4. The transformation of the global financial system and flows and its impact on financial markets and their regulation

There have been both the internal factors that have influenced the dynamics of the US economy over a long run and the external pressures that have impinged on the stability and growth of the US economy. We look at both these group of factors in order to better understand the causality of the crisis. The analysis runs to first outline and present the internal stressors that have caused structural changes in the US economy and then details the significant external or global paradigm shifts that necessitated the systemic responses from the US economy and newly emerging fast-growing economies, the BRIC nations (Brazil, Russia, India, China), that are becoming dominant players in the global growth and stability scenario. Some of these external changes have indeed been the result of its own agenda of globalization and the economic policies it pursued and propagated abroad to carry the process of globalization.

Internal Stressors on the Dynamics of US Economy

American Capitalism: Mature and Migrating

A characteristic feature of the current state of the US economy is that it has entered the mature stage of capitalism. The capital accumulation, a process which is vital for its success, is no longer occurring in traditional sector of manufacturing. The share of manufacturing in the GDP is steadily declining. The thrust of the economy is on the service sector and high-technology industries. Yet, notwithstanding the dramatic shift in global economic power in the last few decades, the share of the USA in global economy has not only remained stable but marginally improved. The share of the USA in global economy GDP has marginally gone up from 26.3% in 1975 to 27.6% in 2009. Despite large increases in growth rates in Asia with countries like China, India, and South Korea at or near double-digit growth, the share of the USA has been steady primarily due to technological advances improving the productivity sharply. However, the share of manufacturing in GDP which was at its high in 1953 at 28% has been steadily declining. The decades of 1950s and 1960s were the heydays of industrial growth in the USA with flourishing manufacturing sector. Since then, it declined to 20% in 1980, 16% in 1990, and 12% in 2005.

American capitalism is in the postindustrial stage. It has exported industrial phase to emerging market economies led by China which are now accumulating capital through rapid industrial growth and mass production. The share of service sector has gone up from 60% in 1950 to 77% in 2010. The government and real estate have grown with each having 12.4 and 12.5% shares in GDP, respectively. The agriculture which was 7% of GDP in 1945 declined to 2.3% in 1970 and 1.2% in 2011. However, the agriculture, despite being low employment generator because of mechanization and technology, has enjoyed maximum productivity growth 1.9% per annum over 1948–1999. The two sectors which give perennial strength to the US economy are the oil and agriculture. The US industrialization did run very fast on cheap oil, the advantage which its European partners did not possess. The other strongest aspects of the US economy, in addition to its oil output and reserves, are its bountiful agriculture and horticulture. It accounts for 9.2% of its exports and is also a net exporter in these sectors. Despite being net importer of goods, the USA continues to maintain its status of net exporter of agricultural products. Its buoyant agriculture and horticulture is another feature of its economy which keeps it stable from the vicissitudes of the global economy. It gives resounding strength, stability, and resilience to the US economy against the inflationary tendencies. Since growth and employment are urgent issues which the policymakers and political parties are addressing, any policy suggestion has to be focused on this reality of changing structure of the economy in the wake of globalization and ongoing technological leaps.

Slopping Savings and Eroding Capital

A disturbing trend in the US economy is that of paucity of savings. Until the onset of globalization in the second half of 1980s, the US personal savings rate ranged between 7 and 9% in the 1960s and surprisingly high range of 8–11% during the uncertain economic age of 1970s. The reason for the high rate of savings despite higher inflation in 1970s was that the economic uncertainty tended the households to save more than before. During the first half of the 1980s, the personal savings rate remained high in the range of 8.5% to a high of 11.5%. By 1990, the rate came down to 6.5% but rose to a high of 7.5% in 1992 and then began sliding to a low of 3% in

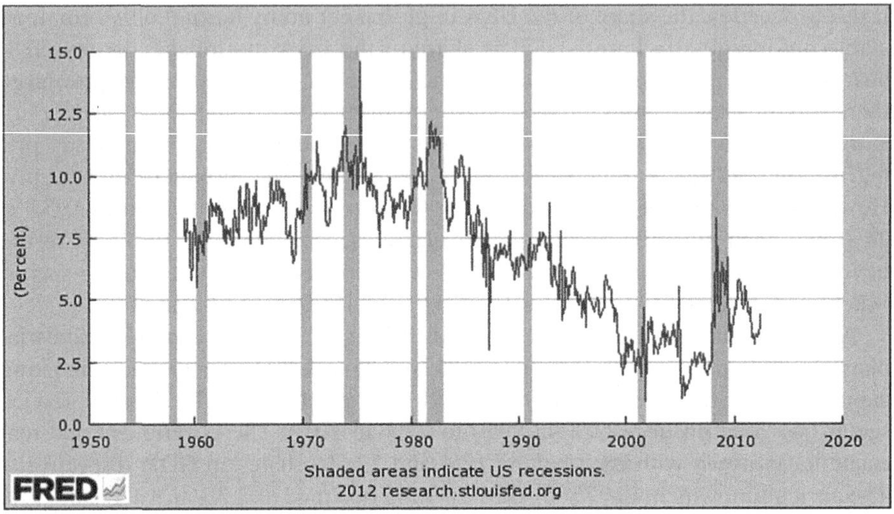

Fig. 11.1 Personal Saving Rate (PSAVERT). *Shaded areas* indicate US recessions. 2012 research.stlouisfed.org (Source: U.S. Department of Commerce: Bureau of Economic Analysis)

2000. It hovered between 1.5 and 2.5% during 2001–2007 but reached a low of 1.3% in 2005. Coincidentally, the USA faced negative savings rate only in 1932 and 1933, the years of the Great Depression when it was negative 0.9 and 1.5%. During the crisis year of 2008, the savings rate improved to 6% but declined to 4% in 2011 (Fig. 11.1).

A number of factors have contributed to this phenomenon. Among the most important ones are availability of cheap housing; auto, consumer, and credit card finance; low or negative real interest rates; rising prices of assets such as stocks, houses, and real estate; and demographic changes in the job market such as rising retiring population which won't save more and entry of younger people in the job market who also don't save more because of their independence from family savings or parental support. The employment–population ratio which was going up from 58% in 1982 to 64% in 2000 began declining and reached 59% in 2009. Yet another lifestyle change that has caused the decline in the household family saving rate is the considerable rise in the number of families in the last two decades arising from single-parent family. Demographic and lifestyle changes, asset price booms, cheap consumer finance, and low to zero or negative real interest rate have all contributed to the decline in the personal savings rate.

Consumption Dominant Economy

The US economy is a continental economy. It does not depend on exports for its growth, although exports until 1970s did contribute to the strength of the dollar in the global currency market. Since the early 1970s after the collapse of the Bretton Woods, the US dollar has declined in the international currency markets. The dollar strengthened briefly during early 1980s during Fed's dear money and high interest rate policy. But since then, the dollar has been consistently falling in the foreign exchange markets due to its growing trade and current account deficit. With the population of 314 million comprising 117 million households, consumption spending touched $11 trillion in 2010, accounting for 70% of GDP. The US consumer market is even larger than the Eurozone which, with population of 500 million, spent 60% of GDP on consumption totaling seven trillion euro. Europe is thriftier, but the US economy is driven more by the strength of growth in consumer spending. Higher propensity to consume makes the economy more sensitive to the changes in growth in consumer spending.

Predominance of Permanent Income and Wealth Effect

The classical economists theorized savings to be determined by the rate of interest and consumption to be the residual. Keynes saw a glaring flaw in this thinking and theory. By proposing the concept of propensity to consume, which established a functional relationship between consumption and income, he revolutionized the macroeconomic theory and policy. The consumption and savings he stated depend on the level of income and not rate of interest. Although he identified current consumption to be influenced by current income, he also mentioned other factors such as wealth and wealth effect also determining consumption. Extending Keynes's concept further, Friedman postulated the permanent income hypothesis in which he identified the role of not only the current income but permanent income comprising expected future income flows to be governing the level of consumption. The concept is very relevant to the US economy. The US economy and its growth in recent years have been driven by permanent income-induced consumption. The availability of credit card debt and cheap consumer credit further strengthen the consumption on permanent income. This has been the redeeming feature of the US economy due to which the savings rate has been traditionally low. The consumption growth in the US economy was fueled by the wealth effect of stock market boom during the 1990s and housing and real estate boom during 2002–2007. While in a booming economy the wealth effect brings positive impact on growth, the depression in prices of financial and real assets results in negative effect on consumption, thereby retarding the growth momentum of the economy. This is a major handicap in the revival of growth following the crisis. So long as the hole in the balance sheets of households remains unfilled, the momentum of growth tends to be slower.

Income Inequality

Income inequality is a measure of economy's distress level. The capitalist development of the global economy over the last more than two and half decades of globalization and reforms has raised the growth rate and also reduced poverty levels but has increased the income inequalities. Between 1950 and 1960, the median family income in the USA went up by 38%. The same rose by 37% between 1960 and 1970. But increases between 1970 and 1980 and 1980 and 1990 were meager 7 and 6%, respectively. It demonstrates poor growth in incomes of the bottom 50% of households. Again between 1970 and 1990, incomes of top 5% of households rose by 35% and top 20% of households by 31%. Next 20% of households by 21%. But bottom 20% household had only 3% rise, while the next 20% by 7%. Since the 1970s, the income distribution in the USA has become more skewed. Gini index, which measures the degree of and change in inequality, for the USA has gone up from 39.7 in 1967 to 46.9 in 2005, showing 18% increase in income inequality.[1]

Return on Capital Under Squeeze

Declining rate of profit is the trump card in Marx's theory of collapse of capitalism. The phenomenon stops accumulation of capital and causes capital decay and eventual collapse of the system due to rampant obsolescence of capital, bankruptcies, and failures. It is ironical that Marx's prophecy became reality not in a mature capitalist state but manifested in the crumbling of the very first communist experiment, the USSR. All the capitalist democracies have survived the other crises. Yet the declining rate of profit is a phase which capitalist economies do face and are facing now. The rate of profit in the USA which increased from 25% in the early 1950s to 30% declined to 15% in the late 1950s. It recovered again in the 1960s, the heyday of manufacturing in the USA, and rose to 30% by mid-1960s to fall again below 15% by 1970. It declined to below 10% by 1980. The 1980s saw profit rates rising to 17%. The rate rose to 19% in the 1990s but fell to 15% in 2000. Japan witnessed much sharper decline in profit rates from the peak of 43% in 1960s and 1970s to a low of 7% in 2000. Peak rate of profit in Germany has been 35% in the early 1950s. But the rate has fallen steadily thereafter and much sharper on German unification to a low of near 0% in 1993 but has recovered to 5% in 2005 [1]. Profit is the engine of growth of capitalism. Declining rate of profit is a feature and trend of capitalism which keeps it alive and kicking. The decline in the profit rate is a reflection of lower prices and better quality of goods and services and efficient allocation of resources achieved by the pulls and pushes of capitalism. It is the result of the competition, another vital ingredient and lifeblood of healthy capitalism. The competition it engenders ensures the survival of the fittest, the economic Darwinism. Declining

[1] US Census, 2006.

rate of profit is the stepping stone for the next round of growth on the business front. The capital is waiting for another bout of technological advance initiating a new round of capital accumulation. At this stage, new and old savings and existing financial and real assets are used for capital accumulation. It is this process which starts the new cycle of growth: new products, new services, new ways of doing old things and new things, new utilities, and new luxuries. That is what economics is all about, and it can happen in free societies with scope for individualism. Schumpeter's creative destruction restarts the engine of capitalism moving its wheels faster and keeps it on the path of sustained progress. This is what makes capitalism healthy, robust, and resilient. Capitalism that halts this progress of innovation digs its own grave. It can evoke stagnation and economic decay later. Marx prophesized this to be the process of the decline of capitalism. Instead his theory manifested itself in the demise of bureaucratic communism in USSR and Eastern Europe. In fact, the capitalism after Keynes reformed dramatically. The postwar-enlightened capitalism that achieved tremendous productivity growth improved wages, contrary to the Marxian theory. The state also redressed the problem of grave economic inequalities and social injustice through the welfare measures. The class divide disappeared, and social unrest became a remote possibility in American capitalism. Erstwhile communist states turned into market-oriented capitalistic economies. The institution of capitalism thrives on innovation. Without innovation and creative destruction, the capitalism is likely to stagnate and decay.

Structural Trade Deficit

The continental nature of the US economy makes American capitalism unique and quite different from other geographically smaller European economies and Japan. In the 1960s, the trade status of the USA changed from the export surplus nation to import surplus or trade deficit nation. Since then, the USA has been facing a propensity to import which is higher than the rate of growth of its exports. Resultantly, the US trade deficit has been rising rapidly. Since the model of globalization centered on higher growth in exports of labor-intensive emerging market economies, the US trade deficit is benign for the global economy.

The phase of globalization has heightened the foreign trade orientation of the US economy. The shares of both the imports and exports in the national economy have increased. The share of foreign trade in the US economy has gone up from 12.2% GDP (imports + exports/2 as % of GDP) in 1980 to 18.2% in 2010. The foreign trade orientation of the US economy has grown by half in three decades. Globalization raised the share of US imports in its GDP from 12.1% in 1980 to 19.5% in 2010. The exports grew at a much slower rate. The share of exports in GDP went up from 12.3 to 17% during the same period. Since the US income elasticity of imports is higher than the rest of the world's income elasticity of imports from the USA, the US exports are growing slower than its imports, leading to its enlarging trade and current account deficit (Table 11.1).

Table 11.1 US foreign trade dynamics

	Exports	Imports	GDP	APM	MPM
	($ billion)			(%)	
1960	30.6	23.7	526.4	4.5	
1970	68.4	66.4	1,038.3	6.4	8.5
1980	344.4	333.8	2,788.1	12.1	15.3
1990	707	759.3	5,800.5	13.1	14.1
2000	1,425.3	1,782.8	9,951.5	17.9	22.2
2010	2,518.8	2,829.7	14,498.9	19.5	22.8

Data source: Bureau of Economic Analysis, US Department of Commerce
Exports = Exports of goods and services and income receipts
Imports = Imports of goods and services and income payments
APM = Average propensity to import = imports/GDP
MPM = Marginal propensity to import = d imports/d GDP

The US trade and current account deficits went up from $111 billion and $79 billion in 1990 to the record highs of $753 billion and $800 billion in 2006. The current account deficit went up from 1.4% of GDP in 1990 to 6.5% of GDP in 2006. Trade deficit declined thereafter to $697 billion in 2008 and to $379 billion in 2009. The current account deficit has been primarily financed by foreign holding of US government securities. Both the foreign official and private holdings of US treasury bills and government securities have gone up from $530 billion in 1990 to $1.1 trillion in 1996 and further jumped to $5.1 trillion in 2011, accounting for 50% of public debt.

Slowing Exports Growth

Loss of competitiveness of US exports in international market was a natural effect of the philosophy of globalization. Under the process of globalization, the USA had to export the capital and technology to the emerging market economies which enjoyed more competitive edge in cost of production due to the lower cost of unskilled as well as skilled labor. By exporting capital and technology, the USA not reduced its exports but also imported goods which it was producing at a higher cost.

The annual rate of exports growth which was 12% in 1960s remained steady at 10.5% during the 1980s and 10% in 1990s. During the new millennium, exports growth declined to 8%. Table 11.2 shows composition of US exports over the last more than three decades. The share of agriculture in the total exports has fallen from 11.3% in 1989 to 9.4% in 2011. Sharper fall was experienced in auto exports whose share fell from 9.6 to 2.2%. Capital goods, computers and chips, and aircrafts and engines also showed marginal declines. The sectors which showed growth in the share were fuels and lubricants and consumer goods.

Table 11.2 Composition of US exports (In billions of $)

	1989		2000		2011	
		% of total		% of total		% of total
Total exports	362,999		784,781		1,480,432	
Agriculture	41,080	11.3	52,801	6.7	140,023	9.4
Industrial materials	97,880	26.9	177,135	22.5	500,342	33.8
Fuels and lubricants	13,251	3.6	21,121	2.7	139,605	9.4
Chemicals	27,082	7.4	52,242	6.6	123,148	8.3
Capital goods	136,098	37.5	357,000	45.5	492,988	33.3
Computers and chips	36,298	10.0	115,619	14.7	93,115	6.3
Aircrafts and engines	26,935	7.4	48,091	6.1	97,989	6.6
Automotive	35,141	9.6	80,356	10.2	33,372	2.2
Consumer goods	35,872	9.9	89,341	11.3	174,957	11.8

Source: Bureau of Economic Analysis, US Department of Commerce

The USA has to rejuvenate its declining sectors in exports, like agriculture, automobiles, aircrafts, and capital goods, in order to raise the rate of growth of exports. If it achieves its secular growth rate of exports of 10%, it would considerably moderate the pressure on its BoP deficit and also the liquidity glut arising in the global market from the growth in forex reserves of the central banks of emerging market economies.

Most Favored Nation (MFN) for Global Capital

The redeeming feature of American capitalism and the dollar is that it still continues to be most attractive destination for global capital. Not only is it the most preferred target for lucrative returns in risk capital, but it is also globally safest and most secure for fixed-income securities and also the real estate. Despite the current lowest return on the US T bills and government securities, they remain the most preferred bond investment. Although the rising trade and current account deficit has been a concern since the beginning of 1990s, the overall BoP situation has been much stable due to inflow of foreign capital both in equity and debt, including the investments in T bills and other government securities.

While the current account deficit shows how much produce and services are sourced from abroad on net basis, the capital account gives the movements of capital which also support the overall BoP. The inflow of capital from abroad both private account and official investment account is adequately large to balance the current account deficit. Since the private capital inflows occur largely on economic and financial considerations, the actual BoP of the USA can only be measured by the foreign official investments in US T bills and government securities. Table 11.3 shows the US current account deficit and foreign investments in the USA over 1980–2011. Despite rising current account deficit from $79 billion in 1990 to the peak of $746 billion in 2005 and lower level of

Table 11.3 US current account deficit and foreign capital inflow (in million $)

	1980	1990	2000	2005	2007	2008	2009	2010	2011
Balance on current account	**2,317**	**−78,968**	**−416,338**	**−745,774**	**−710,303**	**−677,135**	**−381,896**	**−441,951**	**−465,926**
Balance on goods	−25,500	−111,037	−445,787	−780,730	−818,886	−830,109	−505,758	−645,124	−738,413
Balance on services	6,093	30,173	69,038	72,106	122,158	131,770	126,603	150,387	178,533
Balance on goods and services	−19,407	−80,864	−376,749	−708,624	−696,728	−698,338	−379,154	−494,737	−559,880
Balance on income	30,073	28,550	19,178	68,591	101,485	147,089	119,717	183,859	227,007
Unilateral current transfers, net	−8,349	−26,654	−58,767	−105,741	−115,061	−125,885	−122,459	−131,074	−133,053
Foreign-owned assets in the USA	**62,037**	**139,357**	**1,038,224**	**1,247,347**	**2,064,642**	**431,406**	**314,390**	**1,308,279**	**1,000,990**
Foreign official assets in the USA	16,649	33,910	42,758	259,268	481,043	554,634	480,286	398,188	211,826
US government securities	**11,895**	**30,243**	**35,710**	**213,334**	**269,897**	**591,381**	**437,324**	**353,294**	**158,735**
US treasury securities	9,708	29,576	−5,199	112,841	98,432	548,653	569,893	442,012	171,179
Foreign private investments in the USA	45,388	105,447	995,466	988,079	1,583,599	−123,228	−165,896	910,091	789,164
Direct investment	16,918	48,494	321,274	112,638	221,166	310,092	150,442	205,831	233,988
US treasury securities	2,645	−2,534	−69,983	132,300	66,845	162,944	−15,451	297,797	240,878
Other US securities	5,457	1,592	459,889	450,386	605,414	−165,639	1,855	139,316	−56,442
US currency	2,773	16,586	−3,357	8,447	−10,675	29,187	12,632	28,319	54,996

Source: Bureau of Economic Analysis, US Department of Commerce

Table 11.4 US international investment position

	1980 (in billion $)	1990	2000	2005	2008	2011
Net international investment position	360	–230	–1,337	–1,932	–3,260	–4,030
US investment abroad	930	2,179	6,239	11,962	19,465	21,132
US official reserves	171	174	128	188	293	536
Gold	156	102	71	134	227	400
US private investments abroad	693	1,920	6,025	10,506	12,419	15,712
Foreign assets in the USA	570	2,409	7,576	13,894	22,724	25,162
Official holdings in govt. secs.	118	291	756	1,725	3,265	4,277
Foreign private investments	388	2,029	6,538	10,448	12,813	15,333
Private holdings of treasury secs.	16	152	382	644	852	1,418
US currency	19	64	205	280	301	397

Source: Bureau of Economic Analysis, US Department of Commerce

$466 billion in 2011, the actual BoP deficit measured by the official investment in US government securities was only $213 billion in 2005 but rose to record $591 billion in 2008, the year of the crisis. This shows considerable shift toward the US government securities in foreign official investments. By 2011, this investment reduced to $159 billion. The upshot of the matter is that despite higher current account deficit in the 2000s, the robust capital market in the USA which attracts both the risk and debt capital, including the investment in US gilt-edged securities, adequate enough to offset the current account deficit, keeps the overall BoP situation of the USA sustainable, without damaging the strength of the dollar international market.

Over the decade of 2000s on account of the persistent growth in the current account deficit, the foreign investment in the USA has exceeded the US investment abroad, leading to the status of the USA as the net debtor and the largest debtor nation in the world. Table 11.4 above shows the trend in the US international investment position since 1980. The overall US net foreign investments rose from –$230 billion in 1990 to –$4,030 billion in 2011. This has primarily the result of sharp spurt in the foreign holdings of US T bills and government securities from $443 billion in 1990 to $5,695 in 2011 under the impact of globalization that raised the current account deficit.

The situation is analogous to the historical sterling balances which the colonies of the British Empire held in London after Britain abandoned the gold standard in 1931. After the Second World War when the colonies attained independence, they used these balances for financing their trade deficit. The decline of pound sterling as the international currency replaced by the dollar also led to the gradual end of the sterling balances and the sterling area. Today, we are in the dollar area where the BoP surplus nations are holding dollar balances. The situation is sustainable so long as the dollar remains strong in the international market.

Political Economy of Ideology of Capitalism: Size of Government

The phenomenon of larger government involvement has been a feature of modern capitalism since the advent of Keynesianism. It has manifested itself in its size in relation to the economy, regulation and supervision apparatus, welfare obligations and commitments, and counter cyclical fiscal and monetary policies. The experience of the 1980s shows that, notwithstanding the onslaught of Thatcherism in UK which took shape the of Reaganomics in the USA attempting to downsize the government along with economic liberalization, privatization, and reform, the size of government has not come down significantly. Despite the rhetoric of downsizing the government, the size of government in US economy has increased during both the Democratic as well as Republican administrations. The juggernaut of government expenditure can hardly be reduced without seriously jeopardizing the growth dynamics of American capitalism. The government expenditure has continued to be the pump primer as well as the driver of American capitalism. The economic and social infrastructure it builds and maintains triggers and boosts the faster growth in private enterprise. To what extent the government expenditure can be rationalized to avoid waste and unproductive activities is an issue which needs to be and is being addressed by all governments due overriding need to reduce budgetary deficits and rising public debt.

The size of government is currently an issue which has invited considerable debate and discussion not only among the economists but also among the political parties. Elections are contested on this issue. Economically, the right or optimal size of government is intrinsically linked to the structure and institutional makeup of each economy. There isn't a fixed size for all economies. When Keynes brought in the deficit financing and larger government spending, it was advocated in special circumstances. Since then the size of government and deficit financing has increased due to its positive impact on sustaining growth and enhancing economic welfare. What is not desirable is the fiscal profligacy that is unproductive and does not contribute to either growth or higher economic welfare. At that stage, the size of the government and deficit financing has to be lowered. But one cannot reduce government and leave the economy entirely to market forces. In fact, leaving the economy totally to the commands of the unregulated market forces led to the crisis that in fact, with its aftereffects, increased the size of the government further. The experience of recent crisis is the case in point. The free markets, especially the financial markets, still require more prudential regulation to avert excesses and their aftereffects.

The single most important indicator of this change in the influence of government in the economic life is the size of government budget in the economy.

While Roosevelt succeeded in prescribing the Keynesian medicine by adopting the New Deal and raising the government spending from 3.4% of GDP in 1930 to 10.7% in 1934, during the war years 1939–1945, the government spending shot up to as high as 43.6%. In three out of seven war years, the spending was nearing 42–43%. While the budget deficit in 1934 rose to a high of 5.9% of GDP, in 1943, it went up to 30%. In the early postwar years of the 1950s, the share of government expenditure in GDP was in the range of 15–18%. It remained in 17–20% range in the 1960s and 19–20% in the 1970s.

Despite the rhetoric of Reaganomics of reducing the size of the government, the total government expenditure rose to 33.3% of GDP in 1983 with the budget deficit of 6% of GDP. The Clinton years, 1992–2000, saw the decline in government spending to 28.8% of GDP with the budget surplus of 2.4% of GDP. The tax receipts went up by 2% of GDP, and government expenditure came down by 3.2% of GDP. Due to low interest rates, the interest payments on public debt came down by 1.1% of GDP and defense spending by 1.4% of GDP.

The US government expenditure which was $2.7 trillion (30.9% of GDP) in 2007 and $2.98 trillion (32.6% of GDP) in 2008 jumped to $3.5 trillion in 2009 and $3.6 trillion in 2011. The budget deficit escalated from $161 billion in 2007 and $458 billion in 2008 to $1.4 trillion (37.1% of GDP) in 2009 and $1.3 trillion (35.4% of GDP) in 2011. Total government budget deficit which was 2.1% of GDP in 2007 rose to the record 12% of GDP in 2009 and was 9.9% in 2011. The record government expenditure and deficits after the crisis have succeeded in preventing the onset of depression but has increased the federal debt from $9 trillion in 2007 to $14.7 trillion in 2011.[2] The debt ceiling of $16.394 trillion imposed by the Congress as the legal borrowing limit is likely to be crossed in early 2013 as the debt figure reached $15.97 trillion in August, 2012.

Welfare Capitalism and the Fiscal Cliff

The second aspect of American capitalism, which makes it socially more responsible than pure free market, profit-oriented, and greed-driven economy, is the institutional framework legislated from time to time to regulate and supervise the functioning of capitalism, be it in banking, trade, industry, services, labor, and consumer interest. It is not that the system is foolproof and always provides a fail-safe mechanism that will prevent failures. This has been evident from the economic setbacks and crises experienced over time. Every failure is a learning lesson and experience arising from some weaknesses in the system that did not show up earlier. And with every unsavory experience, action for legislative changes has improved the systemic functionality, efficiency, and strength to withstand unexpected shocks.

[2] Office of Management and Budget, The White House.

The Great Depression was an eye opener for governments to realize its social obligation. Although the right to work and engage in productive activity to earn income is enshrined in the constitutions of all nations, after the experience of depression and massive unemployment it caused, the government took upon itself the responsibility to create an economic environment for every able-bodied man and woman to have a job and ensure full employment. Failing this, the government is committed to provide unemployment benefits. In order to fulfill its social obligations, governments also spend on providing free school education, health care, and social security for the old citizens. The American capitalism took the shape of welfare state since the New Deal in 1933 and has been constantly working in perfecting its system in ensuring economic security and welfare.

The process of welfare obsession of America capitalism needs to be buttressed with fiscal prudence. There is no lunch except in private charity and government protection. While the private charity is a zero-sum game, Keynes gave the economic logic for free lunch to usurp the depressed economy. However, even the Keynesian pill and medicine have their adverse side effects in heavy doses. Keynes' medicine was an antidepression or antirecession medicine to be used only when the economies are in the grip of these syndromes. Unfortunately, the overdosing of Keynesianism has unfolded another economic threat. It has unleashed fiscal imprudence, piling public debt, and brought the government finances on a fiscal cliff. While the social security, unemployment benefits, Medicaid, and Medicare give American capitalism a large coverage on welfare issues, the recent health-care extensions have further improved the welfare benefits. What the American capitalism needs now is to achieve the fiscal sustainability of its welfarism. Unfortunately, Obama's election rhetoric on health care came at the time when the economy was in its worst shape, requiring a heavy dose of Keynesianism with large fiscal support.

Sixty-Year Cycle of American Capitalism

After the Great Depression and the Keynesian prescription for this intractable economic malady, government expenditure through deficit financing went on increasing. This naturally raised the public debt in size and also in relation to the GDP. The public debt rose from 17% of GDP in predepression year of 1929 to 50% in 1940. The Second World War raised the government expenditure sharply and public debt to the record level of 120% of GDP by 1945. Since then, the peacetime progress reduced the military expenditure and also caused a decline in the level of public debt.

The 60-year postwar progress of American capitalism in terms of its debt profile is shown in Fig. 11.2. The graph of national debt of the USA as a percentage of GDP shows a declining trend from 1950 till 1980. The unusual growth of debt in 1943–1945 was the result of the war expenditure when the ratio reached the peak of 120%. However, since 1950, it declined from 80% over the next three decades to 33% in 1980. This three decadal period was Bretton Woods era till 1971 and transition

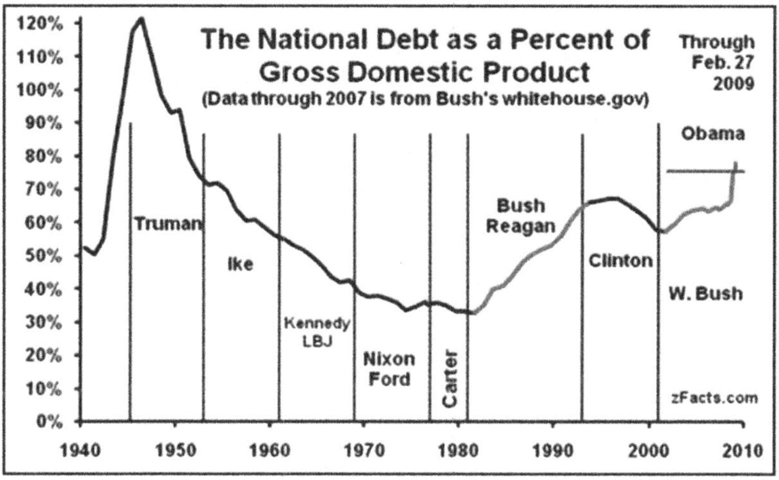

Fig. 11.2 US national debt growth

phase later. Since 1980, the debt steadily rose from a low of 33% and doubled to 66% by 1990 under the Reagan–Bush regimes. The Clinton era of 1993–2001 showed a marginal decline to 60%. But debt rose thereafter and reached 80% of GDP in 2008. Unprecedented budget deficits after the crisis have led to the federal debt crossing 100% of GDP in 2012.

We see a similar but reverse trend in the interest rates. The effective federal funds rate rose from 1% in 1950 to a record high of 21% in 1980 and gradually declined thereafter to less than 1% by 2009. These two symmetric patterns reflect the two different institutional frameworks through which the US economy was passing in the last 60 years since 1950. If we relate the two graphs, we discern that when the interest rates were rising from 1950 to 1980, the debt was falling in relative terms, in terms of GDP. In contrast, when the phase of declining interest rates began, the debt was rising in relative terms (Figs. 11.3 and 11.4).

It is interesting to see that the unemployment rate also steadily rose from 2.5% in 1953 till 1980 after dipping in 1969 to 3%. Unemployment rate crossed 10% in 1982. Since then, it fell to 4% in 2000, but it rose again to 10% in 2009. The difference between 1982 and 2009 is that in 1982, interest rates were high because of inflation and it led to high unemployment. In contrast, in 2009, interest rates were near zero, but the problem is inadequate growth in effective demand and high unemployment persisted.

From low interest rates and low unemployment but high national debt caused by the war expenditure in 1945, the economy has traversed the first 30 years through high interest and low public debt, back to low interest rate over the next 30 years with high unemployment. The economy is, therefore, in a major structural problem of high unemployment, declining rate of profit, and rising personal and public debt.

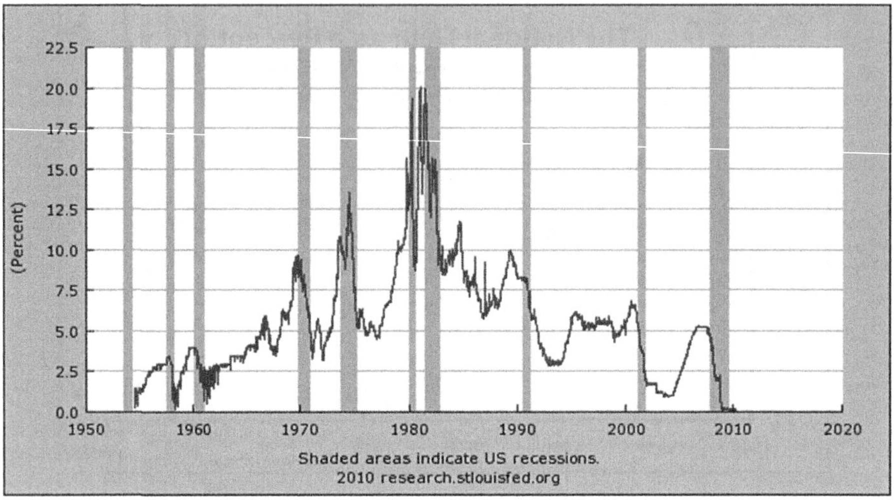

Fig. 11.3 Effective Federal Funds Rate (FF). *Shaded areas* indicate US recessions. 2012 research. stlouisfed.org (Source: Board of Governors of the Federal Reserve System)

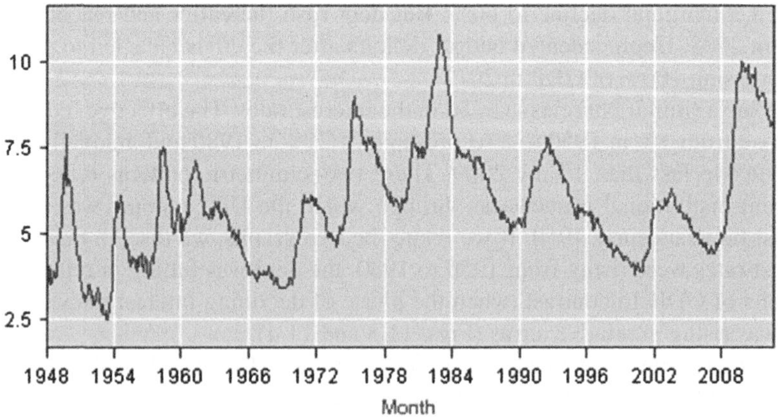

Fig. 11.4 Unemployment rate in the USA (Source: US Department of Labor)

The second aspect of American capitalism, which makes it socially more responsible than pure free market, profit-oriented, and greed-driven economy, is the institutional framework legislated from time to time to regulate and supervise the functioning of capitalism, be it banking, trade, industry, services, labor, and consumer interest. The system is not foolproof and does not provide a fail-safe mechanism that will prevent failures. This has been evident from the economic setbacks and crises experienced over time. Every failure is a learning lesson and experience arising from some weaknesses in the system that did not show up earlier. And with every unsavory experience, action for legislative changes has improved the systemic functionality, efficiency, and strength to withstand unexpected shocks.

Lastly, since the capitalism is known to suffer from the systemic problem of cyclicality whose depth cannot be gauged, counter cyclical fiscal and monetary policies have been adopted to skip the downward phase of the economic cycle. The Fed aims at monetary stimulus through monetary expansion and cheap money and credit by following low interest rate policy, and the government gives tax reliefs and increases expenditure to give the fiscal stimulus to reverse the recessionary trends in the economy and avert the economy slipping into downward spiral.

In a system where the critical component of growth is private investment expenditure, which due to its dynamics but volatile nature governed by the animal spirits takes swings under the domination of changing expected risk–return matrix, the onset of countercyclical fiscal and monetary policy has played a crucial role in sustaining growth and full employment.

Market Failure: Microanalysis and Macro Picture

Two institutions that have played a critical and constructive role in economic activities and development over centuries have been money and markets. Both the institutions have been the facilitators of economic progress. Both have contributed immensely to the technological and economic heights we have reached today. Both money and markets have also evolved rapidly with technological as well as organizational developments. While the main purpose of these institutions is to contribute to the societal welfare, they can sometimes work to the detriment of the society due to their own internal deficiencies or inefficiencies, or weaknesses and drawbacks. The subprime debt crisis is a classic representation of the failure of both money and markets in their excesses.

The free market capitalist economies staged a definite lead over the communist countries but suffered from the other problems of markets. They related to the abuse, inefficiencies, imperfections, and inadequacies of the markets. These came to be exploited by a few institutions at the cost and expense of a wider body of stakeholders and community at large. While the communism failed due to the absence of markets, the capitalism is threatened by the excesses and resultant failures of markets. At the microlevel, a segment of the financial market, the subprime debt securities market, failed, triggering a bigger banking and financial crisis.

While the deficiencies of the banking system and financial system were discussed in Chaps. 1 and 2, the structure of financial markets, their character and peculiarities, and their dynamics and its impact will be discussed later in a separate chapter. It is necessary, however, to mention here this aspect of the financial markets due to its relevance and in fact its critical importance in the current crisis.

Market Versus State: Growing Institutional Mismatch

The metamorphosis of American capitalism displays its adaptability and resilience for seven decades since the Great Depression. Under the overpowering influence of technology, media, legislative boundaries, and regulatory mechanisms, the edifice of capitalism underwent a slow change in its shape and structure. The evolution in corporate structure and management influenced by sophistication in investment banking altered the dynamics of capitalism. Rapid growth and diversity in financial and capital market sophistication gave a new face to the twentieth-century capitalism. The metamorphosis of American capitalism permitted the march of sustained economic progress and prosperity for more than half a century without any serious sign of malaise. Anachronistic capitalism ravaged by depression gave way to more dynamic model with new ideology and functionality. Armed with better legislative safeguards and regulatory structures and guidelines, American capitalism was prepared to thwart any crisis culminating into deep economic malaise. The system was thought to have its fail-safe mechanism in place. This belief was shattered by the breakout of the subprime crisis in 2008.

The weakness which is now evident from the crisis is that the supervisory and regulatory mechanism in its banking sector and financial markets was lagging far behind the enormous growth in volume, products, diversity, and complexity in banking and financial markets. This growing mismatch in the growth, induced by private demand and supply on the one hand and its supervisory setup on the other, has taken the system on a riskier path more vulnerable to crisis. American capitalism needs yet another institutional adjustment and upgradation to deal with demands of modern finance.

Ideological Convergence

Is American capitalism socialism in disguise? It depends on how you define the concepts of capitalism and socialism. The capitalism today is no longer the capitalism of nineteenth- or even twentieth-century ideology, so is socialism. Old-fashioned Marxist–Leninist and then Stalinist bureaucratic, autocratic socialism in the USSR have give way to modern capitalism. China also moved away gradually from Maoist socialism, reforming it by instilling the vital ingredients of capitalism of market-dominated economy, private property, and freedom of choice. When Chinese Premier Deng Xiaoping remarked, "It doesn't matter if a cat is black or white, so long as it catches mice, it is a good cat," and "Socialism is not the same as shared poverty. To be rich is glorious." He effectively closed the chapter of Maoism and class divide and reinvented the Chinese socialism with a new leaf. He called reform a second revolution. He described the annexation of Hong Kong to China as "One country, Two systems," implying the phase as a transition toward the way each of them will perform, until it finally merges into one which is better. When Gorbachev courageously denounced the Marxist–Leninist model as the impractical disaster for the Soviet economy and pleaded to reform it toward market economy with the right to private property, he also echoed the reality which the leadership was refusing to recognize. Two large communist states moved to the right and so is capitalism moving toward the left.

What it reveals is that the political reality of abandoning the ideological dogmatism in favor of pragmatism for economic growth and stability has been captured by the leaderships in both the communist as well as capitalist nations. The communist nations have adopted market mechanism and private property, and capitalism has embraced planning and state intervention in the real interest of salvaging the crisis-ridden economy by massive state intervention. Both the systems are converging. American capitalism is adapting under its systemic stress. It has now pumped enough financial adrenaline in its fight-or-flight response to come out triumphantly defeating the crisis. The Fed, SEC, and government have used the most potent and unorthodox weapons in their armory to deal with the housing loan-borne financial meltdown. With the boldest, historic, and biggest ever fiscal package and monetary creation, American capitalism is now entering a new phase. Not only has the fiscal stimulus from the state proved to be inevitable, but the public–private partnership is also indispensable for restoration of stability in banking system. The market mechanism hereafter will be guided by the state until the system returns to normalcy. The state, with its intervention and financial support, will also oversee the private financial system to ensure that Adam Smith's "invisible hand" of market plays visibly more purposeful social role. American capitalism is evolving and now emerging with a face of socialistic lipstick. Since the 1980s, communist states have adopted capitalism in different shades. This change is a manifestation of slow and gradual convergence of two contrasting ideologies. The compulsions of systemic crises emanating from strains of inherent dynamics of two ideologies are overbearing in bringing them closer.

External Pressures on the US Economy: Global Economic Adjustment

Dominance of Pacific Trade Triangle

Since the onset of globalization which took real momentum in the 1990s, the global trade structure has undergone a rapid transformation and witnessed an unprecedented change. The most dramatic change has occurred in trade between USA, Japan, and China, referred to here as the Pacific trade triangle that has dominated the global scene. Such has been the scale of change that it has not only created a new structure of investment and trade but also given a new direction to the impulses of growth and stability among these economies. China, which was until 1980 an isolationist, an autarkic communist regime, and also not a member of World Trade

Organization until December 2001, has emerged as the one of the largest exporters in the world and the second largest trade partner of the USA next to Canada. China has transformed itself from an autarkic regime into an export-oriented economic juggernaut by ushering export-led growth strategy in its economic development. The double-digit economic growth which it achieved would not have been possible but for the export-dominated growth. Undoubtedly, the change has been the result of massive US and Japanese investment and technology transfer to China, comparable only to the Marshall Plan, burying the historic enmity between China and Japan and ideological hiatus between the USA and China.

In 2009, China emerged as the world's largest exporter with $1,202 billion overtaking Germany at $1,121 and the USA at $1,057 billion. In comparative terms, China's exports were three times the exports of Africa, one and half times the exports of Middle East, and more than two times the exports of Central and South America. China has overshadowed the global trade and growth scenario over the last one decade. The share of China in world trade has gone up from 2.5% in 1993 to 9.1% in 2008, while that of the USA has fallen from 12.6 to 8.2% and of Japan from 9.9 to 5%, with Germany losing marginally from 10.3 to 9.3%. China has also achieved the highest annual rate of growth in exports of 25% among all nations during 2000–2007. In contrast, Japan's exports growth rate declined to 6% during the period. World trade in merchandise rose from $3.7 trillion in 1993 to $13.6 trillion in 2007.

During the 1980s, Japan was the major trading partner of the USA. In 1985, the US imports from Japan accounted for 20.4% of its total imports. The US imports from Germany were 6% and China 1%. China's export-oriented foreign capital and technology-induced growth model changed the scenario. China enjoys considerable advantage in labor cost vis-a-vis Japan and USA. Although the wage rates in China are lower than in Japan by a ratio of 1:10 to 15, due to lower productivity of labor, the wage cost still works out 25% of that in Japan, and the Chinese labor is not as much a stickler for quality as the Japanese.

The US imports from China rose to 16.8% of its total imports in 2007 from 8.5% in 2000, while its imports from Japan fell to 7.4% from 12%. The US imports from Germany have, however, fallen only marginally from 6 to 5% of the total. Despite the decline in Japan's share in US imports, the USA still remains the major destination for Japan's exports accounting for 20% in 2007. The share of Japan's exports to USA was as high as 31% in 1999. Over the period of the last one and half decades, China has replaced Japan as one of its top trading partners. In 2007, China's exports to the USA accounted for 25% of its total exports. China is today in the same position as the USA with respect to its exports as Japan was in the late 1990s. Because of the advantage of low-cost labor, China's exports are more diversified than Japan's. While Japan's exports were dominated in consumer durables and capital goods, China's exports range from footwear, furniture, and ready-made garments to electronic goods and cell phones, and also steel, power equipment, and electrical machinery. While the Japanese exports rendered a great threat to the American industry, mainly in automobile, electronics, and consumer durables, the Chinese exports at low prices helped lower inflation in the USA without being injurious to the US industry (Table 11.5).

Table 11.5 US trade with partners

	China			Germany			Japan			
	In billion $									US total
	Imports	Exports	Balance	Imports	Exports	Balance	Imports	Exports	Balance	imports
1985	3.86	3.85	−0.01	20.2	9.1	−11.1	68.8	22.6	−46.2	337
1990	15.2	4.8	−10.4	28.2	18.8	−9.4	89.7	48.6	−41.1	495
1995	45.5	11.7	−33.8	36.8	22.4	−14.4	123.5	64.5	−59	743
2000	100	16.2	−83.8	58.5	29.5	−29	146	64.9	−81.1	1,218
2005	243.5	41.1	−202.4	84.7	34.2	−50.5	138	54.7	−83.3	1,673
2009	296.4	69.5	−226.9	71.5	43.5	−28	95.8	51.1	−44.7	1,559

Source: World Trade Organization

Table 11.6 China's trade with the United States ($ billions)

	2000	2001	2002	2003	2004	2005	2006	2007	2008	2009
US exports	16.3	19.2	22.1	28.4	34.7	41.8	55.2	65.2	71.5	69.6
% change	24.4	18.3	15.1	28.5	22.2	20.6	32.1	18.1	9.5	−2.6
US imports	100.0	102.3	125.2	152.4	196.7	243.5	287.8	321.5	337.8	296.4
% change	22.3	2.2	22.4	21.7	29.1	23.8	18.2	11.7	5.1	−12.3
Total	116.3	121.5	147.3	180.8	231.4	285.3	343	386.7	409.2	366.0
% change	22.6	21.4	21.2	22.8	28	23.3	20.2	12.7	5.8	−10.6
US balance	−83.7	−83.0	−103.1	−124.0	−162.0	−201.6	−232.5	−256.3	−266.3	−226.8

Source: US International Trade Commission
Notes: US exports reported on FOB basis; imports on a general customs value, CIF basis

The shift of Pacific trade of the USA from Japan to China has been partly offset by a sharp rise in Japan's trade with China. In 2007, China became Japan's largest trade partner, while Japan emerged as the third largest trade partner of China. While the share of the USA in Japan's exports fell from 30 to 20% over 2000–2007, China's share doubled from 9 to 18% (Table 11.6).

A significant feature of the US–China trade is that not only is the USA the single largest destination for China's exports, but due to China's lower import propensity from the USA, the trade surplus of China with the USA has ballooned from $83 billion in 2000 to the peak of $266 billion in 2008. Further, China's trade surplus with the USA is the major contributor of China's overall trade surplus since it does not have any significant trade surplus with any other trade partner. Until 2007, China's trade surplus with the USA was larger than its overall trade surplus. In 2008, the US–China trade surplus of $266 billion accounted for 89% China's overall trade surplus of $298 billion (Table 11.7).

The US–China trade over the last one decade has not only changed the structure of the global economy but has brought a significant impact on external financial flows of the USA. China's forex reserve growing from $165 billion in 2000 to $2.4 trillion in

Table 11.7 China's trade with the world ($ billions)

	2000	2001	2002	2003	2004	2005	2006	2007	2008	2009
Exports	249.2	266.1	325.6	438.2	593.3	762.0	969.0	1,220.5	1,430.7	1,201.7
% change	27.8	6.8	22.4	34.6	35.4	28.4	27.2	26.0	17.3	−16.0
Imports	225.1	243.6	295.2	412.8	561.2	660.0	791.5	956.1	1,132.6	1,005.6
% change	35.8	8.2	21.2	39.8	36.0	17.6	19.9	20.8	18.5	−11.2
Total	474.3	509.7	620.8	851.0	1,154.6	1,421.9	1,760.4	2,176.6	2,563.3	2,207.2
% change	31.5	7.5	21.8	37.1	35.7	23.2	23.8	23.6	17.8	−13.9
Balance	24.1	22.5	30.4	25.5	32.1	102.0	177.5	264.3	298.1	196.1

Sources: PRC National Bureau of Statistics and PRC General Administration of Customs, *China's Customs Statistics*

Note: PRC exports reported on a free-on-board basis; imports on a cost, insurance, and freight basis

June 2010 and its major holdings in the US treasury securities have given a new dimension to the global savings and liquidity situations. This aspect is separately discussed in the next chapter on the US savings gap and global liquidity reflux. It would be demonstrated here how globalization transforming China's economy into gigantic export-driven juggernaut has changed the structure of balance of payments of the USA. It involved the export of private capital and technology by the USA to support China's emergence as the largest export power and second dominant global economy and import of public capital from China to sustain its trade deficit.

Export of Private Capital and Import of Public Capital

The bigger macro problem of the USA is to sustain the investment rate in economy that keeps its growth momentum. The US economy endowed with rich land, capital, entrepreneurship, and technology but short of labor faces a peculiar problem. It exports private capital, technology, and output capacities but imports public capital. It exports output capacities in a bundle of direct investment, equipment, technology, and know-how and imports goods and services generated by them at prices lower than what they would have produced at home. It also imports public capital from exporting nations to finance its imports of goods and services (Fig. 11.5). The central banks of exporting nations hold their forex reserves in the US treasury bills.

In the new wave of globalization, which has brought about a paradigm shift in structure and flow of global investments, trade, and payments, has taken the Keynesianism international. This underlying principle of Keynesianism financing globalization and economic rewards is discussed earlier. The US BoP deficit financing is sustaining the growth of the global economy under globalization. The strength of US dollar as the global currency and reserve asset is the cornerstone of dynamics and growth of globalization.

Globalization is one aspect of the macroeconomics of the USA which has changed its structure. The share of manufacturing which was already declining earlier has

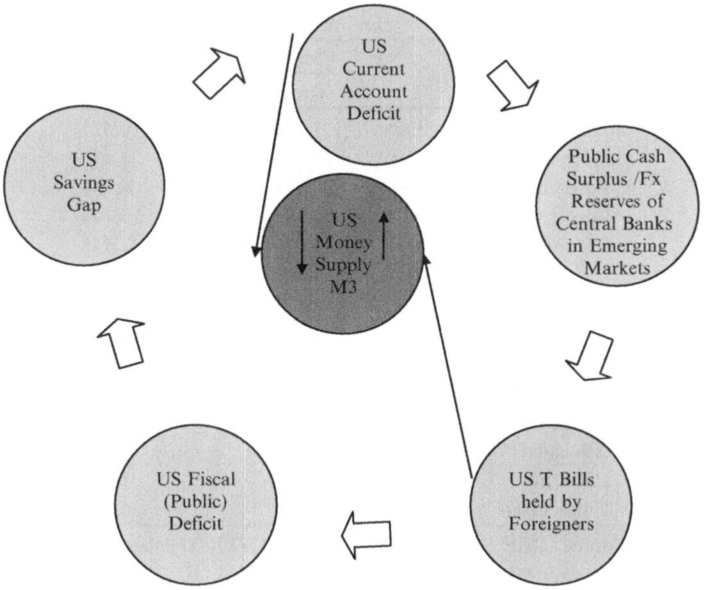

Fig. 11.5 Global funds flow: private savings gap to public savings surplus to public deficit (Source: Globalization and the Indian Economy, by S S Nayak)

declined further. This is nothing unusual about the mature capitalistic economy. The increasing share of service sector in fact brings in efficiencies and productivity gains which would not have otherwise occurred. The enormous growth in the decade of 1990s was caused by a big bout of technological advance in Internet, software, and telecom sectors. It filled the employment gaps created by the migration of commodity production to the more efficient emerging market economies. Then, there was a lull in the sector following the Y2K dot-com bust. It was the cheap money policy and subprime debt securitization that fueled the real estate boom beginning in 2002 that kept the growth rate from declining and signs of recession at bay. The change of guards at the Fed, when the chief architect of unprecedented growth trajectory of the US economy, Alan Greenspan, handed over the charge to Ben Bernanke, the new Fed Chairman, gave new twist to the monetary policy and the behavior of the US economy.

Global Liquidity and Payments Structure

Globalization has brought a dramatic transformation in the global payments flows. The emerging markets have grown at the rates double or treble the rates growth in the developed economies. Not only has the export sector been the engine of growth in these economies, but the net inflow of direct and portfolio

Table 11.8 Global forex reserves

	Mar-00	Mar-12
	(In $ billions)	
Total global forex holdings	1,809	10,421
Advanced nations	1,131	3,437
Emerging markets	678	6,984
Allocated	1,400	5,704
US dollar	1,000	3,548
Unallocated	409	4,717
Advanced nations	1,131	3,437
Allocated	1,017	3,044
US dollar	720	1,999
Unallocated	114	394
Emerging markets	678	6,984
Allocated	382	2,660
US dollar	281	1,548
Unallocated	294	4,324

Source: IMF Statistics Department COFER Database and International Financial Statistics

Note: Allocated reserves are those where the currency composition is identified and unallocated Reserves are those where the currency composition is not identified by the reporting countries

investments into the country along with the technological imports from the developed economies has further contributed to their growth by raising the investment rate and increasing the productivity. The end result of these developments from the standpoint of the global payments flow has been the surpluses in the BoP of the emerging markets. Despite the appreciation in currencies of their currencies, the BoP surpluses of the emerging market economies have continued persistently resulting in the accumulation of forex reserves by the central banks of these nations. Over the last two decades of globalization, these changes have not been small but significant from the viewpoint of global growth as well as liquidity and its distribution (Table 11.8).

Over the last decades, the global forex reserves have expanded from $1.8 trillion in 2000 to $10.4 trillion in March 2012, average annual growth of 40%. The share of the emerging markets in the global reserves which was mere 37% in 2000 has nearly doubled to 67%. The currency composition of allocated reserves shows that 62% of the holdings are in the US dollar. What is most dramatic is that reserves of the emerging markets have grown from $678 billion in 2000 to $6,984 billion in 2012, average annual growth of 71%. Out of the total increase in reserves of $8.6 trillion over this period, about three-fourths have gone to the emerging market economies. This has contributed to liquidity growth in these economies. Since nearly two-thirds of reserves are held in the US dollar, the reserves have also contributed to the inflow of funds and liquidity growth in the US and the offshore foreign currency bank deposits.

Offshore Dollars: Parallel Banking and Dollar System

The phenomenon of offshore dollar deposits and its rapid growth concentrating in nations and banking centers has created parallel banking of the size of the official Federal Reserve banking system. Its growing influence due to its size and its relatively unregulated nature has been matters of great concern among the central banks of major nations and primarily the Federal Reserve. The offshore banking system does not follow the conventional rules and tools of monetary and banking regulation. Also referred to as the shadow banking system, it has been the focus of attention of all the major central banks and the heads of states that assembled recently to analyze the causation the financial crisis and consider measures to prevent its occurrence in future.

In this global offshore banking system, the dollar system dominates offshore bank deposits worldwide. To understand its implications in realistic terms, both in terms of its contribution as well as assessing its potential for the damage it can cause to the system, and also the manner in which it can plausibly be regulated to minimize its adverse growth without jeopardizing its function of contribution to global financial system and economy, it is intended here to give a brief review of its growth and development.

The postwar economic growth and increasing integration in the global economy and financial system coupled with the emergence of the US dollar as the international currency resulted in this phenomenon that began in the early 1960s. The dollars could no longer be contained within the geographical borders of the USA. Over the last half century, the parallel dollar system outside the USA has grown at a rate higher than its growth within the USA. We are here referring to the liquid dollars comprising the US dollar currency and dollar deposits with banks and risk-free US government securities. This has been a natural market phenomenon developing as a part of the systemic growth of the US and global financial systems also guided by the contemporary global and national financial architectures, regulatory structures, and governance practices.

The use of the US dollar as the international currency naturally brought the obligation on the USA to meet the international demand for dollars in form of both the currency and the bank deposits. The US and Federal Reserve had to meet not only its national economic demand for dollar currency and dollar deposits but also the rest of the world's demand for dollars in both these forms. In addition to the rationale for natural demand for dollars outside the US and Federal Reserve complying with this demand, there were several other factors that intensified both the external demand for dollars and supply of dollars from the soil of the USA.

In addition to its use as the international currency because of its continuing strength and universal acceptance, the dollar currency has been widely used in several emerging market economies in conjunction with and as the superior alternative to their local national currencies.

The currency issue is a prerogative of the central banks. The central banking Acts give them the monopoly or the sole right of notes issue. The central banks want to keep the control of currency, which they issue for circulation, within its own jurisdiction and national borders. The Currency Acts of most countries do not permit the export of their currencies in large quantity to foreign countries. Yet good, strong, and widely accepted currencies are usually in demand also outside the countries of their issue and find their way in foreign countries despite legal restriction on such movement. Demand creates its own supply. Good money abhors national borders and travels across counties. Good money also drives bad money out of circulation.

During the early 1960s, the world was not digitally connected as it is today. The USA was not incurring large BoP deficits as it is now, and international banking was just beginning to grow. Many countries including some European economies practiced controls on capital movements and did not have their currencies fully convertible. The global monetary system, although stabilized, remained compartmentalized. The size of the dollar holdings outside the USA was relatively small and held primarily by the foreign central banks serving as a cushion to ward off any exchange rate instability that may arise.

The city of London, being the leading world financial center known for its innovative spirit, was the natural choice for the birth and initial growth of the euro-dollar market. The origin of the market in fact stemmed from geopolitical considerations and Cold War motivations. After the invasion of Hungary by the Soviet Union, it got worried about the confiscation or freezing of its dollar deposits held in the US banks by the US government. The Russians wanted to keep their dollar deposits outside the USA, and London seemed to be the safer choice. It transferred US$800,000 to the Moscow Narodny Bank, the Soviet-owned bank in London, and the first euro-dollars were created. According to another source, euro-dollars were first created in France. In 1921, a few Russian exiles bought a small bank in France and renamed it Banque Commerciale pour l'Europe du Nord (BCEN). The bank failed in 1925 but was taken over the Russian state-owned Gosbank. After the Second World War, it became one of the leading international banks handling international transactions of the communist bloc countries including China and primarily dealt in dollar deposits.

The euro-dollars is a term used to indicate the dollar deposits outside the USA and its banking system. Since the dollar deposits originated and grew in London and then spread to other European financial centers, this market was termed as the euro-dollar. The market, however, spread later to several other banking centers, offshore tax havens. It acquired international character by spreading to other centers such as Tokyo, Hong Kong, Singapore, Bahrain, Bahamas, Bermuda, Panama, Cayman Island, and Antilles.

There are several features of this banking system and market that make it unique: cost and operationally efficient, flexible, dynamic, and innovative. The euro-dollar market or banking engages in wholesale dollar deposits and lending outside the USA and not in retail banking. The foreign currency deposits being outside the purview of many central banks do not attract any cash reserve requirements which the usual bank deposits face. The euro-dollar banking does not carry checking account facility since the central banks offer clearing facilities for checking accounts in their domestic currencies. Hence, the euro-dollar banking does not create credit and engage in multiple credit creation. Since the euro-dollar banking does not attract reserve requirements, the cost of deposits is lower and the spread between the deposit and lending rate is narrower. Being in wholesale banking without checking accounts and less compliance work with the central banks not requiring extensive retail branch network, the cost of operation in the euro-dollar banking is lower. This further reduces the spread between its deposit and lending rates. Working on the lowest spreads, the euro-dollar market is the most efficient wholesale banking system. It offers higher interest rates to depositors and lower rates to borrowers than offered by the domestic banks on similar deposits. The euro-dollar market works on the floating interest rates. The rates for deposits and lending referred to as bid and offered rates change like foreign exchange rates as the deposits are traded in the open markets in major financial centers such as London, Hong Kong, Singapore, and Bahrain; however, the depositors and borrowers can freeze a rate for periods of 1, 3, and 6 months for their deposits and loans. The floating interest rates mechanism offers more market-related rates to the financial market participants than those given by the domestic banking system. The euro-dollar business is essentially international banking since the majority of both depositors and borrowers are cross border individuals and entities and deal in foreign currencies. Involved in international lending, the euro-dollar market has also to monitor and manage country risks in additional to usual banking risks. Because of its nature of foreign currency deposits and floating interest exposures, it has to do more careful management of its interest rate and exchange rate risks. There is no "lender of last resort" for the euro-dollar banking since it is outside the jurisdiction of the Federal Reserve and also other central banks. The euro-dollars are also referred to as "footloose money" or "stateless money" due to the absence of its regulation and control by any central bank.

The oil crisis of 1974 constituted the biggest factor for the rapid growth of the euro-dollar market. The petro-dollar surpluses of the OPEC nations needed an investment outlet, and the euro-dollar market served a potent vehicle of mobilizing as well as recycling the petro-dollar deposits. A large number of oil-importing nations suffered critical deficits in their balance of payments, and this massive disequilibrium needed large external resources to finance the deficits. The euro-dollar market swung in action to exercise one of the largest recycling operation and prevented the oil-importing nations from taking severely restrictive measures detrimental to the growth of their economies and momentum of the global economy. It avoided one of the sharpest and perhaps longest recession in the postwar history.

Developing initially as the euro-dollar market, the parallel dollar deposits with banks outside the USA, the phenomenon influenced the movement of US dollar currency notes outside the USA and, lastly, further enlarged with the growth of foreign holdings of the US government securities. The parallel liquid dollar system as it may be called is now of the size, in its totality and its components, almost equal to the liquid dollar holdings within the USA.

The offshore dollar market has grown consistently in recent years too and totaled the size of $5 trillion in 2010. This is little more than 50% of M2 (money supply, currency, demand deposits, and time deposits) in the USA which was $9 trillion in 2010. A study estimated the foreign holdings of dollar currency notes to be between 50 and 70% of the currency issued and at $500 billion in 2005. The foreign holdings of US government T bills and securities amounted to $5.1 trillion in 2011 accounting for 50% of the US public debt, with China and Japan holding $2.2 trillion. Hence, there is as much dollar liquidity in the rest of the world as there is within the USA. The US current account deficit and short-term capital outflows have been the sources of growth of offshore dollars. The liquidity growth in the global monetary system has been much more than savings growth due the semi-controlled nature of the external payments systems in the emerging market economies with China being largest contributor to this liquidity growth. This phenomenon, developed as a part of the systemic growth of the US and global financial systems, is also guided by the contemporary global and national financial architectures, regulatory structures, and governance practices.

The offshore banking market has played a crucial role in times of oil crises in recycling the surpluses of the oil-exporting nations. It also serves as low-cost, efficient, and liquid market for global finance. Since collectively it does not come under regulation of any authority and is free from stringent banking regulations in tax havens or offshore centers from where it is operating, there is a need for monitoring and regulation in order to avoid any mishaps in the future.

Real Assets and Goods Prices Divide

A very peculiar feature of developments in prices and price structures globally, since the beginning of globalization and more pronounced since the beginning of 1990s when it accelerated with larger number of emerging market economies and transition economies led by China among the Asian tigers, India, Brazil, and Russia joined the phase, is the trend of rising prices of real assets and declining prices of commodity products and manufactures except crude oil and petroleum products. Although countries like China and Russia may not yet officially admit that they have ideologically abandoned communism or socialism, the distinctive features of capitalism discussed earlier are deeply entrenched in their economic system and philosophy. They are already quasi-capitalist states, and the progress they have made over the last two decades is a strong and vivid testimony to the contribution of capitalist ideas in growth and distributive justice. The record transfer of investment and technology in the shift of production of large number of commodity and manufactured goods to the emerging market economies has resulted in a massive buildup of capacities. The higher supply elasticities, productivity gains, and cheap labor cost have brought substantial decline in prices of manufactured products exported from the emerging market economies. "Low consumer price inflation in the face of sharply rising commodity prices implies a considerable change in relative prices: between 1995 and 2004, the prices of consumer goods in the United States fell 30% relative to raw materials. Similar relative price adjustments have taken place in the euro area and Japan."[3]

---

[3] Bank for International Settlement, Annual Report 2008, p.18.

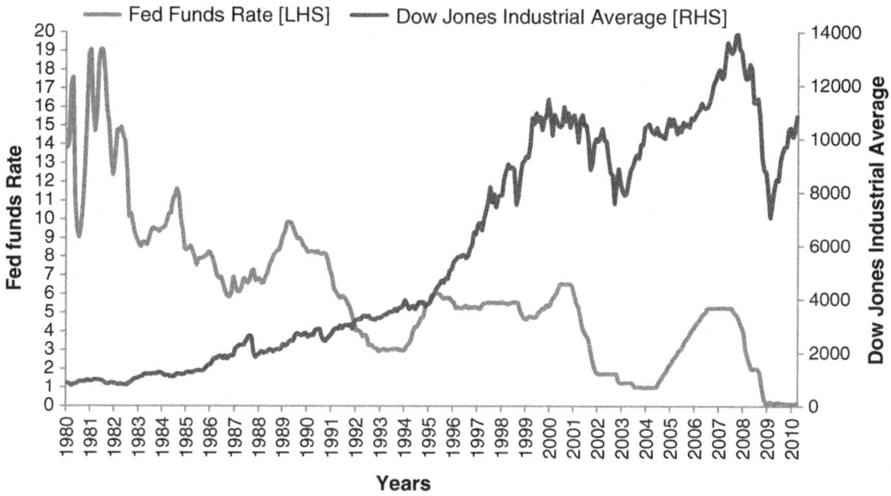

Fig. 11.6 Fed funds rate and Dow Jones Industrial Average

While in the wake of the declining prices of manufactured goods and services, the pressure on prices of real assets has continued unabated with the growth of savings and liquidity globally. The housing boom which began in 1997 gained momentum in 2002 and reaching a peak in June 2006. The S&P/Case–Shiller Home price index for ten cities reached the peak of 226 in June 2006 from 100 in 2000, while 20-city index was also highest at 206 in June 2006 from 100 in 2000. Both the indices reached their 2004 level in October, 2008. At this level, prices were still 70 and 60% higher from the 2000 level.[4]

The equity shares witnessed a greater boom in 1990s. The Dow Jones Industrial Average went up from 2,447 in January 1991 to reach a peak of 11,908 in January 2000, over four times in a 10-year period. The S&P 500 shot up from 309 in January 1991 to a high of 1,552 in March 2000, five times over a 9-year period. The Nasdaq Composite went up from 353 in January 1991 to the peak of 5,133 in March 2000, over a record 14 times in 9 years. The stock market crashed in April 2000 and continued to decline under the bearish spell until October 2002 when the Dow reached the lowest of 7,181, S&P 500 touched the lowest of 769, and Nasdaq Composite at the lowest of 1,108. Since October 2002, the market commenced its bullish phase until October 2007 with Dow reaching its historic high at 14,280, S&P 500 also at an all-time high of 1,576, and Nasdaq at 2,835. The market crash in the wake of the crisis brought the indices tumbling to record lows again by March 2009. The Dow slid to 6,440, S&P fell to 666, and Nasdaq to 1,265 in March 2009. The markets recovered thereafter with Dow at 10,463, S&P 500 at 1,111, and Nasdaq at 2,242 in September 2010 (Fig. 11.6).

---

[4] Standard & Poor's, S&P/Case Shiller Home price Indices, 2008, A Year in Review, January13, 2009.

Global liquidity growth emanating from the US-centric globalization model and compulsions of sustaining the growth momentum, on the one hand, facilitated output growth in the emerging markets that supplied low-cost products to the USA and other developed nations and kept inflation in check. On the other hand, the pent-up liquidity found its way into equity markets and housing and real estate globally. Disproportionately, large exposure of bank credit was to the US housing sector through the securitization of subprime mortgages. When the credit could not serviced by the millions of lowly rated borrowers in the USA under the adverse impact of recession, rising unemployment, and increasing interest rates, the defaults and foreclosures ballooned, having a snowballing effect of defaults, illiquid markets, valuation losses, write-offs, and finally illiquidity and bankruptcy in few large banks and institutions, bringing the wheels of banking and credit to a standstill globally. The tremendous rift between the assets and goods prices finally came to be brought to a reasonable level by crashing housing, real estate, and stock prices.

Global Excess Capacity

In the developed world, while growth remained high and inflation low, the major change created by the structural shift of production of manufactured goods to the market economies has been the sharp change in relative prices. The prices of mass-manufactured consumer goods have come down significantly. A worsening global recessionary trend reveals deficient demand but also reflects substantial excess capacity of output. The buildup of large output capacity following record investments in several industries over the last two decades especially in the emerging market economies has resulted in excess capacities. This is evident in several industries such as textiles, garments, consumer electronics, food processing, auto, metals, petrochemicals, and also services such as shipping, airlines, and telecom. While the capacities were created in expectation of sustained growth in global demand for products, the slowdown in the US economy in 2007 followed by the sudden financial shock in 2008 caused a sharp fall in aggregate global demand. To add fuel to fire, the breakout of the Eurozone crisis in 2010 dampened the global climate when the US economy was in the recovery mode. In the light of these excess capacities, additional private investments in projects are likely to be postponed, delaying further economic recovery. It is in this context that government spending, and especially sectors like infrastructure which has strong backward and forward linkages, is crucial in precipitating and sustaining recovery.

Structural Shift in Global Power

In a recent interview, renowned political scientist, professor, foreign policy expert, former US secretary of state, and Nobel-prize-winner Henry Kissinger, who was instrumental in ending the Vietnam War and later the Cold War with the USSR, succinctly summarized the current crisis as the reflection of shift in center of power from the Atlantic, the USA and Europe, to the Pacific and Indian Ocean, Asia and India. Being the architect of the policy of Detente aiming to end the war against the communism in Vietnam and beginning the new era of peace and prosperity for China and the USA following the historic Nixon–Mao meet in Beijing, Kissinger in fact paved the way for the gradual change in geopolitical change in the balance of global power. Ideological war ended, and the new era of partnership between the USA and China for mutual economic advantage and progress began its course. The process of economic reform began in China in the early 1980s spearheaded by Deng Xiaoping and set the stage for a slow but decisive change in the global economic power structure.

He stressed the new role of China and India vis-a-vis USA in rebuilding the global order. In this tripolar world, US capital and technology, China's competitive mass production machine, and India's talented human capital endowment have to work out the fairest equations of exchange that would sustain the global growth with fairness and stability. The US–China–India tripolar exchanges are so interlinked and mutually reinforcing, as evidenced by the contagion of the current crisis, that it has rendered opportunity not to take global structure for granted but to understand and accept realities and work toward strengthening the systems that bring about synergistic development of these economic interlinkages.

China's great economic leap with double-digit growth for nearly two decades was fueled by American and Japanese investment and technology and cheap Chinese labor. The USA earned handsome returns on their investments in China. Huge imports of low-cost Chinese products of mass consumption helped America to reduce inflation rate. High trade deficit with China also fueled Chinese double-digit growth rate and ballooned her exchange reserves. Investment of bulging Chinese forex reserves into US T bills helped the USA finance its current account as well as budget deficit. The US–China investment and trade partnership was both mutually beneficial and reinforcing and globally benign. The success of the Chinese model set in motion the wave of liberalization and reforms in the other emerging markets. The developed economies also reduced government regulation and liberalized foreign trade and investments. The process of globalization was taking speed and momentum replacing the postwar Bretton Woods architecture.

On the fiscal and balance of payments fronts too, the progress of the US economy in the new millennium has not been healthy. The government budgetary surpluses of the 1990s turned into heavy deficits. Tax breaks and mounting war expenditure made heavy drafts on the already strained budget. Cheap money policy of the Fed, however, kept the cost of borrowing low. Despite the expansionary monetary policy and rising budget deficits, inflation was contained due to large and growing trade deficit. Low-priced imports from China and undervalued Chinese currency, yuan, helped in arresting the pressure of demand from raising consumer prices. The spurt in the crude oil price in 2008 was the only major factor that brought upward pressure on the consumer price index. While the burgeoning trade deficit succeeded in taming inflation, it continued to weaken the balance of payments position. In the era of low interest rate, BoP deficit of the USA tended to weaken the dollar in the forex markets. The euro, pound, and yen touched their all-time highs against the dollar in the global currency markets. Both the budget and BoP deficits took a heavy toll on the dollar, and the twin deficits were financed by the treasury bills investments made by China, Japan, South Korea, Russia, and India.

Henry Kissinger was very perceptive when he added an observation that Asia will have to do to America now what America did to Europe after the Second World War. He was referring to the American Marshall Plan which reconstructed Europe from the ravages of war. Hint was to the Asian Marshall Plan for America's recovery on the growth path. Tremendous liquidity crunch, lull in investments, and declining consumer spending are now driving the global economy into recession. In such situation, nations fall prey to protectionism for narrow and short-term national benefits which bring misery to all. Beggar-thy-neighbor policy can steer the global economy into a deep recession. It is a path that nations must resist. A bailout package to take over distressed assets, two emergency economic stimulus packages by the US government, record liquidity infusion, and record low interest rates set by the Federal Reserves are all aimed to reflate the US economy. But if these measures fail to have stimulating impact, the Asian Marshall Plan led by China and Japan and sufficient large in size will have to be in place to lift the US economy onto growth path.

Three Doctrines of Economic Truth: Determinants of Global Economic Evolution

We have examined the US subprime crisis which occupied the global proportion from the macrolevel as well as the microlevels within the US economy. These tendencies at both the macro and micro standpoints themselves emanate from much broader structural developments within the US and the global economy. The global economy is now functioning under three fundamental doctrines: *Adam Smith's Doctrine of Free Market Mechanism*, *David Ricardo's Doctrine of Comparative Cost Advantage* in global production of goods and services, and *Keynes's Doctrine State Intervention and Countercyclical Policy of Deficit Financing and BoP Financing* by the reserve currency country. Adam Smith's objective of maximum global economic welfare through market mechanism necessitates freer play of David Ricardo's doctrine of comparative cost advantage for global production and trade and Keynes's countercyclical policy of deficit financing for stable and sustainable growth in individual economies and BoP deficit financing policy by the USA, global currency country, to match the global payment imbalances and allow the benefits of the earlier two doctrines to accrue. Keynes's doctrine holds the key for the other two principles to give results in maximizing the welfare of individual economies as well as globally.

If we examine these three economic truths, we observe that the first two are a part of the institution of free market mechanism. In contrast, Keynes's truth does not relate to the markets and their magic but their tyranny. His discovery lies in portraying the role of the institution of state in counteracting the perils of the institution of market and money. The magic of the invisible hand of free markets and the gains from free trade based on production dictated by comparative costs cannot be fairly realized unless the Keynesian principle gives the sustainability to the normal functioning of the US and global economy. Until the formation of the global central bank and global monetary unit, the dollar will have to carry its role as the global currency. Dollar is passing through rough weather both domestically as well as in the international market. It will have to overcome its current economic problems having institutional bearings with structural adjustments and evolve the path for sustainable BoP deficit for global growth and stability. These aspects will be discussed in the last chapter, New Bretton Woods: Agenda for Global Economic Reform.

Reference

1. Brenner R. The economics of global turbulence. London: Verso; 2006. p. 7.

Chapter 12
US Savings Gap Versus Global Liquidity Reflux

> While devaluation (appreciation) of a currency may be appropriate and even necessary help to deal with the consequences of past inflation or serious international imbalances, it cannot be a substitute for more fundamental policies to restore competitiveness, to enhance productivity and savings, and to maintain stability. Repeated time and again, devaluations represent in effect a kind of abdication from necessary policy decisions, and in the end only complicate the job of maintaining growth and stability.
>
> Paul Volcker, *Changing Fortunes: The World's Money and the Threat to American Leadership, 1992.*

Global Savings Glut?

The issue of global savings glut has created quite a stir in the academic, policy making, banking, investment, and market analyst circles. It manifests one of the fundamental changes in the global economy that has occurred over the last two decades under the new economic policy phase of globalization. While the broad hypothesis is indisputably acceptable, there is room for difference on the interpretation and causality of the phenomenon.

In analyzing the phenomenon of rising US current account deficit and its causation, the conventional view is that it was caused by the global savings glut and export surpluses of Asia, Germany, and oil nations. The savings glut was responsible for large investment flows from abroad into the US stock and real estate markets. The resultant boom in these markets created wealth effect leading to growth in consumption, decline in savings rate, and steep increase in imports. Lower competitiveness of US exports and strengthening dollar further widened the US trade deficit [1].

The phase of globalization witnessing more pronounced speed since the 1990s has brought about a profound change in the structure of global economy and financial system. The world is no longer ideologically divided between the free world and the communist regimes. It is divided between the developed and the emerging market economies. Globalization has brought an unprecedented growth

S. Nayak, *The Global Financial Crisis: Genesis, Policy Response and Road Ahead*, DOI 10.1007/978-81-322-0798-6_12, © Springer India 2013

in trade and investment between these two blocs. Higher output and income growth coupled with conventionally high and rising savings rate in the emerging market economies has increased the pool of their savings year after year. In view of their pressure to keep investment rate high to raise the rate of economic growth, they have been using their larger savings internally. Traditionally these economies faced large "savings gap" (investment higher than saving) which was met through foreign capital inflow. Higher savings have enabled them to meet their investment rate and also reduce dependence on capital inflow. Further, their foreign receipts by way of both exports and capital inflows have tended to grow at much faster rate than their foreign payments. Resultantly, they are accumulating more forex reserves, counterpart of which is higher domestic liquidity in their economies. These are cash surpluses of the central banks held in foreign currency securities or liabilities. They are not incomes or savings flows although there is a counterpart to it which merges in the domestic liquidity and savings. The central banks are public institutions and hold and manage country's forex reserves which are used primarily for safeguarding the purchasing power of their currencies in the foreign currency markets against the shocks in their balance of payments (BoP). The rising forex reserves of the emerging market economies mean rising US liquid liabilities held by their central banks, primarily T bills and G secs, since dollar is the most preferred asset of the central banks internationally.

Hence, there is more pronounced "liquidity glut" in the global economy than "savings glut." If there was any excessive "savings glut" in these economies not absorbed by them domestically, it would have been released by way of investments abroad that would have reduced their forex reserves. This is not to deny that there is no savings glut but the liquidity glut is much bigger in its relative magnitude and impact. This is important because the private savings of emerging markets flowing into portfolio, real estate, and direct investments abroad and the investments of forex reserves by their central banks into the same assets have different implications for domestic liquidity in the emerging markets, their savings allocation, and forex reserves.

The argument about the worldwide savings glut is not valid also because many US banks became the victim of the crisis than the foreign banks. The forex reserves of central banks are the counterparts of the savings glut in these countries. These reserves are primarily invested in the US T bills or G secs. The central banks do not keep large deposits with commercial banks, and if the private agencies from these countries kept deposits with the US banks instead of selling dollars in the forex market, it would not increase their forex reserves. But by buying T bills in large numbers, the central banks did improve the liquidity of the banking system in the USA. In fact the USA faced the outgrowth of the liquidity glut. Then, it is also true that banks were unable to manage the liquidity overhang and directed and allocated credit to the new portfolio like subprime debt securities which looked safe on the standing of the issuer, tangible security of mortgage of houses, and credit rating given by the reputed rating agencies but in fact carried higher risks in their sensitivity analysis.

Global Liquidity (Dollar) Reflux

Looking at the data of capital flows of the emerging market economies, we find that during 2003–2007 the inflows of capital (direct and portfolio) into the emerging markets were 6.6% of GDP, while outflows of capital were 4.8% of GDP, resulting in the net inflow of 1.8%. As against this, the current account surplus of the emerging markets was 3.9%. This resulted in the rise in their forex reserves by 5.5% of their GDP.[1] The savings glut in Asia remained within Asia, increasing their domestic financial assets. It did not come to the USA in large measure. What flowed to the USA was the counterpart of forex reserves, investments in T bills and G secs. Not only oil-exporting nations with smaller population but also fastest-growing China has also shown unbelievably high savings rate exceeding 40%, far exceeding their investment rate. This savings glut has not led private flows of capital to the USA because China's forex reserves held by People's Bank of China (counterpart of the Fed) went up from $166 billion in 2000 to $403 billion in 2003, crossed $2 trillion in 2010, and was $3.3 trillion in July 2012. This is the phenomenon of liquidity glut; private savings of China have not flowed into the USA as the Japanese savings did in the 1990s. Majority of Asian nations have capital account controls reintroduced after the Asian crisis. And China has exchange controls on capital outflows. The situation is reflected in huge holdings of US T bills by the central banks of emerging markets. Foreign private and official holdings of the US T bills holdings rose from $1.58 trillion in January 2004 accounting for 44% of all T bills outstanding to $2.19 trillion in January 2006 accounting for 51% of total outstanding bills and to $4.5 trillion in July 2012 [2].[2] What we see as the savings glut in emerging market economies has resulted in global liquidity reflux due to controls on capital movements by the emerging markets. This has led to the rise in the external debt of the USA.

This dollar reflux is the outcome of half free–half controlled nature of the global economy. While the developed world has free economy and convertible currencies, the emerging markets are not yet fully free from controls domestically and also on capital account of BoP. Since the currencies are also not free to move up on market forces, the export and current account surplus continues to grow. And as the exchange rate is fixed and managed, it also promotes high capital inflows from abroad. With the strict controls on outflow of capital, the domestic savings are bottled up inside the economy and results in rising forex reserves of the central banks of these economies. These reserves are largely held in US T bills. Hence, rise in domestic savings in China helps the People's Bank of China finance US budget deficit.

The Asian savings glut is the direct result of the US current account deficit and not its cause. The savings glut of the magnitude would not emerge except from the large and growing US imports from Asia and also its rising import surplus. The US trade and current account deficit is caused by more fundamental and structural factors

---

[1] Source: BIS Annual Report, 2009.

[2] Bernanke, Ben, Chairman, The Federal Reserve Board, The speech on *'Globalization and Monetary Policy'* given at the Fourth Economic Summit, Stanford Institute for Economic Policy Research, Stanford, California, March 2, 2007.

relating to the metamorphosis of the US economy. The trend began under the Bretton Woods system and was further reinforced in the last two decades in the phase of globalization. It is the phenomenon of secular trend of divergence in the income elasticities of the US imports and exports. The income elasticity of US imports has been higher than the rest of the world's income elasticity for imports from USA, which are US exports. The divergence began in the 1950s when the USA emerged as the major export economy in the world and acquired the status of the world's strongest economy from the Great Britain, catapulting dollar by replacing the pound sterling as the global currency. Over the last three decades, this divergence has widened and trend accentuated under the influence of globalization.

Trade Gap Versus Savings Gap

Similar problem was faced by the developing nations during their early development [3–6]. In the 1950s the development economists were designing several models from the springboard of Keynesian economics and capital–output and input–output ratios. The development economists keen to raise the growth rate of economies wanted to know whether the trade gap or savings gap was dominant or constraint on raising the growth rate.

Not all developing countries offered homogeneous economic profiles and hence different countries had different outcomes. Some countries which could supply adequate capital found trade deficit or imports to be limiting their growth, while others which were not having high savings rate did not face any imports induced constraint and found savings gap to be the main constraint on their growth. The most of developing economies in the 1960s faced foreign exchange constraint on their growth and the trade gap was dominant. The question of dominance of the gap is only ex ante, since ex post both the gaps are equal. Ex post they are accounting identities.

The dual gap approach, which was the topic of debate in the 1960s, needs to be examined again now in the context of sharp change in trade and capital movements among the USA and developed world, on the one hand, and the emerging market economies, on the other, in the era of globalization. Today it manifests a schism between the two groups of countries and represents real structural cause of the global problem.

Asian Savings Glut Bottled Up Inside

In the Keynesian national income formula, the current account of BoP is a part of the national income equation. The current account deficit is always equal to the savings gap, i.e., investment being larger than the savings by the size of current account deficit. They are two sides of the same coin and are accounting identities. When we take a global view, the US current account deficit has the counterpart of savings surplus in other nations, primarily Asian export surplus nations and oil-exporting economies. There is savings glut in these economies equivalent to the current account deficit of the USA and Europe. But there is also the liquidity glut because of the surplus in overall BoP. Now the contentious issue is which is the cause and which is the effect. Whether the global savings glut creates the US current account deficit or whether it is vice versa. It is the "chicken or egg" story or the catch-22 situation.

Let us examine the savings glut issue in Keynesian income equation:

$$Y = C + I + X - M$$
$$Y - C = I + X - M$$
$$S = I + X - M$$

$S - I = X - M$ savings glut and current account surplus (China)
$I - S = M - X$ savings gap and current account deficit (USA)

Y=gross national product, C=consumption expenditure, I=investment expenditure, X=exports of goods and services, M=imports of goods and services, and S=savings.

The USA faces the savings gap since the investment is higher than savings and this gap is equivalent to its trade and current account deficit. China on the contrary faces savings surplus or glut, and it is equivalent to its trade and current account surplus. Now if capital transaction between these countries is ignored, then current account surplus would result in the rise in China's forex reserves (+Fx) by the size of current account surplus and savings glut. The USA would have had to use its forex reserves to finance its current account deficit and savings gap. But, in the case of the USA, it does not have to use its forex reserves since dollar itself constitutes reserves for all other central banks. The USA would either have foreign central banks hold dollar balances in the USA or hold US treasury bills. Hence, the USA would finance its foreign trade and savings deficit through its T bills (−Tb) held by the Bank of China:

$$S - I = X - M = \text{Fx (China)}$$
$$I - S = M - X = \text{Tb (US)}$$

Now as we introduce capital movements, its impact on forex reserves in terms of size and movement would be different. What makes difference to the BoP (balance of payments) is the net capital movement which affects forex reserves. In the case of China the capital inflows are higher than outflows. The exchange controls in China do not permit private capital outflows without approvals, and capital investments abroad by individuals are not permitted. Hence, China has net inflows on capital account (Ci) of BoP. This net inflow further adds to its forex reserves. In the case of the USA also on private account, there is net capital inflow since the USA is the safest destination for investments, and corporates and stock market attract large investments from abroad. The advantage of these net capital inflows to the USA is that it eases the pressure on its overall BoP deficit caused by its current account deficit and absorbs the excess supply of dollar in the forex market. Its need to finance the current account deficit through T bills is reduced.

The equation below explains the position with net capital flow:

$$S - I = X - M = \text{Fx} - \text{Ci (China)}$$
$$I - S = M - X = \text{Tb} + \text{Ci (US)}$$

In the case of India the situation is similar to the USA, but despite its current account deficit, it receives net capital from abroad exceeding its current account deficit. This results in the rise in its forex reserves:

$$I - S = M - X = \text{Fx} + \text{Ci (India)}$$

India has gradually allowed its capital account to open up. While corporate investments abroad are substantially liberalized, the individuals are also permitted to invest up to $200,000 per year in foreign currency deposits, securities, mutual funds, and also real estate. This reduces the increase in forex reserves and transfers a part of domestic savings into investments abroad.

Despite some liberalization of capital account in the BoP surplus emerging market economies, controls on capital outflows are common in all emerging market economies. Since the emerging market economies like China, Russia, South Korea, and other Asian and OPEC nations are main contributors of surplus savings or savings glut with the capital account controls, the savings are bottled up within their economies in financial assets, stock market, real estate, and precious metals and stones like gold, silver, and diamonds. It also shows up in ostentatious consumption, like purchase of premium brand cars, planes, and yachts. The counterpart of these savings is the rise in the forex reserves of these savings surplus nations which are held by the central banks of these nations. These central bank reserves are invested either in bank deposits or in US treasury bills. Hence, the Asian savings glut is not finding investment outlet in the developed capital markets but is financing the US budget deficit. What these growing reserves have done is to add liquidity to the US money market by lifting US T bills and holding them as foreign currency assets.

If the forex surplus emerging market economies do not accumulate reserves but liberalize capital outflows (Co) from their countries, their savings would not bottle up in the domestic financial and real assets. It would reduce asset price inflation in their economies and channel their domestic savings in the capital markets of the developed nations. In such an eventuality there could be real savings glut in the developed economies when the excess savings of the emerging markets would inundate their capital markets. The forex reserves of emerging markets would not increase, and the USA will have a situation of lower holdings of its T bills held by foreign central banks. The situation would be as follows:

$$S - I = X - M = \text{Co (China)}$$
$$I - S = M - X = \text{Ci (US)}$$

The situation above assumes the savings glut of the export surplus nations translating to investments in the USA and other developed nations so that there is no growth in their forex reserves and no increase in foreign holdings of US T bills. The actual current savings glut hypothesis can now be restated as the dollar liquidity glut hypothesis. The central banks of the BoP surplus emerging market economies are in effect financing the US BoP as well as the budget deficits. In the event of liberal capital account regimes in the emerging markets, the savings would flow out in the foreign capital markets for investments in stocks and bonds, and phenomenal rise in forex reserves of China and other countries would be abated. In that situation the savings glut of Asia may hit America. Capital flow from China into the USA would increase the supply of dollars in the US capital market and reduce the Bank of China's demand for US T bills. It would also mean lower forex reserves for Bank of China. But with capital account controls what they are today in China, this is not happening. Both the governments in China and the USA are happy to accommodate each other, and both the Fed and Bank of China enjoy being partners in supporting each other's payments.

Divergent US Trade Elasticities

The US trade and current account deficit is an endogenous phenomenon and not the result of the savings glut abroad. This is evident from the long-term trend of US import propensity. The divergence in the US import propensity and the rest of the world's propensity to import from the USA has been creating a rising trade deficit in the USA in the 1960s and 1970s. This trend has further been exacerbated since the 1980s under the forces of globalization which opened up gates for low-cost commodity and manufactured imports from the emerging markets. As we have seen earlier, US average propensity to import (imports of goods and services/GDP) rose from 12.1% in 1980 to 17.9% in 2000 and to 19.5% in 2010. The marginal propensity to import (*d* import/*d* GDP) rose from 15.3% in 1980 to 22.2% in 2000 and further to 22.8% in 2010. The US exports have not grown at the same pace resulting in widening trade and current account deficit. The US trade deficit has gone up from $111 billion in 1990 to record $840 billion in 2008, while the current account deficit has shot up from $79 billion to $706 billion in the same period.[3]

China Syndrome

The same issue of dual gaps is now examined in the context of the global economy. Let us examine whether the global savings glut is dominant or the US current account deficit. Firstly, the USA is the most dominant economy in the world with 30% of global GDP at market exchange rates and 21% on purchasing power parity terms. The growth in the US economy drives the growth in the rest of the world due its

[3] Source of data: Bureau of Economic Analysis, U S Department of Commerce.

interlinkages in global trade, financial flows, and investments. Secondly, looking to the its secular trend of low household savings rate and divergent income elasticities in foreign trade, the US economy is continuing to show higher current account deficit as it grows. This trend is persisting despite substantial depreciation of the US dollar since the breakdown of Bretton Woods and also over last few decades of globalization. Hence, the exchange rate change is not a solution to the US trade deficit problem. Even the revaluation of Chinese yuan may only marginally reduce the US trade deficit and Chinese trade surplus and savings glut, and that too at the cost of inflation in the USA, because US imports from China, which were $337 billion in 2008 forming 16% of US total imports and 2.4% of its GDP, will become costlier. The USA currently spends 20 cents on imports out of its extra dollar of national income, out of which 5 cents go to China. Although the US average propensity to import from China is 2.4%, the marginal propensity to import is almost double at 5%. If we look at the overall US trade deficit, China accounted for 39% of the total in 2008.

Undoubtedly, China has witnessed a sharp rise in its savings rate from 37.5% in 1995 to a whopping 44% in 2005, while the investment rate also going up from 38.4 to 40.4%. The household sector's savings rate declined from 20% in 1995 to 16.2% in 2005, while the corporate savings rate went up from 13.5 to 20.4% and government savings rose marginally from 5.1 to 5.7%.[4] It shows that household accounts for only 37% of national savings and bulk of the savings are of corporate and government. Since the corporate ownership is also with the government, the government itself is the major contributor to national savings. In a communist country the large share of government savings represents Marx's surplus value which has not been distributed among its labor and human resource. This raises an important issue that if the surplus value acquired by the state and state enterprises is more equitably distributed, the overall savings rate may come down and China's export surplus would also come down to a lower level. Such a scenario would partially solve the problem of liquidity glut caused by buildup of forex reserves of China.

US Endogenous Savings Gap

Given that the US current account deficit is endogenous, a question is often asked, is it sustainable and to what extent? Has it reached the limits of its sustainability? It is argued that the increase in US savings rate would reduce its trade deficit. Now we are looking at the dual gap approach within the US economy and not globally.

Firstly, the US economy has traditionally grown, and more so in the last two decades, on buoyant consumption growth and cheap credit. High savings rate would be a deterrent to the dynamics of the US economy now. Secondly, its factor endowments, i.e., abundance of natural resources and capital stock, and shortage of labor

[4] Kuijs Louis, How will China's Savings-Investment Balance Evolve?, World Bank China Research Paper, No.4, May,2006.

do not permit it to engage in the production of mass consumer goods and commodity materials except agricultural products. These production centers have already shifted to the emerging markets. The comparative cost advantage in consumption goods and other commodity sectors is so much in favor of the emerging market economies that it cannot be reversed even with exchange rates adjustment. But unlike any other country, trade deficit for the USA does not limit its economic growth. It finances its trade deficit from its own currency. Thirdly, the above trends manifest in US absorption or spending propensity being higher than its income and output growth. This in fact is the driving force of globalization. The US current account deficit as we have seen is creating growth and savings and higher investments in the emerging market economies. The rising current account deficit creates foreign exchange problem for every country, but not the USA. The other countries acquire dollar balances and US T bills. This is how globalization is financed. Any effort to reduce the US current account deficit would hurt global growth.

The phenomenon reflects the extension of Keynes' General Theory to the global economy. Keynes discussed the *General Theory* in a closed economy framework and advocated government spending and deficit financing for higher growth of an economy. That was the first Keynesian commandment. Extrapolation of the *General Theory* to the global economy brings us to the second Keynesian commandment, of higher spending and current account deficit financing by the dominant economy to generate and sustain higher growth in the global economy. The philosophy of globalization rests on the strong Keynesian strongholds. Keynes has now gone truly international.

Does savings gap limit US growth? No, because US trade deficit creates savings and liquidity in the rest of the world which comes back to the USA as private investments or central bank investments in T bills and G secs. So long as dollar is strong and real rate of interest on risk-free assets and real return on riskier bond and equity securities are higher, the US economy can continue to be the magnate for global savings and investments. The nature and pattern of these financial and savings flows are guided by the sentiment in the US capital market and the direction of the Fed policy.

Figure 12.1 shows how the savings gap in the USA, counterpart of the US current account deficit, creates surplus dollars with the central banks of the emerging market economies that are invested in the US T bills and G secs. It restores liquidity in the US money market, keeps interest rates low, and manages the US government borrowing program without pressure on liquidity. It shows how private savings gap in the USA creates public cash surpluses of the emerging markets and helps finance US public deficit.

Dollar Glut: Bretton Woods to Globalization

To what extent is the US current account deficit sustainable? It depends on two factors, US unemployment and global inflation. The first is the internal limit and second is external limit. So long as the current account deficit due to competitiveness of rising

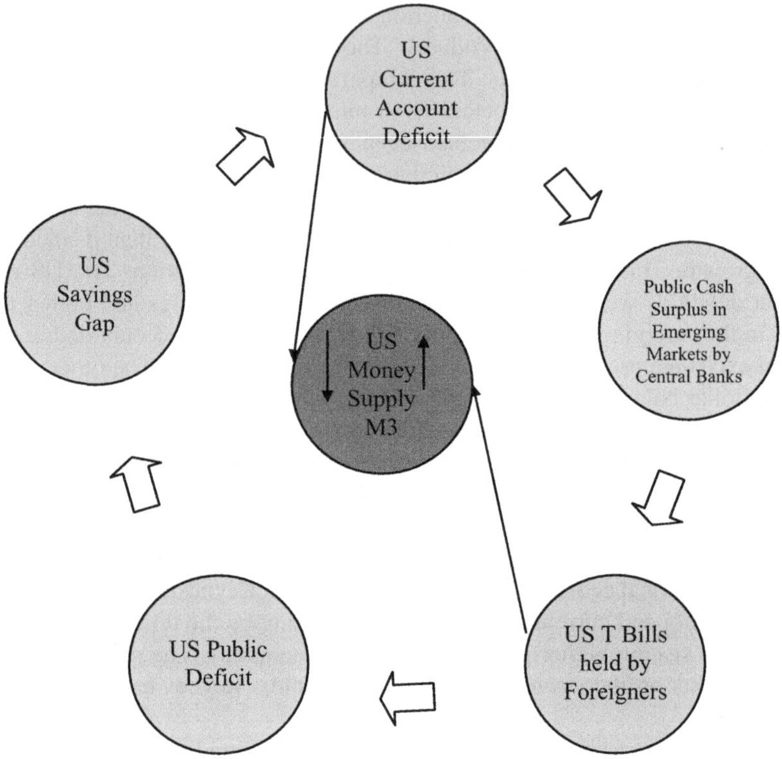

Fig. 12.1 Global funds flow: private savings gap to public savings surplus to public deficit

imports does not pose unemployment problem in the USA or an inflationary concern in the rest of the world due to pressure of US demand on their output capacities, the deficit would be benign and generate global growth.

The situation is to some extent analogous to global monetary situation in the 1960s. After the formation of Bretton Woods in 1945 with dollar linked to gold at $35 per ounce of gold and the USA holding largest gold stocks of $24 billion then (at the recent price of $1,600 per an ounce gold, it was worth $1.1 trillion), there was clamor among economists that world economy was facing shortage of international liquidity. The phenomenon of "dollar shortage" had emerged. The supply of capital and liquidity from the newly created IMF and World Bank was not easy and adequate to meet global demand for dollars. Since the international liquidity comprised gold and dollar holdings of central banks, it was necessary to increase the supply of either or both these components. Since the supply of gold was increasing at a very low rate and central banks also needed resources to acquire gold, the plea was made to increase dollar supply in the world. The dollar supply to the rest of world could be increased only by the USA incurring deficit in its BoP through foreign investments, loans, and aid. The government loans and aid needed budgetary allocation and were a burden on treasury and the budget. Further, the USA could not increase its BoP deficit persistently because dollar was convertible into gold for central banks at the fixed price of $35 and foreign central banks' holdings of dollar liabilities had surpassed the value of US gold stocks. Well-known economist Robert Triffin recommended creation of new money, special drawing rights (SDRs), to be issued by the IMF to solve the problem of both the weakness of dollar and additional liquidity. A few economists, especially French supported by President Charles De Gaulle, advocated increase in the official price of gold from $35 to $70. Finally, President Richard Nixon, in the historic and path-breaking decision, demonetized gold, delinking it from dollar, and let it float in international market. The elimination of the psychological barrier of gold which dollar faced for nearly a century allowed it to be a truly fiat currency and stand in the international market on its own strength. This landmark decision also allowed the global monetary system and economy to move from fixed rates to floating rates and from a stable but rigid financial environment to a more flexible and adjustable one. It also marked the beginning of globalization. Through the uncertain phase of the 1970s triggered by record oil price hikes causing stagflation and imbalance, the global economy moved to more benign phase in the 1980s. Financial deregulation, liberalization, privatization, and reforms allowed the phase of globalization to gather faster momentum. Freer trade and investment flows across all nations galvanized the global economy with unprecedented and sustained economic growth and prosperity.

The Fig. 12.2 shows how globalization is financed. The US excess consumption and outflow of capital create current account and capital account deficit in its balance of payments (BoP). The resultant surplus in the BoPs in emerging market economies causes forex reserves of their central banks to a steep rise. These are invested back into US T bills and G secs. The liquidity crunch caused by the BoP deficit in the USA is restored by investments in T bills and G secs. The process is money supply neutral for the USA. It finances the growth in the emerging markets through their exports and foreign direct and portfolio investments. Money supply and private savings go up in the emerging markets and higher domestic investments mop up both.

Bloated Forex Reserves and Influence of Sovereign Wealth Funds

Globalization has transformed the global economy from rigid and low-growth phase of the Bretton Woods era into dynamic, flexible, adjustable, high-growth economy. At the center of this dynamic global growth lies the US economy. It was argued that the US current account deficit was exogenous and governed by the savings glut of the emerging market economies. On the contrary, the US current account is endogenous and determines and governs the liquidity and savings glut in the emerging markets.

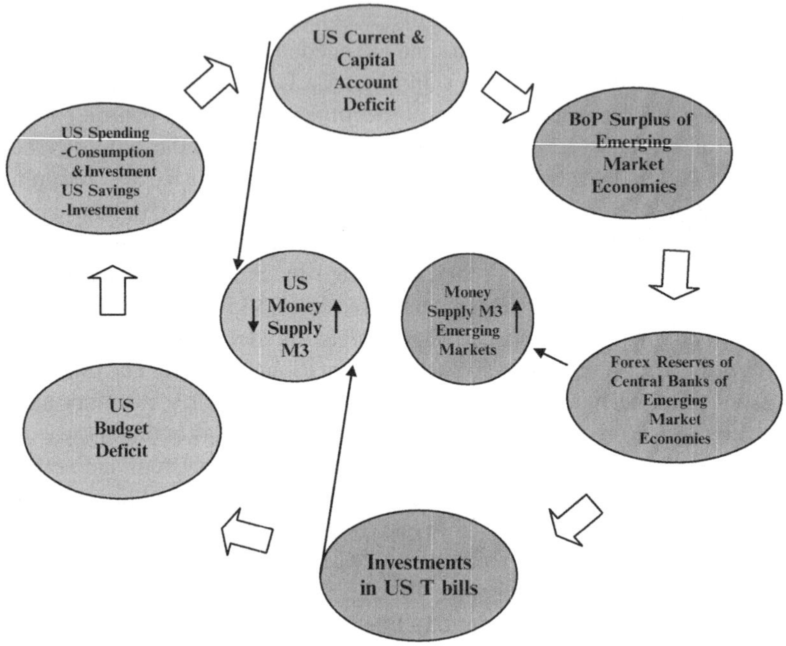

Fig. 12.2 Financing globalization

Because of the dramatic increase in the forex reserves of the central banks, there is also forex glut with the surplus countries and global liquidity glut. The savings glut exists in countries like China, Japan, Germany, South Korea, Malaysia, and some oil-exporting nations where savings rate is higher than the investment rate. Majority of that savings glut has resulted in forex glut. Usually the central bank investments go in the T bills. But this excess liquidity has found way also into equity, bonds, and real estate, including the subprime bonds, through the newly created sovereign wealth funds and other SIVs (structured investment vehicles).

This brings us to the new investment vehicle of sovereign wealth funds which are created out of the forex reserves of export surplus, reserve-gaining countries. These funds, which are SIVs of the central banks and which otherwise would have been invested in US T bill or G secs or such other risk-free investment assets, seek riskier investments including equity and real estate in addition to bonds, for higher returns. An estimate put 47 sovereign wealth funds holding assets totaling $3.1 trillion in 2008 compared to the global forex reserves excluding gold of $4.2 trillion and hedge funds of $1.4 trillion.[5] These funds, in addition to hedge funds, are a new force in the global financial and investment market influencing their dynamics.

[5] Source: OECD Center, Deutsch Bank 2008.

Did the Glut Precipitate Crisis?

Has the current global financial crisis, which originated from defaults in the huge subprime mortgage-securitized debt market in the USA, been caused by the global savings glut? The subprime crisis typifies the characteristic cyclical pattern of twenty-first-century digital free market American capitalism. The great US economic boom of the 1990s fed by telecom, Internet, software, and dot-com revolution attracted large investments from abroad. After the Y2K bust and subsequent economic downturn, the real estate sector, as it has been in the earlier periods, emerged as the booster of economic growth.

By 1990, under the effect of the first round of globalization, the share of manufacturing in total investment of $999 billion in the USA dropped to 13%, while the real estate sector investment with $313 billion formed 31% of total investment and emerged as the rising and critical segment in the growth of the US economy. The share of manufacturing in total investment further dropped to 11% in 2006, and the real estate boom that commenced in 2001 attracted $1,009 billion, accounting for record 40% of total investment. The boom generated by rising investments was facilitated by Fed's cheap money policy and promoted by the wave of subprime lending. The process of securitization and spread of the portfolio of subprimes among larger and more diversified group of commercial banks within the USA and outside recycled the resources of the mortgage banks which could finance more homes at a faster rate. The foreign private investment has been the feature of American capitalism. Even after the dot-com bust in 2000, the USA received foreign private investments in equity and debt (portfolio investment), not including direct investments and T bills and G secs, of $460 billion compared to $299 billion in 1999. It dropped to $221 in 2003 and rose again thereafter to peak at $683 billion in 2006. In addition to these foreign portfolio investments in securities market, including the over-the-counter market for subprime debt which was presumably very liquid till the onset of the crisis in September 2008, the US banks also received record money from abroad. The US banks' foreign liabilities rose from $118 billion in 2000 to $462 billion in 2006 and to record $509 billion in 2007. These may have been either higher supply of foreign deposits or could also be higher borrowings by the US banks due to pressure of demand for funds and inadequate domestic liquidity. After the subprime debt crisis, both these flows reversed. The foreign investments in US securities were -$127 billion and US banks' foreign liabilities –$327 billion, indicating the sale of securities and repayments of claims on US banks.[6]

Hence, in the globalized economy foreign investment is a part of overall economic dynamics, and American capitalism should not be deterred by the global savings glut. It is typical of capitalism entering the phase near the tip of boom to experience excesses under the influence of exuberance or euphoria. It is also a function of the financial system and capital market to allocate resources, may it be a glut or not, efficiently into financial assets that generate productive assets or directly into remunerative real assets. The market is assumed and expected to perform efficiently.

[6] Bureau of Economic Analysis, US Department of Commerce.

The evidence was that it could not. The market structure of the financial system had undergone a remarkable transformation and sophistication which the older regulatory framework and mechanism could not reckon. More broad-based and prudential regulation and monitoring with early warning signals and alarm mechanism should now be in place to avert such excesses and avoid crashes. The enlightened regulator needs to leash the raging horses of chariot of capitalism back onto the safe path and avoid getting derailed into muddy sides of the road ahead.

Alternative Scenarios

It is possible to draw alternative scenarios to see their effects on broad parameters and overall economic situation. Firstly, if forex-reserve-gaining countries had allowed appreciation in their currencies, their exports and capital inflows by way of direct and portfolio investments would have been lower. This would have impacted their growth rate and also lowered the forex accretion of their central banks. The savings and liquidity growth in their economies would have been lower. In the USA there would have been pressure on liquidity due to lack of investments of central banks in T bills. The government borrowings would have had crowding-out effect bringing upward pressure on the interest rates. The costlier imports from emerging markets, primarily China, would have reduced the trade deficit but caused higher rate of inflation. General slowdown in the rate of economic growth in the emerging markets would have been a dampener on the growth in the USA.

The second scenario is to imagine relaxation of controls on capital account in the emerging markets to permit excess savings to flow from the emerging markets to the USA and other developed economies. The private capital flows from the emerging market economies could be of two types: the long-term capital flow of equity and debt by way of direct as well as portfolio investment. There could also be short-term capital flow in debt securities. If these savings had gone to the US securities markets, the forex reserves of their central banks would have gone down. The resultant decline in liquidity in these economies would raise their interest rates. It would lower their growth rate. However, this would not have much of an adverse effect on liquidity in the USA in view of the reverse flow of private capital from the emerging markets. The flow of capital would shift from government securities to private corporate securities market. How much of this capital would go to equity and how much to debt is governed by several factors such as the state of economy and equity market, consumer confidence, corporate earnings forecast, Fed funds rate, yield on 10-year treasury bond, trend and outlook for interest rates and inflation rate, and Fed stance interest rate, money supply growth, and inflation rate target. The flow of private savings and capital would occur only in response to these factors if it is favorable in its risk–return trade-off vis-a-vis that in the home country. When the capital controls are removed, these flows are guided by the market and its signal. The risks and returns change from time to time but also their perception which varies with not only time but also place and institution.

Practical Solutions

The solution to this dual gap problem lies at two levels. There is too much savings and liquidity glut in one part of the world, while there is liquidity crunch and savings shortage in the other part of the world. The savings gap and constraint in the USA and other parts of the developed world except Germany and Japan is overcome by these nations through Keynesian remedy of higher deficit financing and rising public debt. The recent Greek tragedy is an extreme example of this problem, but many European economies are treading the same path closer to its extreme. The emerging market economies on the other hand which are enjoying exports and BoP surpluses are facing relatively high level of liquidity and also savings. The problem is minimized if the USA and other nations facing savings gap try to reduce their gap by raising their savings and also thereby lower their current account deficit. Also the BoP surplus emerging market economies have to reduce their surplus by raising their consumption and reducing savings.

The solution to this conundrum could be addressed at the market or the state levels. The need for state intervention would be the last option. The market-level options are more acceptable and likely to be durable. They would also evolve patterns that would not cause further distortions. In fact the problem is a manifestation of half free–half controlled global balance of payments structure and system. While most of the developed world has free capital account and convertible currencies, the emerging market economies continue to have restrictions on trade and more controls on capital movements. While currencies in the developed world are floating, the emerging market currencies are either fixed or floating but rigidly managed. The most glaring example is that of China which has strict controls on capital movements and fixed exchange rate. Bernanke's hypothesis of savings glut is a clear manifestation of distorted structure of global trade and payments caused by half free–half controlled system. This systemic problem to some extent initiated the current crisis but can be a bigger threat in the future as this lopsided development would lead to adverse trends in both the developed as well as the emerging worlds.

The first line of action would be to allow the market forces to work its way in adjusting or correcting this imbalance. The exchange rates of export surplus emerging market economies which are now regulated need to be left free to float by the market forces. It is also imperative that these export and BoP surplus economies should liberalize capital account transactions, allow freer outflow of surplus savings and capital, and allow residents to hold financial and real assets abroad. The problem of China today is that it has high savings rate coupled with restrictions on private outflow of capital. Resultantly, the domestic savings are bottled up within the country and lead to expansion in the domestic financial assets and money supply. The Bank of China builds up forex reserves and invests them in US T bills. This pressure would be released if private capital outflows are permitted with Chinese residents being allowed to transfer dollar resources abroad to hold financial assets or real estate abroad. This could also to some extent ameliorate the problem of crash in housing demand in the USA. While the Chinese investment in real estate would stabilize the US real estate prices, the private investments in stocks and bonds would also help the US securities market. China would have to allow the exchange rate of its currency to be more flexible and appreciate gradually.

At the state level the imbalance could be redressed by one of the biggest transfer of resources since the Marshall Plan. Henry Kissinger was very perceptive when he recently commented that Asia will have to do to America now what America did to Europe after the Second World War. He was referring to the American Marshall Plan which reconstructed Europe from the ravages of war. Hint was to the Asian Marshall Plan for America's recovery on the growth path. Tremendous liquidity crunch, lull in investments, and declining consumer spending are now driving the global economy into recession. In such situation nations fall prey to protectionism for narrow and short-term national benefits which bring misery to all. Beggar-thy-neighbor policy can steer the global economy into a deep recession. It is a path that nations must resist. A bailout package to take over distressed assets, two emergency economic stimulus packages by the US government, and record liquidity infusion and record low interest rates set by the Federal Reserves were all aimed to reflate the US economy. But if these measures fail to have stimulating impact, the Asian Marshall Plan led by China and Japan sufficiently large in size will have to be in place to lift the US economy onto the growth path. The Eurozone crisis resolution would require similar action from Germany.

Conclusion

We may now conclude. The US current account deficit is endogenous in nature and represents a critical feature of globalization that promotes growth and its financing. It has created global liquidity glut, which has found way in domestic savings growth in BoP surplus countries and also in global market through the forex glut. Neither current account deficit nor savings gap acts as a constraint on the growth of the US economy. The US economic growth is driven by consumption acceleration and investment thrust emanating from its attractiveness determined by innovations, the mix of Fed's monetary policy, and Treasury's fiscal policy.[7] The current financial crisis typifies a feature of American capitalism, which is its inherent cyclicality. Foreign investments and external dollars flowing back to the USA have been an inherent aspect of American capitalism. It is not malignant to cause a crisis if channeled optimally. The market for securitized debt and other derivative products need to move from OTC markets to more organized exchanges so that they can be regulated. What is needed now is broader-based regulation and monitoring to direct and allocate global capital more productively with adequate safeguards to avert any crisis. The crisis also manifests the structural imbalance in the global trade and payments structure created by

[7] This hypothesis is discussed in my earlier book, 'Globalization and Indian Economy: Roadmap to Convertible Rupee', Routledge, Taylor and Francis Group, New York, London, 2009. The figures 1 and 2 are from the author's book, pp. 40, 57.

half free–half controlled nature of developed and emerging worlds. It needs to be redressed first at the market level and then at the state level. To redress this structural problem, China and other export surplus emerging market economies need to adopt full-fledged reform in their domestic economies, float their currencies, and remove capital account controls.

References

1. Bernanke B. The global saving glut and the U.S. current account deficit, Sandridge Lecture, Virginia Association of Economics, Richmond, Virginia, March 10; 2005.
2. Nayak SS. Globalization and the Indian economy: roadmap to convertible rupee. New York: Routledge; 2008. p. 60–1.
3. McKinnon RI. Foreign exchange constraint in economic development and efficient aid allocation. Econ J. 1964;74:388.
4. Chenery HB, Strout AM. Foreign assistance and economic development. Am Econ Rev. 1966;LVI:679–733.
5. Nurkse R. Problem of capital formation in underdeveloped countries. Oxford: Oxford University Press; 1966. p. 97–100.
6. Nayak SS. Global monetary experience and India. Bombay: Kedien; 1991. p. 67–78.

Part IV
Looking Ahead

Chapter 13
Conundrum of Financial Markets: Measuring Risks and Mapping Regulation

> Research reveals that seatbelts encourage drivers to drive more aggressively. Consequently, the number of accidents rises even though the serious injury in any one accident declines. Derivative financial instruments designed as hedges have tempted investors to transform them into speculative vehicles with sleigh-rides for payoffs and involving risks that no corporate risk manager should contemplate.
>
> Bernstein, Peter E., *Against the Gods: The Remarkable Story of Risk*, 1996

With the free world of capitalism beset with stagflation in the late 1970s, the thrust in economic policy was on liberating the markets for regulations and controls. Adam Smith was resurrected and the "invisible hand" was given much freer hand. The postwar experience of the Bretton Woods the world over demonstrated beyond doubt that enlightened free markets are superior to regulation, controls, and planning. Even the supercomputers cannot gauge what the market can, because the markets have the feedback loop which the planning apparatus even with the best technology and computing power cannot replicate efficiently as the market. Since the early 1980s Thatcherism and Reaganomics drove the political economy of the USA and the UK and also influenced Europe and the emerging market economies toward much stronger free market philosophy. This debate over free market was essentially related to the industries covering goods and services and its efficiency in the allocation of physical and financial resources. Unfortunately, the market fundamentalists hijacked the free market argument and philosophy to be extended also to the financial services industry. The case for free markets for more efficient allocation of resources for maximizing consumer welfare and societal good is well taken. And it is preposterous to extend the same argument for the financial markets and also financial services industry.

The object of this chapter is to highlight the differences between the markets for goods and services and the financial markets which deal in securities and paper. It discusses the dynamics of the financial markets which makes it inherently fragile and volatile unless they are well structured and regulated. Some of the recent theories of investment, models, and products are critically analyzed from the viewpoint

S. Nayak, *The Global Financial Crisis: Genesis, Policy Response and Road Ahead*,
DOI 10.1007/978-81-322-0798-6_13,

of their relevance to the real market behavior and experience and their implications for the stability of the markets. This forms the basis of laying the broad contours and structure of prudential regulation reducing the risks of volatility and ensuring stability of markets.

Markets, Free Markets, and Financial Markets: Structure and Dynamics

Are financial markets a boon or a bane? Why do most of the cases of economic turmoil emanate from financial crisis of one sort or another? What is so peculiar about money, banking, and finance that makes it so susceptible to crisis? Is there something special about financial market that distinguishes it from other markets? In what way is the functioning of financial market different from other markets? If this is so, then there is a case for a separate study of the influence of financial market on the economy. The argument of free market is often hijacked by market fundamentalists to allow also the financial markets to be free from any regulatory interference and supervision. The case for free markets as an ideology for efficient real resource allocation, consumer welfare, and societal good is well taken in its micro- as well as macroeconomic realms. But it is preposterous to extend the same argument for noninterference with the financial markets. The structure and dynamics of the financial markets are far different from the markets for goods and services. It is this distinct nature of financial markets which makes them more vulnerable to destabilizing tendencies that can have damaging financial consequences and always lead to more serious economic crisis.

A market in economics is a broad term and is not limited to any physical place and refers to the size of demand and supply for a particular good or service. It goes beyond the physical constraint of space and also does not relate to a particular place. Although space and time are constraints that tend to limit the market size, they are increasingly overcome by technology of transportation and storage. In addition to the natural factors of space and time, the size of market is affected by the constraint of information. The technology of Internet which has provided low-cost and real-time information has been a revolution enlarging the size of market to be global.

For all commodities and services, the market means local market, regional market, national market, and global market. The market for a good or service will have these physical connotations depending upon the type of product and constraints on physical expansion of the market. The delivery mechanism, its cost, and storage capabilities of products also determine the expanse of their markets. The microeconomic theory discusses the price and output behavior, market structure, and its evolution over time for products and services. The theories of perfect competition and several forms of imperfect competition explain the laws of price and output behavior and the distribution of power between the consumers and producers in these market structures. Although one of the keys and central ingredients of capitalism is free and competitive markets, it does accept other imperfections such as monopoly, duopoly, oligopoly, and monopolistic competition as other restrictive market conditions that inhibit consumer welfare. In reality, in many agricultural products, manufactured goods, and services, the market conditions are far from being competitive. The true spirit of capitalism is to preserve the competitiveness of the markets. Hence, all governments have antitrust or monopoly legislations that inhibit the growth of noncompetitive and restrictive economic and trade practices and establish as competitive conditions in markets as possible. The objective is to allow competitive forces to work and flourish for the enrichment of societal welfare.

Market is a mechanism. It gives signals to the systems to allocate resources. Both are interdependent. The markets depend on system for its flows and turnover, and system depends on markets for signals on allocations of the flows. The economic system comprises the households, businesses including corporations, and government. While the households and businesses are the institutions and systems governed by their own motivations of self interest, and trade for value in a society, the government oversees them and provides a broad line of regulation to ensure that nowhere is their behavior inimical to societal interests. In this broad apparatus of institutions and systems, the markets are the meeting place for exchange of information on values of trade.

This is the free market mechanism which Adam Smith talks about, and this is the mechanism which even Keynes supports, accepts, and wishes to be preserved. This is the institution of market which the erstwhile communist regimes have introduced under the reform of their systems to improve their resource efficiency. This aspect of the market is the subject matter of microeconomics. However, it does not mean that the market mechanism has no role in the macroeconomics. Markets and market mechanism also have macroeconomic influence. It discusses how the market mechanism in general can play role in resource allocation and growth in an economy. This body of thought belongs to laissez-faire philosophy and market fundamentalism. The market fundamentalism argues that the market mechanism should not be disturbed even when it produces severe adverse impact on the economy like negative growth and growing unemployment. This they call is the process of cleansing the excesses of the boom. It should not be disturbed. In modern societies this is not practical, and state intervention is a necessity. The macroeconomics of markets is that it can drive growth but needs to be supplemented by the state in economic downturns. This is the Keynesian philosophy. Even Milton Friedman, renowned Chicago School economist and one of the ardent supporters and the champions of free market, admits the role of government in free market functioning. "The existence of a free market does not of course eliminate the need for government. On the contrary, government is essential both as a forum for determining 'the rules of the game' and as an umpire to interpret and enforce the rules decided on. What the market does is to reduce greatly the range of issues that must be decided through political means, and thereby minimize the extent to which government need participate directly in the game" [1].

Apart from the above distinction in the free market mechanism, there is another aspect about the markets which needs closer analysis and distinction, and more so in the light of the current crisis. The idea of free market mechanism has been increasingly hijacked to support market developments and instruments which actually need closer scrutiny since they can cause greater volatility in markets. It has to be reckoned that the entire debate about the free markets and government intervention which was and has been the center of controversy for a long time is not only about the markets for goods and services. It is essential to distinguish between the markets for goods and services and financial markets separately. The financial markets are in a way distinct from the markets for goods and services and need to be assessed and treated on different footing. Both have different characteristics and need to be looked at differently in their functioning as well as the policy angle of the approach of the state toward them.

Why Are Financial Markets Different?

The markets could be broadly classified into two categories on the basis of their distinctive physical characteristic. The markets for goods and services fall in one category because they are actually consumed and used. We may call them physical markets. In contrast the markets for financial assets and securities entirely deal in money and monetary values, documents or contracts of ownership, or debt interests. The peculiar and distinctive features of physical and financial markets underscore the need for looking at them differently and more so for supervising them from regulatory angle in public interest. The markets are a boon because they promote and act as the engines of economic growth. But the bane of the markets is that they can be at times destabilizing and destructive, disrupting the normal growth process it usually encourages. The collapse crises do not occur frequently, but they have shown to have made their periodic appearances in all economies.

Since the dawn of the Keynesian Revolution, the crises of capitalism triggered by the failure of its market and institutional mechanism have been tackled successfully by the efforts of central banks and governments. For the last nine decades since the 1930s, the Keynesian technology has rescued the capitalism from time to time from its crises on to its growth path. It is time now to look beyond the Keynesian technology and preempt the crisis through a new post-Keynesian technology of economic management. The need is for more efficient economic management than adopting the usual crisis-bailout game which is both economically and socially devastating and costly. The greed of the free market and its energy and drive need to be tempered lest it turns destructive after it triggers the crisis. The tipping point of the crisis is a territory in which the market begins to be actually unproductive although apparently it may still continue to look lucrative to the greedy and overoptimistic. This is typically the region of "irrational exuberance."

The key to the logic of adopting new technology of economic management is the understanding and realization of the distinctive characteristics of the physical—goods and services—markets and financial markets.

1. The physical goods and services are constantly produced by the producers and consumed by the consumers. A part of the production until it reaches the consumers is held by the traders as stocks or inventory. Hence, the stocks of commodities at any point in time are a small fraction of annual output or consumption but are usually equivalent to around 1 month's sales. The average monthly inventory to sales ratio for all businesses in the USA was 1.26 in July 2010. For motor cars it was 1.97, grocery 0.77, clothing 2.33, department stores 2.05, and general stores 1.44. During the crisis and recession of 2008, the ratio which is usually between 1.25 and 1.30 had gone up to 1.47, the highest in a decade.[1] The financial markets are the exact opposites. The financial markets deal in the stocks of securities. The very name "stock market" meant they are markets for stocks of equity and debt instruments. It represents instruments of wealth which go on rising in stock year after year as more and more instruments are added every year. Some debt instruments as they mature are redeemed, but new ones are added to the stock. The equity instruments are, however, perpetual unless the company goes bankrupt and is dissolved. This is the fundamental difference in the physical markets and financial markets which needs to be reckoned with in devising strategies and instruments for the regulation of financial markets.
2. The markets for commodities and services are disaggregated since the points of consumption and sales are geographically spread out. The points of production are centered in one or more places but not as disaggregated as sales outlets. They are essentially markets of flows. There is constant flow of goods and services to meet the continuing demand. The markets are spread out geographically where the demand is met. They are physically disaggregated over the geographic regions and serviced from wide network of distribution centers called stores. The Internet has, however, managed to provide a single platform for regional, national, and even global market. Further, there is no single platform for such markets. They are not exchange-based markets. In contrast the financial markets are either recognized exchanges or clearinghouses with a single global platform with the Internet connectivity or OTC (over-the-counter) markets connected by telephones or Internet but may or may not have clearinghouse mechanism, like the markets for many derivatives, securitized debt, or other instruments.
3. The financial markets deal in financial instruments issued by the users of money and held for investment by the suppliers of money at fixed or variable return. Except for the organized markets for standardized agricultural and farm products, metals, minerals, and oil, trading in goods and services is mainly for direct consumption and use by the consumers. Unlike these markets, the financial markets deal in securities which are constantly traded causing shift in their ownership and holding. The investors also have the choice of churning the holdings of their securities. Although the investors can change, the issuers of securities

[1] The US Census Bureau, 2006.

cannot shift their liability. The large volumes in the financial markets impart them a measure of liquidity and stability because of the process of price discovery which high-frequency trading promotes. But large volumes can at times also strike a disaster as they can be destabilizing and cause crash.

4. The price behavior of commodities is discussed in microeconomics in terms of demand and supply analysis. The market conditions form the fundamental basis of price behavior. They vary from the one end of perfect competition to the other extreme of monopoly or monopsony. In reality we have different shades of imperfect or monopolistic competition in different industries. In all the commodities, whether you are buying daily consumables like milk, bread, or fish or complex durables like car or TV, the price is fixed by the sellers, and buyers respond to that price. The sellers may adjust their prices later. The behavior of price over a period is governed by conditions of competition. The economics of prices in the financial markets is totally different. The behavior of security prices is a different ball game. Though the demand–supply analysis is still the crucial and critical determinant of prices, the security markets are believed to be competitive because of large number of players on both sides, supply and demand, and actions of any one player having little influence on the price.
5. The financial markets are markets where financial assets or securities are traded. Unlike the markets of goods and services, the securities markets are single-platform markets. They are exchange-based markets. They are also markets that primarily deal in the stocks of securities. The flow of securities also gets added to the prevailing stocks from time to time. But essentially they deal in stocks which are held and not consumed. These markets are secondary markets run by authorized exchanges dealing in financial instruments and securities. The derivatives markets in stocks and bonds and other financial products are the offshoots of the delivery markets which deal in options and futures. These markets have a trading platform, and institution-like exchanges provide these platforms. These exchanges are institutions which are registered institutions working under the securities regulatory authority in each country. In the USA they are registered with the Securities and Exchange Commission (SEC) and follow its guidelines in their working and operations. They are also supervised and regulated by the SEC. Before the advent of computers and Internet, these markets were physical at a place which used to be the trading floor connected by telephone. The commodity exchanges deal in recognized, standardized commodities, while stock exchanges deal in financial securities, stocks, and bonds, which are listed on the exchanges.

The NYSE (New York Stock Exchange), NASDAQ, and Chicago Board are the official exchanges, where stocks, bonds, and even derivatives are traded. In addition to the recognized exchanges, there are over-the-counter (OTC) markets which provide opportunity for trading of securities that are not listed on the exchanges on telephone or also now Internet. These markets deal not only in delivery-based spot transactions but also in derivatives like futures and options trades. Hence, the market exchanges are far different from the ordinary markets for goods and services. The latter are disaggregated while the exchanges are aggregated. The whole world looks at the NYSE and Dow Jones index to have a feel as to where the economy is heading. This feature of aggregation makes the market mechanism much more volatile thanks to the latest technology which gives global access to the market instantaneously absorbing large volumes in seconds.

6. The trading volumes in financial markets are, therefore, very large and in multiples of the outstanding stock of financial securities. Against the market capitalization of outstanding stocks of companies listed on the New York Stock Exchange (NYSE), the world's largest stock exchange, of $12.5 trillion in 2011, the turnover at the exchange in the same year amounted to $18 trillion. In the financial markets the stocks of securities are churned over so that the turnover is in multiples of market capitalization even if the floating stock of shares traded is smaller percentage of total market capitalization.
7. The financial markets are also considerably different from the other markets, just as services markets are different from commodity markets. The services markets are peculiar because services cannot be stored. They have perishable inventory. While the goods can be stored, the services cannot. The service industries have capacities which need to be used or consumed in time. If unused they expire with time. Hotels, airlines, and electric power providers often offer to supply the services during certain times at unusually low prices on marginal costs plus basis to render additional revenue because unutilized services incur costs that cannot be recovered later. Hence, we find record low prices or high discounts in services when at the last minute they are not likely to be used. Alternatively, when they are more in demand, the prices for last-minute sales could be very high. This is the experience in airline fares and hotel tariffs. This trend is more enhanced now because the Internet has changed the market structure and made markets more transparent, easy, quick, and less costly in information availability and accessibility. In the financial markets you are trading in stocks. Hence, you can be on demand as well as supply side. You can be a buyer or a seller. Unlike this, in commodity markets, there are a few producers and sellers, and the others, the masses, are buyers. Further, the securities market is not homogenous. Each security has its unique characteristic. Each stock and bond is different in its liquidity, return, and risk. The market characteristics such as the volume, floating stock, owner holding, institutional holding, and nature of business are some factors that vary from stock to stock. In contrast the currency markets are more homogeneous than securities markets. For every currency there is only one market, unlike securities where every security has different characteristics and has its own market within the overall stock market. Hence, currency markets offer better scope for studying and researching the behavior of markets and their responses. In fact, because the securities markets are heterogeneous, their behavior and responses are more complex.

Niagara Effect

8. The most important and critical distinction between the financial markets and the physical markets is that the participants in the financial markets can be both buyers and sellers. This is not so in the physical markets where the consumers are the

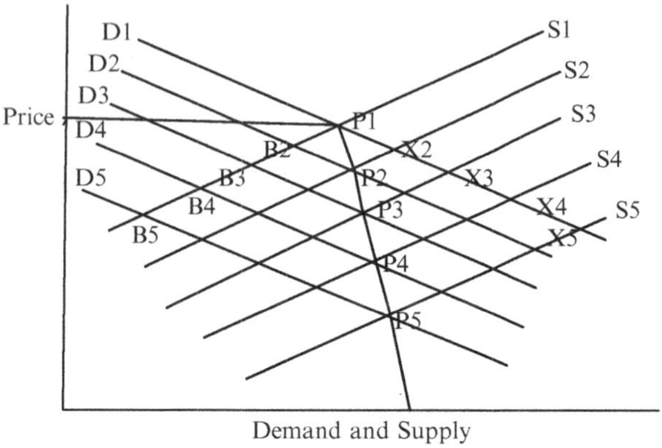

Fig. 13.1 Niagara effect

buyers, and producers and distributors are sellers. In the physical markets the buyers and sellers are two different entities. The consumers do not become sellers, or producers do not become buyers. The participant in the financial markets can be buyers at one price, and the same buyers can be sellers at another price. This distinctive feature of the financial markets makes it vulnerable to volatility.

This is explained in Fig. 13.1 below. D1, D2, D3, D4, and D5 are demand curves, while S1, S2, S3, S4, and S5 are supply curves. D1 and S1 are original demand and supply curves which determine the price P1. In a normal commodity market, whenever there is a selling pressure arising from the rising supplies of goods, the supply curve falls down. With the demand curve D1 remaining stable, the supply curve moves down to S2 and price falls from P1 to X2. If the supply increases further, curve moving to S3, S4, and S5, the price of the commodity falls further to X3 to X4 to X5. The price fall is demonstrated by line P1X5. This is the normal angular fall in the price of a commodity.

In the case of financial securities market, the buyers can become sellers, and sellers can become buyers. We see the same diagram for the financial market. D1 and S1 are demand and supply curves for a security. The price is P1 when market opens. The adverse news on the security results in both lower demand and higher supply. Not only the supply increases and demand reduces but those on the demand side either withdraw or also come to the supply side. Hence, supply increases and demand falls more than normal. Both the curves move down. D2 and S2 are new curves with price P2. The bad news is worse. The demand shifts down to D3 and supply to S3, and then again to D4 and S4, and D5 and S5. The supply increases from S1 to S5, while demand shrinks from D1 to D5. This leads to the price of the security falling sharply from P1 to P2, to P3, to P4, and to P5. The price fall is very sharp from P1 to P5. This fall is much sharper that the one in the physical markets, P1 to X5. This is the Niagara effect. When the prices do not fall but crash almost vertically, the effect is the Niagara effect resembling the waterfall at the Niagara river. The Niagara effect is more common in security prices than the prices of commodities and services. It contrasts the angular fall in prices in commodities from P1 to X5, which is more common. The financial markets are often subject to the Niagara effect, which the physical markets do not experience. The markets for goods and services do not suffer this kind of market and price reaction. Their demand–supply dynamics is more stable and not as volatile as in the financial markets.

If we consider the physical market the price falls on account of continuous fall in demand, it will be P1, B2, B3, B4, and B5. The supply curve S1 remains the same, but demand curve D1 goes on declining downward to D2, D3, D4, and D5. It can be seen that the commodity markets can suffer a price fall of P1X5 due to supply increase from S1 to S5 or of P1B5 due to demand fall from D1 to D5. Both these price falls in commodities are angular in contrast to the sharp fall of P1P5 in a security under the impact of the Niagara effect.

In the recent financial crisis triggered by the subprime debt defaults, illiquidity of debt securities took a heavy toll on the banking system. The market prices of subprime debt suffered the Niagara effect.

9. The extreme Niagara effect can lead to crash in the price of a security to such a low level resulting to illiquidity in the market for the security. This situation arises when the price reaches such a low level that there are only sellers and no buyers or only buyers but no sellers. In the subprime debt crisis, the subprime securities experienced such stage and total illiquidity of all such securities. With no market price available to value these securities, the portfolio had to be written off at huge losses resulting in massive black hole in the banking and financial system. It was not isolated to the USA alone but threatened the financial systems of other countries as well.
10. The financial markets can also be divided into those which are official exchanges registered with the financial regulatory authorities and those which are not official exchanges but over-the-counter (OTC) markets. The OTC markets were traditionally telephone markets, but with the advances in technology and onset of Internet as quick, safe, cheap, and more authentic medium of communication, the Internet has also been used. Some of the OTC markets are registered with the exchanges, but a large portion of OTC markets especially in the derivatives segments whose magnitude has grown astronomically do not have clearinghouse mechanism and facilities, therefore making them vulnerable to collapse and infectious in terms of its spread to other financial markets, banks, and the entire financial system. Many financial products and their derivatives are traded on the OTC markets. The subprime debt securities, CDS, and other exotic options and futures products are traded on the OTC markets. The size of OTC markets in these synthetic or plastic instruments and products has enlarged by leaps and bound in the last decade or so. These are the OTC markets that are not recognized exchanges and therefore not regulated. These markets are causing a great concern and threat because of the funding and involvement of large number of banks, financial institutions, and insurance companies which have larger stakeholders and are "too big fail" in the financial system. If it was only the play of private hedge funds and other private speculative institutions with no counterparty involvement of bank or financial institution with large and public

stakeholders, their involvements or riskier trades would not have caused the systemic damage like it did in the current subprime crisis. Sometimes even the collapse of one large hedge fund can cause systemic damage. This is evident from the LTCM debacle. The counterparty exposures of this single hedge fund were so large that its failure would have caused systemic crisis. Naturally with this impending danger, the collapse or bankruptcy of LTCM was avoided by a bailout by its creditor banks in September 1998 and the crisis was averted. LTCM was carrying a leverage ratio of 25:1. Unfortunately, this did not happen with Lehman Brothers. Their insolvency and illiquidity triggering huge counterparty losses created panic in the market and worsened the crisis instead of ameliorating it. The action in times of crisis like in battlefield and war zone has to be quick. There is not much time for rigorous study. The market does not wait, and judgmental decisions have to fire rapid action. It is in these areas that you need the skills to judge market reaction, take quick effective action, and also provide adequate ammunition or wherewithal supporting the decision to succeed in overcoming the adversity of the market.

Dynamics of Financial Markets: Market Efficiency Versus Vulnerability

Markets are institutions for trading. To serve the purpose of true price discovery, providing liquidity and being fair to both the buyers and sellers without any bias in favor of anyone, they have to be both competitive and transparent. If these parameters are fulfilled, the institution of market per se is not the one that should cause any concern. Yet financial markets have an inherent tendency to be volatile. This tendency is not observed in usual markets for goods and services except in the extraordinary circumstances of endemic shortages or glut.

The financial services industry and markets comprise several elements which share commonalities but also certain diversities. Three critical factors that govern the behavior of financial markets are rate of interest, risk of loss or Value at Risk (VAR), and expected rate of return. All decisions in financial markets and financial calculations or modeling done to guide decisions revolve around these three factors. Of these three factors, the rate of interest is current and known, while risk and return are estimates, and all the three factors are liable to change in the future, i.e., current rate of interest and current estimates of risk and return. Not only are they variable in time but they also follow a peculiar pattern of behavior during the cycles. During the market upswing the interest rate would tend to go up slowly. While the risk is low in upswing, it goes on increasing with the progress of upturn, and the expected return which is initially high also goes on declining with upward phase. When the market is in a cyclical phase, normal distribution of probability is highly inconsistent and unlikely and cannot be relied upon for measurement of risk. The bell-shaped normal distribution curve would take the shape of an angular candle revolving its top tilting to the right side as market moves from the bottom to the top. At the top of the market and on a downward mode, the candle would move its top tilting to the left, indicating the expected losses from investing and profit from disinvesting.

The stock markets are always swayed by sentiments. It is in a continuous process of adjustments of judgments of millions of investors of varying sizes, motivations, and perspectives. Behind the hard economic and financial mathematics of valuations lie the judgmental factors that are governed by the sentiments which actually reflect subjective probabilities. A constant flow of information, favorable and otherwise, changes probabilities on the judgmental factors governing the valuations. A sudden change in probabilities can arise not only from the information external to the market but also from the change in the momentum and the direction of the market itself. The market constantly reestablishes and reassesses itself through its participants. Hence, there are waves which can be observed in a short span of a day or less and also in as long a period as 2–3 years or even longer. *The path of the market is, therefore, charted by the probabilistic view of the judgmental factors that govern valuations.*

Information: Facts and Estimates – Key Determinant of Market Prices

The markets are primarily affected by information and its process of information dissemination and assimilation in price. Information in today's very competitive, sophisticated, and over researched markets is of two types. The first group is of facts and relates to past and present. This is the factual information of past and present available in quantitative and nonquantitative forms. The other group of information is futuristic, although it is based on the past facts and trends. The factual information is not variable, but futuristic information is variable. The analysts, market observers, fund managers, brokers, investment bankers, and others are researching and looking at the markets and stock prices in their own perspective. These estimates may vary within a narrow or a wide range. The market price is a judgmental view of all participants. The buyers are matched by the sellers. The buyers buy because they see a gain in the future, and sellers sell to avoid lower price in the future. The time perspective of prospective gain or loss can be different. A short-term loss can turn into long-term gain, and short-term gain can also move into long-term loss. The buyer may be right in the short and long run, or right in short run but not in long run, or wrong in short run but not in long run, or may be wrong in short as well as long run. Same is the case with the seller. John Bogle, the founder of Vanguard Group and pioneer of index funds, very correctly observed that the stock market works like a voting machine in the short run and weighing machine in the long run. Today's market is dominated by the institutional investors and players both in the spot and derivatives markets. The analyst estimates play market determining role. The markets are made and marred by the analyst estimates and changes in estimates.

Efficient Markets and Random Walk: Do Markets Have Memory?

While the efficiency of free markets and market mechanism is indisputably established in its macroeconomic implications, we are now moving to study the much debated and researched topic of the efficiency of the financial markets. We have already noted how the financial markets are different from the markets for goods and services. Hence, we cannot continue to carry the message of undiluted free markets unqualified to the world of financial markets.

There are two aspects of the financial markets which are subject to considerable research over long periods with different data periods and bases by large number of researchers and the best brains including the Nobel laureates in the subject. The first one is, are the financial markets efficient? And the second is, are the markets predictable? Why are the markets volatile and how do you contain their volatility to make them more constructive than destructive? These are two different and independent issues. Whether markets are efficient or not has nothing to do with its volatility. Similarly, whether markets are volatile or not has nothing to do with its efficiency. The market is said to be efficient if all the information about a stock or security is captured in its price instantly. It presumes that all the participants have equal access to the new information and they behave rationally. This is the technical aspect of the markets. This is determined by the technology of trading in the markets, the institutional and regulatory structure of the markets, disclosure norms and information system, and general behavior of the market participants.

The second aspect of the market is its predictive behavior and how an investor makes or loses money in the market. The well-accepted theory in this regard is the *random walk* hypothesis that states that the past behavior does not tell anything about how the market will behave in the future. The past trend of the market has no predictive quality. The market behavior follows the random walk pattern. Contesting this theory are the recent studies by a number of mathematicians who applied chaos and fractal theory to the market behavior to conclude that the markets have trend-reinforcing forces and that although it is not fully predictable, it is not random behavior but has certain trendy pattern. Mandelbrot who applied fractal analysis to prices in the stock market found the behavior of prices that were trend reinforcing [2]. According to him financial prices have memory. "First, price changes are not independent of each other. Research over the past few decades, by me and then by others, shows that many financial prices have a 'memory' of sorts. Today does in fact, influence tomorrow" [2, p. 11–12]. This phenomenon of positive feedback loop has been presented by several economists in different forms. Hyman Minsky has called it financial instability hypothesis.[2] George Soros has presented his own model of "financial reflexivity" [3].

If the markets are efficient, there would be little or no time available to profit from trade. The opportunity to profit from the market behavior is minimal or nil. But it does not mean that an investor cannot make profit from the efficient market. The

[2] Minsky, Hyman, op.cit.

profit or loss in the market arises from prices in two different points in time. Even if the market is efficient, it does not mean that it is predictable. Tomorrow's price will depend on tomorrow's information, and if investor can anticipate or judge today the information of tomorrow, he will profit from the market. If not, he will lose. Hence, even in efficient market the investor can make money on their predictive judgment. The inefficient markets definitely provide greater opportunity for profit due to a slow response of price sensitive information.

The random walk hypothesis and market efficiency theory are two independent issues. The random walk theory states that the market prices behave in a random fashion and there is no way one can predict the future course of prices on the basis of the past trend. The outcome is that the markets are unpredictable. The past data about the market is of no use to predict the future. This is the statistician view of the market on using his tools of analysis. The random walk hypothesis, however, did not stand the scrutiny of the latest statistical tests with more efficient models. Sometimes even models can be outdated.

Economists, statisticians, and mathematicians are not the only ones to study market price behavior. Another group of researchers, who aim to find a pattern out of chaos of market price behavior or noise therein, are the technical analysts. If economists or quants can go wrong, why can't technical analysts? Nobody is perfect in market prediction. While quants have caused great crises—1987 crash of program trading and 1999 LTCM crisis—the credibility of technical analysts has not been so bad as to cause any crisis. The technical analysts will rubbish the conclusion of the random walk hypothesis since their tools use the past data and find a peculiar trend to predict future course of price behavior. The technical analysts do not use any sophisticated and complex statistical and mathematical tools and analysis but derive trends from visual and graphic presentation of data. The efficiency of market means whether all the publicly available information is quickly embedded in the market price. It does not say anything about the predictability of the market. The inefficient markets give greater scope for profit. The profit you make is because you are among the firsts to enter the market after the news. The efficient market reduces the opportunities for such profits. However, it does not mean the efficient market reduces the profit opportunities from market trading. Knowing and understanding the trend of the market is much complex exercise of seeing or judging the pulse of the market and the securities or stocks you are trading in. While data and number crunching gives you a sense of the past, it is the skill, judgment, and art of interpreting data that determine success in market. It really involves judging the future without having full information about the future. It is not just a guessing game but a calculated guess on available information and knowledge.

The stock market prices have been subject to analysis by statisticians, mathematicians, and physicists who apply their models to understand market behavior and dynamics, derive formulae of their trend, and predict future prices. The finance theorists have been testing the efficiency of markets. The markets are said to be efficient if the information is quickly reflected in the market price. Over the last few years, revolution in information technology and wider and quick dissemination of information at cheaper cost have helped in making markets more efficient. Naturally, the prices are more volatile due to bunching effect. The information effect, instead of coming in a gradual wave, now comes in large packet or cloud and causes price to take much wider amplitude due to bunching of demand or supply. Instead of slow movement in price, it takes a sharp move. The opportunity for profit in an inefficient market is definitely larger than in the efficient market. But ability and skill to make profit does not arise only from exploiting the inefficiencies in the market. It arises from the ability to judge the change in the value of a security in a time frame. The time frame may be 15 min or an hour or a day or a week or a month or a year or 5 years. You may be wrong in one time frame or right in another, or you may be right in more time frames than wrong. Time and events determine value, and gains and losses.

The rationality and homogeneity of investor is another aspect which affects markets prices differently than the standard model. The financial markets are affected by broad macroeconomic parameters. But they are not homogenous and comprise thousands of different markets for different types of securities. Different market participants and investors have different profiles, goals, time frames of investments, risk–return matrix, and liquidity considerations. Again the investors have different scales of operations. In addition to the large number of small investors, today the market is dominated by the smaller number of large institutional investors, hedge funds, and sovereign funds. Their group is also not homogeneous. They comprise a wide spectrum ranging from long-term pension and mutual funds to short-term investment banks and hedge funds. The trading reaction and pattern on any information from these different investors are not uniform. Their trading strategies are different.

Quants and Experiments with Financial Risk

Since the 1960s the capital market theory has undergone a considerable advancement in both theoretical and empirical analysis following the pioneering work by Markowitz in measuring risk and developing the principle of investment diversification. The measurement of risk was the first step toward complex financial modeling which exists today. The risk measure also reflects the behavior of the past and its extrapolation in the future. It is tremendous advantage in comparative statics. It enables the judgment of the degree of riskiness of different assets in exact quantitative terms in different time frames. The static reallocation of assets on measurement of their riskiness in line with the investor's risk appetite and return expectation is a worthwhile exercise. But to build a portfolio for the future on the basis of the results of past data is fraught with serious risks. The concept of beta also relies on past data. CAPM (capital asset pricing model) is based on risk-free rate and beta and mean–variance model. Beta is based on an index, while Markowitz related it to the market portfolio [4].[3] Further, when future probabilities are unknown, the measures

[3] It outlines the critique of random walk hypothesis, market efficiency theory, and capital asset pricing model (CAPM).

need to be modified with subjective probabilities. The investment decisions, therefore, become a judgmental issue and finally an art rather than science which could be based on pure formulae and statistical and mathematical models. We have clear evidence of this from the crises that emanated from model-driven investment policy without the touch of judgment and art and failed to bring positive results but caused disasters. Edmund Phelps, who won the Nobel Prize in Economics in 2006 for his work on inflation–unemployment trade-off in macroeconomic policy, is highly critical of today's financial services industry. "Risk assessment and risk-management models were never well founded. There was a mystique to the idea that market participants knew the price to put on this or that risk. But it is impossible to imagine that such a complex system could be understood in such detail and with such amazing correctness" [5].

In the early 1980s the mathematicians and physicists entered the field of finance to give greater degree of predictability in the wake of volatile markets. The exchange rate started floating in 1973, oil prices recorded fourfold rise in 1974 and another bout of increase in 1979, and gold prices reached highest level and crossed $850 in 1980. These sharp increases in prices offered scope to understand the dynamics of markets and working-out tools to profit or hedge risks. Theoretical research in capital markets, risks, and market volatility known as quantitative finance had also invited the attention of investment and banking institutions to apply some of the theories and tools of physics, mathematics, and statistics to the practical market conditions by developing new products of pricing, trading, and risk management. Considerable research has been made in financial mathematics and statistics that have helped in understanding the markets and their behavior. It has helped in developing the derivatives markets which have enabled investors to hedge their risks. The market has also become more sophisticated and complex with increasing degree of financial engineering and entry of mathematicians and physicists in pricing the derivative products and increasing the range of products offered in the market. "The subject is an interdisciplinary mix of physics inspired models, mathematical techniques, and computer science, all aimed at the valuation of financial securities. The best quantitative finance brings real insight into the relation between value and uncertainty" [6]. The quants, as this group of specialists are known, began their work in valuing securities over time and developed products by pricing instruments that offer hedging of risks inherent in the securities. By that time the Black–Scholes stock option model had become a popular method of pricing options.

The game of knowing the future in economic and financial world is a difficult exercise even with the advanced math and physics. The future is fraught with risks and uncertainties. Risk and uncertainty are not the same thing. Risk is one where the probabilities of loss can be calculated and known, while uncertainty means a dark region where the probabilities are unknown. With known probabilities one could measure risk but measurement of risk in uncertain horizon becomes difficult. Yet statisticians work out measurement of risk in uncertain terrain with subjective definition of probability and, on Bayes' theorem, the basic tool for assigning probabilities to hypotheses combining judgments and experimental information. Bayesian approach is the natural one for analysis of data in the most general sense and for assigning uncertainties to the results of physical measurements. Yet due to the surprise elements that always loom in the economic and financial world, the risk measures are likely to contain an element of error. The black swan events cannot be accurately measured and therefore priced fairly.

Math of Knowing the Future and Game of Risk Trading: Fat Tails and Swinging Tilted Bells

Risk is an inherent aspect of economic activities. Since the future is unpredictable, every economic activity which has a link with the future, whether short term, medium term, or long term, faces risk. In finance risk is inherent because of the changing nature of financial world and financial markets.

The statistical analysis of measurement of risk is based on the Gaussian theory of bell-shaped curve representing normal distribution of events or returns. This is subject to criticism. The estimates of risk which use methods that assume normal distribution are good as standard indicators in normal times but fail to gauge the abnormal events. All the crises that occur are abnormal events. If they were occurring in a regular frequency or manner, they would have been predictable. Hence, all the statistical and mathematical formulae which measure risk fail to account for a sudden event which is abnormal and a crisis. Nissim Taleb calls it *black swan*, one in million events which does not occur with regularity and which is unpredictable [7]. Peter Bernstein, in his brilliant analysis of struggle and attempts of the scientist and economists to quantify risk and predict future economic events, highlights the shortcomings of all these theories, laws, tools, and methods. "We pour data from the past to fuel the decision-making mechanism created by our models, be they linear or nonlinear. But therein lies the logician's trap: past data from real life constitute a sequence of events rather than a set of independent observations, which is what the laws of probability demands. History provides us with only one sample of the economy and the capital markets, not with thousands of separate and randomly distributed numbers. Even though many economic and financial variables fall into distributions that approximate a bell curve, the picture is never perfect. Once again, resemblance to truth is not the same as truth. It is in those outliers and imperfections that the wilderness lurks" [8]. The crisis situations lie in this hidden space uncapturable by the models.

One can use all these tools as the measures of analysis without any practical involvement. But when we apply them in pricing financial products called derivatives which deal with future and engage in large financial exposures for the book writers, they are fraught with risks which are unanticipated and higher than usual. Benoit Mandelbrot, the mathematician who invented fractal theory, calls these events evident in fat tails of bell-shaped distribution. The fat tails discovered by Mandelbrot in financial markets are the evidence of larger frequency of bigger losses than is assumed by the normal distribution [2]. "From 1916 to 2003, the daily index movements of the Dow Jones Industrial Average do not spread out on graph like a simple bell curve.

Fig. 13.2 Bell-shaped probability

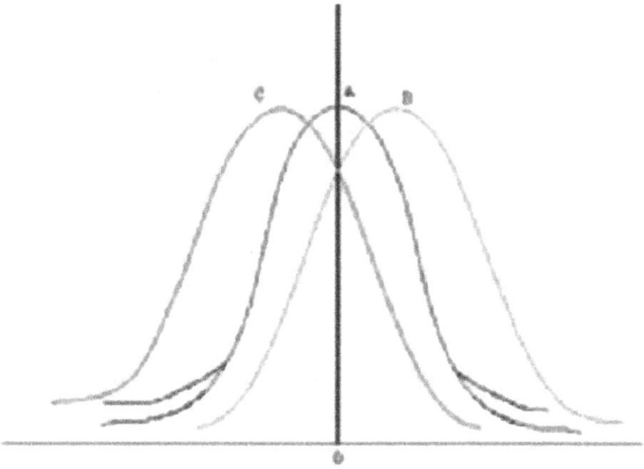

The fat edges flare too high: too many big changes. Theory suggests that over that time, there should be 58 days when the Dow moved more than 3.4%; in fact, there were 1,001. Theory predicts 6 days of index swings beyond 4.5%; in fact there were 366. And index swings of more than 7% should come once every 300,000 years; in fact, the twentieth century saw 48 such days. Truly, a calamitous era that insists on flaunting all predictions. Or, perhaps, our assumptions are wrong" [2, p. 13].

Mandelbrot brings out the flaws in the efficient market and random walk hypotheses and CAPM which are based on the assumption of normal distribution and bell-shaped curve of price changes. These elegant theories, he argued, represented the old financial orthodoxy based on two critical assumptions: price changes are statistically independent and they are normally distributed. Research over the past few decades has demonstrated that both these assumptions are not close to reality of financial markets and price behavior therein. Upshot of the matter is that the statistical or mathematical estimates based on normal theory of distribution do not at all match the reality of stock market or for that matter even forex markets or any other exchange-based markets for securities, commodities, or currencies. It also demonstrates that the markets are not "mildly unstable" but "wildly unstable." The Economist's report writes that the financial markets are not plagued by "black swans" but by "vicious snow-white swans" that make more frequent occurrences than expected. This puts the entire business of risk management and risk trading based on complex models into question.

The Fig. 13.2 above shows normal distribution curve A. The upper lines near the tails of A curve are Mandelbrot's fat tails which indicate higher risks of major crisis. Not only are the tails thick but the bell also gets skewed and tilts on both sides depending on the trend of the market. In a rising market the trend-reinforcing tendency of the market makes the bell curve skewed and tilt to the right and be B curve. The probability of rise is higher than that of a fall. On the contrary, in a falling market the tendency is downward and bell gets skewed and tilts to the left, like C curve. The probability of fall is larger than that of a rise. Similarly, at the bottom of the bear market, we do not face curve A but curve B, and at peak of bull market, we face curve C.

The bell curve, being the basis behind pricing of all risk management tools and derivative products that mainly trade with futures, is the main flaw behind and the bane of decisions of risk management and trading for gains. Leveraging the exposures makes such decisions far more risky than they appear or look. In many cases the crisis is built upon the superstructure of derivative products which give a sense of security to the users who have not reckoned the possibility of abnormal loss in case of abnormal events. The sharpest criticism of the pricing of derivatives comes from Mandelbrot. "If you are going to use probability to model for a financial market, then you had better use the right kind of probability. Real markets are wild. Their price fluctuations can be hair-raising, far greater and more damaging than the mild variations of orthodox finance. That means that individual stocks and currencies are riskier than normally assumed. It means that the stock portfolios are being put together incorrectly; far from managing risk, they may be magnifying it. It means that some trading strategies are misguided, and options mispriced. Anywhere the bell-curve assumption enters the financial calculations, an error can come out" [9].

Failure of the King of Risk Trading

One of biggest setbacks to the derivatives trade in financial markets was received with the Long-Term Capital Management (LTCM) fiasco. LTCM was engaged in arbitrage and options trades in derivatives market based on complex mathematical models. Established as hedge fund in 1993 by well-experienced bond traders from the major investment banking firms and primarily supported by quants, finance practitioners used mathematical models for trading strategy in financial markets, fresh from the business schools. They were guided by renowned Nobel-prize-winning economists for their work on options pricing and whose models were referred and used by the strategists and traders for options trading in the derivatives markets. It was a period in which subjects of finance, financial markets, and investment attracted considerable research in universities on treatments of complex statistical and mathematical tools and models. On the practical side several tools and models were used by the top investment bankers to introduce new products. The launch of derivatives markets with products of futures, options, and swaps offered an open ground for the quants and investment bankers to introduce innovative products in this new market. While the derivatives markets and products offered an excellent opportunity to large corporates, financial, investment, and insurance institutions to hedge the risks inherent in their portfolios and financial exposures, several hedge funds, market trading, and investment banking firms also took exposures in the markets for arbitrage and speculative trade profits.

The LTCM had a capital of $4.4 billion out of which $1.9 billion was held by 16 partners. It established track record of profit for nearly 15 years. Leveraging is at the heart of any business and more in banking and further more in investment banking. Ordinarily businesses do not leverage beyond two times and banks leverage within 10–12 times, and it is not extraordinary for investment banking firms to leverage about 25 times or even 50 times. What is more crucial than simple leverage figure is the risk involved in the leverage. The degree of risk in the leverage is equally important.

High leveraging with low risk has less chance of threatening the liquidity and solvency of an institution. Low leverage with high risk can also destroy an institution. Yet another law of investment is that great profits can come only at the cost of higher risk. Risk and returns are directly related and degree of this relationship varies from asset to asset. Diversification and hedging can reduce the riskiness of your portfolio but not at the same time raise your returns. But the most extraordinary fact of investment is that all the advanced methods of mathematical modeling can go wrong in the estimates of risk and also return, when the results are driven by chance and unusual events. Extraordinary profits or losses can spring up by chance with no relation to earlier estimates of risks. This is the point of inflection when models collapse and normal market behavior becomes abnormal. The market crisis occurs at this point of inflection which has been subject of research by the theorist, practitioners, policy makers, and regulators. The point of inflection is difficult to predict although seasoned traders and market practitioners, analysts, and observers often have an inkling when the market turns into risky zone of collapse. Yet it is next to impossible to time the market crash even with reasonable degree of predictability.

LTCM made 42.8% profit in 1995 and 40.8% in 1996. But it went into turbulent markets thereafter. The losses of LTCM arose from their highly leveraged exposure in interest rate swaps and long-term equity options which carried high risks. Actually the business of arbitrage is not as risky as the option pricing. Arbitrage takes advantage of price differentials in different markets that have tendency to equalize over time. If timed accurately the risk in arbitrage business is little and often nil. Contrary to this, options writing is trading in risk, pricing of which goes up with the degree of risk indicated by the measure of volatility on the basis of the past behavior of price of concerned security, rate of interest or exchange, or index.

When equity options emerged as a popular tool of hedging the loss in equity portfolio due to falling equity prices in the market, institutional as well as large individual investors locked in put options written by the large investment banking firms. In order to cover their risk, the investment banking firms either sought insurance with insurance firms or bought options from other firms. LTCM was a large powerhouse of supply of options trades to investment bankers. The failure of LTCM was not a small failure. It signified the fall of the king of options pricing and risk trading. It was a sad lesson for the quants testifying that there are no perennial routes to profit devoid of risk and they cannot be measured with perfection and predicted without error. Understanding the market cyclicality is both science and art. It needs quantitative measure but has to be tempered with skill and judgment on positions and pricing, which comes only with experience on the quantum of leveraging.

Dynamics of Boom–Bust Cycle of Markets

The phenomena of economic crises, financial collapse, stock market crashes, and boom–bust cycles have been researched in the extensive study by Charles P. Kindleberger and Robert Aliber [10]. The study covers several economic and market booms and crashes from the Tulip mania of 1636 in Amsterdam to more recent Nikkei crash of 1990 and dot-com bust of 2000 highlighting some common elements that underlie the cycles of boom and euphoria that is followed by crash and panic. Although they have not examined the psychological factors and social or group behavioral tendencies and their causes, all the cycles go through a typical behavior due to certain fundamental economic factors or motivation of profit that underlie such tendencies. Firstly, when the asset prices go up, the rise is initially facilitated by easy and cheap credit. Costly credit and difficult credit availability cannot precipitate faster asset price rise. Once the asset price rise gains momentum supported by the positive economic and business environment, the faster price rise encourages higher leveraging. The excess demand for assets fuels higher price rise, and rising prices become self-fulfilling prophecy. This positive feedback loop is further reinforced by the strong and positive wealth effect. The rising asset prices increase the monetary value of wealth of households leading to higher consumption from their realized capital gains, from income against their unrealized capital gains. Rising consumption attracts more investments and, along with growing consumption investment, gives a strong growth stimulus to the economy. This keeps the asset price rise in a positive momentum. It would continue until the point of inflection where further price rise seems economically irrational and unsustainable. While the upward movement is beneficial to all, the trouble starts when the prices begin their downward journey or crash. The panic is more powerful than the greed. The pain of loss is much bigger than the pleasure of gain. Between the pleasure and pain, the tendency is to avoid pain than gain pleasure. The herd mentality is stronger in pain aversion than pleasure seeking. Hence, the crashes are more pronounced and sudden. Further, in leveraged positions loss is magnified and pain intensified. This is the basic dynamics of the markets which is common in all boom–bust cycles.

Asset price inflation acts as an aphrodisiac or an adrenaline that moves the economy in higher tempo of growth. Even the speculative bubbles and booms trigger economic upswing. But they can also have negative influences if not supported or backed by the economic fundamentals. "Did the decline in the prices of tulip bulbs lead to a decline in economic activity? The answer is yes, and the causal connection is that households were less eager spenders as their wealth declined" [10, p. 117]. What is essential is that the economy should not suffer from the withdrawal effects and go in recession when the adrenaline stops generating after the market goes bust. Speculation like atomic fusion can be either productive or destructive. While speculation can set underemployed economy onto a growth path, excessive speculation unwarranted by the potential economic reality can be disastrous after the bubble bursts and cause heavy financial losses that invariably bring the economy into a tailspin. Keynes aptly described this aspect in the General Theory, "Speculator may do no harm as bubbles on a steady stream of enterprise. But the position is serious when enterprise becomes the bubble on a whirlpool of speculation." What is also important is that the economic boom becomes more constructive and not speculative and also not culminate into bubble if economic potential can translate it into real growth not only in price inflation.

The Glass–Steagall Conundrum

The Glass–Steagall Act emerged after the Great Crash and the Depression that followed thereafter. The Great Crash dealt a devastating blow to the banking system which could never recover from its damage until after the New Deal measures and the reform of the banking system and the strengthening of the Federal Reserve. The times were a testing lesson for the banking system. The involvement of banks in the stock and capital market transactions subject to volatility was found to be an undesirable feature of the banking system and needed to be redressed. The economic boom of the 1920s had led to many banks increasing their exposure to stock market and investment-banking-related activities such as margin funding of stockbrokers, investors, and speculators and underwriting of new issues. The Great Crash in stock market in 1929 incurred heavy losses on banks that were involved in the stock market leading to their collapse. Since deposit insurance did not exist in 1929, the depositors lost their money in banks causing a great monetary implosion. The weak Federal Reserve and absence of funding to the illiquid banks led the banking crisis of large proportion which contributed to the sharply declining economy that ended in deep depression. In the light of this experience, the Congressional view of the banking system then prevalent was unequivocal in separating the investment banking from normal commercial banking. It was a measure that was prudent and desirable to ensure stability in the financial system. Since the 1930s the US banking system and also capital market enjoyed more than half a decade of growth and stability primarily due to the prevention of banking excesses ensured by the Glass–Steagall Act.

During the 1980s rapid growth in products and services in financial services industries and technological advance facilitating new product or service growth and their cost efficiency and high productivity broke the traditional barriers between the businesses and offered synergies in their synthesis under single umbrella. The other developed nations in Europe adopted universal banking and posed competition in size and product coverage to the American banks. The share of banking industry in the overall financial services activities was rapidly decreasing. The share of banks in the total assets of all financial intermediaries fell from ¾ in the 1970s to less than ¼ by 2000. The considerable diversification in financial services business and availability of wider range of financial products plus the rapid growth of the securities markets and the popularity of securities-based products reduced the share of pure banking business in a rapidly growing financial services industry. The banking industry was lobbying for the repeal of the Act since the 1980s. The technological gains and eroding share of pure banking business were the two primary considerations weighed heavily in favor of the repeal of the earlier 66-year-old Act that appeared to be a hindrance in the growth and efficiency of the financial services industry.

While there was a growing antipathy of the banking industry and more especially the large banks with the Act and wanted its repeal, by the mid-1980s, the Reaganomics that ruled the economic policy in the USA did give much needed heed to the demands of the banking industry. During the period from 1988 to 1996, four legislative attempts were made to tone down the effect of or repeal the Act. All these attempts failed due to the opposition from the smaller banks who would have faced greater competition with the Act's repeal. This decade-long tussle between the legislators and the industry without much result in favor of the banking industry was a concern to the banking industry. In order to overcome this tangle, the industry leader took initiative on its own that was to be one of the largest and most dramatic mergers in the financial services industry. The Travelers, one of the largest insurance companies; Salomon Smith Barney, one of the largest broking firms on the Wall Street; and the Citibank, the largest commercial bank, merged to be the largest financial conglomerate in the USA, handling banking, broking, and insurance businesses. The merger, although financially well conceived and practically a lucrative option, nevertheless violated the Glass–Steagall Act.

In November 1999 Gramm–Leach–Bliley Act was passed repealing the 66-year-old Glass–Steagall Act of 1933. It allowed the commercial and investment banks to consolidate. The Glass–Steagall prohibited the mixing of commercial banking with investment banking and securities and insurance businesses and permitted universal banking or broad banking. The new Act allowed the financial subsidiaries of the banks to conduct all the financial services businesses. It also allowed the savings and loan and other thrift holding companies to conduct banking, securities, and insurance business.

However, the new Act permitting only holding company option to US banks prevented them from using other organizational options adopted by the European banks. The most important issue in the repeal of the old Act and promotion of broad banking was one of supervision and regulation. The financial services activities came under different regulatory authorities. Hence, the Act advocated the principle of "functional regulation" which meant similar activities to be regulated by the same regulator. The federal and state banking regulators regulate banking, federal and state securities regulators regulate securities activities, and federal and state regulators regulate insurance. The problem of coordination between these multiple regulatory agencies was an important issue that needed to be addressed at the time of the new Act, and concern was raised immediately after the Act was passed in 1999. "How regulators will in practice coordinate their efforts so that the safety and soundness of the banking system is maintained efficiently remains to be seen" [11]. The legislators did not take a tough approach on supervisory and regulatory issues and left the regulation to the existing regulatory apparatus lest it would put unnecessary hindrances on the growth and innovative trends in the industry.

Conclusion

It is imperative to understand that the financial securities and markets behave differently than the commodity markets. The generalized philosophy of free market mechanism cannot be blindly applied to the financial market to keep them totally free and devoid of any regulation or systemic supervision and interference. The financial markets have become more complex, globalized, and increasingly leveraged. Confidence and trust are the anchor of stability of the financial markets. The markets can become highly volatile and in time of severe crisis run the risk of becoming also illiquid. These markets are subject to Niagara effect which can be devastating. A lot of uncertainty and risk emanate from the OTC markets, also including the derivatives markets, which do not have clearinghouse mechanism, capital adequacy, and proper reporting and supervision. A considerable risk of crisis can be eliminated by making the OTC markets follow the rigors of the normal exchanges with clearinghouses, margin requirements, and ongoing reporting and supervision. In avoiding the overheating of the market which later suffers from a crash, the interest policy of the central banks has shown very little restrictive impact. This is due to the fact that several market players are heavily leveraged and institutions are more so. Hence, the interest rate rise is a blunt weapon to arrest excessive financial investments and exposures. Yet the monetary authorities the world over use this weapon with little or no effect. It is more appropriate to enforce stiffer margin requirements, which are more effective instrument of controlling excessive exposures in the bull phases.

References

1. Friedman M. Capitalism and freedom. Chicago: The University of Chicago Press; 1982. p. 15.
2. Mandelbrot BB, Hudson RL. The (mis)behavior of markets: a fractal view of risk, ruin and reward. New York: Basic Books; 2005.
3. Soros G. The alchemy of finance. Hoboken: Wiley; 2003.
4. Beinhocker ED. The origin of wealth: evolution, complexity, and the radical remaking of economics. Boston: Harvard Business School Press; 2006. p. 381–414.
5. A special report on the future of finance, The Economist; January 24, 2009. p. 13.
6. Derman E. My life as a quant: reflections on physics and finance. Hoboken: Wiley; 2004. p. 3.
7. Taleb N. The black swan, Random House, New York, 2007.
8. Bernstein PE. Against the gods: the remarkable story of risk. New York: Wiley; 1996. p. 335.
9. Mandelbrot BB, Hudson RL. The (mis)behaviour of markets: a fractal view of risk, ruin and reward. London: Profile Books Ltd.; 2004. p. 105.
10. Kindlberger C, Aliber R. Manias, panics and crashes: a history of financial crisis. Hoboken: Wiley; 2005.
11. Barth JR, Brumbaugh Jr D, Wilcox JA. The repeal of glass-steagall and advent of broad banking, Economic and policy analysis working paper. Washington, DC: U.S. Office of the Comptroller of the Currency; 2000.

Chapter 14
Rediscovering Keynes

> The story of the decline and fall of the Keynesian Revolution, and what happened to economics generally, is a fascinating intellectual detective story in its own right, which charts the trajectory from President Nixon's 'We are all Keynesians now' in 1971 to Robert Lucas's 2009 remark 'I guess everyone is a Keynesian in the foxhole.'
>
> Robert Skidelsky, *Keynes: The Return of the Master, 2009.*

The Backdrop

The era of liberalization, reforms, and globalization that began in the 1980s marked a paradigm shift in the global economic system from the *Bretton Woods* that survived from 1945 until 1971. The new phase of economic policy was also accompanied by another economic and political philosophical change. It was the ideological thinking about the role of the state. While the postdepression economic policy was dominated by Keynesianism and rising power of the state, the era of globalization gave thrust on minimizing the size and role of the state. This new ideology of privatization and downsizing the government took the form of Thatcherism in the UK and Reaganomics in the USA. Unfortunately, all the rhetoric about reducing the government size and involvement in the economy did not cut much ice with the reality. Despite his goal of achieving the budget surplus by cutting the government size, President Reagan's term ended with the record budget deficit in the USA. The juggernaut of the state continued to rule the economy and drive its growth irrespective of the ideological differences of political parties. The rhetoric on lower government failed to change the reality.

S. Nayak, *The Global Financial Crisis: Genesis, Policy Response and Road Ahead*,
DOI 10.1007/978-81-322-0798-6_14, © Springer India 2013

John Maynard Keynes (1883–1946)

The size of the government hardly reduced, although global economies became more liberalized and closely integrated. The new wave of globalization transformed the world economy beyond anyone's expectations and belief. What is astonishing is that the period of globalization recorded a straight line of higher economic growth without any major break. It was devoid of periods of prolonged slumps. The economic progress did get interrupted periodically by some regional crises, be it an Asian, Mexican, and Russian crises, or dot-com crisis and now subprime debt crisis. Yet economic policy tools were adept and used with speed and diligence to avert market failures culminating into economic catastrophe. It was believed that like small pox, economic depression had been totally eradicated. With the Keynesian medicine at use, the depression, never experienced by the postwar generation, was only a historical event and at the most only a nightmare and not an impending reality. In this not only common public realization but also perception among economists and political thinkers and leadership; the global economy to be hit by depression carried as low a probability as the earth being hit by a large meteorite.

Physical science like astronomy is more advanced and precise in understanding phenomena due to its immutable laws of nature. The availability of most advanced and sophisticated instruments enable the measurements to grasp the reality and draw the future course. On the contrary, economics is subject to laws which are not only imprecise but are liable to experience swings caused by buildup of trends fueled by human emotions and sentiments governing anticipation of gains and greed and abrupt behavioral changes motivated by panic and fear of loss. This has been the bane of market mechanism, which is often subject to herd mentality and instinct, but otherwise also a boon to the economic system.

The instrumentality of information and data collection and monitoring of markets are not yet adequately accurate enough to capture the impending disaster or magnitude of damage it can cause.

The sustained economic growth experienced by the global economy during the 1990s primarily fueled by the USA, China, Southeast Asia, and India continued into the new millennium although at a lesser speed, despite the dot-com bust in 2000. The risk of depression, instead of being negligible getting increasingly greater and becoming a reality and that too with the USA as the center point of the crisis, was unthinkable. Hence, onset of the subprime crisis in the USA spreading the risk of global depression came as the bolt from the blue. Not only the economists but the policy makers and governments were also unprepared for the imminent fallout of the subprime debt crisis. The risk of the US financial crisis culminating into another great depression that earlier appeared to be a remote possibility turned out to be a distinct reality and not a guessing game, if not tackled by timely, decisive, and effective policy action.

It is, therefore, natural that at this critical juncture in 2008, John Maynard Keynes, the savior and hero of postdepression capitalism, was once again remembered. The renowned Cambridge economist wrote *The General Theory of Employment, Interest and Money* in 1936 that revolutionized economics and economic policy paving the way for the postwar depression-free global economic growth and prosperity. *The General Theory* needed to be studied again to deal with the new economic crisis and the impending global depression. Analysis of the genesis of the current subprime mortgage debt crisis and the Great Depression of the 1930s gives the clue to some commonalities, despite the gap of about 80 years and a sea change in economic environment and perspective, leave apart the technological hiatus between the two eras.

Keynes, the Einstein of economics, gave a new lease of life to capitalism in the 1930s and ensured its sustenance out of periodic downturns in the economy which used to turn vicious. With the support of his then unconventional theory, President Roosevelt passed the New Deal in 1933 that totally changed the character of American capitalism, revitalizing it forever into what it is today. While in his own country, Britain, economists and politicians argued and contested the wisdom of his unorthodox ideas breaking the conventional wisdom, America took the lead and displayed the political audacity and wisdom in adopting policies underlying his theory with the lead taken by President Roosevelt. In Britain Prime Minister Churchill did not, or could not, show as much political courage in embracing the ideas of his Cambridge genius first.

Keynesianism: Political Ideology with Economic Significance

Keynesianism is an economic ideology that relies on the main thesis of his *General Theory* that laissez-faireism cannot ensure sustainable growth path for a mature capitalistic economy, which is likely suffering from the malady of depression that can only be remedied by the state by its intervention in the economy by adopting the fiscal policy of deficit financing for pump priming the economy and restoring it on the sustainable growth path. His emphasis on the fiscal policy and deficit financing to cure economic depression stemmed from the theoretical framework of the functioning of a mature capitalistic economy which he developed in the *General Theory*. In fact his *General Theory* was aimed to refute the classical hypothesis about the determinants of income and employment in an economy and provided an alternative framework of interrelationships among the key economic parameters that totally changed the way to look at the macroeconomic aggregates, their behavior, interrelationships, and determinants.

Although he was writing treatise at the time when world was passing through the Great Depression, he did not want it to be primarily a solution or prescription to the malady of depression but something which lays the theoretical foundations of what came to be termed later as the macroeconomics. This is evident from the title which he gave calling it the *General Theory*, something very similar to what Albert Einstein did when he wrote his *General Theory of Relativity* in 1916. Just as Einstein's *General Theory* was a step ahead of Newton's conventional theory after the span of more than 200 years, Keynes' *General Theory* was also a radical departure from and an improvement over the classical theory that ruled the economic policy making for more than two centuries. Keynes wanted his theory to be similar to what Einstein did for physics. Macroeconomics was never the same after Keynes' *General Theory*. So much was his dispassionate approach in dealing with the subject that he probably deliberately avoided the use of the word depression which was the most pressing problem the world was facing and he was destined to provide solution to. Necessity is the mother of invention. Although depression must have precipitated his thinking on the behavior of a mature capitalistic economy and its determinants, his central focus was to develop immutable laws of dynamics of an economy which defy the traditional or conventional thinking or theory. His purpose was to develop a new theory that would revolutionize the thinking on macroeconomic behavior. He is truly the Einstein of Economics. Throughout the entire text of the *General Theory*, he has used the word depression only once. His appendices included the note on trade cycle which also did not make reference to the word depression.

Deficit Financing: A Potent Antidepression Medicine

Keynes is often criticized for his advocacy of deficit financing. To blame Keynes for the ills of deficit financing is like holding Einstein responsible for the devastation from an atomic bomb. Keynesian theory emerged out of depression-ridden economic environment. The single most important concern that must have influenced his mind was the phenomenon of intractable depression. His endeavor was to analyze interrelations among economic factors to develop theory that explained the phenomenon of depression. From the theory he developed the policy prescription to remedy depression and prevent its recurrence. The burden of this prescription fell on the fiscal policy. The expenditure and employment needed to be externally raised by the government to initiate a spurt in private investment and consumption expenditure in the second round. A step-up in government expenditure was the only cure for depression, and it fell in the realm of fiscal policy frame to be executed by the governments. Naturally, it was imperative to have strong political support for Keynesian policy cure.

By turning the classical theory upside down, Keynes also gave a new twist to the theory of interest rate. With his demonstration of impotence of monetary policy in reducing unemployment and curing depression from his new theory of interest rate, the fiscal policy alone remained as the panacea for and enduring salvation from depression. The experience of prolonged recession in Japan in the 1990s going through the new millennium despite low and nearly zero interest rate for a long time vindicates the Keynesian belief in the ineffectiveness of monetary policy in reviving the recession-ridden economy. Low interest rates cannot solve the fundamental and structural problem of inadequacy of aggregate demand to lift the economy from the morass of recession. The zero interest rate and money supply growth can raise neither investment nor consumption, which drives economic growth. The rate of interest fails to be of consideration in boosting investment or consumption. The consumption is low since the income is low. And investment is low despite low interest rate because the volume and growth of sales is more important than the rate of profit.

Writing to President Roosevelt in 1933 at the bottom of depression Keynes urged an action to increase government spending and not to try increasing money supply to end depression. Decrying the use of monetary policy to cure depression, he wrote in his open letter to the President, "Some people seem to infer from this (Quantity Theory of Money) that output and income can be raised by increasing the quantity of money. But this is like trying to get fat by buying a larger belt. In the United States today your belt is plenty big enough for your belly. *It is a most misleading thing to stress the quantity of money, which is only a limiting factor, rather than the volume of expenditure, which is the operative factor*" [1].

It has to be tax cuts and/or lift in government expenditure that would boost aggregate demand in the economy. The monetary policy is designed and pursued by the central banks which have relative autonomy in their functioning. Although there may be some pressure presumably exerted by the governments, the central banks are autonomous institutions. This is not the case with the fiscal policy which is solely within the mandate of the government. Keynes had to undertake an extensive political lobbying to get the support for budgetary deficit financing in order to cure depression. This had to be done in a milieu where balanced budget was the norm and conventional wisdom and government expenditure from deficit financing was abhorred as reckless and inflationary. The Conservatives and Tories in Britain saw Keynes as an iconoclast and ideologically incongruous, and his policy in their perception was politically risky and disastrous. In contrast, the Democrats in the USA understood Keynes much better and had the courage of conviction about his policy. Intellectually also, Keynes had more critics in academic circles in Britain than in the USA. The intellectual opponents of Keynes in the UK were giant theoreticians but had narrow vision and too rigid views incapable of logical revision. Keynesianism, therefore, was more easily assimilated in the US economic thinking and political philosophy and took stronger and deeper roots more quickly there than in his own country.

Keynes Versus Market Fundamentalists: The Role of State Intervention

The ideological status of Keynes lies somewhere between Friedrich Hayek, an Austrian economist, the champion of free market and laissez-faire capitalism, and author of popular book, *The Road to Serfdom,* and Harold Laski, a British economist and the member of Fabian Socialist Society. This makes Keynes neither socialist nor capitalist of Hayek type. Keynes endorsed both private property as well as market mechanism. What he did not agree was the state nonintervention into the dynamics of the economy, especially when it is in deep and long depression. His conviction was deeply rooted into the fresh view, he provided, of the functioning and dynamics of an economy. He clearly brought out the flaws in the classical analysis and argument that inflexibility of wage rates was the main cause of depression and also that the capitalist economy driven by profit motive would automatically overcome temporary depression. Any disequilibrium in the economic system resulting in depression would be remedied by the automatic corrective mechanism of free market. The laissez-faire and free market mechanism were supreme, and no government intervention was needed to correct the disequilibrium in the economy manifesting in depression. Keynes was against this strand of thought. He was against laissez-faire and nonintervention by the state. But he was not against market mechanism in a sense that he never advocated microeconomic tinkering and interference with the market mechanism. But his belief was that the market mechanism was not always supreme and sacrosanct for in its macroeconomic manifestation. The operation of the market mechanism in the labor market was not the panacea for full employment. The threshold spending level in the economy needed to break the vicious circle of depression could only be attained by government intervening to raise its spending in the economy. What kind of government spending was a secondary issue. To carry his argument for government spending strongly, he wrote that the spending for even digging holes and filling them would generate employment and break the cycle and spell of depression. This policy prescription was based on his *General Theory* which gave the most logical and cogent reasoning and analysis of the behavior and dynamics of the economy.

Marx prophesized that the capitalist economy was inherently unstable and a long depression would eventually strike a death knell on the capitalist economy. Hayek gave a contrasting analysis. He presented the case of laissez-faire economy having its own dynamics of correction of its disequilibrium without the state intervention, which he thought to be an artificial and impure attempt to subvert the sanctity and efficiency of market mechanism. The depression of 1930s had proved in demolishing this theory and belief and the policy and philosophy of laissez-faire. And Marx's hypothesis of the demise of capitalism also died its natural death with advent of Keynesianism.

Keynes reiterated that market economy was subject to vicissitudes of uncertainty, irrationality, and psychology of greed and fear and was, therefore, far from being predictable in its collapse and also incapable of repair after the crisis without government intervention. The free market fundamentalists argued that markets are mostly efficient, and price is reflective of inherent prospective returns and risks. Keynes in fact believed that, in their extremities, the markets remain in the grip of sentimental overdrives dominating rather than being governed by rationality. He brought out in the *General Theory* how prospective rate of return is overstretched at the peak of the boom and causes crash when the expectations are not met. Similarly, at the bottom of recession, the rate of return expectations is more pessimistic than realistic and, therefore, fails to revive investment. The market mispricing of returns and risks is the bane of unfettered market mechanism that makes it vulnerable to crash and crisis. The prudential market regulation is the anchor of constructive capitalism and is indispensable if it is not to degenerate into casino capitalism.

Keynesianism Versus Monetarism: Two Sides of the Same Coin

After the initial postwar global economic development, which was primarily a result of Keynesianism, the Keynesian school of thought came under unwarranted and unjustified attack. Another body of thought which developed in the 1960s and championed by Milton Friedman of Chicago School laid emphasis on the monetary aggregates and their influence on the macroeconomic parameters. Friedman developed monetarism, as an alternative school of thought, attempting to demolish some of Keynes' precepts.

Although Friedman's new school of thought of monetarism contrasted the philosophy of Keynesianism, Friedman did contribute in his early days to the ideas of Keynes. After the publication of the *General Theory*, Friedman commented, "We are all Keynesians now." when he was a part of the economic think tank of President Roosevelt working on the New Deal, the biggest Keynesian avatar launched to rescue the US economy and save capitalism from its decay. This quote was further repeated by President Nixon in 1969 when he wanted to defend the budget deficit incurred by his government and accept the reality that the Keynesian precepts went beyond the party ideology and in fact formed the living principles of postwar capitalism.

Further, not only is the *General Theory* essentially monetary theory but Friedman's permanent income hypothesis is also an extension of Keynes's concept of "propensity to consume." One of main themes of the Keynes' *General Theory* is his demonstration of positive functional relationship between consumption and income. This was a new strand of thought for the established theory which had set savings, counterpart of consumption, related to the interest rate and not income.

Friedman further elaborated the Keynesian consumption function and developed "permanent income hypothesis" which stated that consumption is related to not only current income alone but also long-term income of an individual which includes his future income and also wealth. Friedman, therefore, gave a new twist to the Keynesian consumption function. Although Friedman's transmission mechanism of money supply change on macroeconomic aggregates differs from Keynesianism, it does not negate Keynes' theoretical propositions with their attendant presumptions. Keynes demonstrated the futility of using monetary policy for macroeconomic adjustment, especially in the economic depression. Friedman, therefore, revived the use of monetary policy tools not during depression but for control of inflation and sustenance of economic growth in the depression-free post-Keynesian economic era.

A striking difference between the Keynesianism and monetarism is that the former was the offshoot of the basic theoretical exposition of an economy without any empiricism and the latter sprung from considerable empirical evidence supporting the theory it propounded. *The Monetary History of United States, 1867–1960*, written by Milton Friedman and Anna Schwartz formed the empirical basis of monetarism. Over time it became conventionally popular to call the emphasis on fiscal policy measures as Keynesianism and monetary policy tools as monetarism. During depression fiscal policy and deficit financing were the only panacea for recovery, and monetary policy had the role to play only after the recovery began to reinforce it further. Monetarism has more effective role to play in the normal times and also in taming the overheated economy. In long periods of economic growth sustained by Keynesianism, the monetarism helped in monetary targeting and later inflation targeting in keeping price rise under control.

Friedman advocated regulation of macroeconomic parameters like growth, inflation, and employment through monetary management. Since fiscal policy involved government action, Friedman's antigovernment and pro-market philosophy made him active monetarist. Despite his ideological stands and convictions, his greatest contribution to the economic science lies in his work on modern quantity theory of money, which led to monetary targeting, practiced by most central banks. The philosophy of monetary targeting itself has undergone a change over the last 30 years. During the 1990s monetary targeting was discarded in favor of inflation targeting, which has been a standard feature of central bank's monetary management the world over.

Although monetarism positioned itself as an ideology opposite of Keynesianism, in reality this shadowboxing between the two ideologies is little too farfetched. Keynes never denied the importance of monetary factors in his theory, and Friedman also admitted he was also a Keynesian. In fact Keynes himself was a monetary economist with his earlier works, *A Tract on Monetary Reform* (1923) and *A Treatise on Money* (1930), demonstrating how his ideas developed to culminate into the *General Theory*. These works dealt with monetary theory and policy and their role in economic behavior. Nearly half of the *General Theory* is monetary theory. It dwelt at length on money and money supply and their influence on other economic parameters. But Keynes' greatest contribution to monetary theory lies in his revolutionizing the theory of interest rate. He, however, underplayed the role of monetary policy in treating depression because of its impotency in times of deep recession. The monetary parameters of rate of interest and money supply do not help much in reviving the economy on the downhill.

Keynes and Friedman: The State Versus Free Market: Market Rationality Versus Social Good

As a free market fundamentalist, Friedman strongly believed in Adam Smith's *invisible hand* of the market and advocated and supported nonintervention into free market mechanism for its microeconomic allocative efficiency and macroeconomic ability to attain full employment and stability. The government intervention in the economic activities was thought to be inefficient and uncalled for. As an advocate of the free markets, Friedman also criticized the *Bretton Woods* system of fixed but flexible exchange rates and favored floating exchange rates. But he also expressed his skepticism at the floating exchange rates which evolved in 1975 after the collapse of *Bretton Woods* system. He termed it as "dirty floating" due to frequent and significant central bank intervention in the forex market to regulate the exchange rates. This he believed was not only preposterous but also blatantly inefficient method of economic regulation which does not produce healthy economic results.

Keynes was also a believer in the distinct merits of free markets vis-a-vis state regulation or central planning. He was, however, skeptical of ability of the free market mechanism to restore full employment equilibrium following the onset of cyclical depression. In addition to its failure in automatic macroeconomic equilibrium, Keynes also had grave concerns about free market mechanism because of its inherently volatile nature that spurred boom and bust cycle. According to him the macroeconomic linkages and structure were dominated by the microeconomic character of the financial markets. The volatility of the financial markets stemmed from the mass psychology of short-term scenario that overwhelms the long-term expectations. "A conventional valuation which is established as the outcome of the mass psychology of a large number of ignorant individuals is liable to change violently as the result of a sudden fluctuation of opinion due to factors which do not really make much difference to the prospective yield; since there will be no strong roots of conviction to hold it steady. ...the markets will be subject waves of optimistic and pessimistic sentiment, which are unreasoning and yet in a sense legitimate where no solid basis exists for a reasonable calculation. ...It is not sensible to pay 25 for an investment of which you believe the prospective to justify a value of 30, if you also believe that the market will value it at 20 three months hence".[1] Hence, the investor confidence that governs the short-term expectation dominates the long-term rational market and causes sudden and trend-reinforcing changes in the market that are often

[1] Keynes, John Maynard, The General Theory, op. cit., pp 157–8.

bereft of rationality. The markets can quickly turn from *irrational exuberance* to *irrational pessimism or fear psychosis* in no time.

Friedman and market fundamentalists justify markets on the belief in the hypothesis of investor rationality that considers investor irrationality to be short lived and market reverting to rationality. The experiences from the 1987 stock market crash until the recent subprime crisis all support the hypothesis that the rational expectations are overwhelmed by the investor psychology and behavior fuelled by the low credit cost dominates the behavior of the market which is prone to cyclical turns. Arguing the case for state intervention in investment for economic prosperity in times of slump or depression, Keynes states, "I expect to see the State, which is in a position to calculate the marginal efficiency of capital-goods on long views and on the basis of the general social advantage, taking an ever greater responsibility for directly organizing investments; since it seems likely that the fluctuations in the market estimation of the marginal efficiency of different types of capital, calculated on the principles I have described above, will be too great to be offset by any practical changes in the rate of interest".[2]

Capitalism, Democracy, and Communism: Ideological Battle and Demise of Communism

In times of depression of the 1930s until the onset of Keynes' *General Theory*, nobody was able to provide an alternative body of thought, logical analysis, and theory that could provide a burial ground for the classical theory and laissez-faire economics and pave the way for new policy. It was left to the genius mind of Keynes to complete this historic task. The only alternative which seemed feasible was the destruction of the capitalist system to be taken over by the communist ideology as theorized and prophesied by Marx. In the dark days of prolonged depression, the collapse of the capitalist economies seemed a reality. The system had to either recover on its own dynamics, or through a new or unconventional policy measure, or collapse to be replaced or overtaken by a new system. In the 1930s the first alternative was not working, and the second alternative had not emerged until adoption of Keynes' ideas in 1933. The third alternative became a probability with a large body of literature and theory on communism led by Karl Marx and practical success of communism evident in USSR.

The Bolshevik Revolution of 1914 in Russia manifested a striking and successful phenomenon demonstrating an alternative to the capitalist order. The Russian Revolution, however, was not depression resultant. It was an overthrow of feudalism supported by the establishment of monarchy under Tsar by the ideologues like Lenin who led the revolutionary army. Russia was an agrarian and feudal state ruled by the monarchy not a capitalist society. So was the case of Chinese revolution

[2] Ibid., p. 165.

later in 1949. China was also a precapitalist agrarian state ruled by monarchy. Both the USSR and China followed the ideology of Marx to run the system without private property and free market mechanism but through central planning and physical controls. Both the Russian and Chinese societies were not democratic but monarchies with feudal system dominated by the feudal lords and not the mature capitalist societies which Marx characterized as ripe for revolution and replacement by communism. So were Cuba and North Vietnam. Contrary to the prediction by Marx, the communism took roots in preindustrial societies and not in advanced capitalist states.

In contrast all the western capitalist nations were well ahead in the evolution of political system. In the twentieth century the monarchies and colonialism, handicapped by their oppression and inequities, were gradually transforming into democratic societies. Advent of democracies brought considerable power to the people, and therefore, societies remained less susceptible to the phenomenon of ideological overthrow of the system to establish communism. In a democracy, if the system is malfunctioning, the people have the right to bring solution through change of party in power. The whole process is nonviolent. In an enlightened democracy, revolution is nearly impossible. The power effectively lies with the vast majority of population. The western capitalist societies did not see revolution despite prolonged depression due to the prevalence of enlightened democracies which were preexistent better political system for replacement by the totalitarianism.

In the 1930s depression-ridden western capitalist societies were struggling to survive looking for a messiah within the establishment and not become target of Marxism. Keynes is, therefore, often referred to as the savior of capitalism. The global economy survived from the spread of communism, firstly, because of the prevalence of enlightened democracies and, secondly, in the 1930s, in their most critical and weakest times, due to the Keynesian philosophy of enlightened state intervention in the economy rescuing it from economic devastation. The institution of democracy took air out of Marxism, and Keynes flattened the balloon of laissez-faire. Keynes brought Hayek to the left and Laski to the right and became the golden mean between Marxism and orthodox capitalism. "To Anthony Crosland it was Keynes's achievement to have demolished Marx and shown how a private property system could be made to avoid unemployment 'through its metamorphosis into a reformed, planned neo-capitalism'. Crosland attacked the Conservative whitewash in which Harrod painted Keynes, remarking perceptively: 'Truth is that Keynes was strongly hostile to capitalism loosely defined as a system of *laissez faire*. But he was not opposed to capitalism, defined as a system of private property and enterprise'" [2, p. 498].

Keynes was thus the originator of enlightened neo-capitalism that developed in the 1940s. He preserved the human dignity, freedom of choice invariably crushed by Marxism. He secured the innovative spirit and risk-taking instinct almost dead in communist regimes. He insulated individual dreams and vision against the onslaughts of the state. He fostered the spirit of enterprise rare in communist societies. He established the role of a powerful transmitter of private initiative trapped in a vicious circle of depression. He uncovered the potency of the transmitter in lifting the economy from the bottom of depression. He established that the transmitter of spending remains in an unusually low level in depression and goes on diminishing its strength. The government has to intervene to inject an extra amount of spending and evoke the transmitter effect to trigger a higher level of economic activity and then bring about a recovery in the system. Lionel Robbins observes Keynes as "many sided genius who 'shook age-long error and prejudice', but … also sometimes shook essential foundations" [2, p. 494].

Strains of Transition to Globalization

Keynes was the architect of postwar economy throughout the free world. Keynesianism dominated not only the domestic policy but also the *Bretton Woods* international monetary system which he built consistent with the *General Theory* governing the global monetary relations. Both the systems were coherent, consistent, and mutually supportive and provided the framework for the global economy to achieve sustainable economic growth without unemployment and inflation and stable international payments equilibrium. Through the Bretton Woods, Keynes built the international monetary policy route for the postwar global economic prosperity. The decades of the 1950s and 1960s were splendid, looking to experience of the agony of Great Depression and devastation of Second World War. Economic growth, prosperity, and price stability came easily with Keynesianism. Nevertheless, for the international monetary system dependent on gold with its fixed price, two decades was a relatively long period to run smoothly without any breaks and hiccups.

The system came under pressure in the early 1970s due to a variety of national and international factors and strains. Keynesianism and deficit financing did generate trade and balance of payments deficits in the USA. The USA had another global role and responsibility to perform in the postwar economic and global monetary architecture. The *Bretton Woods* system drew its strength from the size of gold reserves at Fort Knox and the capacity of the USA to limit its cumulative BoP deficit within the borders drawn by the size of gold stocks of the Federal Reserve. Both the growth and global monetary stability were in jeopardy in the early 1970s after a long spell of Keynesianism as the inherent gold anchor to which the system was tied came under pressure with the fixed price of gold in terms of dollars. The dollar devaluation was indispensable to remedy the disequilibrium. In fact Keynes had foreseen this problem and, therefore, had suggested in 1944 at the Bretton Woods the creation of a new international money which he named Bancor to be created and managed by the Global Central Bank of all countries. The proposal was turned by the USA in favor of dollar convertible into gold to be the global currency.

What happened during the 1970s does not really negate the validity of Keynesianism. New peripheral theories developed to address the problems of the post-Keynesian economy and global monetary system. Economic policy took swing toward monetarism, floating exchange rates, supply-side economics, Laffer curve, and finally Adam Smithian market-based economic reforms and Ricardian-supported trade liberalization. These policies do not negate validity of Keynesianism and its theoretical framework and philosophy. *General Theory* was born in the midst of depression, and postwar economy in the 1970s presented problems which were post-Keynesian. They were issues and side effects of noncyclical economy. The side effects of the post-Keynesian noncyclical economy needed to be treated with new prescriptions. The post-Keynesian economy needed rectification out of its imperfections by different remedies. The focus had to shift from fiscal policy which remained prime weapon of Keynesianism to the potentials of other policy measures. Minor economic ills of the mature post-Keynesian economies were required to be treated with other pills of economic policy which are more potent in dealing with the most intractable malady of chronic and resistant recession. The productivity and efficiency of the system needed improvement by removing imperfections through liberalization and reforms. Technology and capital were required to be deployed globally to less developed economies which showed promise of higher growth and returns. The stage was set for the strategy of globalization. Keynesianism had to migrate from the national domain to the global arena.

Economic Wisdom and Political Sagacity: Lessons in Economic Policy

Economists are often frustrated when they find they are unable to influence and lobby with political authorities to translate new theories or ideas into economic and political action by means of a change in policy due to the dogmatic attitude based on the conventional wisdom that the political power holds due to their inability to absorb unconventional and novel ideas. Politics deals with power, and any change in policy that may be superior or even the best, if untested, carries an element of risk which is not easily welcomed in the political circles. Keynes' biggest frustration was that the *General Theory* not only faced a number of skeptics in the academic economic circles but also did not have many backers in the ruling Tory party of Britain. In contrast he found much better acceptance of his ideas among economists in the USA and also Democratic party which was in power and, more particularly, President Roosevelt who took personal interest in his ideas and policies and understood the potential of enormously positive political implications of a new direction for the economy which his policies would give.

Keynes wrote an open letter to President Roosevelt in December 1933 after he was elected president, urging him to take action to increase the government spending to trigger economic recovery. The letter changed the economic history of the USA and the world. Despite the physical distance in the 1930s when transport and communications were not as advanced as they are today, the USA became Keynesian much earlier than Britain despite the fact that Keynes' physical presence in his home country carried much greater scope for influence among the academics and politicians there. Americans were on the forefront in adopting the Keynesian nirvana and tasting and trying his recipe first and with resounding success. Despite Harry Dexter's (then US Treasury Secretary) anti-British feeling, he revered Keynes as the greatest living economist of the times. The frustration of the physical scientists is even greater when their theories trigger experimentation and creation of products whose occasional misuse can harm the humanity. The physical theories could be tested in laboratories or smaller spaces. In contrast, the economic theories did not have a testing ground more separate than the economy itself.

Keynes' *General Theory* was published in 1936 when the two largest economies of the world were still not out of grip of depression. The *General Theory*, which prescribed deficit financing as the cure for depression, was not palatable to the conventional economic thought, and a large number of key economists in the UK were still skeptical about the central theme and more so about deficit financing, which they believed will stoke the fires of inflation. Conventional wisdom and political authorities were less inclined to accept the policy of deficit financing as "to most of their elders it was a little more than an inflation tract, 'the dying voice of the bourgeois crying in the wilderness for profits it dare not fight for', as Joseph Schumpeter put it. Most of Keynes's Cambridge colleagues sat on the fence, shaken but skeptical" [2, p. 4]. The political thought and authorities were more congenial in the USA than in the UK for quicker acceptance of the new wave of thought of Keynes and the prescription emanating therefrom. "That Britain, too, was in recession was apparent by December 1937. On this occasion, there was no Keynes Plan. The deepening recession did, though, prompt him to write another of his letters to the American President, Franklin Roosevelt, on 1 February 1938, this time private" [2, p. 12].

After those critical times, during the period of the Second World War, President Roosevelt received another important letter that was also to change the history of mankind and the course of history. That letter came from another brilliant scientist, like Keynes, who had caused a revolution in science by also writing a *General Theory*, not in economics, but in physics. It was Einstein's letter to Roosevelt in 1939 informing him about the progress made by the Nazi under Hitler in developing an atomic bomb with the destructive power beyond anyone's imagination. Coincidentally, both the letters were written by the European scientists and thinkers to the American President urging quick action. Both the scientists had written *General Theory* in their own fields of science, one in economics, a social science, and the other of relativity in physics, a physical science. The power of both the theories from their impact on humanity was initially not only underestimated but also scoffed at. In both the cases, President Roosevelt showed a remarkable degree of sensitivity, farsightedness, leadership, and vision in understanding true implications of their power, when both the theories were not tested for proof. He not only took quick action but backed them with the necessary financial support to bring both the programs to their fruition and make them succeed.

The first was the New Deal passed by the US Congress during 1933–1935 that revitalized the American capitalism with golden lining of social welfare, and the second was the secret code named Manhattan Project to develop atomic bomb that costs $2 billion ($22 billion at the current value) in 1939. The New Deal raised the government spending from $697 million, 1.4% of GDP in 1916, to $9 billion in 1936, 10% of GDP. The distinction between the two programs was that while Keynes' antidepression program was intellectually and publically debated, Einstein's project was not. Skidelsky called New Deal in the US the economic laboratory of the world. The Manhattan Project was on the contrary a secret endeavor. The former ended the economic misery and improved millions of lives; the latter was meant to demonstrate its devastating power by destroying millions of lives to thwart an evil political and military wave.

It now seems that Roosevelt was destined to receive two most valuable and important letters in history, but it was his personality in understanding the gravity of the advice that changed the history twice in a short span of decade that transformed the world.

The classical economists were firm believers in the ability of the free market economy to attain sustainable full employment. Any temporary disturbance away from the full employment was to generate forces like decline in market wage rates that would restore the economy back to full employment. Flexible wage rates would achieve full employment and balanced or surplus budget renders price stability. The laissez-faire free market economy would attain full employment with price stability on its own dynamics. Governmental intervention was believed to be undesirable and unnecessary. Keynes' *General Theory* brought out distinctly the theoretical flaw in the classical reasoning and demonstrated the behavior of economy and broad macroeconomic parameters in completely different angle from the classical view. Spending, and not wage rates, determines employment level. Saving is not a virtue in unemployment-ridden economy. That was the upshot of Keynes' theory. Government intervention by way of extra public expenditure is the only solution to kick off the economy stuck in the morass of unemployment into the full employment Greenland. Keynes' view of an economy and its dynamics was holistic in contrast to the fragmented view of the classical economists. Although Keynes gave a death knell on the laissez-faire economy, he was still an advocate of the free market mechanism. This distinction needs to be watched carefully. Free market economy or laissez-faire economy is one where the government does not intervene to change the course and dynamics of the economy or its macroeconomic aggregates. Keynes was opposed to this state of governmental nonintervention. In contrast, free market mechanism is the system of market and price mechanism that determines prices in microeconomics. Here, Keynes was an ardent advocate of free market mechanism and abhorred government intervention by way of price control or rationing. The consumer freedom of choice continued to remain the cornerstone of his philosophy. Keynes' philosophy rests on the government intervention in macroeconomics and nonintervention in microeconomics.

Skidelsky on Keynes

If one has to name a person, other than Keynes' contemporaries, who has studied and researched extensively Keynes' life, his writings, and his mind, Robert Skidelsky comes on the top of the list.[3] One cannot talk and discuss about Keynes without referring to the work of Skidelsky. Having written three biographical volumes on Keynes' work and life, Skidelsky's contribution in understanding, analyzing, and reinterpreting Keynes has hardly any parallel [3]. Skidelsky's latest book, *Keynes: Return of the Master*, is the most timely and appropriate in rediscovering Keynes and his ideas, their relevance in current crisis, and, most importantly, in thinking about making the capitalism more resilient to the new stresses it has developed over the current phase

[3] Robert Skidelsky is Emeritus Professor of Political Economy at the University of Warwick, member of House of Lords.

of globalization. The short treatise is most opportune in knowing his mind and thoughts in the context of unexpected global financial crisis that took air out of economist profession and policy makers [4]. Very few may have expected the crisis and more so its magnitude, impact, and spread. The fears of Great Depression that engulfed the global economy necessitated the experts, policy makers, and governments the world over to have a relook at Keynes' *General Theory* that revolutionized the economics and policy making since the 1930s. The current crisis is another manifestation of the market failure. It needs to be redressed by establishing a supervisory and regulatory framework that can prevent financial system moving at high speeds and on rough roads and also working out a fail-safe mechanism to avert any major catastrophe from crisis.

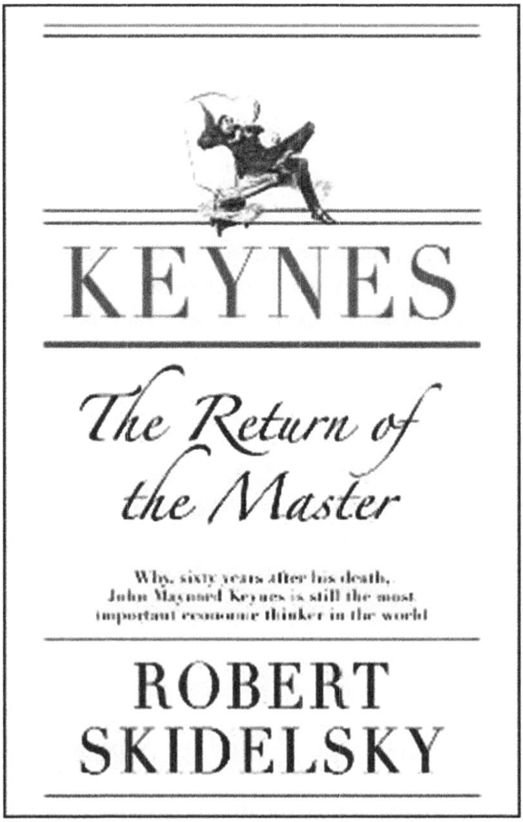

Robert Skidelsky analyzes the above issues in the Keynesian perspective and solutions. The book is divided into three parts. The first part covers the pathology of the crisis and gives account of the crisis in terms of market functioning which emphasizes that neither rationality nor perfect information is reality, and therefore, market dysfunction is periodically common. The second part deals with the heyday of Keynesianism and later its criticism and emergence of alternative philosophies of monetarism, supply-side economics, and Thatcherism or Reaganomics that advocated smaller government. The third part deals with the return of Keynes and the relevance of his ideas and philosophy today in steering the global economy from quicksand of imminent depression. Not only did Keynes oversee his philosophy accepted in the 1930s but he also guided the Allies during the Second World War and contributed in building the postwar international monetary architecture. Keynes died of heart attack in April 1946 at the age of 63 after he returned from Savannah, Georgia, attending the first meeting of the boards of World Bank and IMF where the American negotiating team had finally agreed Keynes to be the managing director of the IMF. Despite the passage of more than half a century, the legacy of Keynes continues unchallenged indefinitely. Finishing the book one is likely to recite, "Long live Keynes! Long live Keynesianism!," paying tribute to the great thinker and philosopher whom we all owe not considerable but immeasurable and invaluable debt.

The recent downturn in the global economy and the financial crisis is a fresh reminder of the principles of Keynesianism which remain undiluted by the test of time. The free market mechanism needs to be nourished but is also at times subject to imperfections, absurdities, irrationality, and excesses from exuberance as well as gloom and, therefore, requires judicious supervision. At the micro level markets, whether financial or commodity, have to be supervised to avert excesses. At the macro level the market economy also cannot function and grow without the benign supervision and support from the state in terms of keeping the aggregate demand growing at a sustainable rate. It does not have inbuilt fail-safe mechanism for economy. The state has to device an inbuilt fail-safe mechanism to avert crashes and crises. The Keynesian philosophy is now further strengthened with the recent experience. Yet it does not constitute or promote a clean overdraft for state profligacy. Keynes never wished the chronic and rising deficit financing, beyond a threshold, continuously inflating the public debt balloon to the point of its burst, the state payments default, and bankruptcy. Like atomic energy, Keynesianism needs to be harnessed for real economic welfare and not for misguided ideals that destroy welfare. Keynes never overtly advocated the bailout of the banks and financial institutions but exhorted the state intervention in any way it can to avert the chain reaction of a collapse that could accentuate the vicious circle of deficient demand culminating in deep depression. The modern banking and financial system is so intricately interwoven within the national economies as well as globally to make any large failure financially highly contagious. Until the animal spirits revive and expectations of consumers and investors revert to normalcy, market-driven economic growth is not possible. The role of the state is in hand holding the economy until that stage when the drive of rational spirits of finance and economics governing the markets returns.

Among the Great Souls of the Twentieth Century

The twentieth century was molded by four great souls and personalities; Marx, Keynes, Einstein, and Gandhi (MKEG). Marx was the champion of equality. He dreamt of an ideal society with minimal inequality in the unequal physical world. For him end was important, no matter the means. His social organization after initial success failed on physical, economic, as well as moral counts. Keynes was the citadel of economic freedom defending the society with private property and organization of markets. He arrested the spread of Marx's ideas by stabilizing the capitalism through intervention by the enlightened state. Knowing the reality of human nature much better, he preserved the economic freedom of mankind by giving the organization of state more stake in our lives. He brought about true economic transformation and emancipation of mankind through his policy prescription and totally changed the way we look at economics. He prevented the spread of totalitarianism by rescuing the capitalism from its crisis and gave it a new shape for its sustained development. Einstein was the champion of the matter, the ultimate creation from the source unknown. He understood the minutest atom as well as the infinite cosmos. He transformed the physical world and demonstrated the immense power of the matter and how it could be harnessed. Gandhi was the trustee of morals, truth, and freedom with peace. For him the means were as important as the end. He believed in cooperation, counseling and consensus, and shunned force. Through this he aimed social transformation and led one of the greatest freedom movements across the time and space.

The Golden Age and Utopia are not dreams but ideals realizable with human intelligence, ingenuity, wisdom, and foresight. MKEG gave us the secrets of nature, human mind, tendencies, and behaviors to build technologies, organizations, and philosophies maximizing the welfare of societies in a fair and just manner. The flaws lie with us in either misunderstanding the concepts or executing them without perfection. Every experience is a new lesson in learning. If the mistakes are not repeated and words of wisdom of MKEG are revisited to realize their true spirits, the path of progress could be much smoother and devoid of occasional disturbances or strain.

The greatness of Keynes lies in his pragmatism in the realms of economic welfare establishing its principles that embody the ideals of both Marx and Gandhi in a manner Einstein probed both atom and universe. Keynes demonstrated how government can harness the economic power and energy of society in a manner Einstein showed the way to harness energy from the matter, viz., the chain reaction. Finally, energy is all that matters, whether in the physical world or the human civilization that inhabits the physical world. In that sense the four great souls of the century made unprecedented advances in unraveling the mysteries of different forms of energy, physical and human, and its harnessing for benign transformation within the limitations of human power miniscule in the context of the vast expanse of cosmos. Collectively, their ideas constituted and resulted in a giant step forward for mankind in its command of its future and the nature.

References

1. Keynes JM. An open letter to President Roosevelt. New York Times. 1933 Dec 31; New York.
2. Skidelsky R. John Maynard Keynes: fighting for freedom, 1937–1949. New York: Penguin Books; 2000.
3. Skidelsky R. John Maynard Keynes, 1983–1946: economist, philosopher, statesman. New York: Penguin Books; 2003.
4. Skidelsky R. Keynes: the return of the master. New York: Allan Lane, Penguin Group; 2009.

Chapter 15
New Bretton Woods: Agenda for Global Economic Reform

> There is a tendency for all knowledge, like all ignorance, to deviate from truth in an opportunistic direction.
>
> Gunnar Myrdal, *The Challenge of World Poverty, 1970.*

It is time now to take stock of the foregoing analysis of the crisis to build the base and architecture for the reform of the present structure. From the post-depression, post-Bretton Woods, and post-floating exchange rates regimes, the global economy has traversed into post-globalization, new capitalism phase devoid of ideology of communism. Free markets, free capital, and technology are ruling the global economy. It is the MOT Revolution which is driving the pace of the global economy. So overwhelming has been the influence of the MOT Revolution on the economic parameters and factors, both globally and also within the national economies, that the number of structural changes and policy adaptations is warranted to direct the energy of MOT Revolution for more sustainable growth with least destabilizing potential. The strong forces of globalization have caused a dramatic realignment in economic structure and power among the developed and emerging worlds. The world can never be flat but is getting flatter.

We have dissected the crisis from both micro and macro angles and also conducted more structural and evolutionary DNA analyses of American capitalism and global economy. This will facilitate us in working out the agenda for reform involving the structural adjustments or reformations and also in new, creative, proactive, and unconventional policy endeavors. Let us take here the essence of the foregoing analysis of the crisis and then consider pragmatic options for the reform of the system that would eliminate the potential for such crisis in future.

The proposals for reform are viewed and recommended from the angle of four regional and global authorities that have bearing on the shape the global economy and monetary system would be taking. They concern the following:

1. US economic and monetary management
2. Economic reforms in China

S. Nayak, *The Global Financial Crisis: Genesis, Policy Response and Road Ahead*,
DOI 10.1007/978-81-322-0798-6_15,

3. Restructuring of IMF and new global money
4. Euro and Eurozone management

Free Market Philosophy, the Fed, and Economic Management

Systemic Risk of Unregulated Financial Markets

The subprime mortgage debt crisis is the manifestation of dynamics of the free market economy which has been driving the global economy. In a free market economy, the private investments flowing into lucrative opportunities keep the growth momentum of the economy stable. The lack of investment opportunities and lackluster investment climate are the bane of the free market economy. Hence, the fiscal and monetary policies have to be always monitored to drive the animal spirits and keep private investments high. In a highly sophisticated and mature American capitalism, the knowledge economy and technology drive private investments. The roaring 1990s has been a fitting demonstration of how technological breakthroughs can drive sustained economic growth. The hardware–software Internet Technology, Media and Telecom (TMT) Revolution transformed the world and brought unprecedented growth from investments in these sectors and tremendous productivity gains. The stock market boom created unparalleled favorable wealth effect in boosting consumption that also contributed to growth. The American economy sped fast like a four-wheeler sophisticated automobile with the investments as the front wheels and the consumption as the rear wheels driving at high speed. With the technology boom petering out in the new millennium and stock market experiencing a bear phase following the crash in 2000, both the front and rear wheels of the sophisticated auto began to speed at the low pace with the risk of auto actually sliding backward into recession. The investment in technology dropped, and consumption growth slid downward under the influence of negative wealth effect from the stock market fall.

The economy was in search of a new growth driver. The Fed policy of record low interest rates made money and credit available at cheap rates, and liquidity flushed the economy from within and out of the USA. The new vehicle and product of subprime loans and their securitization opened a new and large potential market for housing. Unprecedented credit flows drove up the housing prices, and rising housing sales contributed to the higher economic growth. The slowdown in growth and concern on inflation which forced the Fed to raise the interest rates precipitated the defaults on housing loan repayments. Declining housing sales and rising foreclosures bust the boom in housing markets. The subprime securities became illiquid and set in chain of defaults in overexposed and leveraged banks.

The banking crisis of 2008 typically reflected flaw of deregulated free market financial services industry. The existing supervisory mechanism at the federal level comprising the Fed, Department of Treasury, Comptroller of Currency, Deposit Insurance Corporation, and Securities Exchange Commission and at the state level the department of banking failed to notice the practices from the financial services industry beyond the prudential norms of risk and leveraging. The Dodd–Frank Act has attempted to plug the loopholes and improve the regulation to prevent such crisis in future. Although external regulatory mechanism is now in much better and effective shape, the self-disciplinary action is equally essential from the financial services industry in order to avoid the credit profligacy.

The Fed's Monetary Management

With the benefit of hindsight, we are now able to draw some common threads from the analysis of cyclical ups and downs and recessions in the US economy since the 1970s. The decades of 1950s and 1960s were devoid of such economic cyclicality primarily due to the economic institutional framework which was prevalent then and which rendered support to the stable financial milieu internationally. The fixed exchange rates and stable monetary policies did not leave much scope for wide fluctuations in financial parameters and variables. The global economy entered a new phase with the breakaway from stable financial infrastructure of the Bretton Woods in 1971. The new regime of floating exchange rates and greater independence for more autonomous monetary policies by individual central banks changed the rules of the game. Although the global monetary authorities continued to be guided by the Federal Reserve policy stance, the leverage of the Federal Reserve to embark on more flexible policy involved less concern on the dollar's external strength. The flexibility for dollar to move up and down in the exchange market offered a safety valve for the external impact on its more inward-oriented monetary policy.

During the Bretton Woods era, the annual M2 growth in the USA was in the band 2.5–10% (Fig. 15.1). In the post-Bretton Woods period of 1970s, this range went upward from 5 to 13.5%. The period was also characterized by record hikes in oil prices in 1973–1974 and 1979–1980 that warranted unprecedented gesture from the central bankers to expand money supply by a larger margin than done earlier in normal times lest the economy falls into the vicious trap of depression. During the Volcker regime of high interest rates, the monetary growth was lowered considerably and came down from a high 13% in 1983 to a low of 3% in 1987. Greenspan era which began in the aftermath of 1987 stock market crash witnessed higher growth rate in M2 in the range between 3% and 10%. After the Y2K crisis, the M2 growth dropped to 3%. By 2005, the M2 growth began rising again to reach 7.5% in 2008.

The crisis once again reflected a peculiar monetary and economic cycle familiar to the US economy. The earlier but smaller crises of 1966, 1970, 1974–1975, 1979–1980 and 1981–1982, 1991–1993 and 2000–2002 which occurred in a cycle of 4–6 years also followed a similar pattern. They all manifest the typical "cheap money–tight money–crisis–bailout syndrome." The cycle begins with the Fed following the cheap money policy to drive economic growth. The larger, speedier, and cheap credit flows to consumers, households, and businesses promote consumption, housing, and investment demand. The economy grows at a faster pace. When the

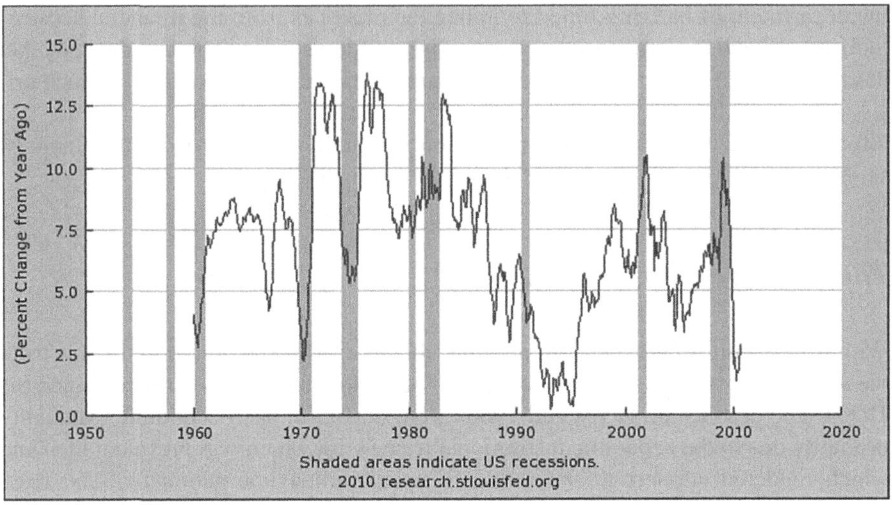

Fig. 15.1 M2 money stock (M2SL). *Shaded areas* indicate US recessions. 2012 research.stiouisfed.org (Source: Board of Governors of the Federal Reserve System)

momentum of growth becomes unsustainable due to the pressure on prices reflecting in rising inflation rate, the Fed is forced to tighten the money flow tap and begin the course of tight money policy. The resultant economic slowdown which culminates in economic recession takes toll on the repayment cycle of credit. Defaults and losses pick holes in the banking system requiring the government bailout of critical institutions that can have snowballing effect on the economy.

The crisis of 2008 was not only the biggest but also a result of the development of sophisticated credit instruments in the credit delivery system that overshot the standard norms of risk management and capital adequacy by the lending banks. In each of the crises, the monetary policy reversal triggered the crisis, but the free market mechanism undeterred by the prudential behavior under the pressure of profit maximization motive resulted in excesses that created imbalances and conditions fit for the crisis.

One of the most crucial commandments of prudent central banking is that when economy is driving on its natural growth momentum, the central bank has to respond quickly nurturing the process of growth. But when the economy begins to falter or shows the signs of overheating, the central bank has to be more predictive and visionary, anticipating the economic adversities and beginning to take proactive measures by fine-tuning the cost of money and its incremental growth. Both in the 2000 and 2008 crises, the Fed was tightening the interest rates a year earlier which strained the economy and financial system. When the markets collapsed under stress at the inflection point, the Fed lowered rates at record levels even below the point when it started its tightening exercise. The exercise of Fed raising rates and then lowering to record lows seems absurd and reactive and not proactive. In contrast, the proactive interest rate policy would have avoided the crisis. The Fed interest rate changes, and open market operations need now to be more proactive in containing the boom without the collapse.

Tackling the Intractable Low Propensity to Save

One of the most intractable propensities of the US economy is toward consumption. Undoubtedly, consumption growth is the key driver of the economy. But for a few years in this decade, it is seen to be crossing the boundaries of economic rationality. The consumption growth is acceptable if it does not lower the investment rate and, also in terms of country's balance of payments considerations, does not generate heavy current account deficit. The counterpart of consumption is savings, and if consumption growth does not make savings rate lower than the investment rate in the economy, there is no savings gap and no current account deficit. But if the consumption growth lowers the savings rate below the investment rate, the emerging savings gap creates current account deficit. Relatively small current account deficit in terms of the economy's GDP of below 2% of GDP is not a BoP concern. Yet the continuing and rising current account deficit is reflection of a structural inadequacy of an economy which needs to be addressed. Since the savings gap is the counterpart of current account deficit and savings remainder from consumption, the problem of rising current account deficit of the USA which rose to a high of 6% of GDP in 2006 needed to be addressed by taking measures to improve the savings rate. The trends in the last few years are encouraging. The current account deficit already witnessed a sharp decline to 2.9% in 2009, the lowest in a decade.

The decline in the personal savings rate from a high of 11.5% in 1982 to 7% in 1990 further to 3% in 2000 and a low of 1.3% in 2005 is disturbing and more so because of a simultaneous rise in the current account deficit. The trend is disconcerting due to slump in the rate of investment in the economy from 20% in 2006 to 14% in 2009 and 15% in 2011. There was bounce in the rate to 5% in 2010 which is a healthy sign. But the current monetary policy is aimed at raising investment rate through QEs and zero interest rate regime which is not conducive to promoting savings. The personal savings rate has to go up to 8–10% level. This would not only give an adequate structural buffer to the economy and improved financing of investments but also improve the current account of deficit.

The savings in an economy comprise those of households, corporates, and governments. In the deficit-financed economies, the government's contribution to the aggregate savings is negative, while the large contributors to savings are the households and corporates. In the USA, not only is the share of household savings in the national savings cake diminishing but the rate of savings of households itself is going down steadily. This is a structural weakness of the US economy that needs to be corrected. It is necessary to gear both monetary and fiscal policies to raise the household savings rate. The interest rate is an important determinant of savings. Under the current close to zero interest rate policy which the Fed is pursuing in order to inject liquidity and make borrowing cheaper, the savings propensity of households is undermined. The overall savings can increase if the corporates plow back more profits and distribute less by way of dividends. The government can give fiscal incentives for retaining profits. It is also imperative to consider fiscal inducements to raise individual savings. The tax breaks for contributions to 401 K, housing, and education loan repayments would help in raising individual savings. After exiting from the current emergency monetary policy of near zero interest rate on the economy gaining its self-sustaining momentum, the level of rate interest should be determined at a higher with view to encourage individual savings. The Fed has to depart from its practice of too frequent changes in the interest rates and replace it by frequent changes in open market operation to control the monetary aggregates with greater frequency.

Stimulating Investment

The continental economies like the USA, which unlike China does not primarily depend on foreign trade for its growth, have internal growth drivers. For so long, the consumption growth has been stimulating the US economic growth. Now in the light of the worsening trend in savings and its implication also for increasing the trade and current account deficit and the attempts to raise the savings rate, it is imperative to drive the other wheel of economic automotive to speed up its momentum. The US economy has always enjoyed robust investment in times of technological breakthroughs. The economic boom of 1990s fueled by new technologies in Internet and telecom demonstrates the spur investments can give to the economy. The cycle of technological discoveries follows its own unpredictable and irregular route. Although larger spending on research in universities and corporates does enhance the frequency of discoveries applied in industries, it is difficult to grasp the contours of saturation and potential in technologies for fresh breakthroughs. The growth in the new millennium was driven by the housing boom fueled by cheap and liberal credit to homeowners who could not earlier afford loans due to stricter loan approval norms. The consumption growth emanating from the wealth effect of the boom and cheap credit also sustained the growth. In the light of the long-term requirement of raising the savings rate, it is more imperative to rely more on investment growth than consumption growth to maintain steady economic growth. The US economy enjoys the long-term potential and dynamics sustaining steady growth at the investment rate of 18% of GDP. The policy measures need to be aimed at economy achieving this rate which should not be left purely to market forces. The state direction and proactive policy action are needed to achieve this rate to help the economy from falling into the trap of recession.

During recession, the negative sales growth faced by industries dampens robust expectations about profitability and rate of return on investment. This hampers the corporate investment programs. In these circumstances, fiscal policy can be used to lift the financial morale of the corporate through tax breaks. The tax on corporate profits could be reduced to leave more resources for investment. This could be made subject to corporates not using these resources to raise dividend to shareholders. A measure in the form of investment allowance is very effective in raising the overall corporate investment rate. Under this provision, the companies would be give tax breaks or exemptions to the extent of their fresh investments made. It serves to boost the posttax expected rate of return which is dampened by temporary economic slowdown.

An area in investment which is long neglected, delayed, and now overdue and in which the state needs to take not only active but proactive role is infrastructure. One of the greatest strengths of the US economy which always abundantly overweighs its some economic weaknesses and some idiosyncrasies of growth is the strength, breadth, and richness of its infrastructure which encompasses the length and the breadth of the geographical expanse of the country. Its infrastructure comprises economic, social, and political structures and their institutions that give it a status that is globally incomparable. It involves its road, highways, bridges, dams, irrigation, power, airways, railroads, and ports, some of which are in the private sector. Apart from these economic areas, education, health, and judiciary excel in standards.

Taming the Chinese Dragon: Half-Baked Economic Reforms in China

Not only is China the world's largest populated nation but following the thrust of globalization it has now emerged as the second largest economy in the world in terms of purchasing power parity GDP soon to rival the USA, the second largest exporter of goods next to Germany overtaking Japan, and also the second largest forex holder after Japan. While the global economy has liberalized, the Chinese economy is still guarded in many respects under the complex regulatory apparatus. Such a structure in a liberalized and open global economy can be tolerated only if the economy is a peripheral economy not having much influence on the global economic variables. Looking to the Chinese rapid growth and its increasing influence in the global economy, it is imperative to reform such dichotomous structure of half-liberalized–half-controlled global economy. With the experimentation and experience of globalization and its success for the last more than two decades, China needs to now face the level playing field in global economy which its competitors encounter. The global economy needs much more balance than the lopsided structure which exists because of its half-controlled nature. The tremendous imbalance in the distribution of flow and stock of global liquidity needs to be more equitably redressed by the forces of market mechanism that drive the capital markets than it is now. China needs to open up its external economy at a faster pace than it is doing now. Although it is a step-by-step process as has been successfully achieved in India, it has to be more expeditious in the light of distinctly favorable position in which China is stationed now.

A number of steps need to be taken to reform the Chinese economy.

1. *Revaluation of Yuan*: The growing exports and trade surplus of China are not only the results of comparative advantage in costs which China enjoys in several commodities due to cheap labor and low other input costs but also due to US higher marginal propensity to import Chinese products and undervaluation of its currency yuan. The Chinese currency has been substantially undervalued, and despite the continuing and growing net inflows of capital and rising current account deficit, the Bank of China has not revalued its currency substantially. This has resulted in the persistent large and growing BoP surpluses by China which are absorbed by Bank of China in the form of dollar reserves. These dollar reserves are then invested in US T bills and government securities. The Bank of China is following a fixed exchange rate policy not allowing the yuan to move as per the forces of demand and supply in its forex market. As a result, the pegged exchange rate policy China's forex reserves have gone up from $30 billion in 1990 to $3.2 in June 2012 and its investments in US government securities from $60 billion in January 2000 to $1.6 trillion in June 2012, accounting for the one-fifth of foreign official holdings of the treasury securities and being the largest investor overtaking Japan at $1.1 trillion. Two-thirds of China's forex reserves are held in US dollar. In 1994, China devalued yuan from 5.76 per dollar to 8.62, i.e., by 50%. That rate cut gave tremendous advantage to China in terms of its exports growth and in attracting foreign capital. Due to growing pressure for revaluation from its trade partners, China revalued yuan to 8.27 per dollar in 1998 and to 8.11 in 2005. Since then, due to a flexible exchange policy, the yuan has revalued to 7.69 in September 2010 and further to 6.30 in September 2012 due to continuing pressure of dollar inflows from net exports and capital inflows and weakening of dollar. Despite this movement, there is still potential for further revaluation. Instead of one-step revaluation, a creeping appreciation of yuan gradually below 6 yuan per dollar would offer more balance in its BoP account and relief in the US trade account. Although the popular perception of revaluation of a currency is that it is injurious to the exports growth and export sector, there are other beneficial impacts on the economy. The revaluation also makes imports cheaper and has a disinflationary impact on the economy which is dependent on imports of raw material and crude oil. Additionally, it benefits foreign investors as their investments valued in foreign currencies appreciate. The revaluation also attracts more foreign investment and short-term capital.
2. *Liberalization of Imports*: While the revaluation or appreciation of yuan would make imports in China cheaper before, it is equally important to remove tariff and quantitative and nonquantitative restrictions on imports to reduce its trade surplus. China needs to be more open to imports and let the consumers have much wider choice of imported products. Openness in trade account would be beneficial in building globally more competitive domestic industry.
3. *Abolition of Export Subsidies*: Although China enjoys comparative cost advantage in several labor-intensive products, the price competitiveness of these goods is further enhanced by fiscal support and provision of lower-priced inputs from the government. These props need to be removed now that the industries have matured and can stand competition in the global market without government aid.

4. *Toward Capital Account Convertibility*: Liberalization cannot be one-way street. Opening up the capital account for foreign capital has brought tremendous economic gains. But now that the surplus on the BoP is bulging and forex reserves are shooting up through the roof, it is imperative to withdraw restrictions on capital outflows. If the Chinese residents have freedom to invest abroad, it would moderate the growth in forex reserves. This would also ease pressure of excess domestic liquidity on prices. Lower money supply growth caused by the export of capital would tend to be naturally disinflationary, so the central bank has not to initiate any measures to tighten money supply growth to control inflation. The road to capital account convertibility is a natural disinflationary route.
5. *Consumption Driven Growth Model*: For the last two decades, China has been riding the wave of globalization primarily on foreign investment-induced export-oriented growth. Exports now formed record 36% of GDP in 2007 compared to 20% in 2001. China has now to enter the second phase of its economic development. The growth model has to be more inwardly driven and accelerated by domestic consumption growth and domestic investment rather than exports growth and foreign investment. This is only way China can make its growth rate sustainable and also reduce the imbalances in the structure of global payments and liquidity. The subprime crisis was a manifestation of excessive global liquidity growth which could not be more prudently allocated. The problem of China's excess domestic and external liquidity growth and its inflationary impact would be more easily tackled and without any further monetary intervention but naturally by the process of the type of economic growth through domestic consumption-oriented growth strategy. The revaluation of yuan, liberalization of imports, capital account convertibility, and larger supplies of domestic products from export surpluses would further due to their disinflationary impact offer tremendous benefit to domestic consumers in terms of prices as well as availability of wider range of products. This is only sustainable model for China's future growth which would also be more compatible with open global economy.
6. *Moderation in Savings Rate*: The driving force of Chinese economic growth is exports. As exports growth rate moderates, it would have negative impact on China's economic growth. Hence, it is advisable to promote growth in domestic consumption to substitute lower demand from exports. We have a classic example in Japan illustrating how the economy can turn into stagnation from a high growth phase when the exports growth drops and is not substituted by the domestic consumption growth. In case of Japan, being a developed economy and record low interest rates touching zero, there was no further scope for growth in domestic consumption. For China, the alternative of domestic consumption growth is open due to its developing nature, large population, where large section of population is yet to increase its standard of living through consumption growth. In order to promote domestic consumption, China needs to make the consumer credit cheaper. Lower savings rate would promote consumption and moderate growth in exports and substitute loss of demand from exports due to revaluation of yuan. It would make the consumption growth model sustainable.

7. *Higher Wage Levels*: One of the causes of high savings rate in China is the high share of corporate profits and governmental institutional surpluses and savings in the overall national savings cake. The rapid rise in the overall savings rate is primarily due to the exceptional growth in institutional savings and not individual or household savings. While the large institutional share in overall savings contributes high rate of capital formation and hence economic growth, there are several handicaps in this trend which needs to be normalized. This surplus value endangers rise in wage levels in the economy. Consequently, it militates against the growth of domestic consumption and forces the economy to be more reliant on corporate investments and exports. While the gross national savings rate as percentage of GDP went up from 37% in 1996 to 44% in 2005, the rate of household savings has come down from 20% GDP to 16% during the same period. The shares of enterprises and government have gone up from 13% of GDP to 20% and from 5% of GDP to 6%.[1] The rise in domestic consumption growth that can emerge from higher wages and lower private and government corporate surpluses would neutralize the overdependence on investment and exports for growth. It would also reduce the growth in trade surplus and ameliorate the US trade deficit and soften the concern on exchange rate of yuan. Even after the fallout of global recession, Chinese economy registered economic growth of 9% in 2009, while the profits of the corporate continued to rise. 1,621 companies listed on Shanghai and Shenzhen exchanges recorded aggregate revenue of RMB 11.31 trillion in 2009, with net profit belonging to parent companies of RMB 1.03 trillion, jumping 25.23% from a year earlier. Among the 1,621 companies, nearly 70% posted an increase in profits, of which 384 companies increased saw profits rise more than 50%.[2] The rising wages would distribute greater purchasing power among wider population and give thrust to the consumption growth model.
8. *Privatization of State Enterprises*: The economic model of Chinese development has been one of state capitalism. Despite the adoption of free market mechanism, right to property, and capital market freedom, large part of the corporate sector is still in the state ownership. Although foreign multinationals and enterprises of private Chinese investors are growing in numbers and size, the state enterprise dominates the overall economic activity. The next move in its reform program is to privatize its state sector. These enterprises need to be partially or fully privatized as was done in India. The state can still retain either dominant or part ownership and offer the rest to the public. This would also revitalize their stock market and spread equity ownership wider in public. It would not only benefit the state treasury but also offer alternative investment vehicle to public and thereby democratize its corporate sector.
9. *Labor Reforms*: Another area of reform which the economy vitally needs is in the labor market. The state capitalism does not engender competition and in its

[1] How will China's Savings-Investment Balance Evolve?, Louis Kuijs, World Bank, 2005, Chinese Economy
Peter Cheung Hung Fai, 2008.

[2] China Securities Journal, April 27, 2010.

present form does give freedom in the labor market. In order to render diversity to the economy and create the countervailing power, it is essential to allow labor unions to function. Labor unions would ensure higher wages and also measures to improve productivity. It would add consumption demand, raise imports, and give the economy some insulation from export domination.

Since China is now emerging as the world's second largest economy, it cannot afford to continue with its regulated economy and has to liberalize both on the domestic as well as external economic fronts to diversify its economy away from export-dominated growth machine. This will not only bring more balance to its economic growth but also render more stability the global economy.

New Bretton Woods: Reform of IMF

The phase of globalization which was primarily financed through private capital flows had relegated the IMF into background. When the equity capital flows and cheap debt flows from competitive international banking and capital markets inundated the emerging markets, the IMF remained on the sidelines. Once powerful source of international funding for countries facing BoP problems, the IMF often showed its muscles dictating stiff and often painful policy conditionalities tied with its assistance. Come globalization and IMF slipped into oblivion except for its annual meet popular as a rendezvous for the global finance ministers, economic policy makers, bankers, and global investors. So much was the drop in its lending due to lack demand for its funds from the member countries and decline in its earnings that it faced serious budgetary constraints. The recent crisis has, however, forced many countries to borrow from the IMF to meet their forex liquidity requirements, revive its lending operations, and sustain its financial viability.

Following the Bretton Woods agreement in July 1944, the IMF was formed more in line with the US plan of making it a pool of financial resources from the member countries with the US dollar as its center and functioning as the reserve currency and much against the proposal of Keynes to form the central bank of central bank with its own currency, Bancor, to be used as the international currency and having powers to create its own money to meet the global demand for international liquidity. Under the Keynes' plan, the global currency system and the IMF would not have to depend on the USA to supply its currency for meeting the global liquidity demand. This would have avoided the pressure on the USA to create deficit in its BoP to finance global liquidity. On the flip side, it would not have given the USA the benefit of seigniorage it enjoyed by using its own currency for global payments. The US proposal was feasible as an alternative due to strong dollar at the end of the Second World War, its large BoP surplus, and its largest gold stocks of 21,678 tons which at the fixed price of $35 an ounce of gold with the value of reserves of $24 billion the ($830 billion at the current price of around $1,200 an ounce), giving enough leverage to defend gold-convertible dollar in the global currency markets. With the global political economy as it was in 1944, the IMF began its journey as the bank of the member nations providing short-term to medium-term assistance to overcome their BoP problems. The capital and resources of the IMF were the gold and currency contributions made by the member nations according to quotas which were determined on the basis of a formula of size, resource requirements, and other economic parameters of each country. The exchange rates were fixed in gold and US dollar.

The IMF began its operations in 1945 with its resource base of gold and the currencies of the member countries to be used for lending out to needy countries to meet their BoP deficits without facing the severe economic hardships for correcting their BoP disequilibria. The use of its financial resources was also meant to preclude competitive depreciations and beggar-thy-neighbor trade policies which were rampant during the interwar period. During the 1950s, the IMF had to face the shortage of international liquidity when availability of external dollars through the US BoP deficits fell short of demand for dollars abroad. The situation reversed in 1960s when the supply of dollars abroad far surpassed its overseas demand. In fact, the more pressing problem of the dollar glut was the dollar overhang which had outstretched the value of US gold reserves at the fixed price of $35 an ounce. This phenomenon lent to a speculation about the devaluation of dollar by raising the price of gold. It had also caused the market price of gold to rise above the official level of $35. To preserve market price at the official level, the Federal Reserve and the European central banks formed a gold pool to sell their gold holdings. Their gold pool, to which contributed 50% of the pool, lost 240 tons of official gold worth $270 million. The US gold stocks more than halved to $10.2 billion compared to $24.4 billion in 1948. To avoid the currency chaos, dollar was finally demonetized from gold in 1971. It was devalued in two stages, however, by raising its price in terms of gold to $38 in 1971 and to $42.22 in 1973. This phase marked a gradual transition of the exchange rates system from the fixed rates to floating beginning in 1975.

While the IMF faced the vicissitudes in exchange rates system without any destabilization and let the global monetary system seek a smooth transition from fixed exchange rates to floating exchange rates and from gold linked to goldless fiat system, it did make an attempt toward the creation of an international money during 1968. The special drawing rights (SDRs) were created.

SDRs: International Settlement Unit

One of the most significant events after the formation of IMF, which established stable exchange rates and mechanism for giving the BoP support to the needy member nations, was the creation of special drawing rights in 1967. Keynes had envisioned a new international currency named, Bancor, to be focal point of the global monetary system. It was to act as the measure of value in which all other currencies were to expressed and also be the means of settling international accounts between the member countries. IMF was to create the Bancor and act as the central bank of the central banks of all member countries. At the Bretton Woods, Keynes' idea of creating an independent international currency, global central bank, and transnational source of global liquidity had to face a retreat, in view of the powerful US lobby to enthrone US dollar as the international reserve currency, monetary unit of measure. Resultantly, the USA enjoyed the seigniorage in the use of its currency as the global reserve asset. During the early 1960s when global liquidity requirements raced faster than the supply of liquidity by the USA through its balance of payments deficit, the global financial community again realized the need to create separate independent source of liquidity from the IMF. By the end of 1960s when US balance of payments suffered heavier deficits, the US dollar repeatedly faced attacks in the currency markets. Averting the exchange crisis required maintaining the gold price at $35 an ounce by the joint action of the US and European central banks to sell gold in the market from their reserves. This alone could maintain the confidence of the market in the US dollar. Both the paucity and redundancy of US dollar created problems in smooth functioning of the global monetary system. During this period, Robert Triffin mooted with idea of reviving Keynes' proposal and argued a strong case for creating a new international monetary unit, means of payments settlements among the member nations, and a source of liquidity called special drawing rights (SDRs).

In 1967, IMF Board of Executive Directors approved the creation of SDRs, as new source of increasing international liquidity by creating a new reserve asset. Initially SDR was equivalent to 1/35th of an ounce of gold. However, later when gold was demonetized by the USA from the global monetary system, SDR was redefined in terms of a basket of 16 currencies. Later, the number of currencies in the SDRs was reduced, and currently, the SDRs comprise only four currencies, with US dollar having 42% weight, euro 38%, pound 11%, and yen 9%. SDRs were created by the IMF and allocated to the members on the basis of their quotas in exchange of their national currencies. For the first time, it meant creation of money by an international agency, international money, to be used by the member countries in times of need. It created international liquidity which was in short supply in the late 1960s. One of the then main criticisms of the SDRs was that it may be inflationary since it created international money and increased the global liquidity. SDRs created and distributed during 1970–1972 were worth SDRs 9.3 billion, and it did provide some respite to the global economy from the inadequate growth in international liquidity. US dollar was the main source of global liquidity, and the USA could provide more dollars to the rest of the world only by incurring deficits in her balance of payments. The ability of the USA to increase its BoP deficit was constrained by its gold–dollar convertibility guarantee which it gave other central banks at $35 an ounce of gold. At this gold price which is established in 1944, the available gold stocks of the USA of 21,678 tons enabled the USA to create global liquidity so long as the holding dollar liabilities of the USA by the other central banks did not exceed the value of the US gold stocks. By the early 1960s, the US liquid liabilities held by the central banks started increasing. This brought upward pressure on the free market gold price. Federal Reserve and other major central banks pooled their gold holdings to sell gold in the market and keep the gold price at $35. By the late 1960s, pressure on the US dollar was so much that central banks began losing gold to the free market and could not meet the market's appetite for gold at $35. In August 1971, President Nixon abolished the age-old gold–dollar link by making the dollar nonconvertible in gold. Gold was thus demonetized from the global monetary system. The exchange rates were not fixed but floated freely by the market mechanism of demand and supply but intervened when necessary by the central banks.

After the first allocation was of SDRs for a total amount of SDRs 9.3 billion, distributed in 1970–1972 in yearly installments, the second allocation, for SDRs 12.1 billion, was distributed in 1979–1981 in yearly installments. The third general allocation was approved on August 7, 2009, for an amount of SDRs 161.2 billion and took place on August 28, 2009. The allocation increased simultaneously members' SDR holdings and their cumulative SDR allocations by about 74.13% of their quota. A proposal for a special one-time allocation of SDRs was approved by the IMF's Board of Governors in September 1997 through the proposed Fourth Amendment of the Articles of Agreement. Its intent was to enable all members of the IMF to participate in the SDR system on an equitable basis and correct for the fact that countries that joined the Fund after 1981—more than one-fifth of the current IMF membership—had never received an SDR allocation. The Fourth Amendment became effective for all members in August 2009 with the support of at least three-fifths of the IMF membership (112 members) and 85% of the total voting power. The special allocation was implemented in September 2009. It increased members' cumulative SDR allocations by SDRs 21.5 billion.

After the demise of the Bretton Woods in 1971 and emergence of floating rates in 1975, the issue of SDRs relegated into background. Further, the SDRs created over the last 35 years remain still a small percentage of international reserves. The SDRs creation has only touched periphery of the global liquidity and has not broached the fundamental issue of creating a source of liquidity and its distribution wherein no single country enjoys seigniorage in its creation and international liquidity is not allocated from the existing size of the member economies but their underdevelopment potential to grow faster and the magnitude of their BoP problems. Developed economies which are large and do not face acute balance of payments problems do not need SDR allocations. There should be a separate criteria than the ones used currently for determining the size of the SDR creation and its allocation among counties.

The issue of the reform of the IMF is twofold. The first relates to the resources of the IMF which comprise (1) the quotas of members: its holdings of gold, 25% of member's quota, and currencies of members, remaining 75%, contributed by the members; (2) the SDRs, money, or drawing rights or accounting balances created by the IMF and allocated among the members; and (3) its borrowings from members under the original GAB (General Agreement to Borrow) and more recent NAB (New Arrangements to Borrow). The second issue relates to the powers of members in the decision making in the IMF. Since the voting rights are proportional to the size of quotas and the quotas were determined by the economic size of member nations in the global economy, the power is concentrated among the big and developed nations. The USA has the voting right of 16.74%, Japan 6%, Germany 5.8%, UK 4.84%, France 4.85%, Italy 3.19%, China 3.65%, Russia 2.69%, and India 1.88%. The quota allocations and voting rights need a revision in the light of the sea change in the global economic, payments, and financial structure over the last three decades of globalization.

Turning SDRs into Global Money: Move from Reserve Currency Standard to International Money Standard

Looking to the growth in global GDP, trade and investments, and money supplies in the last more than half a century, the resources of the IMF look disproportionately shrunk. The offshore banking centers and euro-currency deposits have grown sharply to meet the demand for external resources. After globalization, the direct and portfolio investments from the developed nations to the emerging market economies provided enough liquidity for their BoP needs. There was very little need and demand for funds from the IMF. The member countries only approached the IMF in times of serious forex crisis arising from a critical BoP problem, intractable debt crisis, or severe fiscal crisis. Although the IMF did provide adequate assistance to distressed countries, in several cases, the conditionalities it imposed became a matter of debate and controversy inviting criticism from the liberal economic philosophers.

During the current decade, the total resources of the IMF rose from $280 billion to $840 billion in January 2012, out of which SDRs allocations constituted only $15 billion and gold holdings of 90.5 million ounces (2,814 tons) were $146 billion at current market prices. The IMF is the third largest holder of gold after the USA and Germany. The current NAB has given greater powers to the IMF to raise resources. Under the NAB, the IMF would add $550 billion to its resources. In the light of considerable liquidity addition made by the Fed, the European Central Bank, Bank of China, and Bank of England in tackling the recessionary trend, it seems that there is no dearth of liquidity in the global economy. The global forex reserves totaled $10.4 trillion in 2012. Hence, there is no need for additional liquidity in the form of new international money. The question that needs to be addressed is whether the IMF can continue in its present form of a pool of resources of the member countries or whether it can be transformed into full-fledged global central bank with the powers to issue its own currency and manage its money supply. The forex reserves of central bank also need to be redistributed toward forming much larger IMF.

With respect to the idea of a new global central bank, it needs to be decided whether the money will take form of a physical currency or be an accounting unit or drawing right, like SDR, which can be used only by the central banks. The form which the new international money would take would itself depend on its desired scope in the global monetary system. It could be the following alternative forms.

1. It could take the form of full-fledged money just as the money created by other national central banks. It would have its own currency in paper currency form and also deposit money held by the commercial banks in addition to the central banks. A few commercial banks from each country may be allowed to accept and lend deposits in its currency in their own counties. It would mean the global availability of new money for transactions and as a new asset form. It would globally compete with other currencies mainly, dollar, euro, pound, and yen. If the new money is to take the form of any other national monies in circulation, the IMF will have to impose reserve requirement for the commercial banks. It will have also to set up a global clearing house for settling the transactions between

the banks. Many countries which have exchange controls may not permit the commercial banks to accept such deposits and for new money would function as any other foreign currency available for restricted use along with other foreign currencies like dollar or euro.

2. In a twenty-first-century digital world to create a new money in the form of paper currency will be an anathema of the concept of modern money in view of its evolution over centuries. Hence, there is convincing logic in not pursuing with the idea of new international money in the form of a paper currency. The new money could take form of bank deposits with private banking sector participation and public holding in addition to the holdings by the central banks. It would mean paper currency less use of new money as transaction medium and reserve asset by public and also the central banks.
3. The last alternative is to keep the new money in the realms of only central banks as is the SDR today. The new money could only be traded, transacted, and held by the central banks without the private participation in its operation.

If we look into the objectivity of the need for money or a currency, one view is that since international trade, payments, transactions, and investments are only a part of each nations overall economic and monetary activities, if a currency of large and strong nations serves as the globally accepted means of transaction, payments and reserves without incurring damaging costs to that nation, the necessity of having international money is greatly reduced. The economic argument against this view is that the reserve currency nation enjoys an enormous advantage in form of seigniorage when its currency or money is used internationally. Since the global central bank is not a nation state, it does not have its BoP, and it would not create money to finance its BoP deficit. Nor would it create deficit in its BoP to create its money. It would create money only to meet global demand for its currency, not through its BoP which happens under the current system of reserve currency standard, but through its lines of credit or withdrawal rights from its balance sheet.

The new international money can be held in its currency or deposit forms. But its deposits should not have check-writing facility so that its money supply does not have multiplier effect. Alternatively, IMF need not issue a currency, since currency requirement is usually for public. In a world which is getting increasingly digital, it would be incongruous if the IMF creates a new money also in the form of paper currency in the twenty-first century. The IMF's money, SDRs, has so far been an accounting entry and hence been digital. It could continue to be digital.

Having ruled out the issue of paper currency by the IMF, the next step is to decide whether the SDR deposits can be used for payments and financial settlements and also held as the reserve asset in the public domain.

SDR should work like international money, more traded, more held as asset in private hands and central banks. Currently, it figures in the portfolio of only central banks as a reserve asset. It is used to settle international payments in other important currencies, especially US dollar. Today, SDRs are used to draw dollar balances for making international payments. It is used as an adjunct to the dollar and does not function as an independent means of payment or settlement. Eurodollars developed as a market phenomenon due to its attractiveness and efficiency. It emerged as an important and useful vehicle of recycling the petrodollars in mid-1970s and saved the global economy from plunging into deep recession after the 1974 oil crisis. Euro-currency markets have grown by leaps and bounds since then and have been critical and vital segment of global money and capital markets. There is no reason why SDRs cannot function as a new global currency with a little push from the governments of member countries and initiatives of private commercial and investment banking community. This joint public–private initiative can write a new chapter in evolution of global money, foster the international monetary order, reduce overdependence of global community on the US dollar, and promote more equitable distribution of seigniorage arising from the creation of international money.

The new international money if it is called the Bancor, it will the most befitting tribute to Keynes for his contribution in giving us the tools of economic management that helped create the prosperous postwar global economy. Alternative names could be Ecu (economic currency unit) or Erth, or Gcu (global currency unit) or Laksh, a word derived from the name Lakshmi, the Hindu goddess of wealth, or Brahm (Br), short of Brahma, another Hindu god, the creator of universe. IMF can evolve into a global central bank (GCB). Value of Gcu would be determined by a basket of 4–5 major currencies. Gcu could be traded in the exchange market, and commercial banks could accept Gcu deposits. The use of Gcu as a reserve asset would relieve the pressure on the US dollar, and the central banks could hold a portion of their reserves in Gcu.

Global Monitoring of Crisis and Country-Risk: PreCrisis—Preempting a Crisis

Despite the record economic growth of the global economy over the span of last more than two decades, the crises have occurred like undetected land mines over the global economic landscape increasing the uncertainty in the environment. The sovereignty of nation in its economic policy is supreme and cannot be compromised. Yet today's global economy the individual nations and their economies is so intricately interlinked and hence interdependent that the episodes of economic distress in one economy have immediate and far-reaching ripple effect on all markets and economies even before knowing the gravity of the problem. A crisis even in small economy is now capable of destabilizing the global economic and financial balance. The individual nations cannot any longer afford to ignore the global repercussions of their flagrant fiscal policies. Their sovereignty in policies needs to be tempered by their concern for global stability. In an interconnected global financial system, a small crisis is capable of triggering an avalanche of global dimension. Today's complex global economy requires ongoing monitoring of all economies to detect and diffuse surprise land mines. The recent event of Greek crisis again temporarily destabilized the global economy which was on its way of recovery from the biggest crisis since the 1930s.

A significant step in this direction has already been taken but needs to be more strengthened and made more effective and proactive and not reactive. In 2000 the Executive Board of the IMF decided to set up an Independent Evaluation Office (IEO) with the responsibility for oversight and surveillance of the global economy, monetary systems and developments in the member nations, and policies and actions of the IMF. In order to be more effective in this surveillance task with powers to ring the alarm bells in advance, the IEO needs to have more powers and organizationally and financially strengthened. This will play an important role in avoiding the crises in future and eliminate the losses and damages which they cause. The IMF could play a very constructive role in the bailout of countries before they face the crisis with a package of financial support and policy advice that would blow out the crisis. In the hypersensitive global economy and financial world today, the real contribution which the IMF can make is in making the world free from crises. The economic terrorism emanating from the unhealthy market developments needs to be tackled both at the regulatory level as well as at the macro level of avoiding fiscal and financial profligacy. The IMF can act as the watch guard of the global economy and monetary system which has been its main purpose for which it was decided to be set up in 1944 by great learned men of finance and economics like Keynes at the Bretton Woods. Three-quarters of a century of progress but great jerk in 2008 reflects the imperative need for the institutional reform for a new Bretton Woods.

Euro and Eurozone Management: Harmonization of Monetary Policy—A Tightrope Walking

Soft Money Policy and Softer Euro

The future of euro faces the same fate as many other economic ideas when translated into policy get derailed at some point. Instead of reshaping the reality, the euro went away from its ideal course and was finally overpowered by the reality. The theoretical father of euro, Nobel laureate Robert Mundell, who first wrote about the optimum currency area in 1961 articulating the economic logic for a single currency irrespective of the political boundaries of countries, must have been saddened by the recent fall of euro in the wake of the Greek sovereign debt crisis which is now spreading to other larger members of Eurozone. All is not lost yet, and gains of single currency euro for the Eurozone still heavily outweigh the recent losses. The lesson is learned, and the future would be much more pragmatic than idealistic.

Apart from the common exchange rate which may not be suitable for all Eurozone members, the common currency with separate fiscal budgets has another hurdle which Eurozone has to face. Different political entities have their own fiscal policies and budgetary problems although the effort is always to harmonize the fiscal policies with the common monetary policies. This harmonization is a practical problem since different economies within the Eurozone face different economic situations and fiscal objectives and problems. While the independent fiscal policies are a blessing so that fiscally profligate states will have to tighten their belt and pursue fiscal austerity to bring their house in order. But what has happened is that the fiscal profligacy of some states has gone uncontrolled and the stronger member states have to share the burden of their profligacy and bail them out of their crisis. The Greek crisis is the case in point. Those which may follow are Ireland, Portugal, Spain, and Italy. The practical problem is also in implementation of right shade of common monetary and exchange rate policy. In fact, the seeds of the current Eurozone crisis were sown in pursuing the policy of dear money and strong euro primarily more suited to the stronger members like Germany than to other relatively weaker and some very weak members of the Eurozone like Greece. The Eurozone needed greater harmonization of its monetary and exchange rate policy that was done during 2004–2008. Apart from efforts that support the fiscal budgets of weak members allowing them to gradually eliminate their fiscal profligacy, the ECB needs to continue with low interest and softer exchange rate policy which it is now pursuing in 2012. If this policy had been in place since 2006 when it started hardening the euro, the crisis may have been averted. When the central banks are less perceptive and proactive, the market punishes them to follow the path they should have pursued earlier.

Global Perspective and Holistic View

The global economy is now at the crossroads and is facing potentially most disastrous situation since the Great Depression. The symptoms of the crisis have been managed to rescue the global economy on the path of recovery through the stimulus packages and zero interest policies in the developed world. The predepression era was characterized by balanced government budget, low government and personal debt levels, harsh discipline of gold standard and fixed exchange rates, and government nonintervention in macroeconomic affairs of the country. The current economic environment presents a stark contrast with earlier era. Now it is the Keynesianism, monetarism, and marketization that dominate the global economic management. The budget deficits and public and private debts have reached record levels. While the plethora fiat money and floating exchange rates have enhanced financial volatility, a plethora of banking and government economic regulations have rendered both private as well as public economic affairs more complex.

The Western economies have reached mature state of capitalism where declining rate of profits, demographic transition toward aging population, low or negative population growth, rising inequalities of income and wealth, high cost of labor and cheap availability of capital are undermining their growth potential and growth momentum. Both the investment and consumption demands fail to induce growth. Despite the cheap supply of private capital, the government demand for capital remains unsatiated due to pressure for higher budget deficits. Except Japan and Germany, the Western economies are in chronic and large trade and current account deficits primarily due to higher labor cost in their economies. In contrast, the emerging market economies have younger demographic profile which stimulates high growth of consumer demand. Coupled with inflow of foreign private capital and technology, the emerging market economies have migrated into export surplus economies and accumulated forex reserves to be lent to the Western nations to fund their budget deficits. The forex reserves of the emerging market economies reflect the liquidity they have that commands resources of the rest of the world. The reserves are monetary balances and are usually invested in government securities by the central banks. Hence, they reflect the lines of credit given to the countries whose securities are held. These can be used for recycling the global growth process in current times of sluggish growth and uncertain economic future. The excessive global liquidity growth is not conducive to the current environment of economic uncertainty. It is necessary to recycle some of the forex reserves for asset formation that would accelerate the growth process. Under the current circumstances, it is imperative to convert excess global liquidity into more productive use and regenerate the growth process. This alone can enable the global economy traverse into the phase of stable growth without resorting to measures that could cause double-dip recession.

Index

S. Nayak, *The Global Financial Crisis: Genesis, Policy Response and Road Ahead*,
DOI 10.1007/978-81-322-0798-6, © Springer India 2013

The manufacturer's authorised representative in the EU is Springer Nature Customer Service Centre GmbH, Europaplatz 3, 69115 Heidelberg, Germany. If you have any concerns regarding our products, please contact ProductSafety@springernature.com

Printed and bound by CPI Group (UK) Ltd, Croydon, CR0 4YY
30/09/2026
02225444-0013